S0-AZR-860

Student Solutions Manual

COST ACCOUNTING

Student Solutions Manual

COST ACCOUNTING

Thirteenth Edition

Charles T. Horngren
Srikant Datar
George Foster
Madhav Rajan
Chris Ittner

Margaret Shackell-Dowell

PEARSON

Prentice
Hall

Upper Saddle River, NJ 07458

This work is protected by United States copyright laws and is provided solely for the use of instructors in teaching their courses and assessing student learning. Dissemination or sale of any part of this work (including on the World Wide Web) will destroy the integrity of the work and is not permitted. The work and materials from it should never be made available to students except by instructors using the accompanying text in their classes. All recipients of this work are expected to abide by these restrictions and to honor the intended pedagogical purposes and the needs of other instructors who rely on these materials.

Acquisition Editor: Eric Svendsen
Editorial Project Manager: Kasey Sheehan Madara
Editorial Assistant: Mauricio E. Escoto
Project Manager, Production: Kerri Tomasso
Operations Specialist: Carol O'Rourke
Printer/Binder: Courier/Kendallville
Cover Printer: Coral Graphics

Copyright © 2009 by Pearson Education, Inc., Upper Saddle River, New Jersey, 07458.
Pearson Prentice Hall. All rights reserved. Printed in the United States of America. This publication is protected by Copyright and permission should be obtained from the publisher prior to any prohibited reproduction, storage in a retrieval system, or transmission in any form or by any means, electronic, mechanical, photocopying, recording, or likewise. For information regarding permission(s), write to: Rights and Permissions Department.

Pearson Prentice Hall™ is a trademark of Pearson Education, Inc.
Pearson® is a registered trademark of Pearson plc
Prentice Hall® is a registered trademark of Pearson Education, Inc.

Pearson Education Ltd., London
Pearson Education Singapore, Pte. Ltd
Pearson Education, Canada, Inc.
Pearson Education–Japan
Pearson Education Australia PTY, Limited

Pearson Education North Asia, Ltd., Hong Kong
Pearson Educación de Mexico, S.A. de C.V.
Pearson Education Malaysia, Pte. Ltd
Pearson Education Upper Saddle River, New Jersey

Prentice Hall
is an imprint of

www.pearsonhighered.com

10   9   8   7   6   5   4   3   2

ISBN-13-978-0-13-813042-8
ISBN-10-0-13-813042-6

TABLE OF CONTENTS

Chapter Solutions

1-2   Some people consider that generally accepted accounting principles (GAAP) restrict the choices that accountants can make. When running a business, a manager may want to view information in a specific way that is not allowed by GAAP. Management accounting allows that. Reports can be generated in any way that fits the users' decision making needs. For example:

- a report with a charge interest on owners' capital to help judge a division's performance would be allowed under management accounting, but not GAAP
- a report including internally generated assets or liabilities (e.g. brand names) would be allowed for management accounting, but not GAAP
- a report using present value or fair market value for assets or liabilities is allowed for management accounting, but not GAAP.

1-4   The business functions in the value chain are

Remember	Name	Explanation
R & D	Research and development	generating and experimenting with ideas related to new products, services, or processes.
Design	Design of products, services and processes	After ideas have been researched & developed, the next phase is the detailed planning and engineering of products, services, or processes.
Prod	Production	Once the products & processes have been designed, the firm produces them by acquiring, coordinating, and assembling resources to produce a product or deliver a service.
Mktg	Marketing	Once there is a product or service, it needs to be promoted and sold to customers or prospective customers.
Dist	Distribution	Once the customers agree to purchase, the product or service needs to be delivered to them
C.S.	Customer Service	After the customer purchases the product or service, the firm needs to follow up and provide after-sale support.

1-6 "Management accounting deals only with costs."

- This statement is misleading
- This statement is wrong
- Management accounting includes so much more than cost, e.g.
    - Measurement *non-financial* information
    - Comparison of organizational goals (on financial & non-financial dimensions) & actual outcomes
    - Analysis of revenue and customer profitability

1-8 The five-step decision-making process is
(1) identify the problem and uncertainties
(2) obtain information
(3) make predictions about the future
(4) make decisions by choosing among alternatives and
(5) implement the decision, evaluate performance and learn.

1-10 The three guidelines for management accountants are
1. Employ a cost-benefit approach.
2. Recognize behavioral and technical considerations.
3. Apply the notion of "different costs for different purposes".

1-12 The new controller could include some or all of the following ideas in a discussion:
(a) You can save the plant manager time by providing relevant information
(b) You are not a bean counter, but a person who knows how the plant works. Do your research to make sure this is true!
(c) You can show how you've helped other plants. Examples could include
   - assistance in preparing the budget,
   - assistance in analyzing problem situations and evaluating financial and nonfinancial aspects of different alternatives, and
   - assistance in submitting capital budget requests.
(d) You can ask the corporate controller for advice on how the control function helps at your new plant. *(This approach is a last resort but may be necessary in some cases.)*

1-14 The Institute of Management Accountants (IMA) sets standards of ethical conduct for management accountants in the following areas:
- Competence
- Confidentiality
- Integrity
- Credibility

1-16 (15 min.) **Value chain and classification of costs, computer company.**

Cost Item	Value Chain Business Function
a.	Production
b.	Distribution
c.	Design of products, services or processes
d.	Research and Development
e.	Customer Service or Marketing
f.	Design of products, services or processes (or Research and Development)
g.	Marketing
h.	Production

1-18 (15 min.) **Value chain and classification of costs, fast food restaurant.**

Cost Item	Value Chain Business Function
a.	Production
b.	Distribution
c.	Marketing
d.	Marketing
e.	Marketing
f.	Production
g.	Design of products, services or processes
h.	Customer service

1-20 (10-15 min.) **Planning and control decisions.**

Action	Decision
a.	Planning
b.	Control
c.	Control
d.	Planning
e.	Planning

1-22 (15 min.) **Five-step decision-making process, service firm.**

Action	Step in Decision-Making Process
a.	Obtain information
b.	Identify the problem and uncertainties
c.	Make predictions about the future
d.	Implement the decision, evaluate performance, and learn
e.	Make predictions about the future
f.	Obtain information
g.	Make decisions by choosing among alternatives

1-24 (15 min.) **Planning and control decisions, Internet company.**

1.   **Planning decisions**
        a. Decision to raise monthly subscription fee
        c. Decision to upgrade content of online services (later decision to inform subscribers and upgrade online services is an implementation part of control)
        e. Decision to decrease monthly subscription fee

        Control decisions
        b. Decision to inform existing subscribers about the rate of increase—an implementation part of control decisions
        d. Dismissal of VP of Marketing—performance evaluation and feedback aspect of control decisions

2.   Other planning decisions that may be made at WebNews.com:
        o   decision to raise or lower advertising fees;
        o   decision to charge a fee from on-line retailers when customers click-through from WebNews.com to the retailers' websites.
        Other control decisions that may be made at WebNews.com:
        o   evaluating how customers like the new format for the weather information,
        o   working with an outside vendor to redesign the website, and
        o   evaluating whether the waiting time for customers to access the website has been reduced.

1-26 (15 min.) **Management accounting guidelines.**

1. Cost-benefit approach
2. Behavioral and technical considerations
3. Different costs for different purposes
4. Cost-benefit approach
5. Behavioral and technical considerations
6. Cost-benefit approach
7. Behavioral and technical considerations
8. Different costs for different purposes
9. Behavioral and technical considerations

1-28 (30 min.) **Software procurement decisions, ethics.**

1.   Michael faces an ethical problem.
        o   The trip appears to be a gift which could influence his purchase decision.
        o   Some executives view the meeting as "suspect" from the start given the Caribbean location and its "rest and recreation" tone.
        o   The ethical standard of integrity requires Michaels to refuse the gift.
        o   Companies with "codes of conduct" frequently have a "supplier clause" that prohibits their employees from accepting "material" (in some cases, any) gifts from suppliers. The motivations include
            (a) Integrity/conflict of interest. Suppose Michaels recommends that a Horizon 1-2-3 product should subsequently be purchased by Fiesta. This recommendation could be

because he felt obligated to them as his trip to the Cancún conference was fully paid by Horizon.

(b) The appearance of a conflict of interest. Even if the Horizon 1-2-3 product is the superior one at that time, other suppliers likely will have a different opinion. They may believe that the way to sell products to Fiesta is via "fully-paid junkets to resorts." Those not wanting to do business this way may downplay future business activities with Fiesta even though Fiesta could gain much from such activities.

2.   Attending user meetings per se, is not the problem. The problem is that Horizon 1-2-3 is paying for the trip. The payment of expenses for the trip constitutes a gift that could appear to influence their purchase decision.

Pros of attending user meeting
(a) Opportunity to learn more about Horizon's software products.
(b) Opportunity to interact with other possible purchasers and get their opinions.
(c) Opportunity to influence the future product development plans of Horizon in a way that will benefit Fiesta. An example is Horizon subsequently developing software modules tailored to food product companies.
(d) Saves Fiesta money. Visiting suppliers and their customers typically cost money, whereas Horizon is paying for the Cancún conference.

Cons of Attending
(a) The ethical issues raised in requirement 1.
(b) Negative morale effects on other Fiesta employees who do not get to attend the Cancún conference. These employees may reduce their trust and respect for Michaels's judgment, arguing he has been on a "supplier-paid vacation."

Conditions on Attending that Fiesta Might Impose
(a) Sizable part of that time in Cancún has to be devoted to business rather than recreation.
(b) Decision on which Fiesta executive attends is not made by the person who attends (this reduces the appearance of a conflict of interest).
(c) Person attending (Michaels) does not have final say on purchase decision (this reduces the appearance of a conflict of interest).
(d) Fiesta executives go only when a new major purchase is being contemplated (to avoid the conference becoming a regular "vacation").
(e) Fiesta pays for the trip out of Michaels regular travel budget.

A Conference Board publication on *Corporate Ethics* asked executives about a comparable situation. Following are the results:

- 76% said Fiesta and Michaels face an ethical consideration in deciding whether to attend.
- 71% said Michaels should not attend, as the payment of expenses is a "gift" within the meaning of a credible corporate ethics policy.

3.   The company does not need its own code of ethics. They can use the code of ethics developed by the IMA.

Pros of having a written code
The Conference Board outlines the following reasons why companies adopt codes of ethics:

(a) Signals commitment of senior management to ethics.
(b) Promotes public trust in the credibility of the company and its employees.
(c) Signals the managerial professionalism of its employees.
(d) Provides guidance to employees as to how difficult problems are to be handled. If adhered to, employees will avoid many actions that are unethical or appear to be unethical.
(e) Drafting of the policy (and its redrafting in the light of ambiguities) can assist management in anticipating and preparing for ethical issues not yet encountered.

Cons of having a written code
(a) Can give appearance that all issues have been covered. Issues not covered may appear to be "acceptable" even when they are not
(b) Can constrain the entrepreneurial activities of employees. Forces people to always "behave by the book."
(c) Cost of developing code can be "high" if it consumes a lot of employee time.

1-30 (30 min.) **Professional ethics and earnings management.**

1. The possible motivations for Harvest Day Corporation's CEO to "manage" earnings include
    (a) Stock market reaction. A drop in stock price could upset shareholders, reduce liquidity, and potentially lead to lawsuits.
    (b) Job security. Surprises in the stock market could lead to pressure from the board of directors to resign or they could fire the CEO.
    (c) Management compensation. Top management compensation could include bonuses for income over a certain level or stock options. The options would be worth less, if market price fell.

2. The "Standards for Ethical Conduct..." requires management accountants to
   - Perform professional duties in accordance with relevant laws, regulations, and technical standards.
   - Refrain from engaging in any conduct that would prejudice carrying out duties ethically.
   - Communicate information fairly and objectively.

PROBABLY UNACCEPTABLE

(a) Subscriptions cancelled in December should be recorded in December itself and not delayed until January.

(c) Subscription revenue received in December in advance for magazines that will be sent out in January is a liability. Showing it as revenue falsely reports next year's revenue as this year's revenue.

(d) Office supplies purchased in December should be recorded as an expense of the current year and not as an expense of the next year.

(e) Booking advertising revenues that relate to January in December falsely reports next year's revenue as this year's revenue.

PROBABLY ACCEPTABLE

(b) The choice of when to do repairs or improvements is up to management. A short delay is perfectly acceptable in most cases, if permanent damage is not done. A delay in updating software could be prudent fiscal restraint.

(f) Similar to (b) above, if there is no danger, a delay is not falsification. If building repairs are not done in December, there is no transaction to record in December.

(g) Either depreciation method is acceptable under GAAP. Many companies switch their depreciation policy from one method to another. Often market participants notice a switch in accounting policies, and if it is done solely to hide poor earnings, the firm may be punished through their stock price anyway.

3. Harvest Day's controller should:
   o Directly raise his/her concerns with the CEO.
   o Go to the Audit Committee and the Board of Directors, if the CEO doesn't change.
   o Initiate a confidential discussion with an IMA Ethics Counselor, impartial adviser, or personal attorney.
   o Possibly resign. If the corporate culture of Harvest Day is to reward executives who take "end of fiscal year actions" that the Controller views as unethical and possibly illegal. It was precisely actions along the lines of (a), (c), (d), and (e) that caused Betty Vinson, an accountant at WorldCom, to be indicted for falsifying WorldCom's books and misleading investors.

CHAPTER 2
AN INTRODUCTION TO COST TERMS AND PURPOSES

2-2   **Direct costs** of a cost object can be **traced** to that cost object in a cost-effective way.
       Indirect costs of a cost object are related to the cost object but **cannot be traced** in a
            cost-effective way.
       Cost assignment includes both *tracing* Direct Costs and *allocating* Indirect Costs to a cost
       object.

2-4   Factors affecting the classification of a cost as direct or indirect include
       • the materiality of the cost in question,
       • available information-gathering technology,
       • design of operations

2-6   A *cost driver* is a variable that causally affects total costs over a given time span. A
       change in the **cost driver** results in a **change** in the level of total **costs**. For example, the
       number of vehicles assembled is a driver of the costs of steering wheels on a motor-
       vehicle assembly line.

2-8   A unit cost is computed by $\frac{TotalCosts}{\#Units}$. In many cases, the numerator will include a
       fixed cost that will not change despite changes in the denominator. It is wrong in those
       cases to multiply the unit cost by the change in the number of units to be produced to
       predict changes in total costs at different levels of production or activity.

2-10   Manufacturing companies typically have one or more of the following three types of
       inventory:
       1. *Direct materials inventory.* Direct materials in stock and awaiting use in the
          manufacturing process.
       2. *Work-in-process inventory.* Goods partially worked on but not yet completed. Also
          called *work in progress*.
       3. *Finished goods inventory.* Goods completed but not yet sold.

2-12   No. Most service sector companies do not hold inventories and, hence, have no
       inventoriable costs.

2-14   *Overtime premium* is the wage rate paid to workers in excess of their regular wage rates.
       Idle time is a subset of indirect labor that includes wages paid for unproductive time.
       Unproductive labor may be caused by lack of orders, machine breakdowns, material
       shortages, poor scheduling, etc..

2-16 (15 min.)   **Computing and interpreting manufacturing unit costs**.

1.   July cost per unit:

(in millions)

	Supreme	Deluxe	Regular	Total
Total Direct material cost	$ 84.00	$ 54.00	$ 62.00	$200.00
Total Direct manuf. labor costs	14.00	28.00	8.00	50.00
Total Indirect manuf. costs	42.00	84.00	24.00	150.00
Total manuf. costs	$140.00	$166.00	$ 94.00	$400.00
LESS: Fixed costs allocated at a rate of $20M ÷ $50M (Total direct mfg. labor) equal to $0.40 per dir. manuf. labor dollar (0.40 × $14; 28; 8)	5.60	11.20	3.20	20.00
Total Variable costs	$134.40	$154.80	$ 90.80	$380.00
Units produced (millions)	80	120	100	
Cost per unit (Total manuf. costs ÷ units produced)	$1.7500	$1.3833	$0.9400	
Variable manuf. cost per unit (Total Variable costs ÷ Units produced)	$1.6800	$1.2900	$0.9080	

2. Prediction of August costs based on July cost per unit

(in millions)

	Supreme	Deluxe	Regular	Total
Total manuf. Cost per unit	$1.75	$1.3833	$0.94	
Units produced	X 120	X 160	X 180	
Projected total costs	$210.00	$221.33	$169.20	$600.53
Variable manuf. Cost per unit	$1.68	$1.29	$0.908	
Units produced	X 120	X 160	X 180	
Total projected variable costs	$201.60	$206.40	$163.44	$571.44
Fixed costs				20.00
Total costs				$591.44

The **total** manufacturing cost per unit in requirement 1 includes $20 million of fixed manufacturing costs. Given the unit volume changes for August 2008 (both in total and for each product), the use of total manufacturing cost per unit from the past month at a different unit volume level will yield high estimates of total costs of $600.53 million in August 2008 relative to the more reasonable estimate total manufacturing costs of $591.44 million calculated using variable manufacturing cost per unit times units produced plus the fixed costs of $20 million. This difference of over $9 million could affect a user's decision substantially. That is why we want the best estimates possible. Separating costs into fixed and variable helps with this.

2-18   (15–20 min.)   **Classification of costs, service sector.**

Cost object: Each individual focus group
Cost variability: With respect to the number of focus groups
There may be some debate over classifications of individual items, especially with regard to cost variability.

Cost Item	D or I	V or F
A	D	V
B	I	F
C	I	V[a]
D	I	F
E	D	V
F	I	F
G	D	V
H	I	V[b]

[a]Some students will note that phone call costs are variable when each call has a separate charge. It may be a fixed cost if Consumer Focus has a flat monthly charge for a line, irrespective of the amount of usage.
[b]Gasoline costs are likely to vary with the number of focus groups. However, vehicles likely serve multiple purposes, and detailed records may be required to examine how costs vary with changes in one of the many purposes served.

2-20   (15–20 min.)   **Classification of costs, manufacturing sector.**

Cost object: Type of car assembled (Corolla or Geo Prism)
Cost variability: With respect to changes in the number of cars assembled
There may be some debate over classifications of individual items, especially with regard to cost variability.

Cost Item	D or I	V or F
A	D	V
B	I	F
C	D	F
D	D	F
E	D	V
F	I	V
G	D	V
H	I	F

2-22 (15–20 min.) **Variable costs and fixed costs.**

1. Variable cost per ton of beach sand mined

Subcontractor	$ 80 per ton
Government tax	50 per ton
Total	$130 per ton

Fixed costs per month

0 to 100 tons of capacity per day	=	$150,000
101 to 200 tons of capacity per day	=	$300,000
201 to 300 tons of capacity per day	=	$450,000

2.

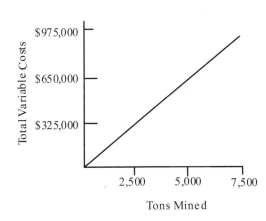 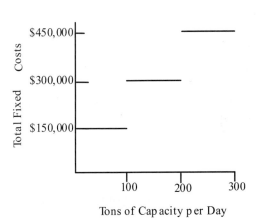

The concept of **relevant range** is potentially relevant for both graphs, but we don't have information restricting the relevant range for **variable** costs. The relevant ranges for the total **fixed** costs are from 0 to 100 tons; 101 to 200 tons; 201 to 300 tons, and so on. Within these ranges, the total fixed costs do not change.

3.

Tons Mined per Day (1)	Tons Mined per Month (2) = (1) × 25	Fixed Unit Cost per Ton (3) = FC ÷ (2)	Variable Unit Cost per Ton (4)	Total Unit Cost per Ton (5) = (3) + (4)
(a) 180	4,500	$300,000 ÷ 4,500 = $66.67	$130	$196.67
(b) 220	5,500	$450,000 ÷ 5,500 = $81.82	$130	$211.82

The unit cost for 220 tons mined per day is $211.82, while for 180 tons it is only $196.67.

Producing only 20 tons per day into the next relevant range causes cost per ton to increase. The closer production is to the top of the relevant range, the lower cost per ton will be.

11

2-24 (20 min.) **Cost drivers and value chain.**

1. Identify the customer need (what do faculty and students want in a book?) – *Product development*
    Find an author – *Product development*
    Market the book to faculty – *Marketing*
    Author writes book – *Product development*
    Process orders from bookstores – *Distribution*
    Editor edits book – *Product development*
    Receive unsold copies of book from bookstore – *Distribution*
    Author rewrites book– *Product development*
    Provide on-line assistance to faculty and students (study guides, test banks, etc.) – *Customer service*
    Print and bind the books – *Production*
    Deliver the book to bookstores – *Distribution*

2. **Value Chain**

Category	Activity	Cost driver
Product Development	Identify the customer need	Number of schools the marketing representative visits to discuss book ideas
	Find an author	Number of potential authors interviewed
	Author writes book	Number of pages of text
		Amount paid to the author (direct labor cost as cost driver)
	Editor edits book	Number of changes editor makes
		Number of pages of text
	Author rewrites book	Number of times author must do rewrites
Production	Print and bind the books	Machine hours for running the printing and binding equipment
Marketing	Market the book to faculty	Number of schools the marketing representative visits to market the book
		Hours spent with prospective customers to sell the book
Distribution	Process orders from bookstores	Number of deliveries made to bookstores
		Number of schools that adopt the new book
		Number of books ordered by bookstores (Note: Number of purchase orders would be a better driver, but it is not on the list of activities.)
	Deliver the book to bookstores	Number of deliveries made to bookstores
	Receive unsold copies of book from bookstores	Number of unsold books sent back from bookstores
Customer service	Provide on-line assistance to faculty and students	Number of faculty that adopt the new book
		Number of books ordered by bookstores (probably net of number of unsold books sent back from bookstores)

2-26 (20 min.) **Total costs and unit costs**

1.

Number of attendees	0	100	200	300	400	500	600
Variable cost per person ($9 caterer charge – $5 student door fee)	$4	$4	$4	$4	$4	$4	$4
Fixed Costs	$1,600	$1,600	$1,600	$1,600	$1,600	$1,600	$1,600
Variable costs (number of attendees × variable cost per person)	0	400	800	1,200	1,600	2,000	2,400
Total costs (fixed + variable)	$1,600	$2,000	$2,400	$2,800	$3,200	$3,600	$4,000

Fixed, Variable and Total Cost of Graduation Party

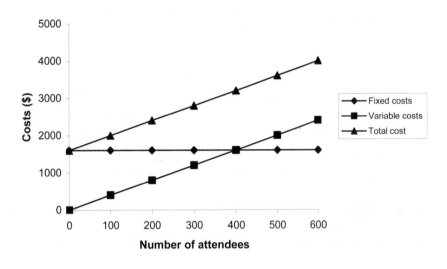

2.

Number of attendees	0	100	200	300	400	500	600
Total costs (fixed + variable)	$1,600	$2,000	$2,400	$2,800	$3,200	$3,600	$4,000
Costs per attendee (total costs ÷ number of attendees)		$20.00	$12.00	$9.33	$ 8.00	$ 7.20	$ 6.67

As shown in the table above, for 100 attendees the total cost will be $2,000 and the cost per attendee will be $20.

3. As shown in the table in requirement 2, for 500 attendees the total cost will be $3,600 and the cost per attendee will be $7.20.

4.   Using the calculations shown in the table in requirement 2, we can construct the cost-per-attendee graph shown below:

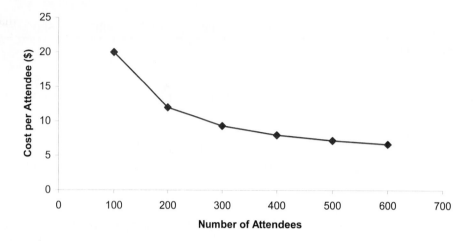

As president of the student association requesting a grant for the party, you should not use the per unit calculations to make your case. The person making the grant may assume an attendance of 500 students and use a low number like $7.20 per attendee to calculate the size of your grant. Instead, you should emphasize the fixed cost of $1,600 that you will incur even if no students or very few students attend the party, and try to get a grant to cover as much of the fixed costs as possible as well as a variable portion to cover as much of the $5 variable cost to the student association for each person attending the party.

2-28   (20–30 min.)   **Inventoriable costs versus period costs.**

1.   *Manufacturing-sector companies* purchase materials and components and convert them into different finished goods.
Merchandising-sector companies purchase and then sell tangible products without changing their basic form.
Service-sector companies provide services or intangible products to their customers—for example, legal advice or audits.

Only manufacturing and merchandising companies have tangible inventories of goods for sale. Some service sector companies can inventory work for a particular client.

2.   *Inventoriable costs* are all costs of a product that are regarded as an asset when they are incurred and then become cost of goods sold when the product is sold. These costs for a manufacturing company are included in work-in-process and finished goods inventory (they are "inventoried") to build up the costs of creating these assets.

Period costs are all costs in the income statement other than cost of goods sold. These costs are treated as expenses of the period in which they are incurred because they are presumed not to benefit future periods (or because there is not sufficient evidence to conclude that such benefit exists). Expensing these costs immediately best matches expenses to revenues.

3.	(a) Mineral water purchased for resale by Safeway—<u>inventoriable</u> cost of a merchandising company. It becomes part of cost of goods sold when the mineral water is sold.

(b) Electricity used at GE assembly plant—<u>inventoriable</u> cost of a manufacturing company. It is part of the manufacturing overhead that is included in the manufacturing cost of a refrigerator finished good.

(c) Depreciation on Google's computer equipment—<u>period cost</u> of a service company. Google has no inventory of goods for sale and, hence, no inventoriable cost.

(d) Electricity for Safeway's store aisles—<u>period cost</u> of a merchandising company. It is a cost that benefits the current period and it is not traceable to goods purchased for resale.

(e) Depreciation on GE's assembly testing equipment—<u>inventoriable</u> cost of a manufacturing company. It is part of the manufacturing overhead that is included in the manufacturing cost of a finished appliance.

(f) Salaries of Safeway's marketing personnel—<u>period cost</u> of a merchandising company. It is a cost that is not traceable to goods purchased for resale. It is presumed not to benefit future periods (or at least not to have sufficiently reliable evidence to estimate such future benefits).

(g) Bottled water consumed by Google's engineers—<u>period cost</u> of a service company. Google has no inventory of goods for sale and, hence, no inventoriable cost.

(h) Salaries of Google's marketing personnel—<u>period cost</u> of a service company. Google has no inventory of goods for sale and, hence, no inventoriable cost.

2-30 (20 min.)	**Computing cost of goods purchased and cost of goods sold.**

(1)	**Marvin Department Store**
Schedule of Cost of Goods Purchased
For the Year Ended December 31, 2008
(in thousands)

Purchases		$155,000
Add transportation-in		7,000
		162,000
Deduct:		
Purchase return and allowances	$4,000	
Purchase discounts	6,000	10,000
Cost of goods purchased		$152,000

(2)	**Marvin Department Store**
Schedule of Cost of Goods Sold
For the Year Ended December 31, 2008
(in thousands)

Beginning merchandise inventory 1/1/2008	$ 27,000
Cost of goods purchased (above)	152,000
Cost of goods available for sale	179,000
Ending merchandise inventory 12/31/2008	34,000
Cost of goods sold	$145,000

2-32 (25–30 min.) **Income statement and schedule of cost of goods manufactured.**

Howell Corporation
Income Statement for the Year Ended December 31, 2009
(in millions)

Revenues		$950
Cost of goods sold:		
Beginning finished goods, Jan. 1, 2009	$ 70	
Cost of goods manufactured (below)	645	
Cost of goods available for sale	715	
Ending finished goods, Dec. 31, 2009	55	660
Gross margin		290
Marketing, distribution, and customer-service costs		240
Operating income		$ 50

Howell Corporation
Schedule of Cost of Goods Manufactured
for the Year Ended December 31, 2009
(in millions)

Direct materials costs:		
Beginning inventory, Jan. 1, 2009	$ 15	
Purchases of direct materials	325	
Cost of direct materials available for use	340	
Ending inventory, Dec. 31, 2009	20	
Direct materials used		$320
Direct manufacturing labor costs		100
Indirect manufacturing costs:		
Indirect manufacturing labor	60	
Plant supplies used	10	
Plant utilities	30	
Depreciation—plant and equipment	80	
Plant supervisory salaries	5	
Miscellaneous plant overhead	35	220
Manufacturing costs incurred during 2009		640
Add beginning work-in-process inventory, Jan. 1, 2009		10
Total manufacturing costs to account for		650
Deduct ending work-in-process, Dec. 31, 2009		5
Cost of goods manufactured		$645

2-34 (25–30 min.)   **Income statement and schedule of cost of goods manufactured.**

Chan Corporation
Income Statement
for the Year Ended December 31, 2009
(in millions)

Revenues		$350
Cost of goods sold:		
Beginning finished goods, Jan. 1, 2009	$ 40	
Cost of goods manufactured (below)	204	
Cost of goods available for sale	244	
Ending finished goods, Dec. 31, 2009	12	232
Gross margin		118
Marketing, distribution, and customer-service costs		90
Operating income		$ 28

Chan Corporation
Schedule of Cost of Goods Manufactured
for the Year Ended December 31, 2009
(in millions)

Direct material costs:		
Beginning inventory, Jan. 1, 2009	$ 30	
Direct materials purchased	80	
Cost of direct materials available for use	110	
Ending inventory, Dec. 31, 2009	5	
Direct materials used		$105
Direct manufacturing labor costs		40
Indirect manufacturing costs:		
Plant supplies used	6	
Property taxes on plant	1	
Plant utilities	5	
Indirect manufacturing labor costs	20	
Depreciation—plant and equipment	9	
Miscellaneous manufacturing overhead costs	10	51
Manufacturing costs incurred during 2009		196
Add beginning work-in-process inventory, Jan. 1, 2009		10
Total manufacturing costs to account for		206
Deduct ending work-in-process inventory, Dec. 31, 2009		2
Cost of goods manufactured (to income statement)		$204

2-36 (20 min.) **Labor cost, overtime and idle time.**

1.(a) Direct labor is charged only at regular rates, and only for productive time, regardless of what is paid to employees. **Total cost of hours worked at regular rates**

42 hours × 12 per hour	$ 504.00
42 hours × 12 per hour	504.00
43 hours × 12 per hour	516.00
40 hours × 12 per hour	480.00
	2,004.00
Minus idle time (5.2 hours × $12 per hour)	62.40
Direct manufacturing labor costs	**$1,941.60**

(b) **Idle time** = 5.2 hours × 12 per hour = $62.40

(c) Overtime and holiday premiums are calculated over and above regular pay. **Overtime and holiday premium.**

Week 1: Overtime (42-40) hours × Premium, $6 per hour	$ 12.00
Week 2: Overtime (42-40) hours ×Premium, $6 per hour	12.00
Week 3: Overtime (43-40) hours × Premium, $6 per hour	18.00
Week 4: Holiday 8 hours × Premium, $12 per hour	96.00
Total overtime and holiday premium	**$138.00**

(d) If we add direct labor, plus idle time, plus overtime & holiday premium, we will get total earnings. **Total earnings in May**

Direct manufacturing labor costs	$1,941.60
Idle time	62.40
Overtime and holiday premium	138.00
Total earnings	**$2,142.00**

2.   **Idle time** caused by equipment breakdowns and scheduling mixups is an indirect cost of the job because it is not related to a specific job.

Overtime premium caused by the heavy *overall* volume of work is also an indirect cost. If, however, the overtime is the result of a demanding "rush job," the overtime premium is a direct cost of that job.

2-38 (30 min.) **Comprehensive problem on unit costs, product costs.**

1. The **cost** of direct materials used is $140,000. The **quantity** of direct materials used is 2 pounds X 100,000 units = 200,000 lbs. Taking cost divided by quantity, we get $0.70 per pound.   Therefore, the **ending inventory** of direct materials is 2,000 lbs. × $0.70 = $1,400.

2. To complete this section, we will first calculate **Average Cost** per unit. Since we know the value for ending inventory in dollars ($20,970 using average unit manufacturing cost), we can then compute the number of units.

	Manufacturing Costs for 100,000 units		
	Variable	**Fixed**	**Total**
Direct materials costs	$140,000	$ –	$140,000
Direct manufacturing labor costs	30,000	–	30,000
Plant energy costs	5,000	–	5,000
Indirect manufacturing labor costs	10,000	16,000	26,000
Other indirect manufacturing costs	8,000	24,000	32,000
Cost of goods manufactured	$193,000	$40,000	$233,000

Average unit manufacturing cost: $233,000 ÷ 100,000 units
                                                             = $2.33 per unit

Finished goods inventory in units: $= \dfrac{\$20,970 \text{ (given)}}{\$2.33 \text{ per unit}}$

                                                             = 9,000 units

3. Units sold in 2009 = Beginning inventory + Production – Ending inventory
                                    = 0 + 100,000 – 9,000 = 91,000 units
   Selling price in 2009 = $436,800 ÷ 91,000
                                    = $4.80 per unit

4.

Revenues (91,000 units sold × $4.80)		$436,800
Cost of units sold:		
Beginning finished goods, Jan. 1, 2009	$ 0	
Cost of goods manufactured	233,000	
Cost of goods available for sale	233,000	
Ending finished goods, Dec. 31, 2009	20,970	212,030
Gross margin		224,770
Operating costs:		
Marketing, distribution, and customer-service costs	162,850	
Administrative costs	50,000	212,850
Operating income		$ 11,920

2-40 (20–25 min.) **Finding unknown amounts.**

For case 1, we need to calculate the cost of goods sold from the gross margin & revenue. Then we need to compute the cost of goods manufactured, so that we can use it to infer ending inventory in the COGS formula.

For case 2, we need to first calculate the gross margin, given revenue & COGS. Then, using the COGS formula, we can infer the cost of goods manufactured, and go backwards to step 2 to solve for indirect manufacturing costs.

Let G = given, I = inferred

Step 1: Use gross margin formula	Case 1	Case 2
Revenues	$ 32,000 G	$31,800 G
Cost of goods sold	**A 20,700** I	20,000 G
Gross margin	$ 11,300 G	**C $11,800** I

Step 2: Use schedule of cost of goods manufactured formula		
Direct materials used	$ 8,000 G	$ 12,000 G
Direct manufacturing labor costs	3,000 G	5,000 G
Indirect manufacturing costs	7,000 G	**D 6,500** I
Manufacturing costs incurred	18,000 I	23,500 I
Add beginning work in process, 1/1	0 G	800 G
Total manufacturing costs to account for	18,000 I	24,300 I
Deduct ending work in process, 12/31	0 G	3,000 G
Cost of goods manufactured	$ 18,000 I	$ 21,300 I

Step 3: Use cost of goods sold formula		
Beginning finished goods inventory, 1/1	$ 4,000 G	$ 4,000 G
Cost of goods manufactured	18,000 I	21,300 I
Cost of goods available for sale	22,000 I	25,300 I
Ending finished goods inventory, 12/31	**B** 1,300 I	5,300 G
Cost of goods sold	$ 20,700 I	$ 20,000 G

CHAPTER 3
COST-VOLUME-PROFIT ANALYSIS

NOTATION USED IN CHAPTER 3 SOLUTIONS

  SP: Selling price
VCU: Variable cost per unit
CMU: Contribution margin per unit
  FC: Fixed costs
 TOI: Target operating income

3-2   The assumptions underlying the CVP analysis outlined in Chapter 3 are
1. **Changes** in the level of **revenues** and **costs** arise only because of **changes** in the **number** of **product** (or service) units sold.
2. **Total costs** can be **separated** into a **fixed** component that does not vary with the units sold and a component that is **variable** with respect to the units sold.
3. When represented graphically, the behavior of **total revenues and total costs are linear** (represented as a straight line) in relation to units sold **within a relevant range** and time period.
4. The **selling price, variable cost per unit, and fixed costs** are **known** and constant.

3-4
Contribution margin is the difference between total revenues and total variable costs.
        (CM = Revenue – Variable Cost)
Contribution margin per unit is the difference between selling price and variable cost per unit.
        (CM/unit = Revenue per unit – Variable Cost per unit)
Contribution-margin percentage is the contribution margin per unit divided by selling price.
        (CM% = CM/unit ÷ Revenue per unit)

3-6   Cost-volume-profit analysis includes analysis of the breakeven point. However, C-V-P includes much more, for example sensitivity of profit to small changes in price.

3-8   An increase in the income tax rate does not affect the breakeven point. Operating income at the breakeven point is zero, and no income taxes are paid at this point.

3-10   Examples include:
    Manufacturing—substituting a robotic machine for hourly wage workers.
    Marketing—changing a sales force compensation plan from a percent of sales dollars to a fixed salary.
    Customer service—hiring a subcontractor to do customer repair visits on an annual retainer basis rather than a per-visit basis.

3-12   **Operating Leverage (OL)** compares Contribution Margin to Operating Income, at a given level of sales. If OL is high, then a small change in contribution margin will lead to a large change in operating income. This change is driven by the level of fixed costs included in operating income. Knowing the degree of operating leverage at a given level of sales helps managers calculate the effect of fluctuations in sales on operating incomes.

3-14 A company with multiple products can compute a breakeven point by assuming there is a constant sales mix of products at different levels of total revenue.

3-16 (10 min.) **CVP computations.**

	Revenues	Variable Costs	Fixed Costs	Total Costs	Operating Income	Contribution Margin	Contribution Margin %
a.	**$2,000**	$ 500	$300	$ 800	$1,200	$1,500	**75.0%**
b.	2,000	**1,500**	300	**1,800**	200	500	**25.0%**
c.	1,000	700	**300**	1,000	**0**	300	**30.0%**
d.	1,500	**900**	300	**1,200**	300	600	40.0%

3-18 (35–40 min.) **CVP analysis, changing revenues and costs.**

1a. SP $= 8\% \times \$1,000 = \$80$ per ticket (Sunshine's revenue is the commission paid to them by the airline company)

VCU $= \$35$ per ticket

CMU $= \$80 - \$35 = \$45$ per ticket

FC $= \$22,000$ a month

$$Q = \frac{FC}{CMU} = \frac{\$22,000}{\$45 \text{ per ticket}}$$

$$= 489 \text{ tickets (rounded up)}$$

1b. $$Q = \frac{FC + TOI}{CMU} = \frac{\$22,000 + \$10,000}{\$45 \text{ per ticket}}$$

$$= \frac{\$32,000}{\$45 \text{ per ticket}}$$

$$= 712 \text{ tickets (rounded up)}$$

2a. SP $= \$80$ per ticket

VCU $= \$29$ per ticket

CMU $= \$80 - \$29 = \$51$ per ticket

FC $= \$22,000$ a month

$$Q = \frac{FC}{CMU} = \frac{\$22,000}{\$51 \text{ per ticket}}$$

$$= 432 \text{ tickets (rounded up)}$$

2b. $Q = \dfrac{FC + TOI}{CMU} = \dfrac{\$22,000 + \$10,000}{\$51 \text{ per ticket}}$

$= \dfrac{\$32,000}{\$51 \text{ per ticket}}$

$= 628$ tickets (rounded up)

3a. SP   = \$48 per ticket
VCU = \$29 per ticket
CMU = \$48 − \$29 = \$19 per ticket
FC   = \$22,000 a month

$Q = \dfrac{FC}{CMU} = \dfrac{\$22,000}{\$19 \text{ per ticket}}$

$= 1,158$ tickets (rounded up)

3b. $Q = \dfrac{FC + TOI}{CMU} = \dfrac{\$22,000 + \$10,000}{\$19 \text{ per ticket}}$

$= \dfrac{\$32,000}{\$19 \text{ per ticket}}$

$= 1,685$ tickets (rounded up)

The reduced commission sizably increases the breakeven point and the number of tickets required to yield a target operating income of \$10,000:

	8% Commission (Requirement 2)	Fixed Commission of \$48
Breakeven point	432	1,158
Attain OI of \$10,000	628	1,685

4a. The \$5 delivery fee can be treated as either an extra source of revenue (as done below) or as a cost offset. Either approach increases CMU \$5:

SP   = \$53 (\$48 + \$5) per ticket
VCU = \$29 per ticket
CMU = \$53 − \$29 = \$24 per ticket
FC   = \$22,000 a month

$Q = \dfrac{FC}{CMU} = \dfrac{\$22,000}{\$24 \text{ per ticket}}$

$= 917$ tickets (rounded up)

4b. $Q = \dfrac{FC + TOI}{CMU} = \dfrac{\$22,000 + \$10,000}{\$24 \text{ per ticket}}$

$= \dfrac{\$32,000}{\$24 \text{ per ticket}}$

$= 1,334$ tickets (rounded up)

The $5 delivery fee results in a higher contribution margin which reduces both the breakeven point and the tickets sold to attain operating income of $10,000.

3-20 (20 min.) **CVP exercises.**

1a. [Units sold × (Selling price – Variable costs)] – Fixed costs   = Operating income
                   [5,000,000 × ($0.50 – $0.30)] – $900,000   = $100,000

1b. Fixed costs ÷ Contribution margin per unit   = Breakeven units
              $900,000 ÷ [($0.50 – $0.30)] = 4,500,000 units
            Breakeven units × Selling price = Breakeven revenues
         4,500,000 units × $0.50 per unit   = $2,250,000

   or,

$$\text{Contribution margin ratio} = \frac{\text{Selling price - Variable costs}}{\text{Selling price}}$$

$$= \frac{\$0.50 - \$0.30}{\$0.50} = 0.40$$

            Fixed costs ÷ Contribution margin ratio   = Breakeven revenues
                     $900,000 ÷ 0.40   = $2,250,000

Follow the formulae above to compute the changed Operating Income & Breakeven units

2.   5,000,000 × ($0.50 – $0.34) – $900,000   = $ (100,000)

3.   [5,000,000 × (1.1) × ($0.50 – $0.30)] – [$900,000 (1.1)]   = $ 110,000

4.   [5,000,000 (1.4) (($0.50 × 0.8) – ($0.30 × 0.9))] – [$900,000 × 0.8]   = $ 190,000

5. $900,000 (1.1) ÷ ($0.50 – $0.30)   = 4,950,000 units

6.   ($900,000 + $20,000) ÷ (($0.50 × 1.1) – $0.30)   = 3,680,000 units

3-22 (20–25 min.) **CVP analysis, income taxes.**

1. Variable cost percentage is $3.20 \div \$8.00 = 40\%$

    $$\text{Let } R = \text{Revenues needed to obtain target net income}$$

    $$R - 0.40R - \$450{,}000 = \frac{\$105{,}000}{1 - 0.30}$$

    $$0.60R = \$450{,}000 + \$150{,}000$$

    $$R = \$600{,}000 \div 0.60$$

    $$R = \$1{,}000{,}000$$

    or,

    $$\text{Breakeven revenues} = \frac{\dfrac{\text{Target net income}}{1 - \text{Tax rate}}}{\text{Contribution margin percentage}} = \frac{\$450{,}000 + \dfrac{\$105{,}000}{1 - 0.30}}{0.60} = \$1{,}000{,}000$$

Proof:		
Revenues		$1,000,000
Variable costs (at 40%)		400,000
Contribution margin		600,000
Fixed costs		450,000
Operating income		150,000
Income taxes (at 30%)		45,000
Net income		$ 105,000

2.a.   Customers needed to break even:

Contribution margin per customer = $8.00 – $3.20 = $4.80

Breakeven number of customers = Fixed costs ÷ Contribution margin per customer

= $450,000 ÷ $4.80 per customer

= 93,750 customers

2.b.   Customers needed to earn net income of $105,000. Because we already computed the revenue needed to earn net income of $105,000, we can just use total revenue ÷ Revenue per customer.

Total revenues ÷ Sales check per customer

$1,000,000 ÷ $8 = 125,000 customers

3. Using the shortcut approach:

$$\text{Change in net income} = \left(\begin{array}{c}\text{Change in}\\\text{number of customers}\end{array}\right) \times \left(\begin{array}{c}\text{Unit}\\\text{contribution}\\\text{margin}\end{array}\right) \times (1 - \text{Tax rate})$$

$$= (150,000 - 125,000) \times \$4.80 \times (1 - 0.30)$$
$$= \$120,000 \times 0.7 = \$84,000$$

New net income $= \$84,000 + \$105,000 = \$189,000$

The alternative approach is:

Revenues, 150,000 × $8.00	$1,200,000
Variable costs at 40%	480,000
Contribution margin	720,000
Fixed costs	450,000
Operating income	270,000
Income tax at 30%	81,000
Net income	$ 189,000

3-24 (10 min.) CVP analysis, margin of safety.

1. $$\text{Breakeven point revenues} = \frac{\text{Fixed costs}}{\text{Contribution margin percentage}}$$

$$\text{Contribution margin percentage} = \frac{\$600,000}{\$1,500,000} = 0.40 \text{ or } 40\%$$

2. $$\text{Contribution margin percentage} = \frac{\text{Selling price} - \text{Variable cost per unit}}{\text{Selling price}}$$

$$0.40 = \frac{SP - \$15}{SP}$$
$$0.40\,SP = SP - \$15$$
$$0.60\,SP = \$15$$
$$SP = \$25$$

3. Breakeven sales in units $=$ Revenues $\div$ Selling price $= \$1,500,000 \div \$25 = 60,000$ units
   Margin of safety in units $=$ sales in units $-$ Breakeven sales in units
   $$= 80,000 - 60,000 = 20,000 \text{ units}$$

Revenues, 80,000 units × $25	$2,000,000
Breakeven revenues	1,500,000
Margin of safety	$ 500,000

3-26 (15 min.) **CVP analysis, international cost structure differences.**

Country	Sales price to retail outlets (1)	Annual Fixed Costs (2)	Variable Manufacturing Cost per Sweater (3)	Variable Marketing & Distribution Cost per Sweater (4)	Contribution Margin Per Unit (5)=(1)-(3)-(4)	Breakeven Units (6)=(2)÷(5)	Breakeven Revenues (6) × (1)	Operating Income for Budgeted Sales of 800,000 Sweaters (7)=[800,000 × (5)] − (2)
Singapore	$32.00	$ 6,500,000	$ 8.00	$11.00	$13.00	500,000	$16,000,000	$3,900,000
Thailand	32.00	4,500,000	5.50	11.50	15.00	300,000	9,600,000	7,500,000
United States	32.00	12,000,000	13.00	9.00	10.00	1,200,000	38,400,000	(4,000,000)
						Requirement 1		Requirement 2

Thailand has the lowest breakeven point since it has both the lowest fixed costs ($4,500,000) and the lowest variable cost per unit ($17.00). Hence, for a given selling price, Thailand will always have a higher operating income (or a lower operating loss) than Singapore or the U.S.

The U.S. breakeven point is 1,200,000 units. Hence, with sales of only 800,000 units, it has an operating loss of $4,000,000.

Keep this problem in mind as we move on in the book. Although the cost is least in Thailand, there are other inputs to the decision making. For example, Knitwear needs to consider whether they can sell more units, or raise the price with a "Made in the USA" label. In addition, they need to consider the timing of shipments and response to demand. They need to consider quality in each country. I'm sure that you can think of other factors that would impact this decision.

27

3-28   (20 min.)   **CVP analysis, multiple cost drivers.**

1a.   Operating
     income

Revenues, $45 × 40,000	$1,800,000
Variable cost of frames, $30 × 40,000	1,200,000
Variable cost of shipment $60 × 1,000	60,000
Contribution margin	540,000
Fixed costs	240,000
Operating income	$ 300,000

1b.

Revenues, $45 × 40,000	$1,800,000
Variable cost of frames, $30 × 40,000	1,200,000
Variable cost of shipment $60 × 800	48,000
Contribution margin	552,000
Fixed costs	240,000
Operating income	$ 312,000

2.   *Once she knows the shipment cost, we treat that as a "fixed cost" in the analysis. The only things that now vary with quantity are revenue and direct variable costs.* Denote the number of picture frames sold by Q, then

$$\$45Q - \$30Q - (500 \times \$60) - \$240,000 = 0$$
$$\$15Q = \$30,000 + \$240,000 = \$270,000$$
$$Q = \$270,000 \div \$15 = 18,000 \text{ picture frames}$$

3.   Suppose Susan had 1,000 shipments.

$$\$45Q - \$30Q - (1,000 \times \$60) - \$240,000 = 0$$
$$15Q = \$300,000$$
$$Q = 20,000 \text{ picture frames}$$

The breakeven point is not unique because there are two cost drivers—quantity of picture frames and number of shipments. Various combinations of the two cost drivers can yield zero operating income.

3-30 (15 min.) **Contribution margin, decision making.**

1. Revenues $500,000
    Deduct variable costs:

Cost of goods sold	$200,000	
Sales commissions	50,000	
Other operating costs	40,000	290,000
Contribution margin		$210,000

2. Contribution margin percentage $= \dfrac{\$210,000}{\$500,000} = 42\%$

3. Incremental revenue (20% × $500,000) = $100,000

Incremental contribution margin	
(42% × $100,000)	$42,000
Incremental fixed costs (advertising)	10,000
Incremental operating income	$32,000

If Mr. Schmidt spends $10,000 more on advertising, the operating income will increase by $32,000, converting an operating loss of $10,000 to an operating income of $22,000.

Most companies will do this analysis in P&L statement format, so it is good to feel comfortable with the following optional method.

Revenues (120% × $500,000)		$600,000
Cost of goods sold (40% of sales)		240,000
Gross margin		360,000
Operating costs:		
Salaries and wages	$150,000	
Sales commissions (10% of sales)	60,000	
Depreciation of equipment and fixtures	12,000	
Store rent	48,000	
Advertising	10,000	
Other operating costs:		
Variable ($40,000 × 120%)	48,000	
Fixed	10,000	338,000
Operating income		$ 22,000

3-32 (30 min.) **Uncertainty and expected costs.**

The cost of each plan for each quantity of monthly orders takes the fixed cost of the plan and multiplies the variable cost of the plan by the expected number of orders.

1.

Monthly Number of Orders	Cost of Current System
300,000	$1,000,000 + $40(300,000) = $13,000,000
400,000	$1,000,000 + $40(400,000) = $17,000,000
500,000	$1,000,000 + $40(500,000) = $21,000,000
600,000	$1,000,000 + $40(600,000) = $25,000,000
700,000	$1,000,000 + $40(700,000) = $29,000,000

Monthly Number of Orders	Cost of Partially Automated System
300,000	$5,000,000 + $30(300,000) = $14,000,000
400,000	$5,000,000 + $30(400,000) = $17,000,000
500,000	$5,000,000 + $30(500,000) = $20,000,000
600,000	$5,000,000 + $30(600,000) = $23,000,000
700,000	$5,000,000 + $30(700,000) = $26,000,000

Monthly Number of Orders	Cost of Fully Automated System
300,000	$10,000,000 + $20(300,000) = $16,000,000
400,000	$10,000,000 + $20(400,000) = $18,000,000
500,000	$10,000,000 + $20(500,000) = $20,000,000
600,000	$10,000,000 + $20(600,000) = $22,000,000
700,000	$10,000,000 + $20(700,000) = $24,000,000

2. *To calculate the expected cost of each plan, take the figures above for the cost of each plan at a given order level multiplied by the probability that that order level will occur. The expected cost of the plan will be the sum of those calculations.*

Current System Expected Cost:
$13,000,000 × 0.1 = $ 1,300,000
17,000,000 × 0.25 =   4,250,000
21,000,000 × 0.40 =   8,400,000
25,000,000 × 0.15 =   3,750,000
29,000,000 × 0.10 =   2,900,000
                    $ 20,600,000

Partially Automated System Expected Cost:
$14,000,000 × 0.1 = $ 1 ,400,000
17,000,000 × 0.25 =   4,250,000
20,000,000 × 0.40 =   8,000,000
23,000,000 × 0.15 =   3,450,000
26,000,000 × 0.1 =   2,600,000
                     $19,700,000

Fully Automated System Expected Cost:

$16,000,000 \times 0.1 = \$\ 1,600,000$
$18,000,000 \times 0.25 = \ \ \ 4,500,000$
$20,000,000 \times 0.40 = \ \ \ 8,000,000$
$22,000,000 \times 0.15 = \ \ \ 3,300,000$
$24,000,000 \times 0.10 = \ \ \underline{\ \ 2,400,000}$
$\ \underline{\$19,800,000}$

3. Dawmart should consider
   - The impact of the different systems on its relationship with suppliers. The interface with Dawmart's system may require that suppliers also update their systems. Suppliers may drop Dawmart or raise prices and lose customers.
   - The reliability of different systems
   - The effect on employee morale if employees have to be laid off as it automates its systems.
   - The precision of the probability estimates
   - The precision of the cost estimates
   - Whether new technology is expected soon
   - Software support for the new system
   - Training for operators of the new system (how much is required, who pays, etc.?)
   - Other

3-34 (30 min.) **CVP, target income, service firm.**

1.
Revenue per child	$600
Variable costs per child	200
Contribution margin per child	$400

$$\text{Breakeven quantity} = \frac{\text{Fixed costs}}{\text{Contribution margin per child}}$$

$$= \frac{\$5,600}{\$400} = 14 \text{ children}$$

2.
$$\text{Target quantity} = \frac{\text{Fixed costs} + \text{Target operating income}}{\text{Contribution margin per child}}$$

$$= \frac{\$5,600 + \$10,400}{\$400} = 40 \text{ children}$$

3. Both the increase in the rent and the field trips result in additional fixed costs. Thus, we divide them by the number of children enrolled, and can compute the additional fee per child.

Increase in rent ($3,000 – $2,000)	$1,000
Field trips	1,000
Total increase in fixed costs	$2,000
Divide by the number of children enrolled	÷ 40
Increase in fee per child	$ 50

Therefore, the fee per child will increase from $600 to $650.

3-36 (30–40 min.) **CVP analysis, income taxes.**

1.

Revenues, $25 × 20,000	$500,000
Variable costs $13.75 × 20,000	275,000
Contribution margin	225,000
Fixed costs	135,000
Net income before taxes	90,000
Income taxes (40%)	36,000
Operating income	$ 54,000

2. $$\text{Breakeven quantity} = \frac{\text{Fixed costs}}{\text{Contribution margin per unit}}$$

Contribution margin per unit = Revenue per unit $25 – Variable cost per unit $13.75
$$= \$11.25$$

$$= \frac{\$135,000}{\$11.25} = 12,000 \text{ units}$$

3.

Revenues, $25 × 22,000	$550,000
Variable costs $13.75 × 22,000	302,500
Contribution margin	247,500
Fixed costs ($135,000 + 11,250)	146,250
Net income before taxes	101,250
Income taxes (40%)	40,500
Operating income	$ 60,750

4. $\text{Breakeven quantity} = \dfrac{\text{Fixed costs}}{\text{Contribution margin per unit}}$

We will repeat the calculation from above, but we need to add the $11,250 in advertising to fixed costs.

$$= \dfrac{\$146,250}{\$11.25} = 13,000 \text{ units}$$

Breakeven revenue = Selling price $25 × Breakeven units 13,000
= $\underline{\$325,000}$

5. Let S = Required sales units to equal 2008 net income

$$\$25.00S - \$13.75S - \$146,250 = \dfrac{\$54,000}{0.60}$$

$$\$11.25S = \$236,250$$
$$S = 21,000 \text{ units}$$
$$\text{Revenues} = 21,000 \text{ units} \times \$25 = \$525,000$$

6. Let A = Amount spent for advertising in 2009

$$\$550,000 - \$302,500 - (\$135,000 + A) = \dfrac{\$60,000}{0.60}$$

$$\$550,000 - \$302,500 - \$135,000 - A = \$100,000$$
$$\$550,000 - \$537,500 = A$$
$$A = \$12,500$$

3-38 (20–30 min.)   ***CVP analysis, shoe stores.***

1. CMU (SP – VCU = $30 – $21)	$ 9.00
a. Breakeven units (FC ÷ CMU = $360,000 ÷ $9 per unit)	40,000
b. Breakeven revenues	
(Breakeven units × SP = 40,000 units × $30 per unit)	$1,200,000
2. Pairs sold	35,000
Revenues, 35,000 × $30	$1,050,000
Total cost of shoes, 35,000 × $19.50	682,500
Total sales commissions, 35,000 × $1.50	52,500
Total variable costs	735,000
Contribution margin	315,000
Fixed costs	360,000
Operating income (loss)	$ (45,000)

3. Unit variable data (per pair of shoes)

Selling price	$ 30.00
Cost of shoes	19.50
Sales commissions	0
Variable cost per unit	$ 19.50
Annual fixed costs	
Rent	$ 60,000
Salaries, $200,000 + $81,000	281,000
Advertising	80,000
Other fixed costs	20,000
Total fixed costs	$ 441,000
CMU, $30 – $19.50	$ 10.50
a. Breakeven units, (FC ÷ CMU = $441,000 ÷ $10.50 per unit)	42,000
b. Breakeven revenues, 42,000 units × $30 per unit	$1,260,000

4. Unit variable data (per pair of shoes)

Selling price	$ 30.00
Cost of shoes	19.50
Sales commissions	1.80
Variable cost per unit	$ 21.30
Total fixed costs	$ 360,000
CMU, $30 – $21.30	$ 8.70
a. Break even units (FC ÷ CMU = $360,000 ÷ $8.70 per unit)	41,380 (rounded up)
b. Break even revenues = 41,380 units × $30 per unit	$1,241,400

5. Pairs sold   50,000

Recall that the original breakeven point was 40,000 pair of shoes.

Revenues (50,000 pairs × $30 per pair)	$1,500,000
Total cost of shoes (50,000 pairs × $19.50 per pair)	$ 975,000
Sales commissions on first 40,000 pairs (40,000 pairs × $1.50 per pair)	60,000
Sales commissions on additional 10,000 pairs	
[10,000 pairs × ($1.50 + $0.30 per pair)]	18,000
Total variable costs	$1,053,000
Contribution margin	$ 447,000
Fixed costs	360,000
Operating income	$ 87,000

Alternative approach:

Breakeven point in units = 40,000 pairs

Store manager receives commission of $0.30 on 10,000 (50,000 – 40,000) pairs.

Because the breakeven point has Revenue – Variable Costs – Fixed Costs = 0, any sales beyond breakeven result in the firm profit equal to the contribution margin beyond breakeven. Therefore, Contribution margin per pair beyond breakeven point of 10,000 pairs = $8.70 ($30 – $21 – $0.30) per pair.

Operating income = 10,000 pairs × $8.70 contribution margin per pair = $87,000.

3-40 (40 min.) **Alternative cost structures, uncertainty, and sensitivity analysis.**

1. Contribution margin assuming fixed rental arrangement = $50 – $30 = $20 per bouquet
Fixed costs = $5,000
Breakeven point = $5,000 ÷ $20 per bouquet = 250 bouquets

   Contribution margin assuming $10 per arrangement rental agreement
= $50 – $30 – $10 = $10 per bouquet
Fixed costs = $0
Breakeven point = $0 ÷ $10 per bouquet = 0
Because there are no fixed costs, selling only 1 bouquet will generate profit for EB. Any sales will generate contribution margin of $10 per unit.

2. Let x denote the number of bouquets EB must sell for it to be indifferent between the fixed rent and royalty agreement.

   To calculate x we solve the following equation.
$$\$50\,x - \$30\,x - \$5,000 = \$50\,x - \$40\,x$$
$$\$20\,x - \$5,000 = \$10\,x$$
$$\$10\,x = \$5,000$$
$$x = \$5,000 \div \$10 = 500 \text{ bouquets}$$

   For sales between 0 to 500 bouquets, EB prefers the royalty agreement because in this range, $\$10\,x > \$20\,x - \$5,000$. Because EB makes profit on each sale, they will be better off without the fixed costs in the low range.

   For sales greater than 500 bouquets, EB prefers the fixed rent agreement because in this range, $\$20\,x - \$5,000 > \$10\,x$. Because the contribution margin increases under the fixed rental agreement, EB will be better off with the fixed fee once their contribution margin covers the fixed fee. They get to keep an extra $10 per basket after that point.

3. The $5 reduction in variable costs applies to both scenarios, thus the difference in contribution margin per unit between the fixed rent and the variable rent remains the same ($10). We solve the   following equation for x.
$$\$50\,x - \$25\,x - \$5,000 = \$50\,x - \$35\,x$$
$$\$25\,x - \$5,000 = \$15\,x$$
$$\$10\,x = \$5,000$$
$$x = \$5,000 \div \$10 \text{ per bouquet} = 500 \text{ bouquets}$$

   The answer is the same as in Requirement 2, that is, for sales between 0 to 500 bouquets, EB prefers the royalty agreement because in this range, $\$15\,x > \$25\,x - \$5,000$. For sales greater than 500 bouquets, EB prefers the fixed rent agreement because in this range, $\$25\,x - \$5,000 > \$15\,x$.

4. Fixed rent agreement:

# Bouquet Sold	200	400	600	800	1,000
Revenue $50 per unit	$10,000	20,000	30,000	40,000	$50,000
Variable Costs $30 per unit	6,000	12,000	18,000	24,000	30,000
Contribution Margin	4,000	8,000	12,000	16,000	20,000
Fixed Costs	5,000	5,000	5,000	5,000	5,000
Operating Income (Loss)	($1,000)	3,000	7,000	11,000	$15,000
Probability of occurrence	.2	.2	.2	.2	.2
Expected Value of each event	($200)	600	1,400	2,200	3,000

Total Expected Value of Rent Agreement	$7,000

Royalty agreement:

# Bouquet Sold	200	400	600	800	1,000
Revenue $50 per unit	$10,000	20,000	30,000	40,000	$50,000
Variable Costs $40 per unit	8,000	16,000	24,000	32,000	40,000
Contribution Margin	2,000	4,000	6,000	8,000	10,000
Fixed Costs	0	0	0	0	0
Operating Income (Loss)	$2,000	4,000	6,000	8,000	$10,000
Probability of occurrence	.2	.2	.2	.2	.2
Expected Value of each event	400	800	1,200	1,600	2,000

Total Expected Value of Rent Agreement	$6,000

EB should choose the fixed rent agreement because the expected value is higher than the royalty agreement. EB will lose money under the fixed rent agreement if EB sells only 200 bouquets but this loss is more than made up for by high operating incomes when sales are high. The fixed agreement is RISKIER. Potentially higher losses, but potentially higher upsides, too. In making this decision, however, EB needs to consider other qualitative factors, like is it possible to switch agreements after they begin, in which case, they could start with the less risky option until they were off their feet, and then switch to the more profitable case when they were operating completely.

3-42 (30 min.)   **CVP analysis, income taxes, sensitivity.**

1a.   To break even, revenues must equal total costs. At breakeven, income taxes are zero.

Let Q denote the quantity of canopies sold.

$$
\begin{aligned}
\text{Revenue} &= \text{Variable costs} + \text{Fixed costs} \\
\$400Q &= \$200Q + \$100,000 \\
\$200Q &= \$100,000 \\
Q &= 500 \text{ units}
\end{aligned}
$$

Breakeven can also be calculated using contribution margin per unit.

Contribution margin per unit = Selling price – Variable cost per unit = $400 – $200 = $200

$$
\begin{aligned}
\text{Breakeven} &= \text{Fixed Costs} \div \text{Contribution margin per unit} \\
&= \$100,000 \div \$200 \\
&= 500 \text{ units}
\end{aligned}
$$

1b.   To achieve its net income objective, Almo Company must sell 2,500 units. This amount represents the point where revenues equal total costs plus the corresponding operating income objective to achieve net income of $240,000.

$$
\begin{aligned}
\text{Revenue} &= \text{Variable costs} + \text{Fixed costs} + [\text{Net income} \div (1 - \text{Tax rate})] \\
\$400Q &= \$200Q + \$100,000 + [\$240,000 \div (1 - 0.4)] \\
\$400 Q &= \$200Q + \$100,000 + \$400,000 \\
\$200Q &= \$500,000 \\
Q &= 2,500 \text{ units}
\end{aligned}
$$

2.

Alternative a.	First 5 months	Rest of Year	Total
Description		SP $360	
Revenue	$140,000	972,000	$1,112,000
Variable Costs	70,000	540,000	610,000
Contribution Margin	70,000	432,000	502,000
Fixed Costs			100,000
Net Income Before Taxes			402,000
Income tax expense			160,800
Operating Income			$241,200

Alternative b.	First 5 months	Rest of Year	Total
Description		Lower VC Reduce SP Sales 2,200	
Revenue	$140,000	814,000	$954,000
Variable Costs	70,000	418,000	488,000
Contribution Margin	70,000	396,000	466,000
Fixed Costs			100,000
Net Income Before Taxes			366,000
Income tax expense			146,400
Operating Income			$219,600

Alternative c.	First 5 months	Rest of Year	Total
Description		Reduce FC Lower SP 5% Sales 2,000	
Revenue	$140,000	760,000	$900,000
Variable Costs	70,000	400,000	470,000
Contribution Margin	70,000	360,000	430,000
Fixed Costs			90,000
Net Income Before Taxes			340,000
Income tax expense			136,000
Operating Income			$204,000

To achieve its net income objective, Almo Company should select the first alternative where the sales price is reduced by $40, and 2,700 units are sold during the remainder of the year. This alternative results in the highest net income and is the only alternative that equals or exceeds the company's net income objective.

3-44 (15–25 min.) **Sales mix, three products.**

1. Sales of A, B, and C are in ratio 20,000 : 100,000 : 80,000. So for every 1 unit of A, 5 (100,000 ÷ 20,000) units of B are sold, and 4 (80,000 ÷ 20,000) units of C are sold.

Contribution margin of the bundle = 1 × $3 + 5 × $2 + 4 × $1 = $3 + $10 + $4 = $17

Breakeven point in bundles = $\dfrac{\$255,000}{\$17}$ = 15,000 bundles

Breakeven point in units is:

Product A:	15,000 bundles × 1 unit per bundle	15,000 units
Product B:	15,000 bundles × 5 units per bundle	75,000 units
Product C:	15,000 bundles × 4 units per bundle	60,000 units
Total number of units to breakeven		150,000 units

Alternatively,

Let Q = Number of units of A to break even

5Q = Number of units of B to break even

4Q = Number of units of C to break even

Contribution margin – Fixed costs = Zero operating income

$3Q + $2(5Q) + $1(4Q) – $255,000 = 0

$17Q = $255,000

Q = 15,000 ($255,000 ÷ $17) units of A

5Q = 75,000 units of B

4Q = 60,000 units of C

Total = 150,000 units

2. Contribution margin:

A: 20,000 × $3	$ 60,000	
B: 100,000 × $2	200,000	
C: 80,000 × $1	80,000	
Contribution margin		$340,000
Fixed costs		255,000
Operating income		$ 85,000

3. Contribution margin

A:	20,000 × $3	$ 60,000
B:	80,000 × $2	160,000
C:	100,000 × $1	100,000
	Contribution margin	$320,000
Fixed costs		255,000
Operating income		$ 65,000

Sales of A, B, and C are in ratio 20,000 : 80,000 : 100,000. So for every 1 unit of A, 4 (80,000 ÷ 20,000) units of B and 5 (100,000 ÷ 20,000) units of C are sold.

Contribution margin of the bundle = 1 × $3 + 4 × $2 + 5 × $1 = $3 + $8 + $5 = $16

$$\text{Breakeven point in bundles} = \frac{\$255,000}{\$16} = 15,938 \text{ bundles (rounded up)}$$

Breakeven point in units is:

Product A:	15,938 bundles × 1 unit per bundle	15,938 units
Product B:	15,938 bundles × 4 units per bundle	63,752 units
Product C:	15,938 bundles × 5 units per bundle	79,690 units
Total number of units to breakeven		159,380 units

Alternatively,

Let Q	=	Number of units of A to break even
4Q	=	Number of units of B to break even
5Q	=	Number of units of C to break even

Contribution margin – Fixed costs = Breakeven point

$3Q + $2(4Q) + $1(5Q) – $255,000	=	0
$16Q	=	$255,000
Q	=	15,938 ($255,000 ÷ $16) units of A (rounded up)
4Q	=	63,752 units of B
5Q	=	79,690 units of C
Total	=	159,380 units

Breakeven point increases because the new mix contains less of the higher contribution margin per unit, product B, and more of the lower contribution margin per unit, product C.

3-46 (20–25 min.) **Sales mix, two products.**

1. Sales of standard and deluxe carriers are in the ratio of 150,000 : 50,000. So for every 1 unit of deluxe, 3 (150,000 ÷ 50,000) units of standard are sold.

Product Line	Standard	Deluxe
Revenue per unit	$20	$30
Variable cost per unit	14	18
Contribution margin per unit	$6	$12

Use the contribution margins above, plus the relative mix of the products to determine a "Contribution Margin of the Bundle". From that, you can determine the breakeven number of bundles, and from that, the breakeven number of units of each product.

Contribution margin of the bundle = $3 \times \$6 + 1 \times \$12 = \$18 + \$12 = \$30$

$$\text{Breakeven point in bundles} = \frac{\text{Fixed costs}}{\text{Bundle contribution margin}}$$

$$= \frac{\$1,200,000}{\$30} = 40,000 \text{ bundles}$$

Breakeven point in units is:
Standard carrier:	40,000 bundles × 3 units per bundle	120,000 units
Deluxe carrier:	40,000 bundles × 1 unit per bundle	40,000 units
Total number of units to breakeven		160,000 units

Alternatively,

Let Q = Number of units of Deluxe carrier to break even

3Q = Number of units of Standard carrier to break even

Revenues – Variable costs – Fixed costs = Zero operating income

$\$20(3Q) + \$30Q - \$14(3Q) - \$18Q - \$1,200,000 = 0$

$\$60Q + \$30Q - \$42Q - \$18Q = \$1,200,000$

$\$30Q = \$1,200,000$

$Q = 40,000 \text{ units of Deluxe}$

$3Q = 120,000 \text{ units of Standard}$

The breakeven point is 120,000 Standard units plus 40,000 Deluxe units, a total of 160,000 units.

2a. Using the fixed costs and contribution margin per unit for Standard Carriers,

Breakeven point in units of Standard $= \dfrac{\text{Fixed costs}}{\text{Contribution Margin}}$

$= \dfrac{\$120,000}{\$6} = 200,000$ units of the Standard Carrier

2b. Using the fixed costs and contribution margin per unit for Deluxe Carriers,

Breakeven point in units of Deluxe $= \dfrac{\text{Fixed costs}}{\text{Contribution Margin}}$

$= \dfrac{\$120,000}{\$12} = 100,000$ units of the Deluxe Carrier

3.

Product Line	Standard	Deluxe	Total
Units Sold	180,000	20,000	200,000
Revenue	$3,600,000	600,000	$4,200,000
Variable costs	2,520,000	360,000	2,880,000
Contribution Margin	1,080,000	240,000	1,320,000
Fixed Costs			1,200,000
Operating Income			$120,000

Alternatively:

3. Operating income = Contribution margin of Standard + Contribution margin of Deluxe - Fixed costs

$$= 180,000(\$6) + 20,000(\$12) - \$1,200,000$$
$$= \$1,080,000 + \$240,000 - \$1,200,000$$
$$= \$120,000$$

Sales of standard and deluxe carriers are in the ratio of 180,000 : 20,000. So for every 1 unit of deluxe, 9 (180,000 ÷ 20,000) units of standard are sold.

Contribution margin of the bundle $= 9 \times \$6 + 1 \times \$12 = \$54 + \$12 = \$66$

Breakeven point in bundles $= \dfrac{\$1,200,000}{\$66} = 18,182$ bundles (rounded up)

Breakeven point in units is:

Standard carrier:	18,182 bundles × 9 units per bundle	163,638 units
Deluxe carrier:	18,182 bundles × 1 unit per bundle	18,182 units
Total number of units to breakeven		181,820 units

Alternatively,

Let Q = Number of units of Deluxe product to break even

9Q = Number of units of Standard product to break even

$$\$20(9Q) + \$30Q - \$14(9Q) - \$18Q - \$1,200,000 = 0$$
$$\$180Q + \$30Q - \$126Q - \$18Q = \$1,200,000$$
$$\$66Q = \$1,200,000$$
$$Q = 18,182 \text{ units of Deluxe (rounded up)}$$
$$9Q = 163,638 \text{ units of Standard}$$

The breakeven point is 163,638 Standard + 18,182 Deluxe, a total of 181,820 units.

The major lesson of this problem is that changes **in the sales mix change breakeven points and operating incomes**. In this example, the budgeted and actual total sales in number of units were identical, but the proportion of the product having the higher contribution margin declined. Operating income suffered, falling from $300,000 to $120,000. Moreover, the breakeven point rose from 160,000 to 181,820 units.

3-48 (30 min.) **Ethics, CVP analysis.**

1.

$$\text{Contribution margin percentage} = \frac{\text{Revenues} - \text{Variable costs}}{\text{Revenues}}$$

$$= \frac{\$5,000,000 - \$3,000,000}{\$5,000,000}$$

$$= \frac{\$2,000,000}{\$5,000,000} = 40\%$$

$$\text{Breakeven revenues} = \frac{\text{Fixed costs}}{\text{Contribution margin percentage}}$$

$$= \frac{\$2,160,000}{0.40} = \$5,400,000$$

2. If variable costs are 52% of revenues, contribution margin percentage equals 48% (100% − 52%)

$$\text{Breakeven revenues} = \frac{\text{Fixed costs}}{\text{Contribution margin percentage}}$$

$$= \frac{\$2,160,000}{0.48} = \$4,500,000$$

3.

Revenues	$5,000,000
Variable costs (0.52 × $5,000,000)	2,600,000
Fixed costs	2,160,000
Operating income	$ 240,000

4.	Incorrect reporting of environmental costs with the goal of continuing operations is unethical. In assessing the situation, the specific "Standards of Ethical Conduct for Management Accountants" (described in Exhibit 1-7) that the management accountant should consider are listed below.

Competence

Clear reports using relevant and reliable information should be prepared. Preparing reports on the basis of incorrect environmental costs to make the company's performance look better than it is violates competence standards. It is unethical for Bush not to report environmental costs to make the plant's performance look good.

Integrity

The management accountant has a responsibility to avoid actual or apparent conflicts of interest and advise all appropriate parties of any potential conflict. Bush may be tempted to report lower environmental costs to please Lemond and Woodall and save the jobs of his colleagues. This action, however, violates the responsibility for integrity. The Standards of Ethical Conduct require the management accountant to communicate favorable as well as unfavorable information.

Credibility

The management accountant's Standards of Ethical Conduct require that information should be fairly and objectively communicated and that all relevant information should be disclosed. From a management accountant's standpoint, underreporting environmental costs to make performance look good would violate the standard of objectivity.

Bush should indicate to Lemond that estimates of environmental costs and liabilities should be included in the analysis. If Lemond still insists on modifying the numbers and reporting lower environmental costs, Bush should raise the matter with one of Lemond's superiors. If after taking all these steps, there is continued pressure to understate environmental costs, Bush should consider resigning from the company and not engage in unethical behavior.

CHAPTER 4
JOB COSTING

4-2 In a *job-costing system,* costs are assigned to a distinct unit, batch, or lot of a product or service. In a *process-costing system,* the cost of a product or service is obtained by using broad averages to assign costs to masses of identical or similar units.

4-4 The seven steps in job costing are:
(1) identify the job that is the chosen **cost object**,
(2) identify the **direct costs** of the job,
(3) select the **cost-allocation bases** to use for allocating indirect costs to the job,
(4) identify the **indirect costs** associated with each cost-allocation base,
(5) compute the **rate per unit of each cost-allocation base** used to allocate indirect costs to the job,
(6) compute the **indirect costs allocated** to the job, and
(7) compute the **total cost of the job** by adding all direct and indirect costs assigned to the job.

4-6 Three major source documents used in job-costing systems are:
(1) **job cost record** or job cost sheet, a document that records and *accumulates all costs* assigned to a specific job, starting when work begins
(2) **materials requisition record**, a document that contains information about the *cost of direct materials used* on a specific job and in a specific department; and
(3) **labor-time record**, a document that contains information about the *labor time used* on a specific job and in a specific department.

4-8 Two reasons for using an annual budget period are
(1) The **numerator** reason—the longer the time period, the *less the influence of seasonal patterns*, and
(2) The **denominator** reason—the longer the time period, the *less the effect of variations in output levels* on the allocation of fixed costs.

4-10 A house construction firm can use job cost information to
(1) determine the **profitability** of individual jobs,
(2) assist in **bidding** on future jobs, or
(3) **evaluate** professionals who are in charge of managing individual jobs.

4-12 Debit entries to Work-in-Process Control represent increases in work in process. Examples of debit entries under normal costing are
(1) direct **materials** used (credit to Materials Control),
(2) direct manufacturing **labor** billed to job (credit to Wages Payable Control), and
(3) manufacturing **overhead** allocated to job (credit to Manufacturing Overhead Allocated).

4-14 A company might use budgeted costs rather than actual costs to compute direct labor rates because it may be *difficult to trace direct labor costs to jobs* as they are completed (for example, because bonuses are only known at the end of the year).

4-16 (10 min) **Job order costing, process costing.**

Situation	Appropriate Costing Method
a. CPA Firm	Job Costing
b. Oil refinery	Process Costing
c. Custom furniture manufacturer	Job Costing
d. Tire manufacturer	Process Costing
e. textbook publisher	Job Costing
f. Pharmaceutical company	Process Costing
g. Advertising agency	Job Costing
h. Apparel Manufacturing plant	Job Costing with some Process Costing
i. Flour mill	Process Costing
j. Paint manufacturer	Process Costing
k. Medical care facility	Job Costing
l. Landscaping company	Job Costing
m. Cola-drink-concentrate producer	Process Costing
n. Movie studio	Job Costing
o. Law firm	Job Costing
p. Commercial aircraft manufacturer	Job Costing
q. Management consulting firm	Job Costing
r. Breakfast-cereal company	Process Costing
s. Catering service	Job Costing
t. Paper mill	Process Costing
u. Auto repair shop	Job Costing

4-18 (20 -30 min.) **Job costing, normal and actual costing.**

1. $$\text{Budgeted indirect-cost rate} = \frac{\text{Budgeted indirect costs}}{\text{Budgeted direct labor-hours}} = \frac{\$8,000,000}{160,000 \text{ hours}}$$

$$= \$50 \text{ per direct labor-hour}$$

$$\text{Actual indirect-cost rate} = \frac{\text{Actual indirect costs}}{\text{Actual direct labor-hours}} = \frac{\$6,888,000}{164,000 \text{ hours}}$$

$$= \$42 \text{ per direct labor-hour}$$

These rates differ because both the numerator and the denominator in the two calculations are different—one based on budgeted numbers and the other based on actual numbers.

2a.

	Laguna Model	Mission Model
Normal costing		
Direct costs		
Direct materials	$106,450	$127,604
Direct labor	36,276	41,410
	142,726	169,014
Indirect costs		
Assembly support ($50 × Actual Labor Hours)	45,000	50,500
Total costs	$187,726	$219,514

2b. Actual costing

	Laguna Model	Mission Model
Direct costs		
Direct materials	$106,450	$127,604
Direct labor	36,276	41,410
	142,726	169,014
Indirect costs		
Assembly support ($42 × Actual Labor Hours)	37,800	42,420
Total costs	$180,526	$211,434

3.   Normal costing enables Anderson to report a job cost as soon as the job is completed, assuming that both the direct materials and direct labor costs are known at the time of use. Once the 900 direct labor-hours are known for the Laguna Model (June 2007), Anderson can compute the $187,726 cost figure using normal costing. Anderson can use this information to manage the costs of the Laguna Model job as well as to bid on similar jobs later in the year. In contrast, Anderson has to wait until the December 2007 year-end to compute the $180,526 cost of the Laguna Model using actual costing.

Although not required, the following overview diagram summarizes Anderson Construction's job-costing system.

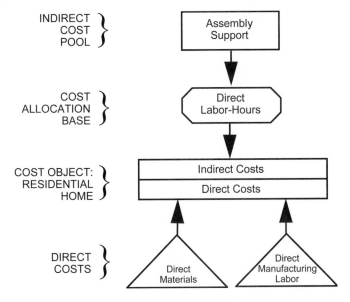

4-20 (20-30 min.) **Job costing, accounting for manufacturing overhead, budgeted rates.**

1.   An overview of the product costing system is

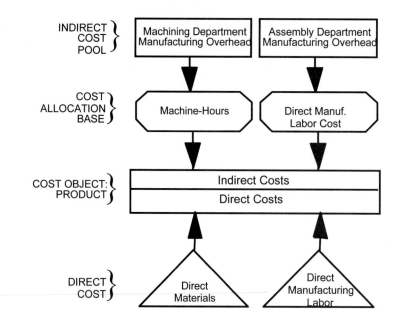

Budgeted manufacturing overhead divided by allocation base:

Machining department overhead $\dfrac{\$1,800,000}{50,000}$ = $36 per machine-hour

Assembly department overhead: $\dfrac{\$3,600,000}{\$2,000,000}$ = 180% of direct manuf. labor costs

2.   Machining department, 2,000 machine hours × $36 $72,000
      Assembly department, 180% × $15,000 labor cost   27,000
      Total manufacturing overhead allocated to Job 494 $99,000

3.

	Machining	**Assembly**
Actual manufacturing overhead	$2,100,000	$ 3,700,000
Manufacturing overhead allocated,		
55,000 machine hours × $36	1,980,000	—
180% × $2,200,000 labor cost	—	3,960,000
Underallocated (Overallocated)	$ 120,000	$ (260,000)

4-22 (15–20 min.) **Service industry, time period used to compute indirect cost rates.**

1. The first step is to compute the budgeded overhead rate for each quarter and for the total year. The rate is calculated by taking TOTAL overhead and dividing it by Direct Labor costs. So, calculate total overhead, by computing variable overhead in dollars and adding it to fixed overhead.

	Jan–March	April–June	July–Sept	Oct–Dec	Total
Direct labor costs	$400,000	$280,000	$250,000	$270,000	$1,200,000
Variable overhead costs as a percentage of direct labor costs	90%	60%	60%	60%	
Variable overhead costs (Percentage × direct labor costs)	$360,000	$168,000	$150,000	$162,000	$ 840,000
Fixed overhead costs	300,000	300,000	300,000	300,000	1,200,000
Total overhead costs	$660,000	$468,000	$450,000	$462,000	$2,040,000
Budgeted overhead rate (Total overhead costs as a percentage of direct labor Costs)	165%	167%	180%	171%	170%
Budgeted Fixed overhead rate (Budgeted Fixed costs ÷ Budgeted Direct Labor costs)					100%

	Budgeted Overhead Rate Used		
Job 332	Jan–March Rate (165%)	July–Sept Rate (180%)	Average Yearly Rate (170%)
Direct materials	$10,000	$10,000	$10,000
Direct labor costs	6,000	6,000	6,000
Overhead allocated (Budgeted overhead rate × Direct labor costs)	9,900	10,800	10,200
Full cost of Job 332	$25,900	$26,800	$26,200

(a) The full cost of Job 332, using the budgeted overhead rate of 165% for January–March, is $25,900.

(b) The full cost of Job 332, using the budgeted overhead rate of 180% for July–September, is $26,800.

(c) The full cost of Job 332, using the annual budgeted overhead rate of 170%, is $26,200.

2.

	Budgeted Variable Overhead Rate Used	
	January–March Rate (From problem 90%)	July–Sept Rate (From Problem 60%)
Job 332		
Direct materials	$10,000	$10,000
Direct labor costs	6,000	6,000
Variable overhead allocated (VOH rate × Direct labor costs)	5,400	3,600
Fixed overhead allocated (100% X Direct labor costs)	6,000	6,000
Full cost of Job 332	$27,400	$25,600

(a)   The full cost of Job 332, using the budgeted variable overhead rate of 90% for January–March and an annual fixed overhead rate of 100%, is $27,400.

(b)   The full cost of Job 332, using the budgeted variable overhead rate of 60% for July–September and an annual fixed overhead rate of 100%, is $25,600.

3.   The dual rate method (requirement 2) arrives at costs that are greater during the congested period of Jan-March. Therefore, using cost + markup pricing, Printers Inc., would be better to use the dual rate by quarters. It would be more effective in deterring clients from sending in last-minute, congestion-causing orders in the January–March time frame. In this calculation, more variable manufacturing overhead costs are allocated to jobs in the first quarter, reflecting the larger costs of that quarter caused by higher overtime and facility and machine maintenance. Printers Inc. could consider an explicit "congestion charge" for orders in January to March, thus clearly giving budget-conscious customers with flexibility of timing an option to switch.

4-24   (35–45 min.)   **Job costing, journal entries.**

1.   An overview of the product costing system is:

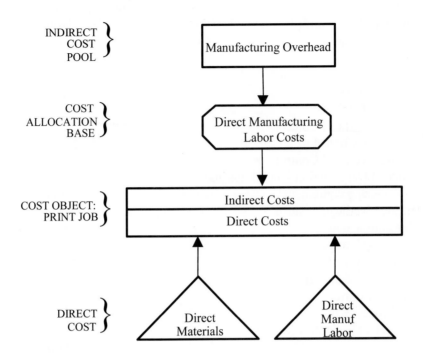

INDIRECT COST POOL } → Manufacturing Overhead

COST ALLOCATION BASE } → Direct Manufacturing Labor Costs

COST OBJECT: PRINT JOB } → Indirect Costs / Direct Costs

DIRECT COST } → Direct Materials / Direct Manuf Labor

2. & 3.

This answer assumes COGS given of $4,020 does not include the writeoff of overallocated manufacturing overhead.

2.	(1)	Materials Control	800	
		Accounts Payable Control		800
	(2)	Work-in-Process Control	710	
		Materials Control		710
	(3)	Manufacturing Overhead Control	100	
		Materials Control		100
	(4)	Work-in-Process Control	1,300	
		Manufacturing Overhead Control	900	
		Wages Payable Control		2,200
	(5)	Manufacturing Overhead Control	400	
		Accumulated Depreciation—buildings and		
		manufacturing equipment		400
	(6)	Manufacturing Overhead Control	550	
		Miscellaneous accounts		550
	(7)	Work-in-Process Control	2,080	
		Manufacturing Overhead Allocated		2,080
		$(1.60 \times \$1,300 = \$2,080)$		
	(8)	Finished Goods Control	4,120	
		Work-in-Process Control		4,120
	(9)	Accounts Receivable Control (or Cash)	8,000	
		Revenues		8,000
	(10)	Cost of Goods Sold	4,020	
		Finished Goods Control		4,020
	(11)	Manufacturing Overhead Allocated	2,080	
		Manufacturing Overhead Control		1,950
		Cost of Goods Sold		130

3.

Materials Control

Bal. 12/31/2008	100	(2)	Issues	710
(1) Purchases	800	(3)	Issues	100
Bal. 12/31/2009	90			

Work-in-Process Control

Bal. 12/31/2008	60	(8) Goods completed	4,120
(2) Direct materials	710		
(4) Direct manuf. labor	1,300		
(7) Manuf. overhead allocated	2,080		
Bal. 12/31/2009	30		

Finished Goods Control

Bal. 12/31/2008	500	(10) Goods sold	4,020
(8) Goods completed	4,120		
Bal. 12/31/2009	600		

Cost of Goods Sold

(10) Goods sold	4,020	(11) Adjust for overallocation	130
Bal. 12/31/2009	3,890		

Manufacturing Overhead Control

(3) Indirect materials	100	(11) To close	1,950
(4) Indirect manuf. labor	900		
(5) Depreciation	400		
(6) Miscellaneous	550		
Bal.	0		

Manufacturing Overhead Allocated

(11) To close	2,080	(7) Manuf. overhead allocated	2,080
		Bal.	0

4-26 (45 min.) **Job costing, journal entries.**

1.   An overview of the product-costing system is

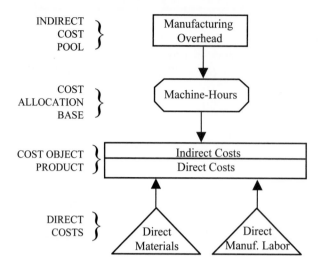

2.   Amounts in millions.

(1)	Materials Control	150	
	Accounts Payable Control		150
(2)	Work-in-Process Control	145	
	Materials Control		145
(3)	Manufacturing Department Overhead Control	10	
	Materials Control		10
(4)	Work-in-Process Control	90	
	Wages Payable Control		90
(5)	Manufacturing Department Overhead Control	30	
	Wages Payable Control		30
(6)	Manufacturing Department Overhead Control	19	
	Accumulated Depreciation		19
(7)	Manufacturing Department Overhead Control	9	
	Various liabilities		9
(8)	Work-in-Process Control	63	
	Manufacturing Overhead Allocated		63
(9)	Finished Goods Control	294	
	Work-in-Process Control		294
(10a)	Cost of Goods Sold	292	
	Finished Goods Control		292
(10b)	Accounts Receivable Control (or Cash)	400	
	Revenues		400

The posting of entries to T-accounts is as follows:

Materials Control			
Bal.	12	(2)	145
(1)	150	(3)	10

Work-in-Process Control			
Bal.	2	(9)	294
(2)	145		
(4)	90		
(8)	63		
Bal.	6		

Finished Goods Control			
Bal.	6	(10a)	292
(9)	294		

Cost of Goods Sold			
(10a)	292		
(11)	5		

Manufacturing Department Overhead Control			
(3)	10	(11)	68
(5)	30		
(6)	19		
(7)	9		

Manufacturing Overhead Allocated			
(11)	63	(8)	63

Accounts Payable Control			
		(1)	150

Wages Payable Control			
		(4)	90
		(5)	30

Accumulated Depreciation			
		(6)	19

Various Liabilities			
		(7)	9

Accounts Receivable Control			
(10b)	400		

Revenues			
		(10b)	400

The ending balance of Work-in-Process Control is $6.

3.　(11)　Manufacturing Overhead Allocated　　　　　　63
　　　　　Cost of Goods Sold　　　　　　　　　　　　5
　　　　　　　　Manufacturing Department Overhead Control　　　　68

Entry posted to T-accounts in Requirement 2.

4-28 (20–30 min.) **Job costing; actual, normal, and variation from normal costing.**

1. Actual direct cost rate for professional labor = $58 per professional labor-hour

$$\text{Actual indirect cost rate} = \frac{\$744,000}{15,500 \text{ hours}} = \$48 \text{ per professional labor-hour}$$

$$\begin{array}{l}\text{Budgeted direct cost rate} \\ \text{for professional labor}\end{array} = \frac{\$960,000}{16,000 \text{ hours}} = \$60 \text{ per professional labor-hour}$$

$$\text{Budgeted indirect cost rate} = \frac{\$720,000}{16,000 \text{ hours}} = \$45 \text{ per professional labor-hour}$$

	(a) Actual Costing	(b) Normal Costing	(c) Variation of Normal Costing
Direct-Cost Rate	$58 (*Actual* rate)	$58 (*Actual* rate)	$60 (**Budgeted** rate)
Indirect-Cost Rate	$48 (*Actual* rate)	$45 (**Budgeted** rate)	$45 (**Budgeted** rate)

2.

	(a) Actual Costing	(b) Normal Costing	(c) Variation of Normal Costing
Direct Costs	$58 × 120 = $ 6,960	$58 × 120 = $ 6,960	$60 × 120 = $ 7,200
Indirect Costs	48 × 120 = 5,760	45 × 120 = 5,400	45 × 120 = 5,400
Total Job Costs	$12,720	$12,360	$12,600

All three costing systems use the actual professional labor time of 120 hours. The budgeted 110 hours for the Pierre Enterprises audit job is not used in job costing. However, Chirac may have used the 110 hour number in bidding for the audit.

The actual costing figure of $12,720 exceeds the normal costing figure of $12,360 because the actual indirect-cost rate ($48) exceeds the budgeted indirect-cost rate ($45). The normal costing figure of $12,360 is less than the variation of normal costing (based on budgeted rates for direct costs) figure of $12,600, because the actual direct-cost rate ($58) is less than the budgeted direct-cost rate ($60).

Although not required, the following overview diagram summarizes Chirac's job-costing system.

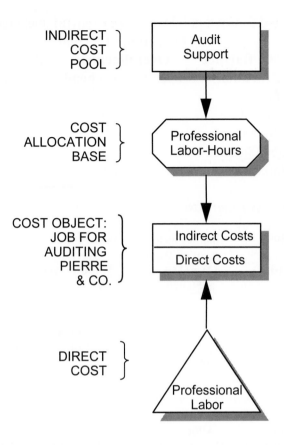

4-30 (30 min.) **Proration of overhead**.

1. Budgeted manufacturing overhead rate $= \dfrac{\text{Budgeted manufacturing overhead cost}}{\text{Budgeted direct manufacturing labor cost}}$

$$= \frac{\$100,000}{\$200,000} = 50\% \text{ of direct manufacturing labor cost}$$

2. Overhead allocated $= 50\% \times$ Actual direct manufacturing labor cost
$= 50\% \times \$220,000 = \$110,000$

Overallocated plant overhead = Actual plant overhead costs – Allocated plant overhead costs
$= \$106,000 - \$110,000 = -\$4,000$

Overallocated plant overhead = \$4,000

3a. All overallocated plant overhead is written off to cost of goods sold.

Both work in process (WIP) and finished goods inventory remain unchanged.

		Proration of $4,000	
	Dec. 31, 2009 Balance (Before Proration)	**Overallocated Manuf. Overhead**	**Dec. 31, 2009 Balance (After Proration)**
Account	**(1)**	**(2)**	**(3) = (1) – (2)**
WIP	$ 50,000	0	$ 50,000
Finished Goods	240,000	0	240,000
Cost of Goods Sold	560,000	4,000	556,000
Total	$850,000	$4,000	$846,000

3b. Overallocated plant overhead prorated based on ending balances:

	Dec. 31, 2009 Balance (Before Proration)	**Balance as a Percent of Total**	**Proration of $4,000 Overallocated Manuf. Overhead**	**Dec. 31, 2009 Balance (After Proration)**
Account	**(1)**	**(2) = (1) ÷ $850,000**	**(3) = (2) × $4,000**	**(4) = (1) – (3)**
WIP	$ 50,000	0.0588	0.0588 × $4,000 = $ 235	$49,765
Finished Goods	240,000	0.2824	0.2824 × $4,000 = 1,130	238,870
Cost of Goods Sold	560,000	0.6588	0.6588 × $4,000 = 2,635	557,365
Total	$850,000	1.0000	$4,000	$846,000

3c. Overallocated plant overhead prorated based on 2009 overhead in ending balances:

	Dec. 31, 2009 Balance (Before Proration)	**Allocated Manuf. Overhead in Dec. 31, 2009 Balance**	**Allocated Manuf. Overhead in Dec. 31, 2009 Balance as a Percent of Total**	**Proration of $4,000 Overallocated Manuf. Overhead**	**Dec. 31, 2009 Balance (After Proration)**
Account	**(1)**	**(2)**	**(3) = (2) ÷ $110,000**	**(4) = (3) × $4,000**	**(5) = (1) – (4)**
WIP	$ 50,000	$ 10,000[a]	0.0909	0.0909 × $4,000 = $ 364	$ 49,636
Finished Goods	240,000	30,000[b]	0.2727	0.2727 × $4,000 = 1,091	238,909
Cost of Goods Sold	560,000	70,000[c]	0.6364	0.6364 × $4,000 = $2,545	557,455
Total	$850,000	$110,000	1.0000	$4,000	$846,000

[a,b,c] Overhead allocated = Direct manuf. labor cost × 50% = $20,000; 60,000; 140,000 × 50%

4. Writing off all of the overallocated plant overhead to Cost of Goods Sold (CGS) is usually warranted when CGS is large relative to Work-in-Process and Finished Goods Inventory and the overallocated plant overhead is immaterial. Both these conditions apply in this case. ROW should write off the $4,000 overallocated plant overhead to Cost of Goods Sold Account.

4-32 (15–20 min.) **Service industry, job costing, law firm.**

1.

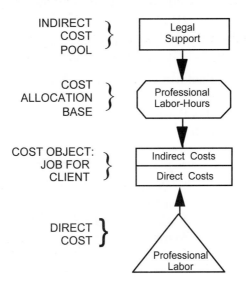

2. $$\begin{aligned}\text{Budgeted professional} \\ \text{labor-hour direct cost rate}\end{aligned} = \frac{\text{Budgeted direct labor compensation per professional}}{\text{Budgeted direct labor-hours per professional}}$$

$$= \frac{\$104,000}{1,600 \text{ hours}}$$

$$= \$65 \text{ per professional labor-hour}$$

3. $$\begin{aligned}\text{Budgeted indirect} \\ \text{cost rate}\end{aligned} = \frac{\text{Budgeted total costs in indirect cost pool}}{\text{Budgeted total professional labor-hours}}$$

$$= \frac{\$2,200,000}{1,600 \text{ hours} \times 25}$$

$$= \frac{\$2,200,000}{40,000 \text{ hours}}$$

$$= \$55 \text{ per professional labor-hour}$$

4.

	Richardson **100 Hours**	**Punch** **150 Hours**
Direct costs $65 per professional labor hour:	$ 6,500	$ 9,750
Indirect costs: Legal support, $55 per professional labor hour:	5,500	8,250
	$12,000	$18,000

4-34 (20–25 min.) **Proration of overhead.**

1. Budgeted manufacturing overhead rate is $4,800,000 ÷ 80,000 hours = $60 per machine-hour.

2.   Allocated overhead = $60 per MH × 75,000 actual machine hours

Manufacturing overhead underallocated	=	Manufacturing overhead incurred	−	Manufacturing overhead allocated
	=	$4,900,000 – $4,500,000		
	=	$400,000		

a.   Write-off to Cost of Goods Sold

Account (1)	Account Balance (Before Proration) (2)	Write-off of $400,000 Underallocated Manufacturing Overhead (3)	Account Balance (After Proration) (4) = (2) + (3)
Work in Process	$ 750,000	$ 0	$ 750,000
Finished Goods	1,250,000	0	1,250,000
Cost of Goods Sold	8,000,000	400,000	8,400,000
Total	$10,000,000	$400,000	$10,400,000

b.   Proration based on ending balances (before proration) in Work in Process, Finished Goods and Cost of Goods Sold.

Account (1)	Account Balance (Before Proration) (2)		Proration of $400,000 Underallocated Manufacturing Overhead (3)	Account Balance (After Proration) (4) = (2) + (3)
Work in Process	$ 750,000	(7.5%)	0.075 × $400,000 = $ 30,000	$ 780,000
Finished Goods	1,250,000	(12.5%)	0.125 × $400,000 = 50,000	1,300,000
Cost of Goods Sold	8,000,000	(80.0%)	0.800 × $400,000 = 320,000	8,320,000
Total	$10,000,000	100.0%	$400,000	$10,400,000

c. *Proration based on the allocated overhead amount (before proration) in the ending balances of Work in Process, Finished Goods, and Cost of Goods Sold.*

Account (1)	Account Balance (Before Proration) (2)	Allocated Overhead (Machine Hours × Overhead Rate) Included in the Account Balance (Before Proration) (3)	(4)	Proration of $400,000 Underallocated Manufacturing Overhead (5)	Account Balance (After Proration) (6) = (2) + (5)
Work in Process	$ 750,000	$ 240,000	(5.33%)	0.0533 × $400,000 = $ 21,320	$ 771,320
Finished Goods	1,250,000	660,000	(14.67%)	0.1467 × $400,000 = 58,680	1,308,680
Cost of Goods Sold	8,000,000	3,600,000	(80.00%)	0.8000 × $400,000 = 320,000	8,320,000
Total	$10,000,000	$4,500,000	100.00%	$400,000	$10,400,000

3. Alternative (c) is theoretically preferred over (a) and (b). Alternative (c) yields the same ending balances in work in process, finished goods, and cost of goods sold that would have been reported had actual indirect cost rates been used.

Chapter 4 also discusses an adjusted allocation rate approach that results in the same ending balances as does alternative (c). This approach operates via a restatement of the indirect costs allocated to all the individual jobs worked on during the year using the actual indirect cost rate.

4-36 (40 min.) **Proration of overhead with two indirect cost pools.**

1.a. C & A department:

Overhead allocated = $40×4,000 Machine hours = $160,000

Underallocated overhead = Actual overhead costs – Overhead allocated
= $163,000 – 160,000 = $3,000 underallocated

1.b. Finishing department:

Overhead allocated = $50 per direct labor-hour ×2,000 direct labor-hours = $100,000

Overallocated overhead = Actual overhead costs – Overhead allocated
= $87,000 – 100,000 = $13,000 overallocated

2a. All over or under allocated overhead is written off to cost of goods sold.

Both Work in Process and Finished goods inventory remain unchanged.

Account	Dec. 31, 2008 Balance (Before Proration) (1)	Proration of $10,000 Overallocated Overhead (2)	Dec. 31, 2008 Balance (After Proration) (3) = (1) + (2)
WIP	$ 150,000	0	$ 150,000
Finished Goods	250,000	0	250,000
Cost of Goods Sold	1,600,000	+$3,000 –$13,000	1,590,000
Total	$2,000,000	$ 10,000	$1,990,000

2b. Overallocated overhead prorated based on ending balances

Account	Dec. 31, 2008 Balance (Before Proration) (1)	Balance as a Percent of Total (2) = (1) ÷ $2,000,000	Proration of $10,000 Overallocated Overhead (3) = (2) × 10,000	Dec. 31, 2008 Balance (After Proration) (4) = (1) – (3)
WIP	$ 150,000	0.075	$0.075 \times \$10,000 = \$$ 750	$ 149,250
Finished Goods	250,000	0.125	$0.125 \times \$10,000 =$ 1,250	248,750
Cost of Goods Sold	1,600,000	0.800	$0.800 \times \$10,000 =$ 8,000	1,592,000
Total	$2,000,000	1.000	$10,000	$1,990,000

2c. Overallocated overhead prorated based on overhead in ending balances. (Note: overhead must be allocated separately from each department. This can be done using the number of machine hours/direct labor hours as a surrogate for overhead in ending balances.)

For C & A department:

Account	Allocated Overhead in Dec. 31, 2008 Balance (1)	Allocated Overhead in Dec. 31, 2008 Balance as a Percent of Total (2) = (1) ÷ $160,000	Proration of $3,000 Underallocated Overhead (3) = (2) × $3000
WIP	$200 \times \$40 = \$$ 8,000	0.05	$0.05 \times \$3,000 = \$$ 150
Finished Goods	$600 \times \$40 =$ 24,000	0.15	$0.15 \times \$3,000 =$ 450
Cost of Goods Sold	$3,200 \times \$40 =$ 128,000	0.80	$0.80 \times \$3,000 =$ 2,400
Total	$160,000	1.00	$3,000

For finishing department:

Account	Allocated Overhead in Dec. 31, 2008 Balance (4)	Allocated Overhead in Dec. 31, 2008 Balance as a Percent of Total (5) = (4) ÷ $100,000	Proration of $13,000 Underallocated Overhead (6) = (5) × $13,000
WIP	100 × $50 = $ 5,000	0.05	0.05 × $13,000 = $ 650
Finished Goods	400 × $50 = 20,000	0.20	0.20 × $13,000 = 2,600
Cost of Goods Sold	1,500 × $50 = 75,000	0.75	0.75 × $13,000 = 9,750
Total	$100,000	1.00	$13,000

Account	Dec. 31, 2008 Balance (Before Proration) (7)	Underallocated/ Overallocated Overhead (8) = (3) – (6)	Dec. 31, 2009 Balance (After Proration) (9) = (7) + (8)
WIP	$ 150,000	$150 – $650 = $ (500)	$ 149,500
Finished Goods	250,000	$450 – $2,600 = (2,150)	247,850
Cost of Goods Sold	1,600,000	$2,400 – $9,750 = (7,350)	1,592,650
Total	$2,000,000	$(10,000)	$1,990,000

3. The first method is simple and Cost of Goods Sold accounts for 80% of the three account amounts. The amount of overallocated and underallocated overhead is also immaterial. Allocation to the other two accounts is minimal. Therefore, write-off to cost of goods sold is the most cost effective alternative.

4-38 (40–55 min.) **Overview of general ledger relationships.**

1. & 3. An effective approach to this problem is to draw T-accounts and insert all the known figures. Then, working with T-account relationships, solve for the unknown figures (here coded by the letter X for beginning inventory figures and Y for ending inventory figures).

Materials Control

X	15,000	(1)	70,000
Purchases	85,000		
	100,000		70,000
Y	30,000		

Work-in-Process Control

X			10,000	(4)	305,000
(1)	DM	70,000			
(2)	DL	150,000			
(3)	Overhead	90,000	310,000		
			320,000		305,000
(a)			5,000		
(c)			3,000		
Y			23,000		

Finished Goods Control

X	20,000	(5)	300,000
(4)	305,000		
	325,000		300,000
Y	25,000		

Cost of Goods Sold

(5)	300,000	(d)	6,000

Manufacturing Department Overhead Control

	85,000	(d)	87,000
(a)	1,000		
(b)	1,000		

Manufacturing Overhead Allocated

(d)	93,000	(3)	90,000
		(c)	3,000

Manufacturing overhead cost rate = $90,000 \div $150,000 = 60\%$

Wages Payable Control

	(a)	6,000

Various Accounts

	(b)	1,000

2. Adjusting and closing entries:

(a) Work-in-Process Control   5,000
        Manufacturing Department Overhead Control   1,000
            Wages Payable Control   6,000
        To recognize payroll costs

(b) Manufacturing Department Overhead Control   1,000
            Various accounts   1,000
        To recognize miscellaneous manufacturing overhead

(c) Work-in-Process Control   3,000
            Manufacturing Overhead Allocated   3,000

To allocate manufacturing overhead

Note: Students tend to forget entry (c) entirely. Make sure that you remember that a budgeted overhead allocation rate is used consistently throughout the year. This point is a major feature of this problem.

(d) Manufacturing Overhead Allocated   93,000
        Manufacturing Department Overhead Control   87,000
        Cost of Goods Sold   6,000
      To close manufacturing overhead accounts and overallocated overhead to cost of goods sold

An overview of the product-costing system is

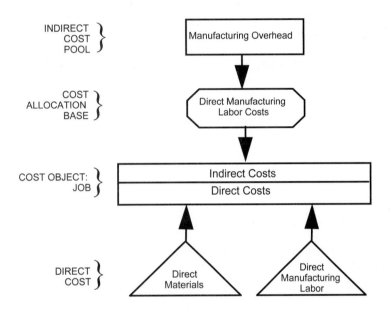

3.   See the answer to 1.

4-40   (20 min.) **Job costing, contracting, ethics.**

1.   Direct manufacturing costs:

Direct materials	$25,000	
Direct manufacturing labor	6,000	$31,000
Indirect manufacturing costs,		
150% × $6,000		9,000
Total manufacturing costs		$40,000

Aerospace bills the Navy $52,000 ($40,000 × 130%) for 100 X7 seats or $520 ($52,000 ÷ 100) per X7 seat.

2. Direct manufacturing costs:

Direct materials	$25,000	
Direct manufacturing labor[a]	5,000	$30,000
Indirect manufacturing costs,		
150% × $5,000		7,500
Total manufacturing costs		$37,500

[a]$6,000 − $400 ($25 × 16) setup − $600 ($50 × 12) design

Aerospace should have billed the Navy $48,750 ($37,500 × 130%) for 100 X7 seats or $487.50 ($48,750 ÷ 100) per X7 seat.

3. The problems the letter highlights (assuming it is correct) include the following:

a. Costs included that should be excluded (design costs)
b. Costs double-counted (setup included as both a direct cost and in an indirect cost pool)
c. Possible conflict of interest in Aerospace Comfort purchasing materials from a family-related company

Steps the Navy could undertake include the following:

(i) Use only contractors with a reputation for ethical behavior as well as quality products or services.
(ii) Issue guidelines detailing acceptable and unacceptable billing practices by contractors. For example, prohibiting the use of double-counting cost allocation methods by contractors.
(iii) Issue guidelines detailing acceptable and unacceptable procurement practices by contractors. For example, if a contractor purchases from a family-related company, require that the contractor obtain quotes from at least two other bidders.
(iv) Employ auditors who aggressively monitor the bills submitted by contractors.
(v) Ask contractors for details regarding determination of costs.

CHAPTER 5
ACTIVITY-BASED COSTING AND ACTIVITY-BASED MANAGEMENT

5-2 **Overcosting** may result in *competitors entering* a market and taking market share for products that a company erroneously believes are low-margin or even unprofitable. **Undercosting** may result in companies *selling products* on which they are in fact *losing money*, when they erroneously believe them to be profitable.

5-4 An **activity-based approach** *refines* a costing system by focusing on individual activities as the fundamental cost objects. It uses the cost of these activities as the basis for assigning costs to other cost objects such as products or services.

5-6 It is important to classify costs into a **cost hierarchy** because costs in *different cost pools relate to different cost-allocation bases* and not all cost-allocation bases are unit-level. For example, an allocation base like setup hours is a batch-level allocation base, and design hours is a product-sustaining base, both insensitive to the number of units in a batch or the number of units of product produced. If costs were not classified into a cost hierarchy, the alternative would be to consider all costs as unit-level costs, leading to misallocation of those costs that are not unit-level costs.

5-8 Four decisions for which **ABC information** is useful are
   1. *pricing and product mix* decisions,
   2. *cost reduction and process improvement* decisions,
   3. *product design* decisions, and
   4. decisions for *planning and managing* activities.

5-10 "Tell-tale" signs that indicate when **ABC systems** are likely to **provide** the most **benefits** are as follows:
   1. Significant *indirect costs* are allocated using only *one or two cost pools*.
   2. All or most *indirect costs* are identified as *output-unit-level* costs (i.e., few indirect costs are described as batch-level, product-sustaining, or facility-sustaining costs).
   3. *Products make diverse demands on resources* because of differences in volume, process steps, batch size, or complexity.
   4. Products that a company is *well suited* to make and sell show *small profits*, whereas products that a company is *less suited* to produce and sell show *large profits*.
   5. *Operations staff* has significant *disagreements* with the *accounting staff* about the costs of manufacturing and marketing products and services.

5-12 No, ABC systems apply equally well to service companies such as banks, railroads, hospitals, and accounting firms, as well merchandising companies such as retailers and distributors.

5-14 Increasing the number of indirect-cost pools does NOT guarantee increased accuracy of product or service costs. If the existing cost pool is already homogeneous, increasing the number of cost pools will not increase accuracy. If the existing cost pool is not homogeneous, accuracy will increase only if the increased cost pools actually vary with the increased cost drivers.

5-16   (20 min.)   **Cost hierarchy.**

Cost	Hierarchy level	Explanation
Indirect manufacturing labor $1,200,000	Output unit level	Direct manufacturing labor generally increases with output units, and so will the indirect costs to support it.
Purchase order-related costs (including costs of receiving materials and paying suppliers) of $600,000	Batch-level costs.	Batch-level costs are costs of activities that are related to a group of units of a product rather than each individual unit of a product.
Cost of indirect materials of $350,000	output unit-level costs.	The use of indirect materials generally changes with labor hours or machine hours which are unit-level costs.
Setup costs of $700,000	batch-level costs	Setup costs relate to a group of units of product produced after the machines are set up.
Costs of designing processes, drawing process charts, and making engineering changes for individual products, $900,000	product-sustaining	Design and engineering costs are product-sustaining because they relate to the costs of activities undertaken to support individual products regardless of the number of units or batches in which the product is produced.
Machine-related overhead costs (depreciation and maintenance) of $1,200,000	output unit-level costs	Machine-related overhead costs are output unit-level costs because they change with the number of units produced.
Plant management, plant rent, and insurance costs of $950,000	facility-sustaining costs	Plant costs are facility-sustaining costs because the costs of these activities cannot be traced to individual products or services but support the organization as a whole.

2.   The **complex boom box** made in many batches will *use significantly more batch-level overhead resources* compared to the simple boom box that is made in a few batches. In addition, the complex boom box will use more product-sustaining overhead resources because it is complex. Because each boom box requires the *same number of machine-hours*, both the simple and the complex boom box will be *allocated the same overhead costs per boom box* if Teledor uses only machine-hours to allocate overhead costs to boom boxes. As a result, the *complex boom box will be undercosted* (it consumes a relatively high level of resources but is reported to have a relatively low cost) and the *simple boom box will be overcosted* (it consumes a relatively low level of resources but is reported to have a relatively high cost).

3.   Using the **cost hierarchy** to calculate activity-based costs can help Teledor to identify both the costs of individual activities and the cost of activities demanded by individual products. Teledor can use this information to manage its business in several ways:

   a.   Pricing and product mix decisions. Knowing the resources needed to manufacture and sell different types of boom boxes can help Teledor to *price the different boom boxes* and also identify *which boom boxes are more profitable*. It can then emphasize its more profitable products.
   b.   Teledor can use information about the costs of different activities to *improve processes and reduce costs of the different activities*. Teledor could have a target of reducing costs of activities (setups, order processing, etc.) by, say, 3% and constantly seek to eliminate activities and costs (such as engineering changes) that its customers perceive as not adding value.
   c.   Teledor management can identify and *evaluate new designs to improve perfor*mance by analyzing how product and process designs affect activities and costs.
   d.   Teledor can use its ABC systems and cost hierarchy information to *plan and manage activities*. What activities should be performed in the period and at what cost?

5-18   (15 min.)   **Alternative allocation bases for a professional services firm.**

1.

| | Direct Professional Time | | | Support Services | | Amount |
| Client | Rate per Hour | Number of Hours | Total | Rate | Total | Billed to Client |
(1)	(2)	(3)	(4) = (2) × (3)	(5)	(6) = (4) × (5)	(7) = (4) + (6)
SEATTLE DOMINION						
Wolfson	$500	15	$7,500	30%	$2,250	$ 9,750
Brown	120	3	360	30	108	468
Anderson	80	22	1,760	30	528	2,288
						$12,506
TOKYO ENTERPRISES						
Wolfson	$500	2	$1,000	30%	$300	$1,300
Brown	120	8	960	30	288	1,248
Anderson	80	30	2,400	30	720	3,120
						$5,668

2.

Client	Direct Professional Time			Support Services		Amount Billed to Client
	Rate per Hour	Number of Hours	Total	Rate per Hour	Total	
(1)	(2)	(3)	(4) = (2) × (3)	(5)	(6) = (3) × (5)	(7) = (4) + (6)
SEATTLE DOMINION						
Wolfson	$500	15	$7,500	$50	$ 750	$ 8,250
Brown	120	3	360	50	150	510
Anderson	80	22	1,760	50	1,100	2,860
						$11,620
TOKYO ENTERPRISES						
Wolfson	$500	2	$1,000	$50	$ 100	$1,100
Brown	120	8	960	50	400	1,360
Anderson	80	30	2,400	50	1,500	3,900
						$6,360

	Requirement 1	Requirement 2
Seattle Dominion	$12,506	$11,620
Tokyo Enterprises	5,668	6,360
	$18,174	$17,980

Both clients use 40 hours of professional labor time. However, Seattle Dominion uses a higher proportion of Wolfson's time (15 hours), which is more costly. This attracts the highest support-services charge when allocated on the basis of direct professional labor costs.

3. Assume that the Wolfson Group uses a cause-and-effect criterion when choosing the allocation base for support services. You could use several pieces of evidence to determine whether professional labor costs or hours is the driver of support-service costs:

a. *Interviews with personnel.* For example, staff in the major cost categories in support services could be interviewed to determine whether Wolfson requires more support per hour than, say, Anderson. The professional labor costs allocation base implies that an hour of Wolfson's time requires 6.25 ($500 ÷ $80) times more support-service dollars than does an hour of Anderson's time.

b. *Analysis of tasks undertaken for selected clients.* For example, if computer-related costs are a sizable part of support costs, you could determine if there was a systematic relationship between the percentage involvement of professionals with high billing rates on cases and the computer resources consumed for those cases.

5-20 (10–15 min.) **ABC, process costing.**

Note to students: Your professor should have told you to change the "number of production runs" for the financial calculator should to 50 from 0. The solution assumes that you have made the change.

Rates per unit cost driver.

Activity	Cost Driver	Rate
Machining	Machine-hours	$375,000 ÷ (25,000 + 50,000) = $5 per machine-hour
Set up	Production runs	$120,000 ÷ (50 + 50) = $1,200 per production run
Inspection	Inspection-hours	$105,000 ÷ (1,000 + 500) = $70 per inspection-hour

Overhead cost per unit:

	Mathematical	Financial
Machining: $5 per machine hour	$125,000	$250,000
Set up: $1,200 per production run	60,000	60,000
Inspection: $70 per inspection hour	70,000	35,000
Total manufacturing overhead costs	$255,000	$345,000
Divide by number of units	÷ 50,000	÷100,000
Manufacturing overhead cost per unit	$ 5.10	$ 3.45

2.

	Mathematical	Financial
Manufacturing cost per unit:		
Direct materials		
$150,000 ÷ 50,000	$3.00	
$300,000 ÷ 100,000		$3.00
Direct manufacturing labor		
$50,000 ÷ 50,000	1.00	
$100,000 ÷ 100,000		1.00
Manufacturing overhead (from requirement 1)	5.10	3.45
Manufacturing cost per unit	$9.10	$7.45

5-22 (25 min.)   **Allocation of costs to activities, unused capacity.**

1.

	Percentage of Costs Used by Each Activity				
Indirect Resources	**Academic Instruction**	**Administration**	**Sports Training**	**Community Relationships**	**2009 Expenditures**
Teachers' salaries and benefits	60%	20%	8%	12%	$4,000,000
Principals' salaries and benefits	10%	60%	5%	25%	400,000
Facilities cost	35%	15%	45%	5%	2,600,000
Office staff salaries and benefits	5%	60%	10%	25%	300,000
Sports program staff salaries and benefits	35%	10%	45%	10%	500,000
					$7,800,000

	Actual Resource Cost Used by Each Activity				
Indirect Resources	**Academic Instruction**	**Administration**	**Sports Training**	**Community Relationships**	**2006 Expenditures**
Teachers' salaries and benefits	$2,400,000	$ 800,000	$ 320,000	$480,000	$4,000,000
Principals' salaries and benefits	40,000	240,000	20,000	100,000	400,000
Facilities cost	910,000	390,000	1,170,000	130,000	2,600,000
Office staff salaries and benefits	15,000	180,000	30,000	75,000	300,000
Sports program staff salaries and benefits	175,000	50,000	225,000	50,000	500,000
Total	$3,540,000	$1,660,000	$1,765,000	$835,000	$7,800,000
No. of students	500	500	500	500	500
Cost per student	$7,080	$ 3,320	$3,530	$1,670	$15,600
Percent of total cost by activity	45%	21%	23%	11%	100%

The overall cost of educating each student is $15,600. Of this, $7,080 (or 45%) is spent on academic instruction and $3,320 (or 21%) is spent on administration.

2. Cost of ice hockey program $ 300,000
    Total cost of activities without ice hockey program = $7,800,000 – $300,000 = $7,500,000
    Per student cost of educational program without hockey = $7,500,000 ÷ 500 = $ 15,000

3. Net cost of ice hockey program with $1,000 fee = $300,000 – (30 × $1,000) = $ 270,000
    Total cost of activities with ice hockey program fee = $7,500,000 + $270,000 = $7,770,000
    Per student cost of educational program with hockey fee = $7,770,000 ÷ 500 = $ 15,540

Charging a fee helps a bit but the net cost of the ice hockey program is still high and significantly increases the cost of educating each student. Smith also needs to understand whether the costs for the hockey program are fixed or variable. If much of the cost for hockey is the ice rink, that cost won't go away if the program goes away.

4.

Academic instruction capacity		600 students
Cost of academic instruction activity (from requirement 1 calculations)		$3,540,000
Cost of academic instruction per student at full utilization = $3,540,000 ÷ 600		$ 5,900
Academic instruction resource costs used by current student population = 500 × $5,900		$2,950,000
Cost of excess academic instruction capacity = $3,540,000 – $2,950,000		$ 590,000

Most of the costs at Harmon school are fixed in the short-run. So, Smith must try to recruit more students to the school. If, in the long run, it seems like the student population is going to be stable at around 500, he should plan how some of the excess capacity can be cut back so that the fixed school capacity is better utilized, that is, he should work to reduce the cost of excess capacity. One problem with that plan is that "cutting excess academic instruction capacity" may eventually mean reducing the number of sections in each grade and letting teachers go, and if this involves the loss of experienced teachers, that could cause long-term damage to the school.

Unrelated to the excess capacity issue, but with the aim of improving the school's economics, he should consider doing away with expensive activities like the ice hockey program which raises the cost per student substantially, even after a large fee is charged from students who choose to play the sport.

5-24 (15–20 min.) **ABC, wholesale, customer profitability.**

	Chain			
	1	**2**	**3**	**4**
Gross sales	$50,000	$30,000	$100,000	$70,000
Sales returns	10,000	5,000	7,000	6,000
Net sales	40,000	25,000	93,000	64,000
Cost of goods sold (80%)	32,000	20,000	74,400	51,200
Gross margin	8,000	5,000	18,600	12,800
Customer-related costs:				
Regular orders				
$20 × 40; 150; 50; 70	800	3,000	1,000	1,400
Rush orders				
$100 × 10; 50; 10; 30	1,000	5,000	1,000	3,000
Returned items				
$10 × 100; 26; 60; 40	1,000	260	600	400
Catalogs and customer support	1,000	1,000	1,000	1,000
Customer related costs	3,800	9,260	3,600	5,800
Contribution (loss) margin	$ 4,200	$ (4,260)	$ 15,000	$ 7,000
Contribution (loss) margin as percentage of gross sales	8.4%	(14.2%)	15.0%	10.0%

The analysis indicates that customers' profitability (loss) contribution varies widely from (14.2%) to 15.0%. Immediate attention to Chain 2 is required which is currently showing a loss contribution. The chain has a disproportionate number of both regular orders and rush orders. Villeagas should work with the management of Chain 2 to find ways to reduce the number of orders, while maintaining or increasing the sales volume. If this is not possible, Villeagas should consider dropping Chain 2, if it can save the customer-related costs.

Chain 1 has a disproportionate number of the items returned as well as sale returns. The causes of these should be investigated so that the profitability contribution of Chain 1 could be improved.

5-26 (20–25 min.) **Activity-based costing, job-costing system.**

1.   An overview of the activity-based job-costing system is:

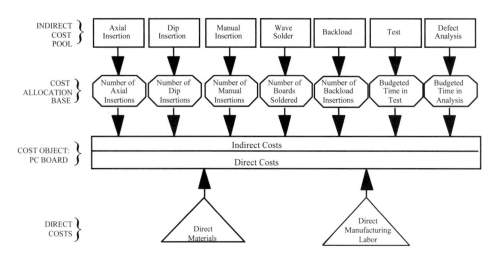

2.

Activity Area	Indirect Manufacturing Costs Allocated		
1. Axial insertion	$ 0.08	× 45	= **$ 3.60**
2. Dip insertion	0.25	× **24**	= 6.00
3. Manual insertion	**0.50**	× 11	= 5.50
4. Wave solder	3.50	× **1**	= 3.50
5. Backload	**0.70**	× 6	= 4.20
6. Test	90.00	× .25	= **22.50**
7. Defect analysis	**80.00**	× .10	= 8.00
Total			$53.30

Direct manufacturing costs:		
Direct materials	$75.00	
Direct manufacturing labor	15.00	$ 90.00
Indirect manufacturing costs:		
Manufacturing overhead (see above)		**53.30**
Total manufacturing costs		**$143.30**

3.   The **manufacturing manager** likely would find the ABC job-costing system useful in *cost management*. Unlike direct manufacturing labor costs, the seven indirect cost pools are systematically linked to the activity areas at the plant. The result is more accurate product costing. Productivity measures can be developed that directly link to the management accounting system.

Marketing managers can use ABC information to *price jobs* as well as to advise customers about how selecting different product features will affect price.

5-28   (15 min.)   **Job costing with single direct-cost category, single indirect-cost pool, law firm.**

1.   Pricing decisions at Wigan Associates are heavily influenced by reported cost numbers. Suppose Wigan is **bidding against another firm** for a client with a job similar to that of Widnes Coal. If the costing system overstates the costs of these jobs, Wigan may bid too high and fail to land the client. If the costing system understates the costs of these jobs, Wigan may bid low, land the client, and then lose money in handling the case.

2.

	Widnes Coal 104 hours	St. Helen's Glass 96 hours	Total 200 hours
Direct professional labor, $70 per hr.	$ 7,280	$ 6,720	$14,000
Indirect costs allocated, $105 per hr.	10,920	10,080	21,000
Total costs to be billed	$18,200	$16,800	$35,000

5-30   (30 min.)   **Job costing with multiple direct-cost categories, multiple indirect-cost pools, law firm (continuation of 5-28 and 5-29 solution not provided. Items from 5-29 italicized).**

1.

	Widnes Coal	St. Helen's Glass	Total
Direct costs:			
Partner professional labor, $100 × 24; $100 × 56	$ 2,400	$ 5,600	$ 8,000
Associate professional labor, $50 × 80; $50 × 40	4,000	2,000	6,000
Research support labor	*1,600*	*3,400*	*5,000*
Computer time	*500*	*1,300*	*1,800*
Travel and allowances	*600*	*4,400*	*5,000*
Telephones/faxes	*200*	*1,000*	*1,200*
Photocopying	*250*	*750*	*1,000*
Total direct costs	9,550	18,450	28,000

Indirect costs allocated:
    Indirect costs for partners,
        $57.50 × 24; $57.50 × 56   1,380   3,220   4,600
    Indirect costs for associates,
        $20 × 80; $20 × 40   1,600   800   2,400
    Total indirect costs   2,980   4,020   7,000
    Total costs to be billed $12,530 $22,470 $35,000

Comparison	Widnes Coal	St. Helen's Glass	Total
Single direct cost/			
Single indirect cost pool	$18,200	$16,800	$35,000
Multiple direct costs/			
Single indirect cost pool	*$14,070*	*$20,930*	*$35,000*
Multiple direct costs/			
Multiple indirect cost pools	$12,530	$22,470	$35,000

The higher the percentage of costs directly traced to each case, and the greater the number of homogeneous indirect cost pools linked to the cost drivers of indirect costs, the more accurate the product cost of each individual case.

The Widnes and St. Helen's cases differ in how they use "resource areas" of Wigan Associates:

	Widnes Coal	St. Helen's Glass
Partner professional labor	30.0%	70.0%
Associate professional labor	66.7	33.3
Research support labor	32.0	68.0
Computer time	27.8	72.2
Travel and allowances	12.0	88.0
Telephones/faxes	16.7	83.3
Photocopying	25.0	75.0

The Widnes Coal case makes relatively low use of the higher-cost partners but relatively higher use of the lower-cost associates than does St. Helen's Glass. As a result, it also uses less of the higher indirect costs required to support partners compared to associates. The Widnes Coal case also makes relatively lower use of the support labor, computer time, travel, phones/faxes, and photocopying resource areas than does the St. Helen's Glass case.

2.   The specific areas where the multiple direct/multiple indirect (MD/MI) approach can provide better information for decisions at Wigan Associates include:

Pricing and product (case) emphasis decisions. In a bidding situation using single direct/single indirect (SD/SI) or multiple direct/single indirect (MD/SI) data, Wigan may win bids for legal cases on which it will subsequently lose money. It may also not win bids on which it would make money with a lower-priced bid.

From a strategic viewpoint, SD/SI or MD/SI exposes Wigan Associates to cherry-picking by competitors. Other law firms may focus exclusively on Widnes Coal-type cases and take sizable amounts of "profitable" business from Wigan Associates. MD/MI reduces the likelihood of Wigan Associates losing cases on which it would have made money.

Client relationships. MD/MI provides a better "road map" for clients to understand how costs are accumulated at Wigan Associates. Wigan can use this road map when meeting with clients to plan the work to be done on a case *before* it commences. Clients can negotiate ways to get a lower-cost case from Wigan, given the information in MD/MI—for example, (a) use a higher proportion of associate labor time and a lower proportion of a partner time, and (b) use fax machines more and air travel less. If clients are informed in advance how costs will be accumulated, there is less likelihood of disputes about bills submitted to them *after* the work is done.

Cost control. The MD/MI approach better highlights the individual cost areas at Wigan Associates than does the SD/SI or MD/SI approaches:

	MD/MI	SD/SI	MD/SI
Number of direct cost categories	7	1	7
Number of indirect cost categories	2	1	1
Total	9	2	8

MD/MI is likely to promote better cost-control practices than SD/SI or MD/SI, as the nine cost categories in MD/MI give Wigan a better handle on how to effectively manage different categories of both direct and indirect costs.

5-32 (30-40 min.) **Department and activity-cost rates service sector.**

1. Compute the total overhead costs. Divide the total by the allocation basis, Direct Labor Cost. Multiply the Overhead Rate by the direct labor costs to get the amount allocated to each product line. Add all direct costs plus the allocated overhead to get the total cost. Divide by the budgeted number of procedures to get the budgeted cost per procedure.

Overhead	*Cost*
Administration	$20,610
Maintenance	247,320
Sanitation	196,180
Utilities	134,350
Total	$598,460

$$\frac{\text{Budgeted overhead}}{\text{rate}} = \frac{\$598,460}{\$368,040} = \$1.626 \text{ per DL }\$$$

	X-rays	Ultrasound	CT scan	MRI	Total
Technician labor	$ 61,440	$105,600	$ 96,000	$ 105,000	$ 368,040
Depreciation	32,240	268,000	439,000	897,500	1,636,740
Materials	22,080	16,500	24,000	31,250	93,830
Allocated overhead*	99,901	171,706	156,096	170,730	598,433
Total budgeted costs	$215,661	$561,806	$715,096	$1,204,480	$2,697,043
Budgeted number of procedures	÷3,840	÷4,400	÷3,000	÷2,500	
Budgeted cost per service	$ 56.16	$ 127.68	$ 238.37	$ 481.79	

* Allocated overhead = Budgeted overhead rate × Technician labor costs

2. Budgeted Information. You need to calculate the total number of cleaning minutes, the total number of procedures, and the total procedure minutes to use as allocation bases.

	X-rays	Ultrasound	CT scan	MRI	Total
Number of procedures	3,840	4,400	3,000	2,500	13,740
Cleaning minutes per procedure	×5	×5	×15	×35	
Total cleaning minutes	19,200	22,000	45,000	87,500	173,700
Number of procedures	3,840	4,400	3,000	2,500	13,740
Minutes for each procedure	×5	×15	×20	×45	
Total procedure minutes	19,200	66,000	60,000	112,500	257,700

Activity	Budgeted Cost (1)	Cost Driver (2)	Units of Cost Driver (3)	Activity Rate (4) = (1) ÷ (3)
Administration	$ 20,610	Total number of procedures	13,740	$1.50 per procedure
Maintenance	$247,320	Total dollars of depreciation	$1,636,740	$0.151105 per dollar of depreciation
Sanitation	$196,180	Total cleaning minutes	173,700	$1.12942 per cleaning minute
Utilities	$134,350	Total procedure minutes	257,700	$0.52134 per procedure minute

	X-rays	Ultrasound	CT scan	MRI	Total
Technician labor	$ 61,440	$105,600	$ 96,000	$ 105,000	$ 368,040
Depreciation	32,240	268,000	439,000	897,500	1,636,740
Materials	22,080	16,500	24,000	31,250	93,830
Allocated activity costs:					
Administration ($1.50×3,840; 4,400; 3,000; 2,500)	5,760	6,600	4,500	3,750	20,610
Maintenance ($0.151105×$32,240; $268,000; $439,000; $897,500)	4,872	40,496	66,335	135,617	247,320
Sanitation ($1.12942×19,200; 22,000; 45,000; 87,500)	21,685	24,847	50,824	98,824	196,180
Utilities ($0.52134×19,200; 66,000; 60,000; 112,500)	10,010	34,409	31,280	58,651	134,350
Total budgeted cost	$158,087	$496,452	$711,939	$1,330,592	$2,697,070
Budgeted number of procedures	÷3,840	÷4,400	÷3,000	÷2,500	
Budgeted cost per service	$ 41.17	$ 112.83	$ 237.31	$ 532.24	

3. Using the disaggregated activity-based costing data, managers can see that the MRI actually costs substantially more and x-rays and ultrasounds substantially less than the traditional system indicated. In particular, the MRI activity generates a lot of maintenance activity and sanitation activity. Managers should examine the use of these two activities to search for ways to reduce the activity consumption and ultimately its cost.

5-34 (30–40 min.) **Activity-based costing, merchandising.**

1.

	General Supermarket Chains	Drugstore Chains	Mom-and-Pop Single Stores	Total
Revenues	$3,708,000	$3,150,000	$1,980,000	$8,838,000
Cost of goods sold	3,600,000	3,000,000	1,800,000	8,400,000
Gross margin	$ 108,000	$ 150,000	$ 180,000	$ 438,000
Other operating costs				301,080
Operating income				$ 136,920
Gross margin %	2.91%	4.76%	9.09%	4.96%

The operating income margin of Pharmacare, Inc., was 1.55% ($136,920 ÷ $8,838,000).

2.   The per-unit cost driver rates are:

Activity	Cost	Cost Driver	Cost Driver Rate
Customer purchase order processing	$80,000	140+360+1500=**2,000**	$40 per order
Line item ordering	63,840	1,960+4,320+15,000=**21,280**	$3 per line item
Store delivery	71,000	120+360+1,000=**1,480**	$47.973 per delivery
Cartons shipped	76,000	36,000+24,000+16,000=**76,000**	$1 per carton
Shelf stocking	10,240	360+180+100=**640**	$16 per hour

3. The activity-based costing of each distribution market for August 2008 is:

	General Supermarket Chains	Drugstore Chains	Mom-and-Pop Single Stores	Total
1. Customer purchase order processing ($**40** × 140; 360; 1,500)	$ 5,600	$14,400	$ 60,000	$ 80,000
2. Line item ordering ($**3** × 1,960; 4,320; 15,000)	5,880	12,960	45,000	63,840
3. Store delivery, ($**47.973** × 120; 360; 1,000)	5,757	17,270	47,973	71,000
4. Cartons shipped ($**1** × 36,000; 24,000; 16,000)	36,000	24,000	16,000	76,000
5. Shelf-stocking ($**16** × 360; 180; 100)	5,760	2,880	1,600	10,240
	$58,997	$71,510	$170,573	$301,080

The revised operating income statement is:

	General Supermarket Chains	Drugstore Chains	Mom-and-Pop Single Stores	Total
Revenues	$3,708,000	$3,150,000	$1,980,000	$8,838,000
Cost of goods sold	3,600,000	3,000,000	1,800,000	8,400,000
Gross margin	108,000	150,000	180,000	438,000
Operating costs	58,997	71,510	170,573	301,080
Operating income	$ 49,003	$ 78,490	$ 9,427	$ 136,920
Operating income margin 1.32%		2.49%	0.48%	1.55%

4.   The ranking of the three markets are:

Using Gross Margin		Using Operating Income	
1. Mom-and-Pop Single Stores	9.09%	1. Drugstore Chains	2.49%
2. Drugstore Chains	4.76%	2. General Supermarket Chains	1.32%
3. General Supermarket Chains	2.91%	3. Mom-and-Pop Single Stores	0.48%

The activity-based analysis of costs highlights how the Mom-and-Pop Single Stores use a larger share of Pharmacare's resources per revenue dollar than do the other two markets. The ratio of the operating costs to revenues across the three markets is:

General Supermarket Chains	1.59%	($58,997 ÷ $3,708,000)
Drugstore Chains	2.27%	($71,510 ÷ $3,150,000)
Mom-and-Pop Single Stores	8.61%	($170,573 ÷ $1,980,000)

This is a classic illustration of the maxim that "all revenue dollars are not created equal." The analysis indicates that the Mom-and-Pop Single Stores are the least profitable market. Pharmacare should work to increase profits in this market through: (1) a possible surcharge, (2) decreasing the number of orders, (3) offering discounts for quantity purchases, etc.

Other issues for Pharmacare to consider include

a. *Choosing the appropriate cost drivers for each area.* The problem gives a cost driver for each chosen activity area. However, it is likely that over time further refinements in cost drivers would occur. For example, not all store deliveries are equally easy to make, depending on parking availability, accessibility of the storage/shelf space to the delivery point, etc. Similarly, not all cartons are equally easy to deliver—their weight, size, or likely breakage component are factors that can vary across carton types.

b. *Developing a reliable data base on the chosen cost drivers.* For some items, such as the number of orders and the number of line items, this information likely would be available in machine readable form at a high level of accuracy. Unless the delivery personnel have hand-held computers that they use in a systematic way, estimates of shelf-stocking time are likely to be unreliable. Advances in information technology likely will reduce problems in this area over time.

c. *Deciding how to handle costs that may be common across several activities.* For example, (3) store delivery and (4) cartons shipped to stores have the common cost of the same trip. Some organizations may treat (3) as the primary activity and attribute only incremental costs to (4). Similarly, (1) order processing and (2) line item ordering may have common costs.

d. *Behavioral factors are likely to be a challenge to Flair.* He must now tell those salespeople who specialize in Mom-and-Pop accounts that they have been less profitable than previously thought.

5-36 (40 min.) **ABC, health care.**

Activity	Cost	Cost Driver	Cost Driver Rate
Medical supplies	$300,000	150 patient years	$2,000 per patient year
Rent & maintenance	180,000	30,000 square feet	$6 per square foot
Admin cost for charts, etc.	600,000	150 patient years	$4,000 per patient year
Laboratory services	100,000	2,500 laboratory tests	$40 per test

These cost drivers are chosen as the ones that best match the descriptions of why the costs arise. Other answers are acceptable, provided that clear explanations are given.

1b.   Activity-based costs for each program and cost per patient-year of the alcohol and drug program follow:

	Alcohol	**Drug**	**After-Care**	**Total**
Direct labor				
Physicians at **$150,000** × 0; 4; 0	—	$ 600,000	—	$ 600,000
Psychologists at **$75,000** × 6; 4; 8	$450,000	300,000	$ 600,000	1,350,000
Nurses at **$30,000** × 4; 6; 10	120,000	180,000	300,000	600,000
Direct labor costs	570,000	1,080,000	900,000	2,550,000
Medical supplies[1] **$2,000** × 40; 50; 60	80,000	100,000	120,000	300,000
Rent and clinic maintenance[2]				
$6 × 9,000; 9,000; 12,000	54,000	54,000	72,000	180,000
Administrative costs to manage				
patient charts, food, and laundry[3]				
$4,000 × 40; 50; 60	160,000	200,000	240,000	600,000
Laboratory services[4] **$40** × 400; 1,400; 700	16,000	56,000	28,000	100,000
Total costs	$880,000	$1,490,000	$1,360,000	$3,730,000

Cost per patient-year $\dfrac{\$880,000}{40} = \$22,000$ $\dfrac{\$1,490,000}{50} = \$29,800$

[1] Allocated using patient-years
[2] Allocated using square feet of space
[3] Allocated using patient-years
[4] Allocated using number of laboratory tests

1c.   The ABC system more accurately allocates costs because it identifies better cost drivers. The ABC system *chooses cost drivers for overhead costs that have a cause-and-effect relationship* between the cost drivers and the costs. Of course, Clayton should continue to evaluate if better cost drivers can be found than the ones they have identified so far.

By implementing the ABC system, Clayton can gain a more detailed *understanding* of costs and cost drivers. This is valuable information from a *cost management* perspective. The system can yield insight into the efficiencies with which various activities are performed. Clayton can then examine if redundant activities can be eliminated. Clayton can study trends and work toward improving the efficiency of the activities.

In addition, the ABC system will help Clayton determine *which programs are the most costly to operate*. This will be useful in making *long-run decisions* as to which programs to offer or emphasize. The ABC system will also assist Clayton in setting prices for the programs that more accurately reflect the costs of each program.

3.   The concern with using costs per patient-year as the rule to allocate resources among its programs is that it emphasizes "input" to the exclusion of "outputs" or effectiveness of the programs. After-all, *Clayton's goal is to cure patients while controlling costs, not minimize costs per-patient year*. The problem, of course, is measuring outputs.

Unlike many manufacturing companies, where the outputs are obvious because they are tangible and measurable, the outputs of service organizations are more difficult to measure. Examples are "cured" patients as distinguished from "processed" or "discharged" patients, "educated" as distinguished from "partially educated" students, and so on.

5-38   (40–50 min.)   **Activity-based job costing, unit-cost comparisons.**

This is not required, but you might find it helpful to do an overview of the product-costing system when the system is complex.

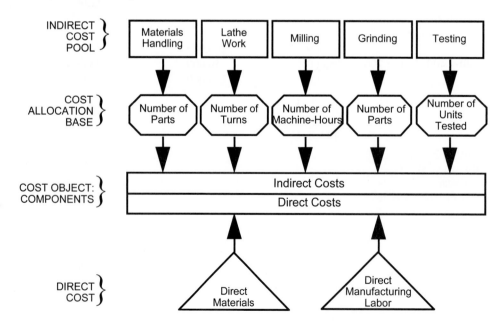

1.

	Job Order 410 25 Labor hours		Job Order 411 375 Labor hours	
Direct manufacturing cost				
Direct materials	$9,700		$59,900	
Direct manufacturing labor $30 per DLH	750	$10,450	11,250	$ 71,150
Indirect manufacturing cost $115 per DLH		2,875		43,125
Total manufacturing cost		$13,325		$114,275
Number of units		÷ 10		÷ 200
Manufacturing cost per unit		$ 1,332.50		$ 571

2.

	Job Order 410 25 Labor Hours		Job Order 411 375 Labor Hours	
Direct manufacturing cost				
Direct materials	$9,700		$59,900	
Direct manufacturing labor $30 per DLH	750	$10,450	11,250	$ 71,150
Indirect manufacturing cost				
Materials handling				
$0.40 × 500; **$0.40** × 2,000	200		800	
Lathe work				
$0.20 × 20,000; **$0.20** × 60,000	4,000		12,000	
Milling				
$20.00 × 150; **$20.00** × 1,050	3,000		21,000	
Grinding				
$0.80 × 500; **$0.80** × 2,000	400		1,600	
Testing				
$15.00 × 10; **$15.00** × 200	150	7,750	3,000	38,400
Total manufacturing cost		$18,200		$109,550
Number of units		÷ 10		÷ 200
Manufacturing cost per unit		$ 1,820		$ 547.75

3.

	Job Order 410	Job Order 411
Number of units in job	10	200
Costs per unit with prior costing system	$1,332.50	$571.375
Costs per unit with activity-based costing	1,820.00	547.750

Job order 410 has an increase in reported unit cost of 36.6% [($1,820 − $1,332.50) ÷ $1,332.50], while job order 411 has a decrease in reported unit cost of 4.1% [($547.75 − $571.375) ÷ $571.375].

A *common finding* when activity-based costing is implemented is that *low-volume products have increases in their reported costs while high-volume products have decreases in their reported cost*. This result is also found in requirements 1 and 2 of this problem. Costs such as materials-handling costs vary with the number of parts handled (a function of batches and complexity of products) rather than with direct manufacturing labor-hours, an output-unit level cost driver, which was the only cost driver in the previous job-costing system.

The product cost figures computed in requirements 1 and 2 differ because
  a. the job *orders differ in the way they use each of five activity areas*, and
  b. the *activity areas differ* in their indirect cost *allocation bases* (specifically, each area does not use the direct manufacturing labor-hours indirect cost allocation base).

The *differences* in product cost figures might be important to Tracy Corporation for *product pricing* and *product emphasis* decisions. The activity-based accounting approach indicates that job order 410 is being undercosted while job order 411 is being overcosted. Tracy Corporation may erroneously bid on jobs like job order 410 and deemphasize bidding on jobs like job order 411. Moreover, by its actions, Tracy Corporation may encourage a competitor to enter the market for jobs like job order 411 and take market share away from it.

4.   Information from the ABC system can also help Tracy manage its business better in several ways.
  a. *Product design*. Product designers at Tracy Corporation likely will find the numbers in the activity-based costing approach more believable and credible than those in the simple system. In a machine-paced manufacturing environment, it is unlikely that direct labor-hours would be the major cost driver. Activity-based costing provides more credible signals to product designers about the ways the costs of a product can be reduced—for example, use fewer parts, require fewer turns on the lathe, and reduce the number of machine-hours in the milling area.
  b. *Cost management*. Tracy can reduce the cost of jobs both by making process improvements that reduce the activities that need to be done to complete jobs and by reducing the costs of doing the activities.
  c. *Cost planning*. ABC provides a more refined model to forecast costs and to explain why actual costs differ from budgeted costs.

5-40   (30-40 mins.) **Activity-based costing, cost hierarchy**.

1.

| | Super Bookstore Income Statement For the Year Ended 31 December, 2010 | | | |
	Book	CDs	Café	Total
Revenues	$3,720,480	$2,315,360	$736,216	$6,772,056
Cost of Merchandise	2,656,727	1,722,311	556,685	4,935,723
Cost of Café Cleaning			18,250	18,250
Allocated Selling, General and Administration Costs[a]				
(0.300986 per Merchandise $)	799,638	518,392	167,554	1,485,584
Operating income	$ 264,115	$ 74,657	$ (6,273)	$ 332,499

[a]Overhead Rate = $1,485,584 ÷ $4,935,723 = 0.300986 per cost of merchandise $

2. Selling, general and administration (S,G & A) is comprised of a variety of costs that are unlikely to be consumed uniformly across product lines based on the cost of merchandise. Super Bookstore should consider an activity-based costing system to clarify how each product line uses these S, G & A resources.

	Books	CDs	Café	Total
Number of purchase orders	2,800	2,500	2,000	7,300
Number of deliveries received	1,400	1,700	1,600	4,700
Hours of shelf-stocking time	15,000	14,000	10,000	39,000
Items sold	124,016	115,768	368,108	607,892

Purchasing	$474,500 ÷ 7,300 orders placed = $65 per purchase order
Receiving	$432,400 ÷ 4,700 deliveries = $92 per delivery
Stocking	$487,500 ÷ 39,000 hours = $12.50 per stocking hour
Customer support	$91, 184 ÷ 607,892 items sold = $0.15 per item sold

	Books	CDs	Café	Total
Revenues	$3,720,480	$2,315,360	$ 736,216	$6,772,056
Cost of Merchandise	2,656,727	1,722,311	556,685	4,935,723
Gross margin	1,063,753	593,049	179,531	1,836,333
Cost of Café Cleaning			18,250	18,250
Purchasing ($65 × 2,800; 2,500; 2,000)	182,000	162,500	130,000	474,500
Receiving ($92 × 1,400; 1,700; 1,600)	128,800	156,400	147,200	432,400
Shelf-stocking ($12.50 × 15,000; 14,000; 10,000)	187,500	175,000	125,000	487,500
Customer support ($0.15 × 124,016; 115,768; 368,108	18,603	17,365	55,216	91,184
Total S, G & A costs	516,903	511,265	475,666	1,503,834
Operating income	$ 546,850	$ 81,784	$(296,135)	$ 332,499

Comparing product line income statements in requirements 1 and 2, it appears that books are much more profitable and café loses a lot more money under the ABC system compared to the simple system. The reason is that books use far fewer S,G & A resources relative to its merchandise costs and café uses far greater S, G & A resources relative to its merchandise costs.

3.

To: Super Bookstore Management Team
From: Cost Analyst
Re: Costing System

The current accounting system allocates indirect costs (S,G & A) to product lines based on the Cost of Merchandise sold. Using this method, the S, G & A costs are assigned 54%, 35%, 11%, to the Books, CDs, and Café product lines, respectively.

I recommend that the organization switch to an activity-based costing (ABC) method. With ABC, the product lines are assigned indirect costs based on their consumption of the activities that give rise to the costs. An ABC analysis reveals that the Café consumes considerably more than 11% of indirect costs. Instead, the café generally requires 25-35% of the purchasing, receiving and stocking activity and 60% of the customer support.

The current accounting technique masks the losses being produced by the café because it assumes all indirect costs are driven by the dollar amount of merchandise sold. By adopting ABC, management can evaluate the costs of operating the three product lines and make more informed pricing and product mix decisions. For example, management may want to consider increasing prices of the food and drinks served in the café. Before deciding whether to increase prices or to close the café, management must consider the beneficial effect that having a cafe has on the other product lines.

An ABC analysis can also help Super Bookstore manage its costs by reducing the number of activities that each product line demands and by reducing the cost of each activity. These actions will improve the profitability of each product line. ABC analysis can also be used to plan and manage the various activities.

CHAPTER 6
MASTER BUDGET AND RESPONSIBILITY ACCOUNTING

6-2 The *master budget* expresses management's operating and financial plans for a specified period (usually a fiscal year) and includes a set of budgeted financial statements. It is the initial plan of what the company intends to accomplish in the period.

6-4 We **agree** that budgeted performance is a better criterion than past performance for judging managers, because *inefficiencies included in past results can be detected* and eliminated in budgeting. Also, *future conditions may be expected to differ from the past*, and these can also be factored into budgets.

6-6 We **agree** that budgets meet the cost benefit test. They force managers to act differently. For example, in many organizations, *budgets encourage managers to plan*. Without budgets, managers drift from crisis to crisis. Research also shows that *budgets can motivate managers* to meet targets and improve their performance.

6-8 The steps in preparing an operating budget are as follows:
1. Prepare the **revenues** budget
2. Prepare the **production** budget (in units)
3. Prepare the **direct material usage** budget and **direct material purchases** budget
4. Prepare the **direct manufacturing labor** budget
5. Prepare the **manufacturing overhead** budget
6. Prepare the **ending inventories** budget
7. Prepare the **cost of goods sold** budget
8. Prepare the **nonmanufacturing costs** budget
9. Prepare the budgeted **income statement**

6-10 **Sensitivity** analysis adds an extra dimension to budgeting. It enables managers to examine *how budgeted amounts change with changes in the underlying assumptions*. This assists managers in *monitoring those assumptions that are most critical* to a company in attaining its budget and allows them to *make timely adjustments* to plans when appropriate.

6-12 Nonoutput-based cost drivers can be incorporated into budgeting by the use of *activity-based budgeting* (ABB). ABB focuses on the *budgeted cost of activities* necessary to produce and sell products and services. Nonoutput-based cost drivers, such as the number of part numbers, number of batches, and number of new products can be used with ABB.

6-14 Budgeting in **multinational** companies may involve budgeting in several different *foreign currencies*. Further, management accountants must translate operating performance into a single currency for reporting to shareholders, by *budgeting for exchange rates*. Managers and accountants must understand the factors that impact exchange rates, and where possible, *plan financial strategies to limit the downside* of unexpected unfavorable moves in currency valuations. In developing budgets for operations in different countries, they must also have *good understanding of political, legal and economic issues in those countries*.

6-16 (15 min.) **Sales budget, service setting.**

1.

McGrath & Sons	2009 Volume	At 2009 Selling Prices	Expected 2010 Change in Volume	Expected 2010 Volume
Radon Tests	11,000	$250	+5%	11,550
Lead Tests	15,200	$200	-10%	13,680

McGrath & Sons Sales Budget
For the Year Ended December 31, 2010

	Selling Price	Units Sold	Total Revenues
Radon Tests	$250	11,550	$2,887,500
Lead Tests	$200	13,680	2,736,000
			$5,623,500

2.

McGrath & Sons	2009 Volume	Planned 2010 Selling Prices	Expected 2010 Change in Volume	Expected 2010 Volume
Radon Tests	11,000	$250	+5%	11,550
Lead Tests	15,200	$190	-5%	14,440

McGrath & Sons Sales Budget
For the Year Ended December 31, 2010

	Selling Price	Units Sold	Total Revenues
Radon Tests	$250	11,550	$2,887,500
Lead Tests	$190	14,440	2,743,600
			$5,631,100

Expected revenues at the new 2010 prices are $5,631,100, which are greater than the expected 2010 revenues of $5,623,500 if the prices are unchanged. So, if the goal is to maximize sales revenue and if Jim McGrath's forecasts are reliable, the company should lower its price for a lead test in 2010.

6-18 (5 min.)   **Direct materials purchases budget.**

Direct materials to be used in production (bottles)	2,500,000
Add target ending direct materials inventory (bottles)	80,000
Total requirements (bottles)	2,580,000
Deduct beginning direct materials inventory (bottles)	50,000
Direct materials to be purchased (bottles)	2,530,000

6-20 (30 min.)   **Revenues and production budget.**

1.

	Selling Price	Units Sold	Total Revenues
12-ounce bottles	$0.25	4,800,000[a]	$1,200,000
4-gallon units	1.50	1,200,000[b]	1,800,000
			$3,000,000

[a] 400,000 × 12 months = 4,800,000
[b] 100,000 × 12 months = 1,200,000

2.

Budgeted unit sales (12-ounce bottles)	4,800,000
Add target ending finished goods inventory	600,000
Total requirements	5,400,000
Deduct beginning finished goods inventory	900,000
Minimum Units to be produced	4,500,000

3.

Budgeted unit sales (12-ounce bottles)	1,200,000
Add target ending finished goods inventory	200,000
Total requirements	1,400,000
Production budget	1,300,000
Inventory on hand January 1, 2010	100,000

6-22 (15–20 min.)   **Revenues, production, and purchases budget.**

1.   Revenue budget:
900,000 motorcycles × selling price of 400,000 yen = 360,000,000,000 yen ¥

2.

Budgeted sales (motorcycles)	900,000
Add target ending finished goods inventory	80,000
Total requirements	980,000
Deduct beginning finished goods inventory	100,000
Units to be produced	880,000

3.

Direct materials to be used in production,		
880,000 × 2 (wheels)		1,760,000
Add target ending direct materials inventory		60,000
Total requirements		1,820,000
Deduct beginning direct materials inventory		50,000
Direct materials to be purchased (wheels)		**1,770,000**
Cost per wheel in yen		16,000
Direct materials purchase cost in yen		**28,320,000,000**

Note the relatively small inventory of wheels. In Japan, suppliers tend to be located very close to the major manufacturer. Inventories are controlled by just-in-time and similar systems. Indeed, some direct materials inventories are almost nonexistent.

6-24 (20–30 min.) **Activity-based budgeting.**

1. This question links to the ABC example used in the Problem for Self-Study in Chapter 5 and to Question 5-23 (ABC, retail product-line profitability).

Activity	Cost Hierarchy	Soft Drinks	Fresh Produce	Packaged Food	Total
Ordering					
$90 × 14; 24; 14	Batch-level	$1,260	$ 2,160	$1,260	$ 4,680
Delivery					
$82 × 12; 62; 19	Batch-level	984	5,084	1,558	7,626
Shelf-stocking	Output-unit-				
$21 × 16; 172; 94	level	336	3,612	1,974	5,922
Customer support	Output-unit-				
$0.18 × 4,600; 34,200; 10,750	level	828	6,156	1,935	8,919
Total budgeted indirect costs		**$3,408**	**$17,012**	**$6,727**	**$27,147**
Percentage of total indirect costs (subject to rounding)		13%	**63%**	25%	

2. Refer to the last row of the table in requirement 1. Fresh produce, which probably represents the smallest portion of COGS, is the product category that consumes the largest share (63%) of the indirect resources. Fresh produce demands the highest level of ordering, delivery, shelf-stocking and customer support resources of all three product categories—it has to be ordered, delivered and stocked in small, perishable batches, and supermarket customers often ask for a lot of guidance on fresh produce items. However, a supermarket without fresh produce would probably lose many customers for its other product lines.

3.   An **ABB** approach recognizes how *different products require different mixes of support activities*. The relative percentage of how each product area uses the cost driver at each activity area is:

Activity	Cost Hierarchy	Soft Drinks	Fresh Produce	Packaged Food	Total
Ordering	Batch-level	27%	46%	27%	100%
Delivery	Batch-level	13	67	20	100
Shelf-stocking	Output-unit-level	6	61	33	100
Customer support	Output-unit-level	9	69	22	100

By recognizing these differences, FS managers are *better able to budget for different unit sales* levels and different mixes of individual product-line items sold. Using a single cost driver (such as COGS) assumes homogeneity in the use of indirect costs (support activities) across product lines which does not occur at FS. Other benefits cited by managers include: (1) better *identification of resource needs*, (2) clearer *linking of costs with staff responsibilities*, and (3) *identification of budgetary slack*.

6-26   (15 min.)   **(a) Responsibility and (b) controllability. (c) What might be done.**

1. (a)   Salesman
   (b)   VP of Sales
   (c)   Permit the salesman to offer a reasonable discount to customers, but require that he clear bigger discounts with the VP. Also, base his bonus/performance evaluation not just on revenues generated, but also on margins (or, ability to meet budget).

2. (a)   VP of Sales
   (b)   VP of Sales
   (c)   VP of Sales should compare budgeted sales with actuals, and ask for an analysis of all the sales during the quarter. Discuss with salespeople why so many discounts are being offered—are they really needed to close each sale. Are our prices too high (i.e., uncompetitive)?

3. (a)   Manager, Shipping department
   (b)   Manager or Director of Operations (including shipping)
   (c)   Shipping department manager must report delays more regularly and request additional capacity in a timely manner. Operations manager should ask for a review of shipping capacity utilization, and consider expanding the department.

4. (a)   HR department
   (b)   Production supervisor
   (c)   The production supervisor should devise his or her own educational standards that all new plant employees are held to before they are allowed to work on the plant floor. Offer remedial in-plant training to those workers who show promise. Be very specific about the types of skills required when using the HR department to hire plant workers. Test the workers periodically for required skills.

5. (a) Production supervisor
    (b) Production supervisor
    (c) Get feedback from the workers, analyze it, and act on it. Get extra coaching and training from experienced mentors.

6. (a) Maintenance department
    (b) Production supervisor
    First, get the requisite maintenance done on the machines. Make sure that the maintenance department head clearly understands the repercussions of poor maintenance. Discuss and establish maintenance standards that must be met (frequency of maintenance and tolerance limits, for example). Test and keep a log of the maintenance work.

6-28 (40 min.) **Budget schedules for a manufacturer.**

1a. Revenues Budget

	Executive Line	Chairman Line	Total
Units sold	740	390	
Selling price	$ 1,020	$ 1,600	
Budgeted revenues	$754,800	$624,000	$1,378,800

b. Production Budget in Units

	Executive Line	Chairman Line
Budgeted unit sales	740	390
Add budgeted ending fin. goods inventory	30	15
Total requirements	770	405
Deduct beginning fin. goods. inventory	20	5
Budgeted production	750	400

c. Direct Materials Usage Budget (units)

	Oak	Red Oak	Oak Legs	Red Oak Legs	Total
Executive Line:					
1. Budgeted input per f.g. unit	16	–	4	–	
2. Budgeted production	750	–	750	–	
3. Budgeted usage (1 × 2)	12,000	–	3,000	–	
Chairman Line:					
4. Budgeted input per f.g. unit	–	25	–	4	
5. Budgeted production	–	400	–	400	
6. Budgeted usage (4 × 5)	–	10,000	–	1,600	
7. Total direct materials usage (3 + 6)	12,000	10,000	3,000	1,600	
Direct Materials Cost Budget					
8. Beginning inventory	320	150	100	40	
9. Unit price (FIFO)	$18	$23	$11	$17	
10. Cost of DM used from beginning inventory (8 × 9)	$5,760	$3,450	$1,100	$680	$10,990
11. Materials to be used from purchases (7 − 8)	11,680	9,850	2,900	1,560	
12. Cost of DM in March	$20	$25	$12	$18	
13. Cost of DM purchased and used in March (11 × 12)	$233,600	$246,250	$34,800	$28,080	$542,730
14. Direct materials to be used (10 + 13)	$239,360	$249,700	$35,900	$28,760	$553,720

Direct Materials Purchases Budget

	Oak	Red Oak	Oak Legs	Red Oak Legs	Total
Budgeted usage (from line 7)	12,000	10,000	3,000	1,600	
Add target ending inventory	192	200	80	44	
Total requirements	12,192	10,200	3,080	1,644	
Deduct beginning inventory	320	150	100	40	
Total DM purchases	11,872	10,050	2,980	1,604	
Purchase price (March)	$20	$25	$12	$18	
Total purchases	$237,440	$251,250	$35,760	$28,872	$553,322

d. Direct Manufacturing Labor Budget

	Output Units Produced	Direct Manuf. Labor-Hours per Output Unit	Total Hours	Hourly Rate	Total
Executive Line	750	3	2,250	$30	$ 67,500
Chairman Line	400	5	2,000	$30	60,000
			4,250		$127,500

93

e. Manufacturing Overhead Budget

Variable manufacturing overhead costs (4,250 direct labor hours × $35) $148,750
Fixed manufacturing overhead costs   42,500
Total manufacturing overhead costs $191,250

$$\text{Total manuf. overhead cost per hour} = \frac{\$191,250}{4,250} = \$45 \text{ per direct manufacturing labor-hour}$$

$$\text{Fixed manuf. overhead cost per hour} = \frac{\$42,500}{4,250} = \$10 \text{ per direct manufacturing labor-hour}$$

f. Computation of unit costs of ending inventory of finished goods

	Executive Line 3 DL Hours	Chairman Line 5 DL Hours
Direct materials		
Oak top ($20 × 16 square feet, 0)	$320	$ 0
Red oak ($25 × 0, 25 square feet)	0	625
Oak legs ($12 × 4 legs, 0)	48	0
Red oak legs ($18 × 0, 4 legs)	0	72
Direct manufacturing labor ($30 per DL hour)	90	150
Manufacturing overhead		
Variable ($35 per DL hour)	105	175
Fixed ($10 per DL hour)	30	50
Total manufacturing cost	$593	$1,072

Ending Inventories Budget

	Cost per Unit	Units	Total
Direct Materials			
Oak top	$ 20	192	$ 3,840
Red oak top	25	200	5,000
Oak legs	12	80	960
Red oak legs	18	44	792
			10,592
Finished Goods			
Executive (computed above)	593	30	17,790
Chairman (computed above)	1,072	15	16,080
			33,870
Total			$44,462

g. Cost of goods sold budget

Budgeted fin. goods inventory, March 1, 2009 ($10,480 + $4,850)		$ 15,330
Direct materials used (from Dir. materials purch. budget)	$553,720	
Direct manufacturing labor (Dir. manuf. labor budget)	127,500	
Manufacturing overhead (Manuf. overhead budget)	191,250	
Cost of goods manufactured		872,470
Cost of goods available for sale		887,800
Deduct ending fin. goods inventory, March 31, 2009 (Inventories budget)		33,870
Cost of goods sold		$853,930

2. Areas where continuous improvement might be incorporated into the budgeting process:

(a) **Direct materials.** Either an improvement in usage or price could be budgeted. For example, the budgeted usage amounts could be related to the maximum improvement (current usage – minimum possible usage) of 1 square foot for either desk:

- Executive: 16 square feet – 15 square feet minimum = 1 square foot
- Chairman: 25 square feet – 24 square feet minimum = 1 square foot

Thus, a 1% reduction target per month could be:

- Executive: 15 square feet + (0.99 × 1) = 15.99
- Chairman: 24 square feet + (0.99 × 1) = 24.99

Be sure to notice that you cannot achieve a standard less than the size of the desk. If you recommended an alternative improvement suggestion, check that it won't go below the square footage requirement at some point.

(b) **Direct manufacturing labor.** The budgeted usage of 3 hours/5 hours could be continuously revised on a monthly basis. Similarly, the manufacturing labor cost per hour of $30 could be continuously revised down. The former appears more feasible than the latter.

(c) **Variable manufacturing overhead.** By budgeting more efficient use of the allocation base, a signal is given for continuous improvement. A second approach is to budget continuous improvement in the budgeted variable overhead cost per unit of the allocation base.

(d) **Fixed manufacturing overhead.** The approach here is to budget for reductions in the year-to-year amounts of fixed overhead. If these costs are appropriately classified as fixed, then they are more difficult to adjust down on a monthly basis.

6-30 (30–40 min.) **Revenue and production budgets.**

This is a routine budgeting problem. The key to its solution is to compute the correct *quantities* of finished goods and direct materials. Use the following general formula:

$$\begin{pmatrix} \text{Budgeted} \\ \text{production} \\ \text{or purchases} \end{pmatrix} = \begin{pmatrix} \text{Target} \\ \text{ending} \\ \text{inventory} \end{pmatrix} + \begin{pmatrix} \text{Budgeted} \\ \text{sales or} \\ \text{materials used} \end{pmatrix} - \begin{pmatrix} \text{Beginning} \\ \text{inventory} \end{pmatrix}$$

1.

Scarborough Corporation
Revenue Budget
for 2010

	Units	Price	Total
Thingone	60,000	$165	$ 9,900,000
Thingtwo	40,000	250	10,000,000
Budgeted revenues			$19,900,000

2.

Scarborough Corporation
Production Budget (in units)
for 2010

	Thingone	Thingtwo
Budgeted sales in units	60,000	40,000
Add target finished goods inventories, December 31, 2010	25,000	9,000
Total requirements	85,000	49,000
Deduct finished goods inventories, January 1, 2010	20,000	8,000
Units to be produced	65,000	41,000

3.

Scarborough Corporation
Direct Materials Purchases Budget (in quantities)
for 2010

	Direct Materials		
	A	B	C
Direct materials to be used in production			
• Thingone (budgeted production of 65,000 units times 4 lbs. of A, 2 lbs. of B)	260,000	130,000	--
• Thingtwo (budgeted production of 41,000 units times 5 lbs. of A, 3 lbs. of B, 1 lb. of C)	205,000	123,000	41,000
Total	465,000	253,000	41,000
Add target ending inventories, December 31, 2010	36,000	32,000	7,000
Total requirements in units	501,000	285,000	48,000
Deduct beginning inventories, January 1, 2010	32,000	29,000	6,000
Direct materials to be purchased (units)	469,000	256,000	42,000

4.

Scarborough Corporation
Direct Materials Purchases Budget (in dollars)
for 2010

	Budgeted Purchases (Units)	Expected Purchase Price per unit	Total
Direct material A	469,000	$12	$5,628,000
Direct material B	256,000	5	1,280,000
Direct material C	42,000	3	126,000
Budgeted purchases			$7,034,000

5.

Scarborough Corporation
Direct Manufacturing Labor Budget (in dollars)
for 2010

	Budgeted Production (Units)	Direct Manufacturing Labor-Hours per Unit	Total Hours	Rate per Hour	Total
Thingone	65,000	2	130,000	$12	$1,560,000
Thingtwo	41,000	3	123,000	16	1,968,000
Total					$3,528,000

6.

Scarborough Corporation
Budgeted Finished Goods Inventory
at December 31, 2010

Thingone:
    Direct materials costs:

A, 4 pounds × $12	$48	
B, 2 pounds × $5	10	$ 58
Direct manufacturing labor costs,		
2 hours × $12		24
Manufacturing overhead costs at $20 per direct		
manufacturing labor-hour (2 hours × $20)		40
Budgeted manufacturing costs per unit	$122	
Finished goods inventory of Thingone		
$122 × 25,000 units		$3,050,000

Thingtwo:
    Direct materials costs:

A, 5 pounds × $12	$60	
B, 3 pounds × $5	15	
C, 1 each × $3	3	$ 78
Direct manufacturing labor costs,		
3 hours × $16		48
Manufacturing overhead costs at $20 per direct		
manufacturing labor-hour (3 hours × $20)		60
Budgeted manufacturing costs per unit	$186	
Finished goods inventory of Thingtwo		
$186 × 9,000 units		1,674,000
Budgeted finished goods inventory, December 31, 2010		$4,724,000

6-32   (15 min.)   **Responsibility of purchasing agent.**

<u>**The time lost in the plant should be charged to the purchasing department**</u>. The plant manager probably should not be asked to underwrite a loss due to failure of delivery over which he had no supervision. Although the purchasing agent may feel that he has done everything he possibly could, he must realize that, in the whole organization, he is *the one* who is in the best position to evaluate the situation. He receives an assignment. He may accept it or reject it. But if he accepts, he must perform. If he fails, the damage is evaluated. Everybody makes mistakes. The important point is to avoid making too many mistakes and also to understand fully that the extensive control reflected in responsibility accounting is the necessary balance to the great freedom of action that individual executives are given.

Discussions of this problem have again and again revealed a tendency among students (and among accountants and managers) to "fix the blame"—as if the variances arising from a responsibility accounting system should pinpoint misbehavior and provide answers. The point is that no accounting system or variances can provide answers. However, variances can lead to questions. In this case, in deciding where the penalty should be assigned, the student might inquire who should be asked—not who should be blamed.

Classroom discussions have also raised the following diverse points:
(a) Is the railroad company liable?
(b) Costs of idle time are usually routinely charged to the production department. Should the information system be fine-tuned to reallocate such costs to the purchasing department?
(c) How will the purchasing managers behave in the future regarding willingness to take risks?

The text emphasizes the following: Beware of overemphasis on controllability. For example, a time-honored theme of management is that responsibility should not be given without accompanying authority. Such a guide is a useful first step, but responsibility accounting is more far-reaching. The basic focus should be on information or knowledge, not on control. The key question is: Who is the best informed? Put another way, "Who is the person who can tell us the most about the specific item, regardless of ability to exert personal control?"

6-34 (25 min.) **(Continuation of 6-33) Cash budget (Appendix)**

Cash Budget
April 30, 20xx

Cash balance, April 1, 20xx	$ 5,360
Add receipts	
Cash sales ($155,000 × 10%)	15,500
Credit card sales ($155,000 × 90% × 97%)	135,315
Total cash available for needs (x)	$156,175
Deduct cash disbursements	
Direct materials ($8,500 + $17,300 × 50%)	$ 17,150
Direct manufacturing labor	29,850
Manufacturing overhead ($59,265 − $20,000 depreciation)	39,265
Nonmanufacturing salaries	18,900
Sales commissions	1,550
Other nonmanufacturing fixed costs ($18,000 − $10,000 deprn)	8,000
Machinery purchase	13,700
Income taxes	5,000
Total disbursements (y)	$133,415
Financing	
Repayment of loan	$ 2,000
Interest at 12% ($2,000 × 12% × $\frac{1}{12}$)	20
Total effects of financing (z)	$ 2,020
Ending cash balance, April 30 (x) − (y) − (z)	$ 20,740

6-36 (30 min.) **Cash budgeting, chapter appendix.**

1.   Projected Sales

	May	June	July	August	September	October
Sales in units	80	120	200	100	60	40
Revenues (Sales in units × $450)	$36,000	$54,000	$90,000	$45,000	$27,000	

Collections of Receivables

	May	June	July	August	September	October
From sales in:						
May (30% × $36,000)			$10,800			
June (50%; 30% × $54,000)			27,000	$16,200		
July (20%; 50%; 30% × $90,000)			18,000	45,000	$ 27,000	
August (20%; 50% × $45,000)				9,000	22,500	
September (20% × $27,000)					5,400	
Total			$55,800	$70,200	$54,900	

Calculation of Payables

	May	June	July	August	September	October
Material and Labor Use, Units						
Budgeted production		200	100	60	40	
Direct materials						
Wood (board feet)		1,000	500	300	200	
Fiberglass (yards)		1,200	600	360	240	
Direct manuf. labor (hours)		1,000	500	300	200	
Disbursement of Payments						
Direct materials						
Wood						
(1,000; 500; 300 × $30)			$30,000	$15,000	$9,000	
Fiberglass						
(1,200; 600; 360 × $5)			6,000	3,000	1,800	
Direct manuf. labor						
(500; 300; 200 × $25)			12,500	7,500	5,000	
Interest payment						
(6% × $30,000 ÷12)			150	150	150	
Variable Overhead Calculation						
Variable overhead rate			$ 7	$ 7	$ 7	
Overhead driver						
(direct manuf. labor-hours)			500	300	200	
Variable overhead expense			$ 3,500	$ 2,100	$1,400	

Cash Budget for the months of July, August, September 2007

	July	August	September
Beginning cash balance	$10,000	$ 5,650	$40,100
Add receipts: Collection of receivables	55,800	70,200	54,900
Total cash available	$65,800	$75,850	$95,000
Deduct disbursements:			
Material purchases	$36,000	$18,000	$10,800
Direct manufacturing labor	12,500	7,500	5,000
Variable costs	3,500	2,100	1,400
Fixed costs	8,000	8,000	8,000
Interest payments	150	150	150
Total disbursements	60,150	35,750	25,350
Ending cash balance	$ 5,650	$40,100	$69,650

2.   Yes. Slopes has a budgeted cash balance of $69,650 on 10/1/2010 and so it will be in a position to pay off the $30,000 1-year note on October 1, 2010.

3.   No. Slopes does not maintain a $10,000 minimum cash balance in July. To maintain a $10,000 cash balance in each of the three months, it could perhaps encourage its customers to pay earlier by offering a discount. Alternatively, Slopes could seek short-term credit from a bank.

6-38 (60 min.) **Comprehensive problem; ABC manufacturing, two products.**

1.

Revenues Budget
For the Year Ending December 31, 2009

	Units	Selling Price	Total Revenues
Chairs	172,000	$ 80	$13,760,000
Tables	45,000	$900	$40,500,000
Total			$54,260,000

2a. Total budgeted marketing costs = Budgeted variable marketing costs + Budgeted fixed marketing costs

$$= \$2,011,200 + \$4,500,000 = \$6,511,200$$

$$\text{Marketing allocation rate} = \frac{\$6,511,200}{\$54,260,000} = \$0.12 \text{ per sales dollar}$$

2b. Total budgeted distribution costs = Budgeted variable distribution costs + Budgeted fixed distribution costs

$$= \$54,000 + \$380,000 = \$434,000$$

Chairs:	172,000 units ÷ 500 units per delivery	344 deliveries
Tables:	45,000 units ÷ 500 units per delivery	90 deliveries
Total		434 deliveries

$$\text{Delivery allocation rate} = \frac{\$434,000}{434 \text{ deliveries}} = \$1,000 \text{ per delivery}$$

3.

Production Budget (in Units)
For the Year Ending December 31, 2009

	Product	
	Chairs	**Tables**
Budgeted unit sales	172,000	45,000
Add target ending finished goods inventory	8,500	2,250
Total required units	180,500	47,250
Deduct beginning finished goods inventory	8,000	2,100
Units of finished goods to be produced	172,500	45,150

4a.

	Chairs	Tables	Total
Machine setup overhead			
Units to be produced	172,500	45,150	
Units per batch	÷500	÷50	
Number of setups	345	903	
Hours to setup per batch	×3	×2	
Total setup hours	1,035	1,806	2,841

Total budgeted setup costs = Budgeted variable setup costs + Budgeted fixed setup costs

$$= \$97,000 + \$300,740 = \$397,740$$

$$\text{Machine setup allocation rate} = \frac{\$397,740}{2,841 \text{ setup-hours}} = \$140 \text{ per setup hour}$$

b.

Chairs:	172,500 units × 3 MH per unit	517,500	MH
Tables:	45,150 units × 5 MH per unit	225,750	MH
Total		743,250	MH

Total budgeted processing costs = Budgeted variable processing costs + Budgeted fixed processing costs

$$= \$789,250 + \$5,900,000 = \$6,689,250$$

$$\text{Processing allocation rate} = \frac{\$6,689,250}{743,250 \text{ MH}} = \$9 \text{ per MH}$$

5.

Direct Material Usage Budget in Quantity and Dollars
For the Year Ending December 31, 2009

	Material Wood	Glass	Total
Physical Units Budget			
Direct materials required for			
Chairs (172,500 units × 5 b.f. and 0 sheets)	862,500 b.f.		
Tables (45,150 units × 7 b.f. and 2 sheets)	316,050 b.f.	90,300 sheets	
Total quantity of direct materials to be used	1,178,550 b.f.	90,300 sheets	
Cost Budget			
Available from beginning direct materials inventory			
(under a FIFO cost-flow assumption)	$ 170,352	$ 109,375	
To be purchased this period			
Wood: (1,178,550 b.f. − 109,200 b.f.) × $1.60 per b.f.	1,710,960		
Glass: (90,300 sheets − 8,750 sheets) × $12 per sheet		978,600	
Direct materials to be used this period	$1,881,312	$1,087,975	$2,969,287

Direct Materials Purchases Budget
For the Year Ending December 31, 2009

| | Material | | |
	Wood	Glass	Total
Physical Units Budget			
To be used in production (requirement 5)	1,178,550 b.f.	90,300 sheets	
Add: Target ending direct material inventory	117,500 b.f.	9,000 sheets	
Total requirements	1,296,050 b.f.	99,300 sheets	
Deduct: Beginning direct material inventory	109,200 b.f.	8,750 sheets	
Purchases to be made	1,186,850	90,550 sheets	
Cost Budget			
Wood: 1,186,850 b.f. × $1.60 per b.f.	$ 1,898,960		
Glass: 90,550 sheets × $12 per sheet		$ 1,086,600	
Purchases	$ 1,898,960	$ 1,086,600	$2,985,560

$$\text{Total budgeted materials-handling costs} = \text{Budgeted variable materials-handling costs} + \text{Budgeted fixed materials-handling costs}$$

$$= \$342,840 + \$600,000 = \$942,840$$

$$\text{Materials handling allocation rate} = \frac{\$942,840}{1,178,550 \text{ b.f.}} = \$0.80 \text{ per b.f.}$$

7.

Direct Manufacturing Labor Costs Budget
For the Year Ending December 31, 2009

	Output Units Produced	Direct Manufacturing Labor-Hours per Unit	Total Hours	Hourly Wage Rate	Total
Chairs	172,500	4	690,000	$15	$10,350,000
Tables	45,150	8	361,200	15	5,418,000
Total					$15,768,000

8.

Manufacturing Overhead Cost Budget
For the Year Ending December 31, 2009

	Variable	Fixed	Total
Materials handling	$ 342,840	$ 600,000	$ 942,840
Machine setup	97,000	300,740	397,740
Processing	789,250	5,900,000	6,689,250
Total	$1,229,090	$6,800,740	$8,029,830

9.

Unit Costs of Ending Finished Goods Inventory
For the Year Ending December 31, 2009

	Cost per Unit of Input	Chair Input per Unit of Output	Total	Table Input per Unit of Output	Total
Wood	$1.60	5 b.f.	$ 8.00	7 b.f.	$ 11.20
Glass	12	—	—	2 sheets	24.00
Direct manufacturing labor	15	4 hrs.	60.00	8 hrs.	120.00
Materials handling	0.80	5 b.f.	4.00	7 b.f.	5.60
Machine setup	140	0.006 hrs. [1]	0.84	0.04 setup-hr[1]	5.60
Processing	9	3 MH	27.00	5 MH	45.00
Total			$ 99.84		$211.40

[1] 1,035 setup-hours ÷ 172,500 units = 0.006 hours per unit; 1,806 setup hours ÷ 45,150 units = 0.04 hours per unit

Ending Inventories Budget
December 31, 2009

	Quantity	Cost per unit	Total	
Direct Materials				
Wood	117,500 b.f.	$1.60	$188,000	
Glass	9,000 sheets	12.00	108,000	$ 296,000
Finished goods				
Chairs	8,500	$99.84	$848,640	
Tables	2,250	211.40	475,650	1,324,290
Total ending inventory				$1,620,290

10.

Cost of Goods Sold Budget
For the Year Ending December 31, 2009

Beginning finished goods inventory, Jan. 1 ($760,000 + $477,000)		$ 1,237,000
Direct materials used (requirement 5)	$ 2,969,287	
Direct manufacturing labor (requirement 7)	15,768,000	
Manufacturing overhead (requirement 8)	8,029,830	
Cost of goods manufactured		26,767,117
Cost of goods available for sale		28,004,117
Deduct: Ending finished goods inventory, December 31 (reqmt. 9)		1,324,290
Cost of goods sold		$26,679,827

11.

Nonmanufacturing Costs Budget
For the Year Ending December 31, 2009

	Variable	Fixed	Total
Marketing	$2,011,200	$4,500,000	$6,511,200
Distribution	54,000	380,000	434,000
Total	$2,065,200	$4,880,000	$6,945,200

12.

Budgeted Income Statement
For the Year Ending December 31, 2009

Revenue	$54,260,000
Cost of goods sold	26,679,827
Gross margin	27,580,173
Operating (nonmanufacturing) costs	6,945,200
Operating income	$20,634,973

13. The budgeted unit cost of the chair is $99.84, which is $20 more than the selling price of $80 per chair.

The company is willing to accept the loss on chairs because of the high markup on tables ($900 $- \$211.40) = \$688.60 \ (\dfrac{\$688.60}{\$900} = 76.5\%)$. Customers who purchase a table will likely want matching chairs. Thus the markup on tables more than recoups the loss on four chairs. Dinette could, of course, reduce the price on tables and increase the price on chairs. If, however, customers care less about the price of the table and more about the price of chairs and buy 4 chairs for every 1 table, Dinette's pricing strategy may well be optimal.

6-40 (60 min.) **Comprehensive budgeting problem; activity-based costing, operating and financial budgets.**

1a.

Revenues Budget
For the Month of June, 20xx

	Units	Selling Price	Total Revenues
Large	3,000	$3	$ 9,000
Giant	1,800	4	7,200
Total			$16,200

b.

Production Budget
For the Month of June, 20xx

	Product	
	Large	Giant
Budgeted unit sales	3,000	1,800
Add: target ending finished goods inventory	300	180
Total required units	3,300	1,980
Deduct: beginning finished goods inventory	200	150
Units of finished goods to be produced	3,100	1,830

c.

Direct Material Usage Budget in Quantity and Dollars
For the Month of June, 20xx

	Material		
	Sugar	Sticks	Total
Physical Units Budget			
Direct materials required for			
Large (3,100 units × 0.25 lb.; 1 stick)	775 lbs.	3,100	
Giant (1,830 units × 0.50 lb.; 1 stick)	915 lbs.	1,830	
Total quantity of direct materials to be used	1,690 lbs.	4,930	
Cost Budget			
Available from beginning direct materials inventory			
(under a FIFO cost-flow assumption)	$ 64	$ 105	
To be purchased this period			
Sugar: (1,690 lbs. – 125 lbs.) × $0.50 per lb.	783		
Sticks: (4,930 – 350) × $0.30 per stick		1,374	
Direct materials to be used this period	$847	$1,479	$2,326

Direct Materials Purchases Budget
For the Month of June, 20xx

	Material		
	Sugar	Sticks	Total
Physical Units Budget			
To be used in production	1,690 lbs.	4,930	
Add: Target ending direct material inventory	240 lbs.	480	
Total requirements	1,930 lbs.	5,410	
Deduct: beginning direct material inventory	125 lbs.	350	
Purchases to be made	1,805 lbs.	5,060	
Cost Budget			
Sugar: (1,805 lbs. × $0.50 per lb.)	$903		
Sticks: (5,060 × $0.30 per stick)		$1,518	
Total	$903	$1,518	$2,421

d.

Direct Manufacturing Labor Costs Budget
For the Month of June, 20xx

	Output Units Produced	Direct Manufacturing Labor-Hours per Unit	Total Hours	Hourly Wage Rate	Total
Large	3,100	0.20	620	$8	$4,960
Giant	1,830	0.25	457.5	8	3,660
Total			1,077.5		$8,620

e.

Manufacturing Overhead Costs Budget
For the Month of June 20xx

	Total
Machine setup	
(Large 310 batches[1] × 0.08 hrs./batch + Giant 183 batches[2] × 0.09 hrs./batch) × $20/hour	$ 825
Processing (1,077.5 DMLH × $1.70)	1,832
Total	$2,657

[1]Large: 3,100 units ÷ 10 units per batch = 310; [2]Giant: 1,830 units ÷ 10 units per batch = 183

f.

Unit Costs of Ending Finished Goods Inventory
For the Month of June, 20xx

	Cost per Unit of Input	Large Input per Unit of Output	Large Total	Giant Input per Unit of Output	Giant Total
Sugar	$ 0.50	0.25 lb	$0.125	0.50 lb.	$ 0.25
Sticks	0.30	1	0.30	1	0.30
Direct manufacturing labor	8.00	0.2 hr.	1.60	0.25 hr.	2.00
Machine setup	20.00	0.008 hr. [1]	0.16	0.009 hr[1]	0.18
Processing	1.70	0.2 hr	0.34	0.25 hr	0.425
Total			$2.525		$3.155

[1] 0.08 hour per setup ÷ 10 units per batch = 0.008 hr. per unit;
0.09 hour per setup ÷ 10 units per batch = 0.009 hr. per unit.

Ending Inventories Budget
June, 20xx

	Quantity	Cost per unit	Total	
Direct Materials				
Sugar	240 lbs.	$0.50	$120	
Sticks	480 sticks	0.30	144	$ 264
Finished goods				
Large	300	$2.525	$757	
Giant	180	3.155	568	1,325
Total ending inventory				$1,589

g.

Cost of Goods Sold Budget
For the Month of June, 20xx

Beginning finished goods inventory, June 1 ($500 + $474)		$ 974
Direct materials used (requirement c)	$2,326	
Direct manufacturing labor (requirement d)	8,620	
Manufacturing overhead (requirement e)	2,657	
Cost of goods manufactured		13,603
Cost of goods available for sale		14,577
Deduct ending finished goods inventory, June 30 (requirement f)		1,325
Cost of goods sold		$13,252

h.

Nonmanufacturing Costs Budget
For the Month of June, 20xx

	Total
Marketing and general administration	
$10\% \times 16,200$	$1,620

2.

Cash Budget
June 30, 20xx

Cash balance, June 30, 20xx	$ 587
Add receipts	
Collections from May accounts receivable	4,704
Collections from June accounts receivable	
($16,200 × 80% × 50%)	6,480
Collections from June cash sales	
($16,200 × 20%)	3,240
Total collection from customers	14,424
Total cash available for needs (x)	$15,011
Deduct cash disbursements	
Direct material purchases in May	$ 696
Direct material purchases in June	
($2,421 × 70%)	1,695
Direct manufacturing labor	8,620
Manufacturing overhead	
($2,657 × 60% because 40% is depreciation)	1,594
Nonmanufacturing costs	
($1,620 × 70% because 30% is depreciation)	1,134
Taxes	500
Total disbursements (y)	$14,239
Financing	
Interest at 12% ($20,000 × 12% × 1 ÷ 12) ($z$)	$ 200
Ending cash balance, June 30 (x) − (y) − (z)	$ 572

3.

Budgeted Income Statement
For the Month of June, 20xx

Revenues		$16,200
Cost of goods sold		13,252
Gross margin		2,948
Operating (nonmanufacturing) costs	$1,620	
Bad debt expense ($16,200 × 80% × 1%)	130	
Interest expense (for June)	200	1,950
Net income		$ 998

Budgeted Balance Sheet
June 30, 20xx

Assets

Cash		$ 572
Accounts receivable ($16,200 × 80% × 50%)	$ 6,480	
Less: allowance for doubtful accounts	130	6,350
Inventories		
Direct materials	$ 264	
Finished goods	1,325	1,589
Fixed assets	$190,000	
Less: accumulated depreciation		
($55,759 + 2,657 × 40% + 1,620 × 30%)	57,308	132,692
Total assets		$141,203

Liabilities and Equity

Accounts payable ($2,421 × 30%)		$ 726
Interest payable		200
Long-term debt		20,000
Common stock		10,000
Retained earnings ($109,279 + $998)		110,277
Total liabilities and equity		$141,203

CHAPTER 7
FLEXIBLE BUDGETS, DIRECT-COST VARIANCES,
AND MANAGEMENT CONTROL

7-2 **Two sources** of information about budgeted amounts are
(a) *past* amounts and
(b) detailed *engineering* studies.

7-4 The **key difference** is the *output level* used to set the budget. A *static budget* is based on the level of output *planned* at the *start of the budget period*. A *flexible budget* is developed using budgeted revenues or cost amounts based on the *actual output* level in the budget period. The actual level of output is not known until the *end of the budget period*.

7-6 The steps in developing a **flexible budget** are:
Step 1: Identify the *actual quantity* of output.
Step 2: Calculate the flexible budget for *revenues* based on *budgeted selling price* and *actual quantity* of output.
Step 3: Calculate the flexible budget for *costs* based on *budgeted variable cost* per output unit, *actual quantity* of output, and *budgeted fixed costs*.

7-8 A manager should **subdivide the flexible-budget variance** for direct materials into a *price variance* (that reflects the difference between actual and budgeted prices of direct materials) and an *efficiency variance* (that reflects the difference between the actual and budgeted quantities of direct materials used to produce actual output). The individual causes of these variances can then be investigated, recognizing possible interdependencies across these individual causes.

7-10 Some possible reasons for an **unfavorable direct manufacturing labor efficiency variance** are:
a) the hiring and use of *underskilled* workers;
b) *inefficient scheduling* of work so that the workforce was not optimally occupied;
c) *poor maintenance* of machines resulting in a high proportion of non-value-added labor;
d) *unrealistic time standards*.

7-12 An individual business function, such as **production**, is **interdependent** with other business functions. Factors outside of production can explain why variances arise in the production area. For example:
- *poor design* of products or processes can lead to a sizable number of defects,
- marketing personnel making *promises for delivery times* that require a large number of rush orders can create production-scheduling difficulties, and
- *purchase of poor-quality materials* by the purchasing manager can result in defects and waste.

7-14 Variances can be calculated at the activity level as well as at the company level. For example, a price variance and an efficiency variance can be computed for an activity area.

7-16 (20–30 min.) **Flexible budget.**

Variance Analysis for Brabham Enterprises for August 2009

	Actual Results (1)	Flexible-Budget Variances (2) = (1) – (3)	Flexible Budget (3)	Sales-Volume Variances (4) = (3) – (5)	Static Budget (5)
Units (tires) sold	2,800[g]	0	2,800	200 U	3,000[g]
Revenues	$313,600[a]	$ 5,600 F	$308,000[b]	$22,000 U	$330,000[c]
Variable costs	229,600[d]	22,400 U	207,200[e]	14,800 F	222,000[f]
Contribution margin	84,000	16,800 U	100,800	7,200 U	108,000
Fixed costs	50,000[g]	4,000 F	54,000[g]	0	54,000[g]
Operating income	$ 34,000	$12,800 U	$ 46,800	$ 7,200 U	$ 54,000

$12,800 U $ 7,200 U

▲ Total flexible-budget variance   Total sales-volume variance ▲

$20,000 U

Total static-budget variance

[a] $112 × 2,800 = $313,600

[b] $110 × 2,800 = $308,000

[c] $110 × 3,000 = $330,000

[d] Given. Unit variable cost = $229,600 ÷ 2,800 = $82 per tire

[e] $74 × 2,800 = $207,200

[f] $74 × 3,000 = $222,000

[g] Given

2. The key information items are:

	Actual	Budgeted
Units	2,800	3,000
Unit selling price	$ 112	$ 110
Unit variable cost	$ 82	$ 74
Fixed costs	$50,000	$54,000

The total static-budget variance in operating income is $20,000 U. There is both an unfavorable total flexible-budget variance ($12,800) and an unfavorable sales-volume variance ($7,200).

The **unfavorable sales-volume variance** arises solely because *actual units* manufactured and *sold were 200 less* than the budgeted 3,000 units. The **unfavorable flexible-budget variance** of $12,800 in operating income is due *primarily to the $8 increase in unit variable costs*. This increase in unit variable costs is only *partially offset by the $2 increase in unit selling price* and the *$4,000 decrease* in fixed costs.

7-18 (25–30 min.) **Flexible-budget preparation and analysis.**

1. Variance Analysis for Bank Management Printers for September 2009

Level 1 Analysis

	Actual Results (1)	Static-Budget Variances (2) = (1) – (3)	Static Budget (3)
Units sold	12,000	3,000 U	15,000
Revenue	$252,000[a]	$ 48,000 U	$300,000[c]
Variable costs	84,000[d]	36,000 F	120,000[f]
Contribution margin	168,000	12,000 U	180,000
Fixed costs	150,000	5,000 U	145,000
Operating income	$ 18,000	$ 17,000 U	$ 35,000

$17,000 U
Total static-budget variance

2. *Level 2 Analysis*

	Actual Results (1)	Flexible-Budget Variances (2) = (1) – (3)	Flexible Budget (3)	Sales Volume Variances (4) = (3) – (5)	Static Budget (5)
Units sold	12,000	0	12,000	3,000 U	15,000
Revenue	$252,000[a]	$12,000 F	$240,000[b]	$60,000 U	$300,000[c]
Variable costs	84,000[d]	12,000 F	96,000[e]	24,000 F	120,000[f]
Contribution margin	168,000	24,000 F	144,000	36,000 U	180,000
Fixed costs	150,000	5,000 U	145,000	0	145,000
Operating income	$ 18,000	$19,000 F	$ (1,000)	$36,000 U	$ 35,000

$19,000 F
Total flexible-budget variance

$36,000 U
Total sales-volume variance

$17,000 U
Total static-budget variance

[a] 12,000 × $21 = $252,000 [d] 12,000 × $7 = $ 84,000
[b] 12,000 × $20 = $240,000 [e] 12,000 × $8 = $ 96,000
[c] 15,000 × $20 = $300,000 [f] 15,000 × $8 = $120,000

3. Level 2 analysis breaks down the static-budget variance into a flexible-budget variance and a sales-volume variance. The primary reason for the static-budget variance being unfavorable ($17,000 U) is the reduction in unit volume from the budgeted 15,000 to an actual 12,000. One explanation for this reduction is the increase in selling price from a budgeted $20 to an actual $21. Operating management was able to reduce variable costs by $12,000 relative to the flexible budget. This reduction could be a sign of efficient management. Alternatively, it could be due to using lower quality materials (which in turn adversely affected unit volume).

7-20 (30–40 min.)   **Flexible budget and sales volume variances.**

1. and 2.

Performance Report for Marron, Inc., June 2009

	Actual (1)	Flexible Budget Variances (2) = (1) – (3)		Flexible Budget (3)	Sales Volume Variances (4) = (3) – (5)		Static Budget (5)	Static Budget Variance (6) = (1) – (5)		Static Budget Variance as % of Static Budget (7) = (6) ÷ (5)
Units (pounds)	525,000	–		525,000	25,000	F	500,000	25,000	F	5.0%
Revenues	$3,360,000	$ 52,500	U	$3,412,500[a]	$162,500	F	$3,250,000	$110,000	F	3.4%
Variable mfg. costs	1,890,000	52,500	U	1,837,500[b]	87,500	U	1,750,000	140,000	U	8.0%
Contribution margin	$1,470,000	$105,000	U	$1,575,000	$ 75,000	F	$1,500,000	$ 30,000	U	2.0%

$105,000 U $ 75,000 F

Flexible-budget variance   Sales-volume variance

$30,000 U

Static-budget variance

[a] Budgeted selling price = $3,250,000 ÷ 500,000 lbs = $6.50 per lb.
Flexible-budget revenues = $6.50 per lb. × 525,000 lbs. = $3,412,500

[b] Budgeted variable mfg. cost per unit = $1,750,000 ÷ 500,000 lbs. = $3.50
Flexible-budget variable mfg. costs = $3.50 per lb. × 525,000 lbs. = $1,837,500

113

3.   The selling price variance, caused solely by the difference in actual and budgeted selling price, is the flexible-budget variance in revenues = $52,500 U.

4.   The flexible-budget variances show that for the actual sales volume of 525,000 pounds, *selling prices were lower and costs per pound were higher*. The favorable sales volume variance in revenues (because more pounds of ice cream were sold than budgeted) helped offset the unfavorable variable cost variance and shored up the results in June 2009. Levine should be more concerned because the small static-budget variance in contribution margin of $30,000 U is actually made up of a favorable sales-volume variance in contribution margin of $75,000, an unfavorable selling-price variance of $52,500 and an unfavorable variable manufacturing costs variance of $52,500. Levine should analyze why each of these variances occurred and the relationships among them. Could the efficiency of variable manufacturing costs be improved? Did the sales volume increase because of a decrease in selling price or because of growth in the overall market? Analysis of these questions would help Levine decide what actions he should take.

7-22 (15 min.) Materials and manufacturing labor variances.

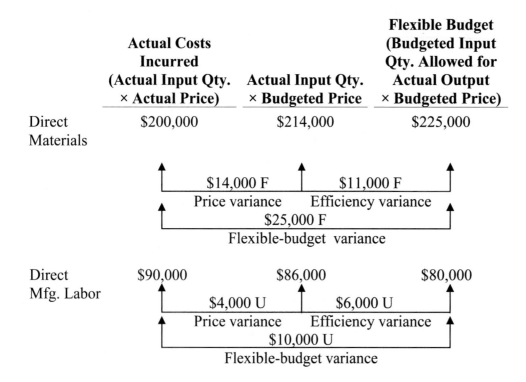

	Actual Costs Incurred (Actual Input Qty. × Actual Price)	Actual Input Qty. × Budgeted Price	Flexible Budget (Budgeted Input Qty. Allowed for Actual Output × Budgeted Price)
Direct Materials	$200,000	$214,000	$225,000

$14,000 F $11,000 F
Price variance   Efficiency variance
$25,000 F
Flexible-budget variance

Direct Mfg. Labor	$90,000	$86,000	$80,000

$4,000 U $6,000 U
Price variance   Efficiency variance
$10,000 U
Flexible-budget variance

7-24 (30 min.) **Price and efficiency variances, journal entries.**

1. Direct materials and direct manufacturing labor are analyzed in turn:

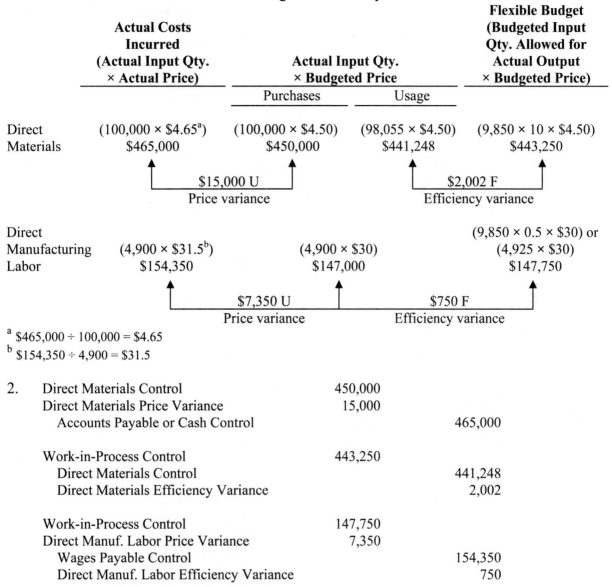

	Actual Costs Incurred (Actual Input Qty. × Actual Price)	Actual Input Qty. × Budgeted Price		Flexible Budget (Budgeted Input Qty. Allowed for Actual Output × Budgeted Price)
		Purchases	Usage	
Direct Materials	(100,000 × $4.65[a]) $465,000	(100,000 × $4.50) $450,000	(98,055 × $4.50) $441,248	(9,850 × 10 × $4.50) $443,250

$15,000 U
Price variance

$2,002 F
Efficiency variance

	Actual Costs Incurred	Actual Input Qty. × Budgeted Price	Flexible Budget
Direct Manufacturing Labor	(4,900 × $31.5[b]) $154,350	(4,900 × $30) $147,000	(9,850 × 0.5 × $30) or (4,925 × $30) $147,750

$7,350 U
Price variance

$750 F
Efficiency variance

[a] $465,000 ÷ 100,000 = $4.65
[b] $154,350 ÷ 4,900 = $31.5

2.
Direct Materials Control	450,000	
Direct Materials Price Variance	15,000	
Accounts Payable or Cash Control		465,000
Work-in-Process Control	443,250	
Direct Materials Control		441,248
Direct Materials Efficiency Variance		2,002
Work-in-Process Control	147,750	
Direct Manuf. Labor Price Variance	7,350	
Wages Payable Control		154,350
Direct Manuf. Labor Efficiency Variance		750

3. A *possibility* is that approximately the same labor force, paid somewhat more, is taking slightly less time with better materials and causing less waste and spoilage. There are other explanations that you may want to consider for this scenario.

   A key point in this problem is that all of these *efficiency variances* are likely to be *insignificant*. They are so small as to be nearly meaningless. Fluctuations about standards are bound to occur in a random fashion. Practically, from a control viewpoint, a standard is a band or range of acceptable performance rather than a single-figure measure.

4. The *purchasing point* is where responsibility for *price variances* is found most often. The *production point* is where responsibility for *efficiency variances* is found most often. The Monroe Corporation may calculate variances at different points in time to tie in with these different responsibility areas.

7-26 (20–30 min.) **Materials and manufacturing labor variances, standard costs.**

1.   Direct Materials

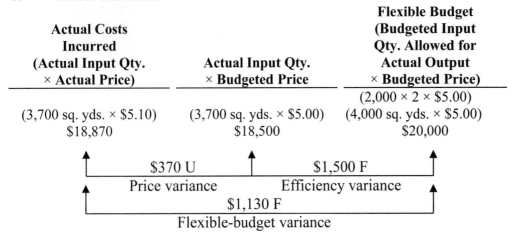

The **unfavorable materials price variance** may be *unrelated* to the **favorable materials efficiency variance**. For example
(a) the purchasing officer may be less skillful than assumed in the budget
(b) there was an unexpected increase in materials price per square yard due to reduced competition
(c) the production manager may have been able to employ higher-skilled workers
(d) the budgeted materials standards were set too loosely.

It is also possible that the two variances are *interrelated*. The higher materials input price may be due to higher quality materials being purchased. Less material was used than budgeted due to the high quality of the materials.

Direct Manufacturing Labor

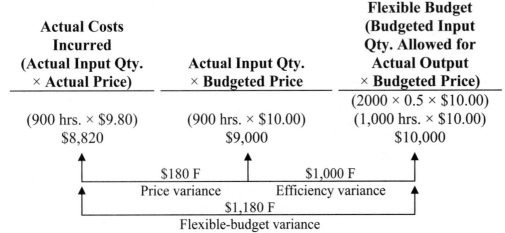

The **favorable labor price variance** may be due to
(a) a reduction in labor rates due to a recession
(b) the standard being set without detailed analysis of labor compensation.
The favorable labor efficiency variance may be due to
(a) more efficient workers being employed

(b) a redesign in the plant enabling labor to be more productive

(c) the use of higher quality materials.

2.

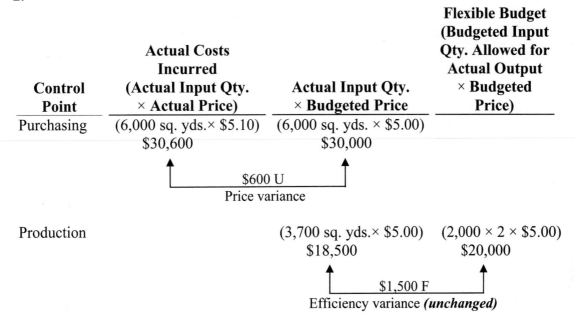

Control Point	Actual Costs Incurred (Actual Input Qty. × Actual Price)	Actual Input Qty. × Budgeted Price	Flexible Budget (Budgeted Input Qty. Allowed for Actual Output × Budgeted Price)
Purchasing	(6,000 sq. yds.× $5.10) $30,600	(6,000 sq. yds. × $5.00) $30,000	
		↑ $600 U ↑ Price variance	
Production		(3,700 sq. yds.× $5.00) $18,500	(2,000 × 2 × $5.00) $20,000
		↑ $1,500 F ↑ Efficiency variance *(unchanged)*	

Direct manufacturing labor variances are the same as in requirement 1.

7-28 (25 min.)   **Flexible budget (Refer to data in Exercise 7-26).**

A more detailed analysis underscores the fact that the world of variances may be divided into three general parts: price, efficiency, and what is labeled here as a sales-volume variance. Failure to pinpoint these three categories muddies the analytical task. The clearer analysis follows (in dollars):

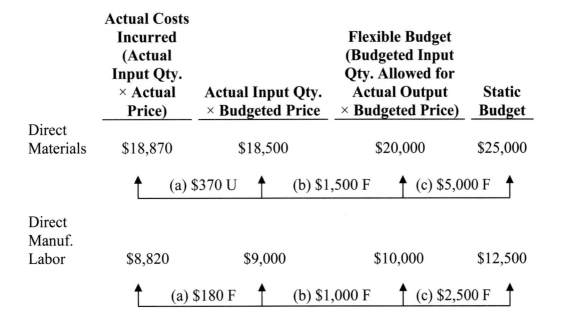

	Actual Costs Incurred (Actual Input Qty. × Actual Price)	Actual Input Qty. × Budgeted Price	Flexible Budget (Budgeted Input Qty. Allowed for Actual Output × Budgeted Price)	Static Budget
Direct Materials	$18,870	$18,500	$20,000	$25,000
	↑ (a) $370 U ↑	(b) $1,500 F ↑	(c) $5,000 F ↑	
Direct Manuf. Labor	$8,820	$9,000	$10,000	$12,500
	↑ (a) $180 F ↑	(b) $1,000 F ↑	(c) $2,500 F ↑	

(a) Price variance

(b) Efficiency variance

(c) Sales-volume variance

The sales-volume variances are favorable here in the sense that less cost would be expected solely because the output level is less than budgeted. However, this is an example of how variances must be interpreted cautiously. Managers may be incensed at the failure to reach scheduled production (it may mean fewer sales) even though the 2,000 units were turned out with supreme efficiency. Looking only at the cost budget doesn't do justice to the situation in which the firm finds itself. If production was down, revenues and profits were down too, and the firm may be worse off, despite these favorable variances.

7-30 (30 min.) **Flexible budget, direct materials and direct manufacturing labor variances.** Note: Since you are only given units sold and costs, you cannot computer variances for operating income. The following are the required variances.

1. Variance Analysis for Tuscany Statuary for 2009

	Actual Results (1)	Flexible-Budget Variances (2) = (1) – (3)	Flexible Budget (3)	Sales-Volume Variances (4) = (3) – (5)	Static Budget (5)
Units sold	6,000[a]	0	6,000	1,000 F	5,000[a]
Direct materials	$ 594,000	$ 6,000 F	$ 600,000[b]	$100,000 U	$ 500,000[c]
Direct manufacturing labor	950,000[a]	10,000 F	960,000[d]	160,000 U	800,000[e]
Fixed costs	1,005,000[a]	5,000 U	1,000,000[a]	0	1,000,000[a]
Total costs	$2,549,000	$11,000 F	$2,560,000	$260,000 U	$2,300,000

$11,000 F $260,000 U

Flexible-budget variance   Sales-volume variance

$249,000 U

Static-budget variance

[a] Given
[b] $100 × 6,000 = $600,000
[c] $100 × 5,000 = $500,000
[d] $160 × 6,000 = $960,000
[e] $160 × 5,000 = $800,000

2. *Note: The price and efficiency variances add together to equal the flexible budget variances above.*

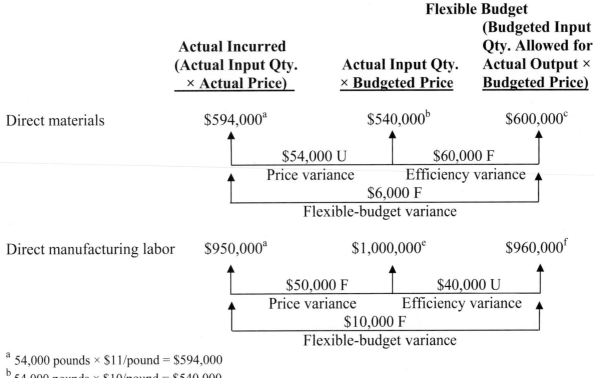

^{a} 54,000 pounds × \$11/pound = \$594,000

^{b} 54,000 pounds × \$10/pound = \$540,000

^{c} 6,000 statues × 10 pounds/statue × \$10/pound = 60,000 pounds × \$10/pound = \$600,000

^{d} 25,000 pounds × \$38/pound = \$950,000

^{e} 25,000 pounds × \$40/pound = \$1,000,000

^{f} 6,000 statues × 4 hours/statue × \$40/hour = 24,000 hours × \$40/hour = \$960,000

7-32 (60 min.) Comprehensive variance analysis, responsibility issues.

1a.   Actual selling price = \$82.00
Budgeted selling price = \$80.00
Actual sales volume = 7,275 units
Selling price variance = (Actual sales price − Budgeted sales price) × Actual sales volume
= (\$82 − \$80) × 7,275 = \$14,550 Favorable

1b. Development of Flexible Budget

	Budgeted Unit Amounts		**Actual Volume**	**Flexible Budget Amount**
Revenues		$80.00	7,275	$582,000
Variable costs				
DM–Frames	$2.20/oz. × 3.00 oz.	6.60[a]	7,275	48,015
DM–Lenses	$3.10/oz. × 6.00 oz.	18.60[b]	7,275	135,315
Direct manuf. labor	$15.00/hr. × 1.20 hrs.	18.00[c]	7,275	130,950
Total variable manufacturing costs				314,280
Fixed manufacturing costs				112,500
Total manufacturing costs				426,780
Gross margin				$155,220

[a]$49,500 ÷ 7,500 units; [b]$139,500 ÷ 7,500 units; [c]$135,000 ÷ 7,500 units

	Actual Results (1)	**Flexible-Budget Variances** (2)=(1)-(3)	**Flexible Budget** (3)	**Sales - Volume Variance** (4)=(3)-(5)	**Static Budget** (5)
Units sold	7,275		7,275		7,500
Revenues	$596,550	$ 14,550 F	$582,000	$ 18,000 U	$600,000
Variable costs					
DM–Frames	55,872	7,857 U	48,015	1,485 F	49,500
DM–Lenses	150,738	15,423 U	135,315	4,185 F	139,500
Direct manuf. labor	145,355	14,405 U	130,950	4,050 F	135,000
Total variable costs	351,965	37,685 U	314,280	9,720 F	324,000
Fixed manuf. costs	108,398	4,102 F	112,500	0	112,500
Total costs	460,363	33,583 U	426,780	9,720 F	436,500
Gross margin	$ 136,187	$19,033 U	$155,220	$ 8,280 U	$163,500

Level 2   ↑ $19,033 U ↑ $ 8,280 U ↑

          Flexible-budget variance   Sales-volume variance

Level 1   ↑ $27,313 U   ↑

            Static-budget variance

1c. Price and Efficiency Variances

DM–Frames–Actual ounces used = 3.20 per unit × 7,275 units = 23,280 oz.

Price per oz. = $55,872 ÷ 23,280 = $2.40

DM–Lenses–Actual ounces used = 7.00 per unit × 7,275 units = 50,925 oz.

Price per oz. = $150,738 ÷ 50,925 = $2.96

Direct Labor–Actual labor hours = $145,355 ÷ 14.80 = 9,821.3 hours

Labor hours per unit = 9,821.3 ÷ 7,275 units = 1.35 hours per unit

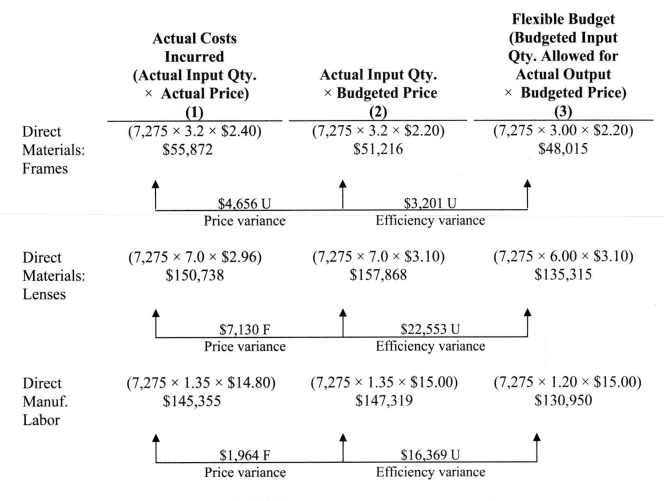

	Actual Costs Incurred (Actual Input Qty. × Actual Price) (1)	Actual Input Qty. × Budgeted Price (2)	Flexible Budget (Budgeted Input Qty. Allowed for Actual Output × Budgeted Price) (3)
Direct Materials: Frames	(7,275 × 3.2 × $2.40) $55,872	(7,275 × 3.2 × $2.20) $51,216	(7,275 × 3.00 × $2.20) $48,015
	↑ $4,656 U Price variance	↑ $3,201 U Efficiency variance	↑
Direct Materials: Lenses	(7,275 × 7.0 × $2.96) $150,738	(7,275 × 7.0 × $3.10) $157,868	(7,275 × 6.00 × $3.10) $135,315
	↑ $7,130 F Price variance	↑ $22,553 U Efficiency variance	↑
Direct Manuf. Labor	(7,275 × 1.35 × $14.80) $145,355	(7,275 × 1.35 × $15.00) $147,319	(7,275 × 1.20 × $15.00) $130,950
	↑ $1,964 F Price variance	↑ $16,369 U Efficiency variance	↑

2.   Possible explanations for the **price variances** are:
(a) Unexpected outcomes from purchasing and labor negotiations during the year.
(b) Higher quality of frames and/or lower quality of lenses purchased.
(c) Standards set incorrectly at the start of the year.

Possible explanations for the uniformly unfavorable **efficiency variances** are:
(a) Substantially higher usage of lenses due to poor quality lenses purchased at lower price.
(b) Lesser trained workers hired at lower rates result in higher materials usage (for both frames and lenses), as well as lower levels of labor efficiency.
(c) Standards set incorrectly at the start of the year.

7-34 (35 min.) **Material cost variances, use of variances for performance evaluation**

1. Materials Variances

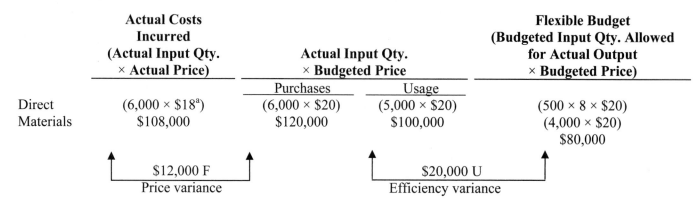

	Actual Costs Incurred (Actual Input Qty. × Actual Price)	Actual Input Qty. × Budgeted Price		Flexible Budget (Budgeted Input Qty. Allowed for Actual Output × Budgeted Price)
		Purchases	Usage	
Direct Materials	$(6,000 \times \$18^{a})$ $108,000	$(6,000 \times \$20)$ $120,000	$(5,000 \times \$20)$ $100,000	$(500 \times 8 \times \$20)$ $(4,000 \times \$20)$ $80,000

$\$12,000$ F
Price variance

$\$20,000$ U
Efficiency variance

^{a} $\$108,000 \div 6,000 = \$18$

2. The **favorable price variance** is due to the $2 difference ($20 - $18) between the standard price based on the previous suppliers and the actual price paid through the on-line marketplace. The **unfavorable efficiency variance** could be due to several factors including inexperienced workers and machine malfunctions. But the likely cause here is that the lower-priced titanium was lower quality or less refined, which led to more waste. The labor efficiency variance could be affected if the lower quality titanium caused the workers to use more time.

3. **Switching suppliers was not a good idea**. The $12,000 savings in the cost of titanium was outweighed by the $20,000 extra material usage. In addition, the $20,000U efficiency variance does not recognize the total impact of the lower quality titanium because, of the 6,000 pounds purchased, only 5,000 pounds were used. If the quantity of materials used in production is relatively the same, Better Bikes could expect the remaining 1,000 lbs to produce 100 more units. At standard, 100 more units should take $100 \times 8 = 800$ lbs. There could be an additional unfavorable efficiency variance of

$(1000 \times \$20)$ $(100 \times 8 \times \$20)$
$20,000$ $16,000$

$\$4,000U$

4. The purchasing manager's **performance evaluation should not be based solely on the price variance**. The short-run reduction in purchase costs was more than offset by higher usage rates. His evaluation should be based on the total costs of the company as a whole. In addition, the production manager's performance evaluation should not be based solely on the efficiency variances. In this case, the production manager was not responsible for the purchase of the lower-quality titanium, which led to the unfavorable efficiency scores. In general, it is important for Stanley to understand that not all favorable material price variances are "good news," because of the negative effects that can arise in the production process from the purchase of inferior inputs. They can lead to unfavorable

efficiency variances for both materials and labor. Stanley should also that understand efficiency variances may arise for many different reasons and she needs to know these reasons before evaluating performance.

5. **Variances** should be used to help Better Bikes *understand what led to the current set of financial results*, as well as how to perform better in the future. They are a way to facilitate the continuous improvement efforts of the company. Rather than focusing solely on the price of titanium, Scott can balance price and quality in future purchase decisions.

6. **Future problems** can arise in the *supply chain*. Scott may need to go back to the previous suppliers. But Better Bikes' relationship with them may have been damaged and they may now be selling all their available titanium to other manufacturers. Lower quality bicycles could *also* affect Better Bikes' *reputation with the distributors*, the *bike shops* and *customers*, leading to higher warranty claims and customer dissatisfaction, and decreased sales in the future.

7-36 (20–30 min.) **Direct materials and manufacturing labor variances, solving unknowns.**

All given items are designated by an asterisk.

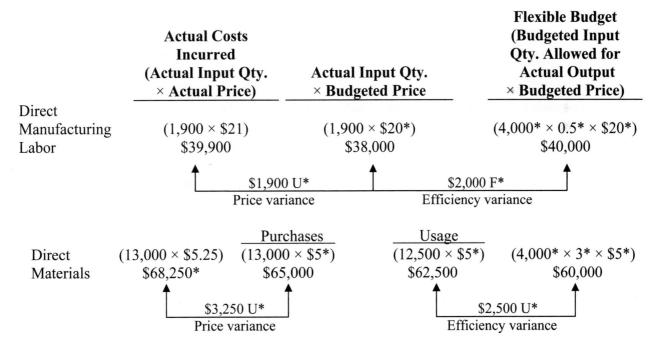

1. 4,000 units × 0.5 hours/unit = 2,000 hours

2. Flexible budget – Efficiency variance = $40,000 – $2,000 = $38,000
   Actual dir. manuf. labor hours = $38,000 ÷ Budgeted price of $20/hour = 1,900 hours

3. $38,000 + Price variance, $1,900 = $39,900, the actual direct manuf. labor cost
   Actual rate = Actual cost ÷ Actual hours = $39,000 ÷ 1,900 hours = $21/hour (rounded)

4. Standard qty. of direct materials = 4,000 units × 3 pounds/unit = 12,000 pounds

5. Flexible budget + Dir. matls. effcy. var. = $60,000 + $2,500 = $62,500
   Actual quantity of dir. matls. used = $62,500 ÷ Budgeted price per lb
   $$= \$62,500 \div \$5/lb = 12,500 \text{ lbs}$$

6. Actual cost of direct materials, $68,250 – Price variance, $3,250 = $65,000
   Actual qty. of direct materials purchased = $65,000 ÷ Budgeted price, $5/lb = 13,000 lbs.

7. Actual direct materials price = $68,250 ÷ 13,000 lbs = $5.25 per lb.

7-38 (30 min.) **Use of materials and manufacturing labor variances for benchmarking**.

1. Unit variable cost (dollars) and component percentages for each firm:

	Firm A		Firm B		Firm C		Firm D	
DM	$10.00	35.7%	$10.73	25.2%	$10.75	36.4%	$11.25	32.3%
DL	11.25	40.2%	17.05	40.0%	12.80	43.3%	14.03	40.3%
VOH	6.75	24.1%	14.85	34.8%	6.00	20.3%	9.56	27.4%
Total	$28.00	100.0%	$42.63	100.0%	$29.55	100.0%	$34.84	100.0%

2. Variances and percentage over/under standard for each firm relative to Firm A:

	Firm B		Firm C		Firm D	
	Variance	% over standard	Variance	% over standard	Variance	% over standard
DM Price Variance	0.98 U	10.0%	- -	0.0%	1.25 F	-10.0%
DM Efficiency Variance	0.25 F	-2.5%	0.75 U	7.5%	2.50 U	25.0%
DL Price Variance	0.55 U	3.3%	0.80 U	6.7%	1.28 U	10.0%
DL Efficiency Variance	5.25 U	46.7%	0.75 U	6.7%	1.50 U	13.3%

To illustrate these calculations, consider the DM Price Variance for Firm B. This is computed as:

Actual Input Quantity × (Actual Input Price – Price paid by Firm A)
= 1.95 oz. × ($5.50 - $5.00)
= $0.98 U

124

The % over standard is just the percentage difference in prices relative to Firm A. Again using the DM Price Variance calculation for Firm B, the % over standard is given by:

(Actual Input Price – Price paid by Firm A)/Price paid by Firm A
= ($5.50 - $5.00)/$5.00
= 10% over standard.

3.

To: Boss
From: Junior Accountant
Re: Benchmarking & productivity improvements
Date: October 15, 2010

Benchmarking advantages
- we can see how productive we are relative to our competition

- we can see the specific areas in which there may be opportunities for us to reduce costs

Benchmarking disadvantages
- some of our competitors are targeting the market for high-end and custom-made lenses. I'm not sure that looking at their costs helps with understanding ours better

- we may focus too much on cost differentials and not enough on differentiating ourselves, maintaining our competitive advantages, and growing our margins

Areas to discuss
- we may want to find out whether we can get the same lower price for glass as Firm D

- can we use Firm B's materials efficiency and Firm C's variable overhead consumption levels as our standards for the coming year?

7-40 (25 min.) **Comprehensive variance analysis.**

1. Variance Analysis for Sol Electronics for the second quarter of 2009

	Second-Quarter 2009 Actuals	Flexible Budget Variance		Flexible Budget for Second Quarter	Sales Volume Variance		Static Budget
	(1)	**(2) = (1) – (3)**		**(3)**	**(4) = (3) – (5)**		**(5)**
Units	4,800	0		4,800	800	F	4,000
Selling price	$ 71.50			$ 70.00			$ 70.00
Sales	$343,200	$7,200	F	$336,000	$56,000	F	$280,000
Variable costs							
Direct materials	57,600	2,592	F	60,192 [a]	10,032	U	50,160
Direct manuf. labor	30,240	1,440	U	28,800 [b]	4,800	U	24,000
Other variable costs	47,280	720	F	48,000 [c]	8,000	U	40,000
Total variable costs	135,120	1,872	F	136,992	22,832	U	114,160
Contribution margin	208,080	9,072	F	199,008	33,168	F	165,840
Fixed costs	68,400	400	U	68,000	0		68,000
Operating income	$139,680	$8,672	F	$131,008	$33,168	F	$97,840

[a] 4,800 units × 2.2 lbs. per unit × $5.70 per lb. = $60,192
[b] 4,800 units × 0.5 hrs. per unit × $12 per hr. = $28,800
[c] 4,800 units × $10 per unit = $48,000

	Second-Quarter 2009 Actuals	Price Variance		Actual Input Qty. × Budgeted Price	Efficiency Variance		Flexible Budget for Second Quarter
Direct materials	$57,600	$2,880	U	$54,720 [a]	$5,472	F	$60,192
Direct manuf. labor (DML)	30,240	4,320	U	25,920 [b]	2,880	F	28,800

[a] 4,800 units × 2 lbs. per unit × $5.70 per lb. = $54,720
[b] 4,800 units × 0.45 DML hours per unit × $12 per DML hour = $25,920

2. The following details, revealed in the variance analysis, should be used to rebut the union if it focuses on the favorable operating income variance:

- Most of the static budget operating income variance of $41,840F ($139,680 – $97,840) comes from a favorable sales volume variance, which only arose because Sol sold more units than planned.
- Of the $8,672 F flexible-budget variance in operating income, most of it comes from the $7,200F flexible-budget variance in sales.
- The net flexible-budget variance in total variable costs of $1,872 F is small, and it arises from direct materials and other variable costs, not from labor. Direct manufacturing labor flexible-budget variance is $1,440 U.
- The direct manufacturing labor price variance, $4,320U, which is large and unfavorable, is indeed offset by direct manufacturing labor's favorable efficiency variance—but the efficiency variance is driven by the fact that Sol is using new, more

expensive materials. Shaw may have to "prove" this to the union which will insist that it's because workers are working smarter. Even if workers are working smarter, the favorable direct manufacturing labor efficiency variance of $2,880 does not offset the unfavorable direct manufacturing labor price variance of $4,320.

3.   Changing the standards may make them more realistic, making it easier to negotiate with the union. But the union will resist any tightening of labor standards, and it may be too early (is one quarter's experience enough to change on?); a change of standards at this point may be viewed as opportunistic by the union. Perhaps a continuous improvement program to change the standards will be more palatable to the union and will achieve the   same result over a somewhat longer period of time.

7-42 **(20 min.)** **Variance analysis with activity-based costing and batch-level direct costs**

1. Flexible budget variances for batch activities

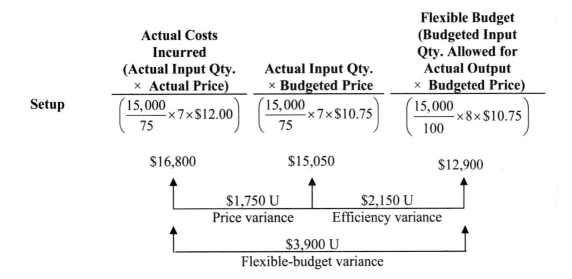

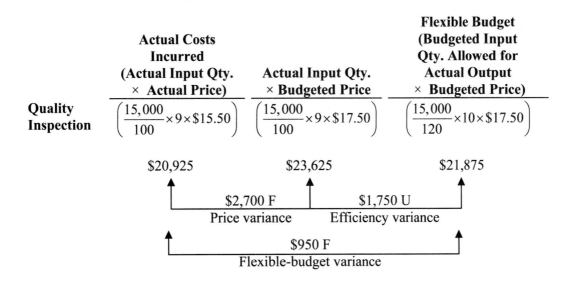

127

2. Re: Explanation of Variances

Below I explain the implications of the variances that I calculated. I would enjoy meeting with you to discuss whether we are following the most efficient policies, given these calculations. Please let me know if there is any way to improve my work or my presentation to you.

1. Our batch sizes for both setups and quality inspection were smaller than planned. Even though we were able to reduce the setup and quality inspection time needed for each batch (because of the smaller batch sizes), these gains were more than offset by the increased number of batches. Overall, we ended up substantially below the level of efficiency at which we wished to operate.
2. The hourly wage for the setup workers went over budget due to the tight labor market in our area for such employees. However, we saved a considerable amount of money because we were able to negotiate reduced wage rates for the quality inspection labor after the expiration of their previous contract.

Overall, given our output level of 15,000 eels, we had a moderately favorable variance for quality inspection costs, and a significant unfavorable variance on setups, for the reasons outlined above.

Thank you.

CHAPTER 8
FLEXIBLE BUDGETS, OVERHEAD COST VARIANCES, AND MANAGEMENT CONTROL

8-2   At the start of an accounting period, a larger percentage of fixed overhead costs are locked-in than is the case with variable overhead costs. When planning fixed overhead costs, a company must choose the appropriate level of capacity or investment that will benefit the company over a long time. This is a strategic decision.

8-4   Steps in developing a budgeted variable-overhead cost rate are:
1. Choose the **period** to be used for the budget,
2. Select the **cost-allocation bases** to use in allocating variable overhead costs to the output produced,
3. Identify the **variable overhead costs** associated with each cost-allocation base, and
4. Compute the **rate per unit** of each cost-allocation base used to allocate variable overhead costs to output produced.

8-6   Possible reasons for a favorable variable-overhead efficiency variance are:
- *Workers more skillful* in using machines than budgeted,
- Production scheduler was able to *schedule jobs better* than budgeted, resulting in lower-than-budgeted machine-hours,
- Machines operated with *fewer slowdowns* than budgeted, and
- Machine time *standards* were overly *lenient*.

8-8   Steps in developing a budgeted fixed-overhead rate are
1. Choose the **period** to use for the budget,
2. Select the **cost-allocation base** to use in allocating fixed overhead costs to output produced,
3. Identify the **fixed-overhead costs** associated with each cost-allocation base, and
4. Compute the **rate per unit** of each cost-allocation base used to allocate fixed overhead costs to output produced.

8-10   For *planning and control purposes*, fixed overhead costs are a lump sum amount that is not controlled on a per-unit basis. In contrast, for *inventory costing purposes*, fixed overhead costs are allocated to products on a per-unit basis.

8-12 **Pros** for writing off the production-volume variance to cost of goods sold:

- Does not "penalize" the units produced (inventory) for the cost of unused capacity, i.e., for the units *not* produced.
- Often not material, so might as well write it off.

Cons against writing of the production volume variance to cost of goods sold:

- The denominator level is only an estimate, never expected to be reached exactly, then it makes more sense to prorate the production volume variance among the inventory stock and cost of goods sold.
- Prorating a favorable variance is also more conservative: it results in a lower operating income than if the variance had been written off to cost of goods sold.
- Finally, prorating also minimizes management's ability to manage income through manipulation of the production volume variance.

8-14 Interdependencies among the variances could arise for the spending and efficiency variances. For example, if the chosen allocation base for the variable overhead efficiency variance is only one of several cost drivers, the variable overhead spending variance will include the effect of the other cost drivers. As a second example, interdependencies can be induced when there are misclassifications of costs as fixed when they are variable, and vice versa.

8-16 (20 min.) **Variable manufacturing overhead, variance analysis.**

1. Variable Manufacturing Overhead Variance Analysis for Esquire Clothing for June 2009

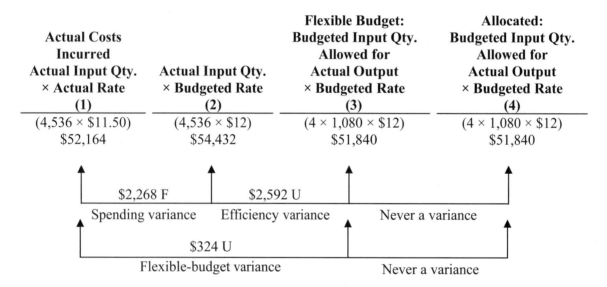

2. Esquire had a favorable spending variance of $2,268 because the actual variable overhead rate was $11.50 per direct manufacturing labor-hour versus $12 budgeted. It had an unfavorable efficiency variance of $2,592 U because each suit averaged 4.2 labor-hours (4,536 hours ÷ 1,080 suits) versus 4.0 budgeted labor-hours.

8-18 (30 min.)   **Variable manufacturing overhead variance analysis.**

1.   Denominator level   = Number of baguettes × Labor hours per baguette
                           = (3,200,000 × 0.02 hours)
                           = 64,000 hours

2.

	Actual Results	Flexible Budget Amounts
1. Output units (baguettes)	2,800,000	2,800,000
2. Direct manufacturing labor-hours	50,400	56,000[a]
3. Labor-hours per output unit (2 ÷1)	0.018	0.020
4. Variable manuf. overhead (MOH) costs	$680,400	$560,000
5. Variable MOH per labor-hour (4 ÷2)	$13.50	$10
6. Variable MOH per output unit (4 ÷1)	$0.243	$0.200

[a]2,800,000 × 0.020= 56,000 hours

Variable Manufacturing Overhead Variance Analysis for French Bread Company for 2009

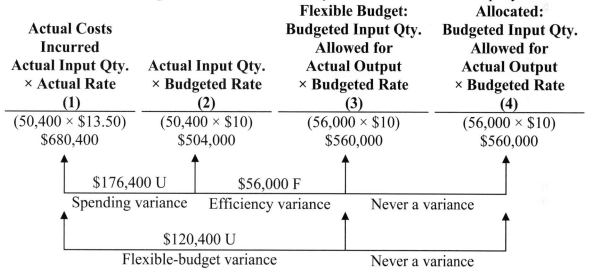

Actual Costs Incurred Actual Input Qty. × Actual Rate (1)	Actual Input Qty. × Budgeted Rate (2)	Flexible Budget: Budgeted Input Qty. Allowed for Actual Output × Budgeted Rate (3)	Allocated: Budgeted Input Qty. Allowed for Actual Output × Budgeted Rate (4)
(50,400 × $13.50) $680,400	(50,400 × $10) $504,000	(56,000 × $10) $560,000	(56,000 × $10) $560,000

$176,400 U $56,000 F
Spending variance   Efficiency variance   Never a variance

$120,400 U
Flexible-budget variance   Never a variance

3.   **Spending variance of $176,400U**. It is unfavorable because variable manufacturing overhead was 35% higher than expected. A possible explanation could be an increase in energy rates relative to the rate per standard labor-hour assumed in the flexible budget.

Efficiency variance of $56,000F. It is favorable because the actual number of direct manufacturing labor-hours required was lower than the number of hours in the flexible budget. Labor was more efficient in producing the baguettes than management had anticipated in the budget. This could occur because of improved morale in the company, which could result from an increase in wages or an improvement in the compensation scheme.

Flexible-budget variance of $120,400U. It is unfavorable because the favorable efficiency variance was not large enough to compensate for the large unfavorable spending variance.

8-20 (30–40 min.) **Manufacturing overhead, variance analysis.**

1.   The summary information is:

The Solutions Corporation (June 2009)	Actual	Flexible Budget	Static Budget
Outputs units (number of assembled units)	216	216	200
Hours of assembly time	411	432[c]	400[a]
Assembly hours per unit	1.90[b]	2.00	2.00
Variable mfg. overhead cost per hour of assembly time	$ 30.20[d]	$ 30.00	$ 30.00
Variable mfg. overhead costs	$12,420	$12,960[e]	$12,000[f]
Fixed mfg. overhead costs	$20,560	$19,200	$19,200
Fixed mfg. overhead costs per hour of assembly time	$ 50.02[g]		$ 48.00[h]

[a] 200 units × 2 assembly hours per unit = 400 hours

[b] 411 hours ÷ 216 units = 1.90 assembly hours per unit

[c] 216 units × 2 assembly hours per unit = 432 hours

[d] $12,420 ÷ 411 assembly hours = $30.22 per assembly hour

[e] 432 assembly hours × $30 per assembly hour = $12,960

[f] 400 assembly hours × $30 per assembly hour = $12,000

[g] $20,560 ÷ 411 assembly hours = $50 per assembly hour

[h] $19,200 ÷ 400 assembly hours = $48 per assembly hour

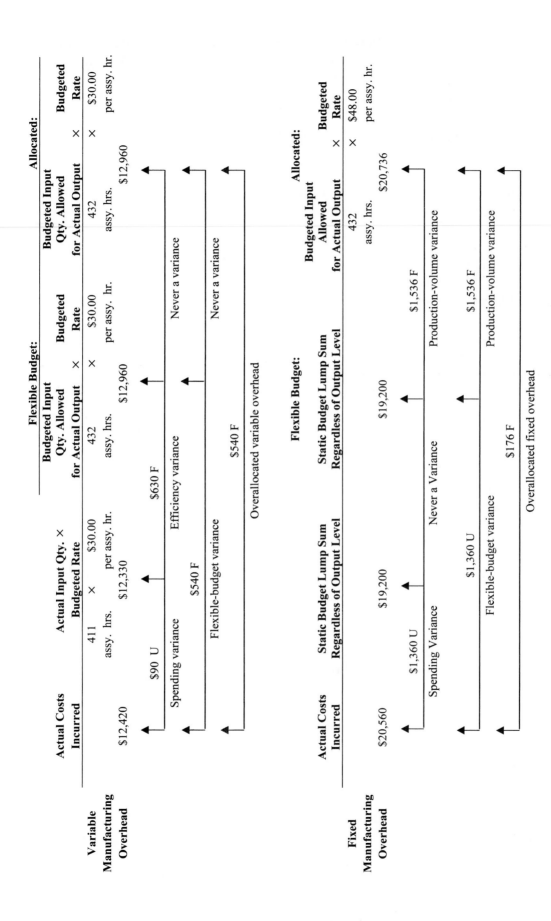

The summary analysis is:

	Spending Variance	Efficiency Variance	Production-Volume Variance
Variable Manufacturing Overhead	$90 U	$630 F	Never a variance
Fixed Manufacturing Overhead	$1,360 U	Never a variance	$1,536 F

2. Variable Manufacturing Costs and Variances

a. Variable Manufacturing Overhead Control   12,420
    Accounts Payable Control and various other accounts   12,420
  To record actual variable manufacturing overhead costs incurred.

b. Work-in-Process Control   12,960
    Variable Manufacturing Overhead Allocated   12,960
  To record variable manufacturing overhead allocated.

c. Variable Manufacturing Overhead Allocated   12,960
  Variable Manufacturing Overhead Spending Variance   90
    Variable Manufacturing Overhead Control   12,420
    Variable Manufacturing Overhead Efficiency Variance   630
  To isolate variances for the accounting period.

d. Variable Manufacturing Overhead Efficiency Variance   630
    Variable Manufacturing Overhead Spending Variance   90
    Cost of Goods Sold   540
To write off variable manufacturing overhead variances to cost of goods sold.

Fixed Manufacturing Costs and Variances

a. Fixed Manufacturing Overhead Control   20,560
    Salaries Payable, Acc. Depreciation, various other accounts   20,560
  To record actual fixed manufacturing overhead costs incurred.

b. Work-in-Process Control   20,736
    Fixed Manufacturing Overhead Allocated   20,736
  To record fixed manufacturing overhead allocated.

c. Fixed Manufacturing Overhead Allocated   20,736
  Fixed Manufacturing Overhead Spending Variance   1,360
    Fixed Manufacturing Overhead Production-Volume Variance   1,536
    Fixed Manufacturing Overhead Control   20,560
  To isolate variances for the accounting period.

d. Fixed Manufacturing Overhead Production-Volume Variance   1,536
    Fixed Manufacturing Overhead Spending Variance   1,360
    Cost of Goods Sold   176
To write off fixed manufacturing overhead variances to cost of goods sold.

3. Planning and control of *variable* manufacturing overhead costs has both a long-run and a short-run focus. It involves Solutions planning to undertake only value-added overhead activities (a long-run view) and then managing the cost drivers of those activities in the most efficient way (a short-run view). Planning and control of *fixed* manufacturing overhead costs at Solutions has primarily a long-run focus. It involves undertaking only value-added fixed-overhead activities for a budgeted level of output. Solutions makes most of the key decisions that determine the level of fixed-overhead costs at the start of the accounting period.

8-22 (20–30 min.) **Straightforward 4-variance overhead analysis.**

1. A detailed comparison of actual and flexible budgeted amounts is:

	Actual	Flexible Budget
Output units (auto parts)	4,400	4,400
Allocation base (machine-hours)	28,400	26,400[a]
Allocation base per output unit	6.45[b]	6.00
Variable MOH	$245,000	$211,200[c]
Variable MOH per hour	$8.63[d]	$8.00
Fixed MOH	$373,000	$360,000[e]
Fixed MOH per hour	$13.13[f]	–

[a]4,400 units × 6.00 machine-hours/unit = 26,400 machine-hours

[b]28,400 ÷ 4,400 = 6.45 machine-hours per unit

[c] 4,400 units × 6.00 machine-hours per unit × $8.00 per machine-hour = $211,200

[d] $245,000 ÷ 28,400 = $8.63

[e] 4,000 units × 6.00 machine-hours per unit × $15 per machine-hour = $360,000

[f] $373,000 ÷ 28,400 = $13.13

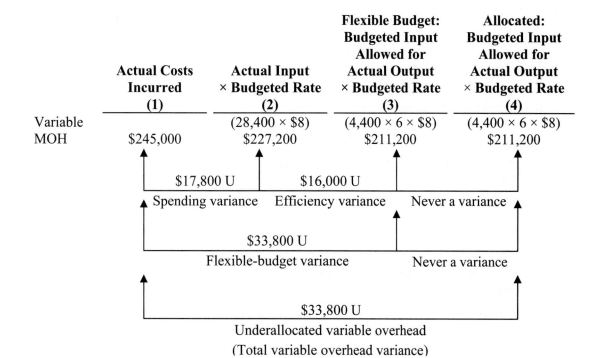

135

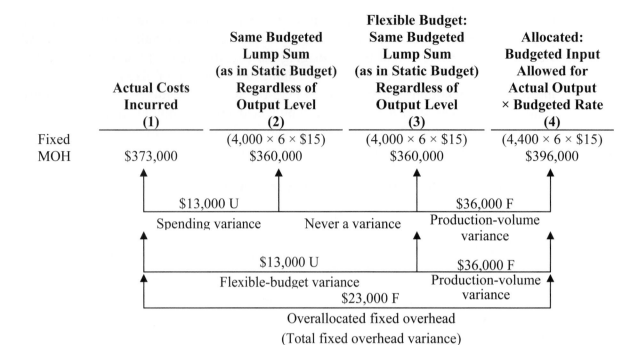

	Actual Costs Incurred (1)	Same Budgeted Lump Sum (as in Static Budget) Regardless of Output Level (2)	Flexible Budget: Same Budgeted Lump Sum (as in Static Budget) Regardless of Output Level (3)	Allocated: Budgeted Input Allowed for Actual Output × Budgeted Rate (4)
Fixed MOH	$373,000	(4,000 × 6 × $15) $360,000	(4,000 × 6 × $15) $360,000	(4,400 × 6 × $15) $396,000

$13,000 U $36,000 F
Spending variance   Never a variance   Production-volume variance

$13,000 U $36,000 F
Flexible-budget variance   Production-volume variance
$23,000 F
Overallocated fixed overhead
(Total fixed overhead variance)

An overview of the 4-variance analysis is:

4-Variance Analysis	Spending Variance	Efficiency Variance	Production-Volume Variance
Variable Manufacturing Overhead	$17,800 U	$16,000 U	Never a Variance
Fixed Manufacturing Overhead	$13,000 U	Never a Variance	$36,000 F

2. Variable Manufacturing Overhead Control   245,000
    Accounts Payable Control and other accounts   245,000

Work-in-Process Control   211,200
    Variable Manufacturing Overhead Allocated   211,200

Variable Manufacturing Overhead Allocated   211,200
Variable Manufacturing Overhead Spending Variance   17,800
Variable Manufacturing Overhead Efficiency Variance   16,000
    Variable Manufacturing Overhead Control   245,000

Fixed Manufacturing Overhead Control   373,000
    Wages Payable Control, Accumulated Depreciation
      Control, etc.   373,000

Work-in-Process Control   396,000
    Fixed Manufacturing Overhead Allocated   396,000

Fixed Manufacturing Overhead Allocated   396,000
Fixed Manufacturing Overhead Spending Variance   13,000
    Fixed Manufacturing Overhead Production-Volume Variance   36,000
    Fixed Manufacturing Overhead Control   373,000

3. Individual fixed manufacturing overhead items are **not usually affected very much by day-to-day control**. Instead, they are controlled periodically through planning decisions and budgeting procedures that may sometimes have horizons covering six months or a year (for example, management salaries) and sometimes covering many years (for example, long-term leases and depreciation on plant and equipment).

4. The **fixed overhead spending variance** is caused by the actual realization of fixed costs differing from the budgeted amounts. Some fixed costs are known because they are contractually specified, such as rent or insurance, although if the rental or insurance contract expires during the year, the fixed amount can change. Other fixed costs are estimated, such as the cost of managerial salaries which may depend on bonuses and other payments not known at the beginning of the period. In this example, the spending variance is unfavorable, so actual FOH is greater than the budgeted amount of FOH.

    The **fixed overhead production volume variance** is caused by production being over or under expected capacity. You may be under capacity when demand drops from expected levels, or if there are problems with production. Over capacity is usually driven by favorable demand shocks or a desire to increase inventories. The fact that there is a favorable volume variance indicates that production exceeded the expected level of output (4,400 units actual relative to a denominator level of 4,000 output units).

8-24 (20–25 min.) **Overhead variances, service sector.**

1.

Meals on Wheels (May 2009)	Actual Results	Flexible Budget	Static Budget
Output units (number of deliveries)	8,800	8,800	10,000
Hours per delivery	0.65[a]	0.70	0.70
Hours of delivery time	5,720	6,160[b]	7,000[b]
Variable overhead costs per delivery hour	$1.80[c]	$1.50	$1.50
Variable overhead (VOH) costs	$10,296	$9,240[d]	$10,500[d]
Fixed overhead costs	$38,600	$35,000	$35,000
Fixed overhead cost per hour			$5.00[e]

[a] 5,720 hours ÷ 8,800 deliveries = 0.65 hours per delivery
[b] hrs. per delivery × number of deliveries = 0.70 × 10,000 = 7,000 hours
[c] $10,296 VOH costs ÷ 5,720 delivery hours = $1.80 per delivery hour
[d] Delivery hours × VOH cost per delivery hour = 7,000 × $1.50 = $10,500
[e] Static budget delivery hours = 10,000 units × 0.70 hours/unit = 7,000 hours;
    Fixed overhead rate = Fixed overhead costs ÷ Static budget delivery hours = $35,000 ÷ 7,000 hours = $5 per hour

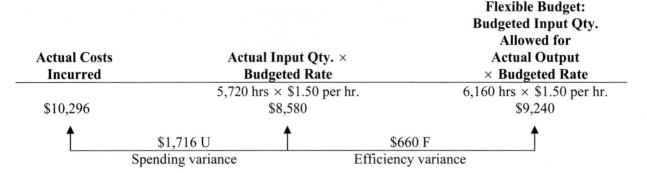

VARIABLE OVERHEAD

Actual Costs Incurred	Actual Input Qty. × Budgeted Rate	Flexible Budget: Budgeted Input Qty. Allowed for Actual Output × Budgeted Rate
	5,720 hrs × $1.50 per hr.	6,160 hrs × $1.50 per hr.
$10,296	$8,580	$9,240

$1,716 U ← Spending variance

$660 F ← Efficiency variance

2.

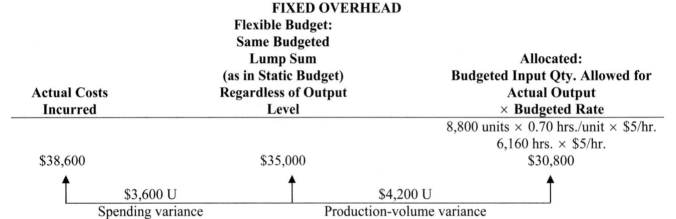

FIXED OVERHEAD

Actual Costs Incurred	Flexible Budget: Same Budgeted Lump Sum (as in Static Budget) Regardless of Output Level	Allocated: Budgeted Input Qty. Allowed for Actual Output × Budgeted Rate
		8,800 units × 0.70 hrs./unit × $5/hr.
		6,160 hrs. × $5/hr.
$38,600	$35,000	$30,800

$3,600 U ← Spending variance

$4,200 U ← Production-volume variance

3. The *spending variances for variable and fixed overhead are both unfavorable*. This means that MOW had increases over budget in either or both the cost of individual items (such as telephone calls and gasoline) in the overhead cost pools, or the usage of these individual items per unit of the allocation base (delivery time). The *favorable efficiency variance* for variable overhead costs results from more efficient use of the cost allocation base—each delivery takes 0.65 hours versus a budgeted 0.70 hours.

MOW can best **manage its fixed overhead costs** by long-term planning of capacity rather than day-to-day decisions. This involves planning to undertake only value-added fixed-overhead activities and then determining the appropriate level for those activities. Most fixed overhead costs are committed well before they are incurred. In contrast, for variable overhead, a mix of long-run planning and daily monitoring of the use of individual items is required to manage costs efficiently. MOW should plan to undertake only value-added variable-overhead activities (a long-run focus) and then manage the cost drivers of those activities in the most efficient way (a short-run focus).

There is no production-volume variance for variable overhead costs. The *unfavorable production-volume variance* for fixed overhead costs arises because MOW has unused fixed overhead resources that it may seek to reduce in the long run.

8-26 (30 min.) **Overhead variances, missing information.**

1.

VARIABLE MANUFACTURING OVERHEAD

Actual Costs Incurred	Actual Input Qty. × Budgeted Rate		Flexible Budget: Budgeted Input Qty. Allowed for Actual Output ×	Budgeted Rate
	15,000 mach. hrs.	× $6.00 per mach. hr.	14,850 mach. hrs. ×	$6.00 per mach. hr.
$89,625[b]		$90,000[a]		$89,100[c]

$375 F
Spending variance

$900 U[d]
Efficiency variance

$525 U[e]
Flexible-budget variance

a.   15,000 machine-hours × $6 per machine-hour = $90,000

b.   Actual VMOH = $90,000 – $375F (VOH spending variance) = $89,625

c.   14,850 machine-hours × $6 per machine-hour = $89,100

d.   VOH efficiency variance = $90,000 – $89,100 = $900U

e.   VOH flexible budget variance = $900U – $375F = $525U

Allocated variable overhead will be the same as the flexible budget variable overhead of $89,100. The actual variable overhead cost is $89,625. Therefore, variable overhead is underallocated by $525.

2.

FIXED MANUFACTURING OVERHEAD

Actual Costs Incurred	Flexible Budget: Static Budget Lump Sum Regardless of Output Level	Allocated: Budgeted Input Qty. Allowed for Actual Output	×	Budgeted Rate
		14,850 mach. hrs.	×	**$1.60^c** per mach. hr.
$30,375^a	**$28,800^b**	**$23,760^c**		

$1,575 U^e
Spending variance

$5,040 U^d
Production-volume variance

$6,615 U$
Underallocated fixed overhead

a. Actual FOH costs = $120,000 total overhead costs − $89,625 VOH costs = $30,375

b. Static budget FOH lump sum = $30,375 − $1,575 spending variance = $28,800

c. *FOH allocation rate = $28,800 FOH static-budget lump sum ÷ 18,000 static-budget machine-hours
= $1.60 per machine-hour
   Allocated FOH = 14,850 machine-hours × $1.60 per machine-hour = $23,760

d. PVV = $28,800 − $23,760 = $5,040U

e. FOH flexible budget variance = FOH spending variance = $1,575 U

Allocated fixed overhead is $23,760. The actual fixed overhead cost is $30,375. Therefore, fixed overhead is underallocated by $6,615.

8-28 (35 min.) Flexible-budget variances, review of Chapters 7 and 8.

1. Overhead variances for Doorknob Design Company (DDC) for April 2009:

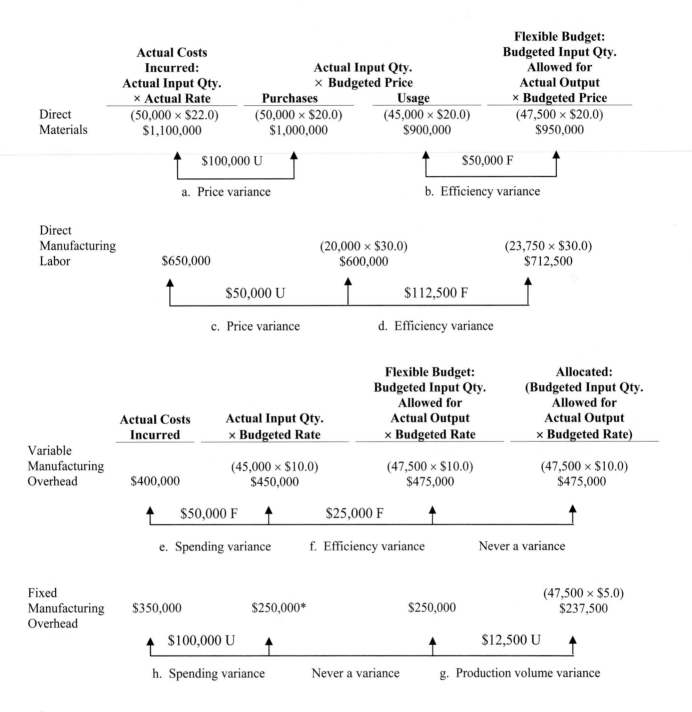

*Denominator level in hours: 100,000 x .5 = 50,000 hours
Budgeted Fixed Overhead: 50,000 x $5/hr = $250,000

2.   The *direct materials price variance* indicates that DDC paid more for brass than they had planned. If this is because they purchased a higher quality of brass, it may explain why they used less brass than expected (leading to a *favorable material efficiency variance*). In turn, since variable manufacturing overhead is assigned based on pounds of materials used, this directly led to the *favorable variable overhead efficiency variance*. The purchase of a better quality of brass may also explain why it took less labor time to produce the doorknobs than expected (the *favorable direct labor efficiency variance*). Finally, the *unfavorable direct labor price variance* could imply that the workers who were hired were more experienced than expected, which could also be related to the positive direct material and direct labor efficiency variances.

8-30   (60 min.)   **Journal entries (continuation of 8-29).**

3.   Key information underlying the computation of variances is:

	Actual Results	Flexible-Budget Amount	Static-Budget Amount
1. Output units (food processors)	960	960	888
2. Machine-hours	1,824	1,920	1,776
3. Machine-hours per output unit	1.90	2.00	2.00
4. Variable MOH costs	$76,608	$76,800	$71,040
5. Variable MOH costs per machine-hour (Row 4 ÷ Row 2)	$42.00	$40.00	$40.00
6. Variable MOH costs per unit (Row 4 ÷ Row 1)	$79.80	$80.00	$80.00
7. Fixed MOH costs	$350,208	$348,096	$348,096
8. Fixed MOH costs per machine-hour (Row 7 ÷ Row 2)	$192.00	$181.30	$196.00
9. Fixed MOH costs per unit (7 ÷ 1)	$364.80	$362.60	$392.00

Variable Manufacturing Overhead

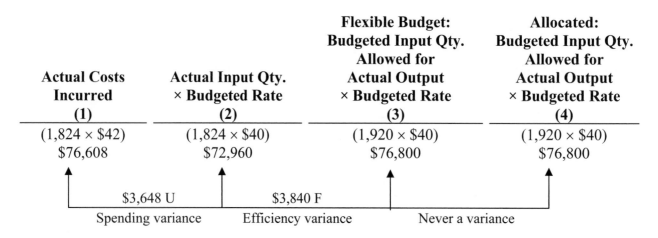

Actual Costs Incurred (1)	Actual Input Qty. × Budgeted Rate (2)	Flexible Budget: Budgeted Input Qty. Allowed for Actual Output × Budgeted Rate (3)	Allocated: Budgeted Input Qty. Allowed for Actual Output × Budgeted Rate (4)
(1,824 × $42)	(1,824 × $40)	(1,920 × $40)	(1,920 × $40)
$76,608	$72,960	$76,800	$76,800

$3,648 U $3,840 F
Spending variance   Efficiency variance   Never a variance

Fixed Manufacturing Overhead

Actual Costs Incurred (1)	Same Budgeted Lump Sum (as in Static Budget) Regardless Of Output Level (2)	Flexible Budget: Same Budgeted Lump Sum (as in Static Budget) Regardless of Output Level (3)	Allocated: Budgeted Input Qty. Allowed for Actual Output × Budgeted Rate (4)
			$(1,920 \times \$196)$
$350,208	$348,096	$348,096	$376,320

$2,112U   Spending variance   Never a variance $28,224 F   Production-volume variance

Journal entries for variable MOH, year ended December 31, 2010:

Variable MOH Control	76,608	
Accounts Payable Control and Other Accounts		76,608
Work-in-Process Control	76,800	
Variable MOH Allocated		76,800
Variable MOH Allocated	76,800	
Variable MOH Spending Variance	3,648	
Variable MOH Control		76,608
Variable MOH Efficiency Variance		3,840

Journal entries for fixed MOH, year ended December 31, 2010:

Fixed MOH Control	350,208	
Wages Payable, Accumulated Depreciation, etc.		350,208
Work-in-Process Control	376,320	
Fixed MOH Allocated		376,320
Fixed MOH Allocated	376,320	
Fixed MOH Spending Variance	2,112	
Fixed MOH Control		350,208
Fixed MOH Production-Volume Variance		28,224

2. Adjustment of COGS

Variable MOH Efficiency Variance	3,840	
Fixed MOH Production-Volume Variance	28,224	
Variable MOH Spending Variance		3,648
Fixed MOH Spending Variance		2,112
Cost of Goods Sold		26,304

8-32 (30 min.) 4-variance analysis, find the unknowns.

	A	B	C
1) Fixed MOH incurred	$26,500	**$16,750**	$30,000
2) Variable MOH incurred	$15,000	**$13,813**	**$15,500**
3) Denominator level in MH	1,250	**1,750**	2,750
4) Standard MH allowed for actual output	**1,250**	1,625	**2,875**
5) Fixed MOH (per standard MH)	**$20**	**$10**	**$10**
6) Variable MOH (per standard MH)	**$15**	$8.50	$5.00
7) Budgeted fixed MOH	$25,000	**$17,500**	$27,500
8) Budgeted variable MOH	**$18,750**	**$13,813**	**$14,375**
9) Total budgeted MOH	**$43,750**	$31,313	**$41,875**
10) Standard variable MOH allocated	$18,750	**$13,813**	**$14,375**
11) Standard fixed MOH allocated	$25,000	**$16,250**	**$28,750**
12) Production-volume variance	**0**	$1,250 U	$1,250 F
13) Variable MOH spending variance	$4,875 F	0	$875 U
14) Variable MOH efficiency variance	**$1,125 U**	0	$250 U
15) Fixed MOH spending variance	**$1,500 U**	$750 U	**$2,500 U**
16) Actual MH used	**1,325**	1,625	2,925

Known figures denoted by an *

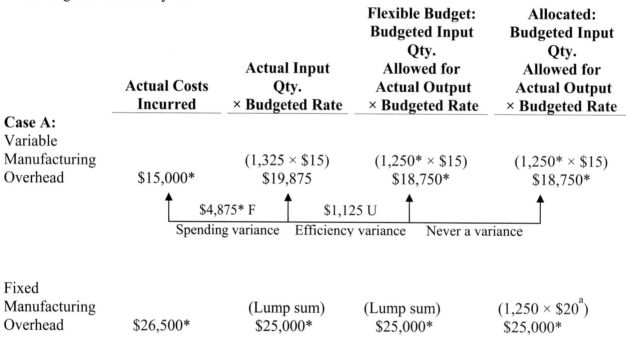

Total budgeted manufacturing overhead = $18,750 + $25,000 = $43,750

Case B:

Variable
Manufacturing
Overhead

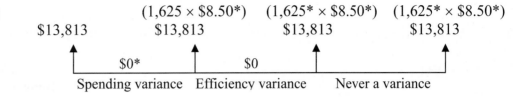

		(1,625 × $8.50*)	(1,625* × $8.50*)	(1,625* × $8.50*)
$13,813		$13,813	$13,813	$13,813

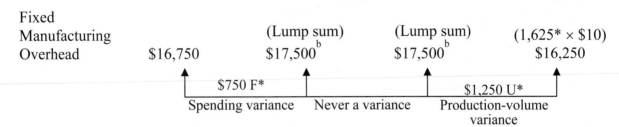

$0* → Spending variance $0 → Efficiency variance   Never a variance

Fixed
Manufacturing
Overhead

		(Lump sum)	(Lump sum)	(1,625* × $10)
$16,750		$17,500[b]	$17,500[b]	$16,250

$750 F* → Spending variance   Never a variance $1,250 U* → Production-volume variance

Denominator level = Budgeted FMOH costs ÷ Budgeted FMOH rate = $17,500 ÷ $10 = 1,750 hours

Case C:

Variable
Manufacturing
Overhead

		(2,925 × $5.00*)	(2,875 × $5.00*)	(2,875 × $5.00*)
$15,500		$14,625	$14,375[c]	$14,375[c]

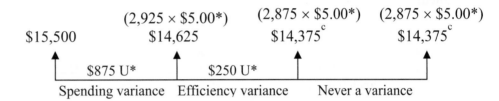

$875 U* → Spending variance $250 U* → Efficiency variance   Never a variance

Fixed
Manufacturing
Overhead

$30,000*		$27,500*	$27,500*	$28,750[d]

$2,500 U → Spending variance   Never a variance $1,250 F* → Production-volume variance

Total budgeted manufacturing overhead = $14,375 + $27,500 = $41,875

[a]Budgeted FMOH rate = Budgeted FMOH costs ÷ Denominator level = $25,000 ÷ 1,250 = $20

[b] Budgeted total overhead = Budgeted fixed manuf. overhead + Budgeted variable manuf. overhead

$31,313* = BFMOH + (1,625 × $8.50)
BFMOH = $17,500

[c] Budgeted hours allowed for actual output achieved must be derived from the output level variance before this figure can be derived, or, since the fixed manufacturing overhead rate is $27,500 ÷ 2,750 = $10, and the allocated amount is $28,750, the budgeted hours allowed for the actual output achieved must be 2,875 ($28,750 ÷ $10).

[d] 2,875 × ($27,500* ÷ 2,750*) = $28,750

8-34 (20 min.) **Direct Manufacturing Labor and Variable Manufacturing Overhead Variances**

1. Direct Manufacturing Labor variance analysis for Sarah Beth's Art Supply Company

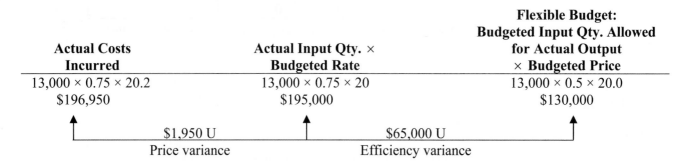

Actual Costs Incurred	Actual Input Qty. × Budgeted Rate	Flexible Budget: Budgeted Input Qty. Allowed for Actual Output × Budgeted Price
13,000 × 0.75 × 20.2	13,000 × 0.75 × 20	13,000 × 0.5 × 20.0
$196,950	$195,000	$130,000

$1,950 U — Price variance

$65,000 U — Efficiency variance

2. Variable Manufacturing Overhead variance analysis for Sarah Beth's Art Supply Company

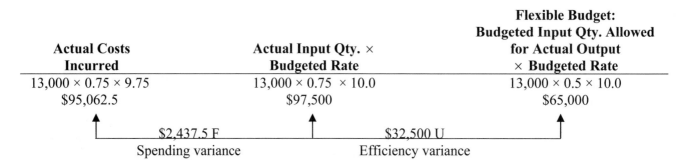

Actual Costs Incurred	Actual Input Qty. × Budgeted Rate	Flexible Budget: Budgeted Input Qty. Allowed for Actual Output × Budgeted Rate
13,000 × 0.75 × 9.75	13,000 × 0.75 × 10.0	13,000 × 0.5 × 10.0
$95,062.5	$97,500	$65,000

$2,437.5 F — Spending variance

$32,500 U — Efficiency variance

3. The *favorable variable MOH spending variance* suggests that less costly items were used, which could have a negative impact on labor efficiency. But note that the workers were paid a higher rate than budgeted, which, if it indicates the hiring of more qualified employees, should lead to favorable labor efficiency variances. Moreover, the price variance and the spending variance are both very small, approximately 1% and 2.5% respectively, while the efficiency variances are very large, each equaling 50% of expected costs. It is clear therefore that the efficiency variances are related to factors other than the cost of the labor or overhead.

4. Sarah has a point. Allocating variable overhead using direct labor as the only base will inflate the effect of inefficient labor usage on the variable overhead efficiency variance. The real effect on firm profitability will be lower, and will likely be captured in a favorable spending variance for variable overhead.

8-36 (20 min.)   **Activity-based costing, batch-level variance analysis**

1.   Static budget number of crates = Budgeted pairs shipped / Budgeted pairs per crate
= 240,000/12
= 20,000 crates

2.   Flexible budget number of crates = Actual pairs shipped / Budgeted pairs per crate
= 180,000/12
= 15,000 crates

3.   Actual number of crates shipped = Actual pairs shipped / Actual pairs per box
= 180,000/10
= 18,000 crates

4.   Static budget number of hours = Static budget number of crates × budgeted hours per box
= 20,000 × 1.2 = 24,000 hours

Fixed overhead rate = Static budget fixed overhead / static budget number of hours
= 60,000/24,000
= $2.50 per hour

5.   Variable Overhead Variance Analysis for Rica's Fleet Feet Inc. for 2008

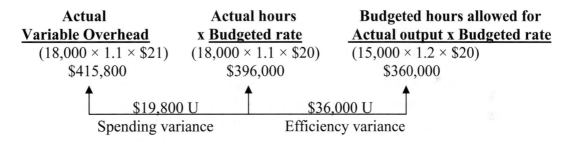

Actual **Variable Overhead**	**Actual hours** **x Budgeted rate**	**Budgeted hours allowed for** **Actual output x Budgeted rate**
(18,000 × 1.1 × $21)	(18,000 × 1.1 × $20)	(15,000 × 1.2 × $20)
$415,800	$396,000	$360,000

$19,800 U — Spending variance $36,000 U — Efficiency variance

6.   Fixed Overhead Variance Analysis for Rica's Fleet Feet Inc. for 2008

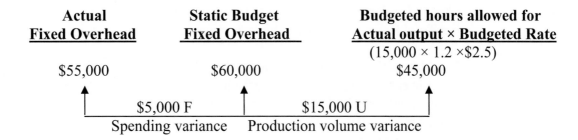

Actual **Fixed Overhead**	**Static Budget** **Fixed Overhead**	**Budgeted hours allowed for** **Actual output × Budgeted Rate**
		(15,000 × 1.2 × $2.5)
$55,000	$60,000	$45,000

$5,000 F — Spending variance $15,000 U — Production volume variance

8-38   (35 min.)   **Production-Volume Variance Analysis and Sales Volume Variance.**

1. and 2.   Fixed Overhead Variance Analysis for Dawn Floral Creations, Inc. for February

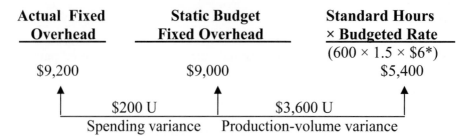

Actual Fixed Overhead	**Static Budget Fixed Overhead**	**Standard Hours × Budgeted Rate**
		(600 × 1.5 × $6*)
$9,200	$9,000	$5,400

$200 U — Spending variance $3,600 U — Production-volume variance

* fixed overhead rate = (budgeted fixed overhead)/(budgeted DL hours at capacity)
                       = $9,000/(1000 x 1.5 hours)
                       = $9,000/1,500 hours
                       = $6/hour

3.   An _unfavorable production-volume variance_ measures the cost of unused capacity. Production at capacity would result in a production-volume variance of 0 since the fixed overhead rate is based upon expected hours at capacity production. However, the existence of an unfavorable volume variance does not necessarily imply that management is doing a poor job or incurring unnecessary costs. Using the suggestions in the problem, two reasons can be identified.

   a.   For most products, _demand varies from month to month_ while _commitment to the factors that determine capacity_, e.g. size of workshop or supervisory staff, tends to remain relatively _constant_. If Dawn wants to meet demand in high demand months, it will have excess capacity in low demand months. In addition, forecasts of future demand contain uncertainty due to unknown future factors. Having some excess capacity would allow Dawn to produce enough to cover peak demand as well as slack to deal with unexpected demand surges in non-peak months.

   b.   Basic economics provides a demand curve that shows a _tradeoff between price charged and quantity demanded_. Dawn could increase sales by lowering price, but Total Revenue could still be less, even with higher quantity.

          In addition, the unfavorable production-volume variance may not represent a feasible cost savings associated with lower capacity. Even if Dawn could shift to lower fixed costs by lowering capacity, the fixed cost may behave as a step function. If so, fixed costs would decrease in fixed amounts associated with a range of production capacity, not a specific production volume. The production-volume variance would only accurately identify potential cost savings if the fixed cost function is continuous, not discrete.

4. The static-budget operating income for February is:

Revenues $55 × 1,000	$55,000
Variable costs $25 × 1,000	25,000
Fixed overhead costs	9,000
Static-budget operating income	$ 21,000

The flexible-budget operating income for February is:

Revenues $55 × 600	$33,000
Variable costs $25 × 600	15,000
Fixed overhead costs	9,000
Flexible-budget operating income	$ 9,000

The sales-volume variance represents the difference between the static-budget operating income and the flexible-budget operating income:

Static-budget operating income	$21,000
Flexible-budget operating income	9,000
Sales-volume variance	$12,000 U

Equivalently, the sales-volume variance captures the fact that when Dawn sells 600 units instead of the budgeted 1,000, only the revenue and the variable costs are affected. Fixed costs remain unchanged. Therefore, the shortfall in profit is equal to the budgeted contribution margin per unit times the shortfall in output relative to budget.

$$\text{Sales-volume variance} = \left[\text{Budgeted selling price} - \text{Budgeted variable cost per unit} \right] \times \text{Difference in quantity of units sold relative to the static budget}$$

$$= (\$55 - \$25) \times 400 = \$30 \times 400 = \$12,000 \text{ U}$$

In contrast, we computed in requirement 2 that the production-volume variance was $3,600U. This captures only the portion of the budgeted fixed overhead expected to be unabsorbed because of the 400-unit shortfall. To compare it to the sales-volume variance, consider the following:

Budgeted selling price		$55
Budgeted variable cost per unit	$25	
Budgeted fixed cost per unit ($9,000 ÷ 1,000)	9	
Budgeted cost per unit		34
Budgeted profit per unit		$ 21
Operating income based on budgeted profit per unit		
$21 per unit × 600 units		$12,600

The $3,600 U production-volume variance explains the difference between operating income based on the budgeted profit per unit and the flexible-budget operating income:

Operating income based on budgeted profit per unit	$12,600
Production-volume variance	3,600 U
Flexible-budget operating income	$ 9,000

Since the sales-volume variance represents the difference between the static- and flexible-budget operating incomes, the difference between the sales-volume and production-volume variances, which is referred to as the operating-income volume variance is:

Operating-income volume variance
= Sales-volume variance – Production-volume variance
= Static-budget operating income - Operating income based on budgeted profit per unit
= $21,000 U – $12,600 U = $8,400 U.

The operating-income volume variance explains the difference between the static-budget operating income and the budgeted operating income for the units actually sold. The static-budget operating income is $21,000 and the budgeted operating income for 600 units would have been $12,600 ($21 operating income per unit × 600 units). The difference, $8,400 U, is the operating-income volume variance, i.e., the 400 unit drop in actual volume relative to budgeted volume would have caused an expected drop of $8,400 in operating income, at the budgeted operating income of $21 per unit. The operating-income volume variance assumes that $50,000 in fixed cost ($9 per unit × 400 units) would be saved if production and sales volumes decreased by 400 units.

8-40 (30–50 min.)   **Review of Chapters 7 and 8, 3-variance analysis.**

1.   Total standard production costs are based on 7,800 units of output.

Direct materials, 7,800 × $15.00
    7,800 × 3 lbs. × $5.00 (or 23,400 lbs. × $5.00) $ 117,000
Direct manufacturing labor, 7,800 × $75.00
    7,800 × 5 hrs. × $15.00 (or 39,000 hrs. × $15.00)   585,000
Manufacturing overhead:
    Variable, 7,800 × $30.00 (or 39,000 hrs. × $6.00)   234,000
    Fixed, 7,800 × $40.00 (or 39,000 hrs. × $8.00)   312,000
    Total $1,248,000

The following is for later use:
    Fixed manufacturing overhead, a lump-sum budget $320,000[*]

$$^{*}\text{Fixed manufacturing overhead rate} = \frac{\text{Budgeted fixed manufacturing overhead}}{\text{Denominator level}}$$

$$\$8.00 = \frac{\text{Budget}}{40,000 \text{ hours}}$$

$$\text{Budget} = 40,000 \text{ hours} \times \$8.00 = \$320,000$$

2.   An overview of the 3-variance analysis using the block format of the text is:

3-Variance Analysis	Spending Variance	Efficiency Variance	Production Volume Variance
Total Manufacturing Overhead	$39,400 U	$6,600 U	$8,000 U

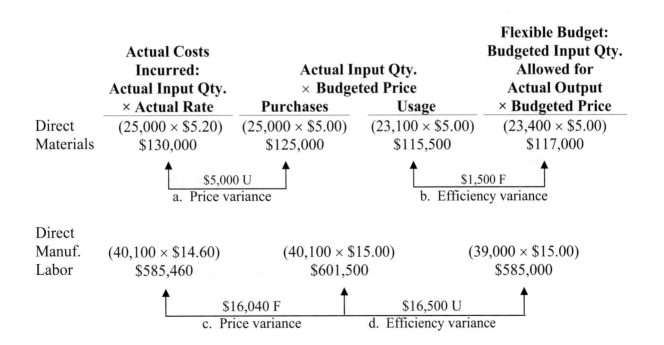

151

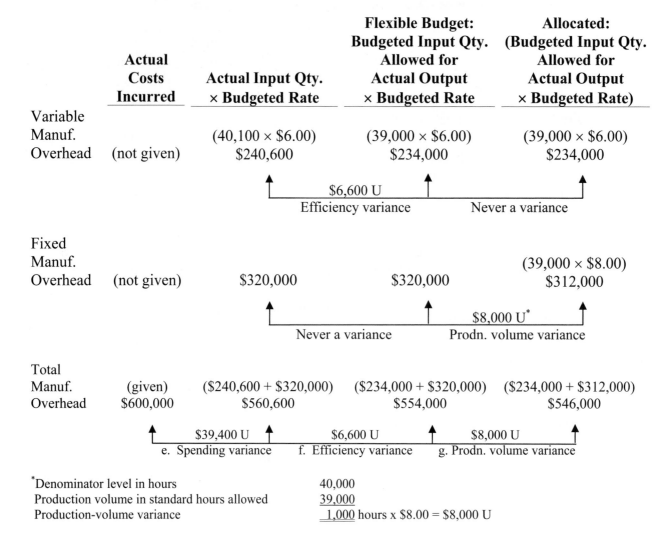

	Actual Costs Incurred	Actual Input Qty. × Budgeted Rate	Flexible Budget: Budgeted Input Qty. Allowed for Actual Output × Budgeted Rate	Allocated: (Budgeted Input Qty. Allowed for Actual Output × Budgeted Rate)
Variable Manuf. Overhead	(not given)	(40,100 × $6.00) $240,600	(39,000 × $6.00) $234,000	(39,000 × $6.00) $234,000

$6,600 U
Efficiency variance   Never a variance

| Fixed Manuf. Overhead | (not given) | $320,000 | $320,000 | (39,000 × $8.00) $312,000 |

Never a variance $8,000 U[*]
                    Prodn. volume variance

| Total Manuf. Overhead | (given) $600,000 | ($240,600 + $320,000) $560,600 | ($234,000 + $320,000) $554,000 | ($234,000 + $312,000) $546,000 |

$39,400 U $6,600 U $8,000 U
e. Spending variance   f. Efficiency variance   g. Prodn. volume variance

[*]Denominator level in hours   40,000
Production volume in standard hours allowed   39,000
Production-volume variance   1,000 hours x $8.00 = $8,000 U

8-42 (20 minutes) Non-financial performance measures

1. The cost of the ball bearings would be indirect materials if it is either not possible to trace the costs to individual products, or if the cost is so small relative to other costs that it is impractical to do so. Since Department B makes a fairly constant number of finished products (400 units) each day, it would be easy to trace the cost of bearings to the wheels completed daily. However, the fact that Rollie measures ball bearings by weight and discards leftover bearings at the end of each day suggests that they are a relatively inexpensive item and not worth the effort to restock or track in inventory. As such, it could be argued that ball bearings should be classified as overhead (e.g., indirect materials).

2. Non-financial performance measures for Department B might include:

    - Number or proportion of wheels sent back for rework and/or amount or proportion of time spent on rework;
    - Number of wheels thrown away, ratio of wheels thrown away to wheels reworked, and/or ratio of bad to good wheels;

- Amount of down time for broken machines during the day;
- Weight of ball bearings discarded, or ratio of weights used and discarded.

3.
If the number of *wheels thrown away is significant* relative to the number of reworked wheels, then it is *not efficient to rework them* and so Rollie should re-examine the rework process or even just throw away all the bad wheels without rework.

If the *amount of rework is significant* then the original process is not turning out quality goods in a timely manner. Rollie might *slow down the process* in Department B so it takes a little longer to make each good wheel, but the number of good wheels will be higher and may even save time overall if rework time drops considerably. They might also need to *service the machines more often* than just after the total daily production run, in which case they will trade off intentional down time for more efficient processing.

If the amount of *unintentional down time* is significant they might bring in the mechanics during the day to fix a machine that goes down during a production run.

Finally, Rollie might consider determining a *better measure of ball bearings to requisition* each day so that fewer are discarded, and might also keep any leftover ball bearings for use the next day.

CHAPTER 9
INVENTORY COSTING AND CAPACITY ANALYSIS

9-2   The term **direct costing is a misnomer** for variable costing for two reasons:

a.   *Variable costing does not include all direct costs* as inventoriable costs. Only variable direct manufacturing costs are included. Any fixed direct manufacturing costs, and any direct nonmanufacturing costs (either variable or fixed), are excluded from inventoriable costs.

b.   *Variable costing includes* as inventoriable costs *not only direct* manufacturing costs *but also some indirect* costs (variable indirect manufacturing costs).

9-4   The **main issue** between variable costing and absorption costing is the proper timing of the release of fixed manufacturing costs as costs of the period:

a.   at the time of incurrence (*Variable Costing*), or

b.   at the time the finished units to which the fixed overhead relates are sold (*Absorption Costing*).

9-6   No. *Variable costing* does not view fixed costs as unimportant or irrelevant, but it *maintains that the distinction between behaviors of different costs is crucial* for certain decisions. The planning and management of fixed costs is critical, irrespective of what inventory costing method is used.

9-8   (a) The factors that affect the breakeven point under **variable costing** are:

1.   Fixed (manufacturing and operating) costs.

2.   Contribution margin per unit.

(b) The factors that affect the breakeven point under **absorption costing** are:

1.   Fixed (manufacturing and operating) costs.

2.   Contribution margin per unit.

3.   *Production level* in units in excess of breakeven sales in units.

4.   *Denominator level* chosen to set the fixed manufacturing cost rate.

9-10   Approaches used to **reduce the negative aspects of absorption costing** include:

a.   *Change the accounting system:*
   - Adopt either variable or throughput costing, both of which reduce the incentives of managers to produce for inventory.
   - Adopt an inventory holding charge for managers who tie up funds in inventory.

b.   *Extend the time period used to evaluate performance.* By evaluating performance over a longer time period (say, 3 to 5 years), the incentive to take short-run actions that reduce long-term income is lessened.

c.   *Include nonfinancial* as well as financial variables in the measures used to evaluate performance.

d.   *Explain the negative cash flow consequences* of inventory buildup to people working in the organization. Knowledge can help them curb the negative aspects of absorption costing.

9-12 The *downward demand spiral* is the continuing reduction in demand for a company's product that occurs when the company prices their products higher than their competitors and (as demand drops further), higher and higher unit costs result in more and more reluctance to meet competitors' prices. Pricing decisions need to consider competitors and customers as well as costs.

9-14 For **tax reporting** in the U.S., the **IRS requires** companies to use the *practical capacity* concept. At year-end, *proration of any variances* between inventories and cost of goods sold is required (unless the variance is immaterial in amount).

9-16 (30 min.) **Variable and absorption costing, explaining operating-income differences.**

1. Key inputs for income statement computations are

	April	May
Beginning inventory	0	150
Production	500	400
Goods available for sale	500	550
Units sold	350	520
Ending inventory	150	30

The budgeted fixed cost and budgeted total manuf. cost per unit under absorption costing are

		April	May
(a)	Budgeted fixed manufacturing costs	$2,000,000	$2,000,000
(b)	Budgeted production	500	500
(c)=(a)÷(b)	Budgeted fixed manufacturing cost per unit	$4,000	$4,000
(d)	Budgeted variable manufacturing cost per unit	$10,000	$10,000
(e)=(c)+(d)	Budgeted total manufacturing cost per unit	$14,000	$14,000

(a) Variable costing

	April 2008		May 2008	
Revenues[a]		$8,400,000		$12,480,000
Variable costs				
Beginning inventory	$ 0		$1,500,000	
Variable manufacturing costs[b]	5,000,000		4,000,000	
Cost of goods available for sale	5,000,000		5,500,000	
Deduct ending inventory[c]	(1,500,000)		(300,000)	
Variable cost of goods sold	3,500,000		5,200,000	
Variable operating costs[d]	1,050,000		1,560,000	
Total variable costs		4,550,000		6,760,000
Contribution margin		3,850,000		5,720,000
Fixed costs				
Fixed manufacturing costs	2,000,000		2,000,000	
Fixed operating costs	600,000		600,000	
Total fixed costs		2,600,000		2,600,000
Operating income		$1,250,000		$3,120,000

[a] $24,000 × 350; $24,000 × 520 [b] $10,000 × 500; $10,000 × 400 [c] $10,000 × 150; $10,000 × 30 [d] $3,000 × 350; $3,000 × 520

155

(b)   Absorption costing

	April 2008		May 2008	
Revenues[a]		$8,400,000		$12,480,000
Cost of goods sold				
Beginning inventory	$ 0		$2,100,000	
Variable manufacturing costs[b]	5,000,000		4,000,000	
Allocated fixed manufacturing costs[c]	2,000,000		1,600,000	
Cost of goods available for sale	7,000,000		7,700,000	
Deduct ending inventory[d]	(2,100,000)		(420,000)	
Adjustment for prod.-vol. variance[e]	0		400,000 U	
Cost of goods sold		4,900,000		7,680,000
Gross margin		3,500,000		4,800,000
Operating costs				
Variable operating costs[f]	1,050,000		1,560,000	
Fixed operating costs	600,000		600,000	
Total operating costs		1,650,000		2,160,000
Operating income		$1,850,000		$ 2,640,000

[a] $24,000 × 350; $24,000 × 520
[b] $10,000 × 500; $10,000 × 400
[c] $4,000 × 500; $4,000 × 400
[d] $14,000 × 150; $14,000 × 30
[e] $2,000,000 – $2,000,000; $2,000,000 – $1,600,000
[f] $3,000 × 350; $3,000 × 520

2. $\frac{\text{Absorption-costing}}{\text{operating income}} - \frac{\text{Variable-costing}}{\text{operating income}} = \frac{\text{Fixed manufacturing costs}}{\text{in ending inventory}} - \frac{\text{Fixed manufacturing costs}}{\text{in beginning inventory}}$

April:

$1,850,000 – $1,250,000   =   ($4,000 × 150) – ($0)
$600,000   = $600,000

May:

$2,640,000 – $3,120,000   =   ($4,000 × 30) – ($4,000 × 150)
– $480,000   = $120,000 – $600,000
– $480,000   =   – $480,000

The difference between absorption and variable costing is due solely to moving fixed manufacturing costs into inventories as inventories increase (as in April) and out of inventories as they decrease (as in May).

9-18   (40 min.)   Variable and absorption costing, explaining operating-income differences.

1.   Key inputs for income statement computations are:

	January	February	March
Beginning inventory	0	300	300
Production	1,000	800	1,250
Goods available for sale	1,000	1,100	1,550
Units sold	700	800	1,500
Ending inventory	300	300	50

The budgeted fixed manufacturing cost per unit and budgeted total manufacturing cost per unit under absorption costing are:

		January	February	March
(a)	Budgeted fixed manufacturing costs	$400,000	$400,000	$400,000
(b)	Budgeted production	1,000	1,000	1,000
(c)=(a)÷(b)	Budgeted fixed manufacturing cost per unit	$400	$400	$400
(d)	Budgeted variable manufacturing cost per unit	$900	$900	$900
(e)=(c)+(d)	Budgeted total manufacturing cost per unit	$1,300	$1,300	$1,300

(a) Variable Costing

	January 2009	February 2009	March 2009
Revenues[a]	$1,750,000	$2,000,000	$3,750,000
Variable costs			
Beginning inventory[b]	$ 0	$270,000	$ 270,000
Variable manufacturing costs[c]	900,000	720,000	1,125,000
Cost of goods available for sale	900,000	990,000	1,395,000
Deduct ending inventory[d]	(270,000)	(270,000)	(45,000)
Variable cost of goods sold	630,000	720,000	1,350,000
Variable operating costs[e]	420,000	480,000	900,000
Total variable costs	1,050,000	1,200,000	2,250,000
Contribution margin	700,000	800,000	1,500,000
Fixed costs			
Fixed manufacturing costs	400,000	400,000	400,000
Fixed operating costs	140,000	140,000	140,000
Total fixed costs	540,000	540,000	540,000
Operating income	$ 160,000	$ 260,000	$ 960,000

a $2,500 × 700; $2,500 × 800; $2,500 × 1,500
b $? × 0; $900 × 300; $900 × 300
c $900 × 1,000; $900 × 800; $900 × 1,250
d $900 × 300; $900 × 300; $900 × 50
e $600 × 700; $600 × 800; $600 × 1,500

157

(b)   Absorption Costing

	January 2009	February 2009	March 2009
Revenues[a]	$1,750,000	$2,000,000	$3,750,000
Cost of goods sold			
Beginning inventory[b]	$ 0	$ 390,000	$ 390,000
Variable manufacturing costs[c]	900,000	720,000	1,125,000
Allocated fixed manufacturing costs[d]	400,000	320,000	500,000
Cost of goods available for sale	1,300,000	1,430,000	2,015,000
Deduct ending inventory[e]	(390,000)	(390,000)	(65,000)
Adjustment for prod. vol. var.[f]	0	80,000 U	(100,000) F
Cost of goods sold	910,000	1,120,000	1,850,000
Gross margin	840,000	880,000	1,900,000
Operating costs			
Variable operating costs[g]	420,000	480,000	900,000
Fixed operating costs	140,000	140,000	140,000
Total operating costs	560,000	620,000	1,040,000
Operating income	$ 280,000	$ 260,000	$ 860,000

[a] $2,500 × 700; $2,500 × 800; $2,500 × 1,500
[b] $? × 0; $1,300 × 300; $1,300 × 300
[c] $900 × 1,000; $900 × 800; $900 × 1,250
[d] $400 × 1,000; $400 × 800; $400 × 1,250
[e] $1,300 × 300; $1,300 × 300; $1,300 × 50
[f] $400,000 – $400,000; $400,000 – $320,000; $400,000 – $500,000
[g] $600 × 700; $600 × 800; $600 × 1,500

2.

$$\begin{pmatrix}\text{Absorption-costing}\\\text{operating income}\end{pmatrix} - \begin{pmatrix}\text{Variable costing}\\\text{operating income}\end{pmatrix} = \begin{pmatrix}\text{Fixed manufacturing}\\\text{costs in}\\\text{ending inventory}\end{pmatrix} - \begin{pmatrix}\text{Fixed manufacturing}\\\text{costs in}\\\text{beginning inventory}\end{pmatrix}$$

January:
$$\$280,000 - \$160,000 = (\$400 \times 300) - \$0$$
$$\$120,000 = \$120,000$$

February:
$$\$260,000 - \$260,000 = (\$400 \times 300) - (\$400 \times 300)$$
$$\$0 = \$0$$

March:
$$\$860,000 - \$960,000 = (\$400 \times 50) - (\$400 \times 300)$$
$$-\$100,000 = -\$100,000$$

The difference between absorption and variable costing is due solely to moving fixed manufacturing costs into inventories as inventories increase (as in January) and out of inventories as they decrease (as in March).

9-20 (40 min) Variable versus absorption costing.

1.

Income Statement for the Zwatch Company, Variable Costing
for the Year Ended December 31, 2009

Revenues: $22 × 345,400		$7,598,800
Variable costs		
Beginning inventory: $5.10 × 85,000	$ 433,500	
Variable manufacturing costs: $5.10 × 294,900	1,503,990	
Cost of goods available for sale	1,937,490	
Deduct ending inventory: $5.10 × 34,500	(175,950)	
Variable cost of goods sold	1,761,540	
Variable operating costs: $1.10 × 345,400	379,940	
Adjustment for variances	0	
Total variable costs		2,141,480
Contribution margin		5,457,320
Fixed costs		
Fixed manufacturing overhead costs	1,440,000	
Fixed operating costs	1,080,000	
Total fixed costs		2,520,000
Operating income		$2,937,320

Absorption Costing Data

Fixed manufacturing overhead allocation rate =
Fixed manufacturing overhead/Denominator level machine-hours = $1,440,000 ÷ 6,000
= $240 per machine-hour

Fixed manufacturing overhead allocation rate per unit =
Fixed manufacturing overhead allocation rate/standard production rate = $240 ÷ 50
= $4.80 per unit

Income Statement for the Zwatch Company, Absorption Costing
for the Year Ended December 31, 2009

Revenues: $22 × 345,400		$7,598,800
Cost of goods sold		
Beginning inventory ($5.10 + $4.80) × 85,000	$ 841,500	
Variable manuf. costs: $5.10 × 294,900	1,503,990	
Allocated fixed manuf. costs: $4.80 × 294,900	1,415,520	
Cost of goods available for sale	$3,761,010	
Deduct ending inventory: ($5.10 + $4.80) × 34,500	(341,550)	
Adjust for manuf. variances ($4.80 × 5,100)[a]	24,480 U	
Cost of goods sold		3,443,940
Gross margin		4,154,860
Operating costs		
Variable operating costs: $1.10 × 345,400	$ 379,940	
Fixed operating costs	1,080,000	
Total operating costs		1,459,940
Operating income		$2,694,920

$$
\begin{aligned}
{}^a \text{ Production volume variance} &= [(6,000 \text{ hours} \times 50) - 294,900] \times \$4.80 \\
&= (300,000 - 294,900) \times \$4.80 \\
&= \$24,480
\end{aligned}
$$

2. Zwatch's operating margins as a percentage of revenues are

Under variable costing:		
Revenues		$7,598,800
Operating income		2,937,320
Operating income as percentage of revenues		38.7%
Under absorption costing:		
Revenues		$7,598,800
Operating income		2,694,920
Operating income as percentage of revenues		35.5%

3. Operating income using variable costing is about 9% higher than operating income calculated using absorption costing.

Variable costing operating income – Absorption costing operating income =
$2,937,320 – $2,694,920 = $242,400

Fixed manufacturing costs in beginning inventory under absorption costing –
Fixed manufacturing costs in ending inventory under absorption costing
= ($4.80 × 85,000) – ($4.80 × 34,500) = $242,400

4. The factors the CFO should consider include
    (a) Effect on managerial behavior.
    (b) Effect on external users of financial statements.

I would recommend absorption costing because it considers all the manufacturing resources (whether variable or fixed) used to produce units of output. Absorption costing has many critics. However, the dysfunctional aspects associated with absorption costing can be reduced by
  - Careful budgeting and inventory planning.
  - Adding a capital charge to reduce the incentives to build up inventory.
  - Monitoring nonfinancial performance measures.
  - Communicating the costs of inventory build up with managers and employees.

9-22 (40 min) **Absorption versus variable costing.**

1. The variable manufacturing cost per unit is $55 + $45 + $120 = $220.

2009 Variable-Costing Based Operating Income Statement

Revenues (8,960 × $1,200 per unit)		$10,752,000
Variable costs		
Beginning inventory	$ 0	
Variable manufacturing costs (10,000 units × $220 per unit)	2,200,000	
Cost of goods available for sale	2,200,000	
Deduct: Ending inventory (1,040[a] units × $220 per unit)	(228,800)	
Variable cost of goods sold	1,971,200	
Variable marketing costs (8,960 units × $75 per unit)	672,000	
Total variable costs		2,643,200
Contribution margin		8,108,800
Fixed costs		
Fixed manufacturing costs	1,471,680	
Fixed R&D	981,120	
Fixed marketing	3,124,480	
Total fixed costs		5,577,280
Operating income		$2,531,520

[a] Beginning Inventory 0 + Production 10,000 – Sales 8,960 = Ending Inventory 1,040 units

161

2.

2009 Absorption-Costing Based Operating Income Statement

Revenues (8,960 units × $1,200 per unit)		$10,752,000
Cost of goods sold		
Beginning inventory	$ 0	
Variable manufacturing costs (10,000 units × $220 per unit)	2,200,000	
Allocated fixed manufacturing costs (10,000 units × $165 per unit)	1,650,000	
Cost of goods available for sale	3,850,000	
Deduct ending inventory (1,040 units × ($220 + $165) per unit)	(400,400)	
Deduct favorable production volume variance	(178,320)[a] F	
Cost of goods sold		3,271,280
Gross margin		7,480,720
Operating costs		
Variable marketing costs (8,960 units × $75 per unit)	672,000	
Fixed R&D	981,120	
Fixed marketing	3,124,480	
Total operating costs		4,777,600
Operating income		$2,703,120

[a] PVV = Allocated $1,650,000 ($165 × 10,000) – Actual $1,471,680 = $178,320

3. 2009 operating **income under absorption** costing is _greater_ than the operating income under variable costing because in 2009 _inventories increased_ by 1,040 units, and under absorption costing _fixed overhead remained in the ending inventory_, and resulted in a lower cost of goods sold (relative to variable costing). As shown below, the difference in the two operating incomes is exactly the same as the difference in the fixed manufacturing costs included in ending vs. beginning inventory (under absorption costing).

Operating income under absorption costing	$2,703,120
Operating income under variable costing	2,531,520
Difference in operating income under absorption vs. variable costing	$ 171,600
Under absorption costing:	
Fixed mfg. costs in ending inventory (1,040 units × $165 per unit)	$ 171,600
Fixed mfg. costs in beginning inventory (0 units × $165 per unit)	0
Change in fixed mfg. costs between ending and beginning inventory	$ 171,600

4. Relative to the alternative of using contribution margin (from variable costing), the absorption-based gross margin has some pros and cons as a performance measure for Electron's supervisors. It takes into account both variable costs and long run fixed costs and therefore it is a more complete measure than contribution margin. The downside of using absorption-based gross margin is the supervisor's temptation to use inventory levels to control the gross margin—e.g., to shore up a sagging gross margin by building up inventories. This can be offset by specifying, or limiting, the inventory build-up that can occur, charging the supervisor a carrying cost for holding inventory, and using nonfinancial performance measures such as the ratio of ending to beginning inventory.

9-24 (40 min.) **Variable and absorption costing, sales, and operating-income changes.**

1. Headsmart's annual fixed manufacturing costs are $1,200,000. It allocates $24 of fixed manufacturing costs to each unit produced. Therefore, it must be using $1,200,000÷$24 = 50,000 units (annually) as the denominator level to allocate fixed manufacturing costs to the units produced.

   We can see from Headsmart's income statements that it disposes off any production volume variance against cost of goods sold. In 2009, 60,000 units were produced instead of the budgeted 50,000 units. This resulted in a favorable production volume variance of $240,000 F ((60,000 – 50,000) units × $24 per unit), which, when written off against cost of goods sold, increased gross margin by that amount.

2. The breakeven calculation for each year is shown below:

Calculation of breakeven volume	2008	2009	2010
Selling price ($2,100,000 ÷ 50,000; $2,100,000 ÷ 50,000; $2,520,000 ÷ 60,000)	$42	$42	$42
Variable cost per unit (all manufacturing)	14	14	14
Contribution margin per unit	$28	$28	$28
Total fixed costs (fixed mfg. costs + fixed selling & admin. costs)	$1,400,000	$1,400,000	$1,400,000
Breakeven quantity = Total fixed costs ÷ contribution margin per unit	50,000	50,000	50,000

3.

Variable Costing

	2008	2009	2010
Sales (units)	50,000	50,000	60,000
Revenues	$2,100,000	$2,100,000	$2,520,000
Variable cost of goods sold			
Beginning inventory $14 × 0; 0; 10,000	0	0	140,000
Variable manuf. costs $14 × 50,000; 60,000; 50,000	700,000	840,000	700,000
Deduct ending inventory $14 × 0; 10,000; 0	0	(140,000)	0
Variable cost of goods sold	700,000	700,000	840,000
Contribution margin	$1,400,000	$1,400,000	$1,680,000
Fixed manufacturing costs	$1,200,000	$1,200,000	$1,200,000
Fixed selling and administrative expenses	200,000	200,000	200,000
Operating income	$ 0	$ 0	$ 280,000

Explaining variable costing operating income

	2008	2009	2010
Contribution margin ($28 contribution margin per unit × sales units)	$1,400,000	$1,400,000	$1,680,000
Total fixed costs	1,400,000	1,400,000	1,400,000
Operating income	$ 0	$ 0	$ 280,000

4.

Reconciliation of absorption/variable costing operating incomes

operating incomes	2008	2009	2010
(1) Absorption costing operating income (ACOI)	$0	$240,000	$ 40,000
(2) Variable costing operating income (VCOI)	0	0	280,000
(3) Difference (ACOI – VCOI)	$0	$240,000	$(240,000)
(4) Fixed mfg. costs in ending inventory under absorption costing (ending inventory in units × $24 per unit)	$0	$240,000	$ 0
(5) Fixed mfg. costs in beginning inventory under absorption costing (beginning inventory in units × $24 per unit)	0	0	240,000
(6) Difference = (4) – (5)	$0	$240,000	$(240,000)

In the table above, row (3) shows the difference between the operating income under absorption costing and the operating income under variable costing, for each of the three years. In 2008, the difference is $0; in 2009, absorption costing income is greater by $240,000; and in 2010, it is less by $240,000. Row (6) above shows the difference between the fixed costs in ending inventory and the fixed costs in beginning inventory under absorption costing, which is $0 in 2008, $240,000 in 2009 and -$240,000 in 2010. Row (3) and row (6) must be equal. The difference in operating income between absorption costing and variable costing arises because of the difference between fixed costs in inventory.

Stuart wants to understand why:
- o positive net income (reported under absorption costing) in 2009, when sales were at the 'breakeven volume' of 50,000;
- o drop in operating income in 2010, when, in fact, sales increased to 60,000 units.

In 2009
- o 60,000 units were produced, 50,000 were sold (10,000 units in ending inventory).
- o The 10,000 units each absorbed $24 of fixed costs (total of $240,000),
- o Ending inventory is an Headsmart's balance sheet until they were sold.
- o Cost of goods sold was reduced by $240,000, the production volume variance, resulting in a positive operating income even though sales were at breakeven levels.
- o The following year, in 2010, production was 50,000 units, sales were 60,000 units i.e., all of the fixed costs that were included in 2009 ending inventory, flowed through COGS in 2010. Hence the drop in operating income under absorption costing, even though sales were greater than the computed breakeven volume.

Note that beginning and ending with zero inventories during the 2008–2010 period, under both costing methods, Headsmart's total operating income was $280,000. The difference in the two methods is the timing of that income.

9-26 (25 min.)   **Denominator-level problem.**

1.   Budgeted fixed manufacturing overhead costs rates:

Denominator Level Capacity Concept	Budgeted Fixed Manufacturing Overhead per Period	Budgeted Capacity Level	Budgeted Fixed Manufacturing Overhead Cost Rate
Theoretical	$ 4,000,000	2,880	$ 1,388.89
Practical	4,000,000	1,920	2,083.33
Normal	4,000,000	1,200	3,333.33
Master-budget	4,000,000	1,500	2,666,67

2.   The **benefit from using theoretical or practical** level concepts is that the variances signal that there is a divergence between the supply of capacity and the demand for capacity. This is useful input to managers; they can respond to this mismatch, and change capacity in the long run. However, it is important not to place undue reliance on the production volume variance as a measure of the economic costs of unused capacity.

3.   Under a **cost-based pricing system**, the choice of a **master-budget level denominator** will lead to *high prices when demand is low* (more fixed costs allocated to the individual product level), further eroding demand; conversely, it will lead to *low prices when demand is high*, forgoing profits. This has been referred to as the downward demand spiral—the continuing reduction in demand that occurs when the prices of competitors are not met and demand drops, resulting in even higher unit costs and even more reluctance to meet the prices of competitors. The **positive** aspects of the master-budget denominator level are that it is based on demand for the product and *indicates the price* at which all *costs per unit would be recovered* to enable the company to make a profit. Master-budget denominator level is also a good benchmark against which to evaluate performance.

9-28 (40 min.) **Variable costing versus absorption costing.**

1.   Absorption Costing:

Mavis Company
Income Statement
For the Year Ended December 31, 2009

Revenues (540,000 × $5.00)		$2,700,000
Cost of goods sold:		
Beginning inventory (30,000 × $3.70[a])	$ 111,000	
Variable manufacturing costs (550,000 × $3.00)	1,650,000	
Allocated fixed manufacturing costs (550,000 × $0.70)	385,000	
Cost of goods available for sale	2,146,000	
Deduct ending inventory (40,000 × $3.70)	(148,000)	
Add adjustment for prod.-vol. variance (50,000[b] × $0.70)	35,000 U	
Cost of goods sold		2,033,,000
Gross margin		667,000
Operating costs:		
Variable operating costs (540,000 × $1)		540,000
Fixed operating costs		120,000
Total operating costs		660,000
Operating income		$ 7,000

[a] $3.00 + ($7.00 ÷ 10) = $3.00 + $0.70 = $3.70

[b] [(10 units per mach. hr. × 60,000 mach. hrs.) − 550,000 units)] = 50,000 units unfavorable

2.   Variable Costing:

Mavis Company
Income Statement
For the Year Ended December 31, 2009

Revenues		$2,700,000
Variable cost of goods sold:		
Beginning inventory (30,000 × $3.00)	$ 90,000	
Variable manufacturing costs		
(550,000 × $3.00)	1,650,000	
Cost of goods available for sale	1,740,000	
Deduct ending inventory (40,000 × $3.00)	(120,000)	
Variable cost of goods sold		1,620,000
Variable operating costs		540,000
Contribution margin		540,000
Fixed costs:		
Fixed manufacturing overhead costs	420,000	
Fixed operating costs	120,000	
Total fixed costs		540,000
Operating income		$ 0

3. The difference in operating income between the two costing methods is:

$$\begin{pmatrix} \text{Absorption-} \\ \text{costing} \\ \text{operating} \\ \text{income} \end{pmatrix} - \begin{pmatrix} \text{Variable-} \\ \text{costing} \\ \text{operating} \\ \text{income} \end{pmatrix} = \begin{pmatrix} \text{Fixed} \\ \text{manuf. costs} \\ \text{in ending} \\ \text{inventory} \end{pmatrix} - \begin{pmatrix} \text{Fixed} \\ \text{manuf. costs} \\ \text{in beginning} \\ \text{inventory} \end{pmatrix}$$

$$
\begin{aligned}
\$7,000 - \$0 &= [(40,000 \times \$0.70) - (30,000 \times \$0.70)] \\
\$7,000 &= \$28,000 - \$21,000 \\
\$7,000 &= \$7,000
\end{aligned}
$$

The absorption-costing operating income exceeds the variable costing figure by $7,000 because of the increase of $7,000 during 2009 of the amount of fixed manufacturing costs in ending inventory vis-a-vis beginning inventory.

4.

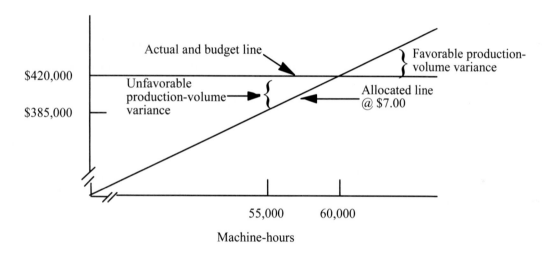

5. **Absorption costing is more likely to lead to buildups of inventory** than does variable costing. Absorption costing enables managers to increase reported operating income by building up inventory which reduces the amount of fixed manufacturing overhead included in the current period's cost of goods sold.
Ways to reduce this incentive include
(a) Careful budgeting and inventory planning.
(b) Change the accounting system to variable costing or throughput costing.
(c) Incorporate a carrying charge for carrying inventory.
(d) Use a longer time period to evaluate performance than a quarter or a year.
(e) Include nonfinancial as well as financial measures when evaluating management performance.
(f) Communicate the cost of producing and holding inventory to managers and employees.

9-30 (30–35 min.)   **Comparison of variable costing and absorption costing.**

1.   Since production volume variance is unfavorable, the budgeted fixed manufacturing overhead must be larger than the fixed manufacturing overhead allocated.

$$\frac{\text{Production - volume}}{\text{variance}} = \frac{\text{Budgeted fixed}}{\text{manufacturing overhead}} - \frac{\text{Fixed manufacturing}}{\text{overhead allocated}}$$

$400,000   = $1,200,000 – Allocated

Allocated   = $800,000, which is 67% of $1,200,000

If 67% of the budgeted fixed costs were allocated, the plant must have been operating at 67% of denominator level in 2009.

2.   The difference between inventory under absorption costing and inventory under variable costing is the fixed costs included in the inventory.

	Absorption Costing	Variable Costing	Fixed Manuf. Overhead in Inventory
Inventories:			
December 31, 2008	$1,720,000	$1,200,000	$520,000
December 31, 2009	206,000	66,000	140,000

3.   Note that the answer to (3) is independent of (1). The difference in operating income of $380,000 ($1,520,000 – $1,140,000) is explained by the release of $380,000 of fixed manufacturing costs when the inventories were decreased during 2009:

	Absorption Costing	Variable Costing	Fixed Manuf. Overhead in Inventory
Inventories:			
December 31, 2008	$1,720,000	$1,200,000	$520,000
December 31, 2009	206,000	66,000	140,000
Release of fixed manuf. costs			$380,000

The above schedule in this requirement is a formal presentation of the equation:

$$\begin{pmatrix} \text{Absorpting} \\ \text{costing} \\ \text{operating} \\ \text{income} \end{pmatrix} - \begin{pmatrix} \text{Variable} \\ \text{costing} \\ \text{operating} \\ \text{income} \end{pmatrix} = \begin{pmatrix} \text{Fixed} \\ \text{manuf. costs in} \\ \text{ending} \\ \text{inventory} \end{pmatrix} - \begin{pmatrix} \text{Fixed} \\ \text{manuf. costs in} \\ \text{beginning} \\ \text{inventory} \end{pmatrix}$$

($1,140,000 – $1,520,000)   =   ($140,000 – $520,000)
– $380,000   =   – $380,000

Alternatively, the presence of fixed manufacturing overhead costs in each income statement can be analyzed:

Absorption costing,
   Fixed manuf. costs in cost of goods sold
     ($5,860,000 − $4,680,000) $1,180,000
    Production-volume variance   400,000
                                                      1,580,000
Variable costing, fixed manuf. costs charged to expense   (1,200,000)
Difference in operating income explained $ 380,000

4.   Under absorption costing, *operating income is a function of both sales and production*. During 2009, Hinkle experienced a severe decline in inventory levels: sales were probably higher than anticipated, production was probably lower than planned (at 67% of denominator level), resulting in much of the 2009 beginning inventory passing through cost of goods sold in 2009. This means that under absorption costing, large amounts of inventoried fixed costs have flowed through 2009 cost of goods sold, resulting in a smaller operating income than in 2008, despite an increase in sales volume.

9-32 (25–30 min.)   **Alternative denominator-level capacity concepts, effect on operating income.**

1.

Denominator-Level Capacity Concept	Budgeted Fixed Manuf. Overhead per Period (1)	Days of Production per Period (2)	Hours of Production per Day (3)	Barrels per Hour (4)	Budgeted Denominator Level (Barrels) (5) = (2) × (3) × (4)	Budgeted Fixed Manufacturing Overhead Rate per Barrel (6) = (1) ÷ (5)
Theoretical capacity	$28,000,000	360	24	540	4,665,600	$ 6.00
Practical capacity	28,000,000	350	20	500	3,500,000	8.00
Normal capacity utilization	28,000,000	350	20	400	2,800,000	10.00
Master-budget utilization						
(a) January-June 2009	14,000,000	175	20	320	1,120,000	12.50
(b) July-December 2009	14,000,000	175	20	480	1,680,000	8.33

The differences arise for several reasons:

a. The theoretical and practical capacity concepts emphasize supply factors, while normal capacity utilization and master-budget utilization emphasize demand factors.

b. The two separate six-month rates for the master-budget utilization concept differ because of seasonal differences in budgeted production.

2.   Using column (6) from above,

	Per Barrel				
Denominator-Level Capacity Concept	Budgeted Fixed Mfg. Overhead Rate per Barrel (6)	Budgeted Variable Mfg. Cost Rate (7)	Budgeted Total Mfg Cost Rate (8) = (6) + (7)	Fixed Mfg. Overhead Costs Allocated (9) = 2,600,000 × (6)	Fixed Mfg. Overhead Variance (10) = $27,088,000 − (9)
Theoretical capacity	$6.00	$30.20[a]	$36.20	$15,600,000	$11,488,000 U
Practical capacity	8.00	30.20	38.20	20,800,000	6,288,000 U
Normal capacity utilization	10.00	30.20	40.20	26,000,000	1,088,000 U

[a] $78,520,000 ÷ 2,600,000 barrels

Absorption-Costing Income Statement

	Theoretical Capacity	Practical Capacity	Normal Capacity Utilization
Revenues (2,400,000 bbls. × $45 per bbl.)	$108,000,000	$108,000,000	$108,000,000
Cost of goods sold			
Beginning inventory	0	0	0
Variable mfg. costs	78,520,000	78,520,000	78,520,000
Fixed mfg. overhead costs allocated			
(2,600,000 units × $6.00; $8.00; $10.00 per unit)	15,600,000	20,800,000	26,000,000
Cost of goods available for sale	94,120,000	99,320,000	104,520,000
Deduct ending inventory			
(200,000 units × $36.20; $38.20; $40.20 per unit)	(7,240,000)	(7,640,000)	(8,040,000)
			1,088,000
Adjustment for variances (add: all unfavorable)	11,488,000 U	6,288,000 U	U
Cost of goods sold	98,368,000	97,968,000	97,568,000
Gross margin	9,632,000	10,032,000	10,432,000
Other costs	0	0	0
Operating income	$ 9,632,000	$ 10,032,000	$ 10,432,000

9-34 (25 min.) **Denominator-level choices, changes in inventory levels, effect on operating income.**

1.

	Theoretical Capacity	Practical Capacity	Normal Utilization Capacity
Denominator level in units	144,000	120,000	96,000
Budgeted fixed manuf. costs	$1,440,000	$1,440,000	$1,440,000
Budgeted fixed manuf. cost allocated per unit	$ 10.00	$ 12.00	$ 15.00
Production in units	104,000	104,000	104,000
Allocated fixed manuf. costs (production in units × budgeted fixed manuf. cost allocated per unit)	$1,040,000	$1,248,000	$1,560,000
Production volume variance (Budgeted fixed manuf. costs – allocated fixed manuf. costs)[a]	$ 400,000 U	$ 192,000 U	$ 120,000 F

[a]PVV is unfavorable if budgeted fixed manuf. costs are greater than allocated fixed costs

2.

	Theoretical Capacity	Practical Capacity	Normal Utilization Capacity
Units sold	112,000	112,000	112,000
Budgeted fixed mfg. cost allocated per unit	$10	$12	$15
Budgeted var. mfg. cost per unit	$ 3	$ 3	$ 3
Budgeted cost per unit of inventory or production	$13	$15	$18

ABSORPTION-COSTING BASED INCOME STATEMENTS

	Theoretical Capacity	Practical Capacity	Normal Utilization Capacity
Revenues ($3 selling price per unit × units sold)	$3,360,000	$3,360,000	$3,360,000
Cost of goods sold			
Beginning inventory (10,000 units × budgeted cost per unit of inventory)	130,000	150,000	180,000
Variable manufacturing costs (104,000 units × $3 per unit)	312,000	312,000	312,000
Allocated fixed manufacturing overhead (104,000 units × budgeted fixed mfg. cost allocated per unit)	1,040,000	1,248,000	1,560,000
Cost of goods available for sale	1,482,000	1,710,000	2,052,000
Deduct ending inventory (2,000[b] units × budgeted cost per unit of inventory)	(26,000)	(30,000)	(36,000)
Adjustment for production-volume variance	400,000 U	192,000 U	(120,000) F
Total cost of goods sold	1,856,000	1,872,000	1,896,000
Gross margin	1,504,000	1,488,000	1,464,000
Operating costs	400,000	400,000	400,000
Operating income	$1,104,000	$1,088,000	$1,064,000

[b]Ending inventory = Beginning inventory + production – sales = 10,000 + 104,000 – 112,000 = 2,000 units
2,000 x $13; 2,000 x $15; 2,000 x $18

3.   Koshu's 2009 beginning inventory was 10,000 units; its ending inventory was 2,000 units. So, during 2009, there was a drop of 8,000 units in inventory levels (matching the 8,000 more units sold than produced). The smaller the denominator level, the larger is the budgeted fixed cost allocated to each unit of production, and, when those units are sold (all the current production is sold, and then some), the larger is the cost of each unit sold, and the smaller is the operating income. *Normal utilization capacity is the smallest capacity of the three*, hence in this year, when production was less than sales, the absorption-costing based operating income is the smallest when normal capacity utilization is used as the denominator level.

4.

Reconciliation

Theoretical Capacity Operating Income – Practical Capacity Operating Income		$16,000
Decrease in inventory level during 2009	8,000	
Fixed mfg cost allocated per unit under practical capacity – fixed mfg. cost allocated per unit under theoretical capacity ($12 – $10)	$2	
Additional allocated fixed cost included in COGS under practical capacity = 8,000 units × $2 per unit =		$16,000

More fixed manufacturing costs are included in inventory under practical capacity, so, when inventory level decreases (as it did in 2009), more fixed manufacturing costs are included in COGS under practical capacity than under theoretical capacity, resulting in a lower operating income.

9-36 (20 min.) Downward demand spiral.

1. and 2.

	Original	Competitive Situation
Practical capacity (units)	7,500	7,500
Budgeted capacity (units)	7,500	6,000
Variable manufacturing cost per unit	$100	$100
Fixed manufacturing costs	$2,250,000	$2,250,000
Markup percentage	100%	100%
Manufacturing cost per unit		
Variable	$100	$100
Fixed (fixed mfg costs ÷ budgeted capacity) ($2,250,000 ÷ 7,500; $2,250,000 ÷ 6,000)	300	375
Full manufacturing cost per unit	$400	$475
Selling Price (200% of full manuf. cost per unit)	$800	$950

3. When budgeted production is used as the denominator level, the changes with demand. The full cost per unit and the selling price are sensitive to the denominator level. In this case, the denominator level has fallen by 20% (from 7,500 to 6,000) and the allocated fixed cost has increased by 25% (from $300 to $375). Thus selling price increases from $800 to $950 (18.75% increase).

If Network's market is more competitive because of entrants, increasing price could further drive away customers, reduce budgeted capacity and increase fixed cost per unit, a downward demand spiral. If Network's plant was built for a practical capacity of 7,500 units, that should be used to focus managerial attention on the unused capacity. If the competitive trends continue, Network will need to cut back its installed capacity to stay competitive.

4. Suppose Network sells x units each year. Its total cost to manufacture the x units would be $100x + $2,250,000$. Its total cost to purchase x units would be $400x + $450,000$. Therefore, Network should manufacture in-house, if $100x + $2,250,000 < $400x + $450,000$; i.e., if $x >$

6,000 units. In-house, the cost structure is a low variable cost, high fixed cost structure, and only worth pursuing for high volumes. The source-outside cost structure is a high variable cost, low fixed cost structure, and only worth pursuing for small volumes. Currently, demand is exactly at 6,000 units. Network should conduct some research to forecast future demand patterns. If it seems likely that demand is going to fall below 6,000, it may be better to shut down its production capacity and outsource all of its needed units. This may also allow the management to examine and pursue other business options, as its current business gets increasingly competitive.

9-38 (35 min.) **Operating income effects of denominator-level choice and disposal of production-volume variance (continuation of 9-37)**

1. Since no beginning inventories exist, if ELF sells all 220,000 bulbs manufactured, its operating income will be the same under all four capacity options.

	Theoretical	Practical	Normal	Master Budget
Revenue	$1,980,000	$1,980,000	$1,980,000	$1,980,000
Less: Cost of goods sold [a]	825,000	990,000	1,430,000	1,650,000
Production volume variance	725,000 U	560,000 U	120,000 U	(100,000) F
Gross margin	430,000	430,000	430,000	430,000
Variable selling [b]	55,000	55,000	55,000	55,000
Fixed selling	250,000	250,000	250,000	250,000
Operating income	$ 125,000	$ 125,000	$ 125,000	$ 125,000

[a]220,000 × 3.75, × 4.50, × 6.50, × 7.50
[b]200,000 × 0.25

2. If the manager of ELF is able to sell only 200,000 of the bulbs produced and if the production-volume variance is closed to cost of goods sold, then the operating income is given as in requirement 3 of 9-37. This is compared to sale of all production, as above.

	Theoretical	Practical	Normal	Master Budget
Income with sales of 220,000 bulbs	$125,000	$125,000	$125,000	$125,000
Income with sales of 200,000 bulbs	25,000	40,000	80,000	100,000
Decrease in income when there is over production	$100,000	$ 85,000	$ 45,000	$ 25,000

Comparing these results, it is clear that for a given level of overproduction relative to sales, the manager's performance will appear better if he/she uses as the denominator a level that is lower. In this example, setting the denominator to equal the master budget (the lowest of the four capacity levels here), minimizes the loss to the manager from being unable to sell the entire production quantity of 220,000 bulbs.

3. In this scenario, the manager of ELF produces 220,000 bulbs and sells 200,000 of them, and the production volume variance is prorated. Given the absence of ending work in process inventory or beginning inventory of any kind, the fraction of the production volume variance that is absorbed into the cost of goods sold is given by 200,000/220,000 or 10/11. The operating income under various denominator levels is then given by the following modification of the solution to requirement 3 of 9-37:

	Theoretical	Practical	Normal	Master Budget
Revenue	$1,800,000	$1,800,000	$1,800,000	$1,800,000
Less: Cost of goods sold	750,000	900,000	1,300,000	1,500,000
Prorated production-volume variance [a]	659,091 U	509,091 U	109,091 U	(90,909) F
Gross margin	390,909	390,909	390,909	390,909
Variable selling [b]	50,000	50,000	50,000	50,000
Fixed selling	250,000	250,000	250,000	250,000
Operating income	$ 90,909	$ 90,909	$ 90,909	$ 90,909

[a] (10/11) × 725,000, × 560,000, × 120,000, × 100,000
[b] 200,000 × 0.25

Under the proration approach, operating income is $90,909 regardless of the denominator initially used. Thus, in contrast to the case where the production volume variance is written off to cost of goods sold, there is no temptation under the proration approach for the manager to play games with the choice of denominator level.

9-40 (20 min.) **Cost allocation, responsibility accounting, ethics (continuation of 9-39).**

1. If Deliman uses its master budget capacity utilization to allocate fixed costs in 2010, it would allocate 806,840 × $1.75 = $1,411,970. Budgeted fixed costs are $1,533,000. Therefore, the production volume variance = $1,533,000 − $1,411,970 = $121,030 U. An unfavorable production volume variance will reduce operating income by this amount. (Note: in this business, there are no inventories. All variances are written off to cost of goods sold).

2.   Hospitals are charged a budgeted variable cost rate and allocated budgeted fixed costs. By overestimating budgeted meal counts, the denominator-level is larger, hence the amount charged to individual hospitals is lower. Consider 2010 where the budgeted fixed cost rate is computed as follows:

$1,533,000/876,000 meals = $1.75 per meal

If in fact, the hospital administrators had better estimated and revealed their true demand (say, 806,800 meals), the allocated fixed cost per meal would have been

$1,533,000/806,800 meals = $1.90 per meal, 8.6% higher than the $1.75 per meal.

Hence, by deliberately overstating budgeted meal count, hospitals are able to reduce the price charged by Deliman for each meal. In this scheme, Deliman bears the downside risk of demand overestimates.

3.   Evidence that could be collected include:
(a) Budgeted meal-count estimates and actual meal-count figures each year for each hospital controller. Over an extended time period, there should be a sizable number of both underestimates and overestimates. Controllers could be ranked on both their percentage of overestimation and the frequency of their overestimation.
(b) Look at the underlying demand estimates by patients at individual hospitals. Each hospital controller has other factors (such as hiring of nurses) that give insight into their expectations of future meal-count demands. If these factors are inconsistent with the meal-count demand figures provided to the central food-catering facility, explanations should be sought.

4.   (a) Highlight the importance of a corporate culture of honesty and openness. Deli One could institute a Code of Ethics that highlights the upside of individual hospitals providing honest estimates of demand (and the penalties for those who do not).
(b) Have individual hospitals contract in advance for their budgeted meal count. Unused amounts would be charged to each hospital at the end of the accounting period. This approach puts a penalty on hospital administrators who overestimate demand.
(c) Use an incentive scheme that has an explicit component for meal-count forecasting accuracy. Each meal-count "forecasting error" would reduce the bonus by $0.05. Thus, if a hospital bids for 292,000 meals and actually uses 200,000 meals, its bonus would be reduced by $0.05 × (292,000 – 200,000) = $4,600.

10-2 Three alternative linear cost functions are
1. **Variable cost** function—total *costs change in proportion* to the changes in the level of activity in the relevant range.
2. **Fixed cost** function—total *costs do not change* with changes in the level of activity in the relevant range.
3. **Mixed cost** function—*both variable and fixed elements*. Total costs change but not in proportion to the changes in the level of activity in the relevant range.

10-4 **No**. High *correlation* merely indicates that the two variables *move together* in the data examined. You need to consider economic plausibility before making inferences about cause and effect.

10-6 The **conference method** *estimates cost functions* on the basis of *analysis and opinions* about costs and their drivers gathered from various departments of a company (purchasing, process engineering, manufacturing, employee relations, etc.). Advantages of the conference method include
    1.   The *speed* with which cost estimates can be developed.
    2.   The *pooling of knowledge* from experts across functional areas.
    3.   The *improved credibility* of the cost function to all personnel.

10-8 The six steps of **past analysis** are
    1.   Choose the *dependent* variable (the variable to be predicted, which is some type of cost).
    2.   Identify the *independent* variable or cost driver.
    3.   *Collect data* on the dependent variable and the cost driver.
    4.   *Plot* the data.
    5.   *Estimate* the cost function.
    6.   *Evaluate the cost driver* of the estimated cost function.
Step 3 typically is the *most difficult* for a cost analyst.

10-10 Three criteria important when **choosing** among alternative cost functions are
    1.   Economic *plausibility*.
    2.   Goodness of *fit*.
    3.   *Slope* of the regression line.

10-12 Frequently encountered **problems** when collecting cost data on variables included in a cost function are

1. The *time period* used to measure the dependent variable is *not* properly *matched* with the time period used to measure the cost driver(s).
2. *Fixed costs* are allocated as if they are variable.
3. *Data* are either not available or are reliable.
4. *Extreme values* of observations occur.
5. A homogeneous *relationship* between the individual cost items in the dependent variable cost pool and the cost driver(s) *does not exist*.
6. The *relationship* between the cost and the cost driver *changes*.
7. *Inflation* has occurred in a dependent variable, a cost driver, or both.

10-14 **No**. A *cost driver* is any factor whose change *causes* a change in the total cost of a related *cost object*. Some users of regression analysis include numerous independent variables in a regression model in an attempt to maximize goodness of fit. Some of the independent variables included may not be cost drivers.

10-16 (10 min.) **Estimating a cost function.**

1. *To compute the slope, recall high school math, rise over run.*

$$\text{Slope coefficient} = \frac{\text{Difference in costs}}{\text{Difference in machine-hours}}$$

$$= \frac{\$5,400 - \$4,000}{10,000 - 6,000}$$

$$= \frac{\$1,400}{4,000} = \$0.35 \text{ per machine-hour}$$

To compute the constant, substitute the slope into either January or February data (both shown here)

Constant = Total cost − (Slope coefficient × Quantity of cost driver)

$$= \$5,400 - (\$0.35 \times 10,000) = \$1,900$$

$$= \$4,000 - (\$0.35 \times 6,000) = \$1,900$$

The cost function based on the two observations is
Maintenance costs = $1,900 + $0.35 × Machine-hours

2. The cost function is an estimate of how costs behave *within the relevant range*. If there are no months with zero machine-hours represented in the maintenance account, data in that account cannot be used to estimate the fixed costs at the zero machine-hours level. Rather, the constant component of the cost function provides the best available starting point for a straight line that approximates how a cost behaves within the relevant range.

10-18 (20 min.)   **Various cost-behavior patterns.**

1. K
2. B
3. G
4. J   Note that A is incorrect because, although the cost per pound eventually equals a constant at $9.20, the total dollars of cost increases linearly from that point onward.
5. I   The total costs will be the same regardless of the volume level.
6. L
7. F   This is a classic step-cost function.
8. K
9. C

10-20 (15 min.) **Account analysis method.**

1.   Variable costs:

Car wash labor	$260,000
Soap, cloth, and supplies	42,000
Water	38,000
Electric power to move conveyor belt	72,000
Total variable costs	$412,000

Fixed costs:

Depreciation	$ 64,000
Salaries	46,000
Total fixed costs	$110,000

Costs are classified as variable because the *total* costs in these categories change in proportion to the number of cars washed. Costs are classified as fixed because the *total* costs in these categories do not vary with the number of cars washed. Different assumptions could lead to different conclusions. For example, if the conveyor belt moves regardless of the number of cars on it, the electricity costs to power the conveyor belt would be a fixed cost.

2.   Variable costs per car $= \dfrac{\$412,000}{80,000} = \$5.15$ per car

Total costs estimated for 90,000 cars $= \$110,000 + (\$5.15 \times 90,000) = \$573,500$

10-22 (30 min.) **Account analysis method.**

1. Manufacturing cost classification for 2009:

Account	Total Costs (1)	% of Total Costs That is Variable (2)	Variable Costs (3) = (1) × (2)	Fixed Costs (4) = (1) – (3)	Variable Cost per Unit (5) = (3) ÷ 75,000
Direct materials	$300,000	100%	$300,000	$ 0	$4.00
Direct manufacturing labor	225,000	100	225,000	0	3.00
Power	37,500	100	37,500	0	0.50
Supervision labor	56,250	20	11,250	45,000	0.15
Materials-handling labor	60,000	50	30,000	30,000	0.40
Maintenance labor	75,000	40	30,000	45,000	0.40
Depreciation	95,000	0	0	95,000	0
Rent, property taxes, admin	100,000	0	0	100,000	0
Total	$948,750		$633,750	$315,000	$8.45

Total manufacturing cost for 2009 = $948,750

Variable costs in 2010:

Account	Unit Variable Cost per Unit for 2009 (6)	Percentage Increase (7)	Increase in Variable Cost per Unit (8) = (6) × (7)	Variable Cost per Unit for 2010 (9) = (6) + (8)	Total Variable Costs for 2010 (10) = (9) × 80,000
Direct materials	$4.00	5%	$0.20	$4.20	$336,000
Direct manufacturing labor	3.00	10	0.30	3.30	264,000
Power	0.50	0	0	0.50	40,000
Supervision labor	0.15	0	0	0.15	12,000
Materials-handling labor	0.40	0	0	0.40	32,000
Maintenance labor	0.40	0	0	0.40	32,000
Depreciation	0	0	0	0	0
Rent, property taxes, admin.	0	0	0	0	0
Total	$8.45		$0.50	$8.95	$716,000

Fixed and total costs in 2010:

Account	Fixed Costs for 2009 (11)	Percentage Increase (12)	Dollar Increase in Fixed Costs (13) = (11) × (12)	Fixed Costs for 2010 (14) = (11) + (13)	Variable Costs for 2010 (10 above)	Total Costs (15) = (14) + (10)
Direct materials	$ 0	0%	$ 0	$ 0	$336,000	$ 336,000
Direct manufacturing labor	0	0	0	0	264,000	264,000
Power	0	0	0	0	40,000	40,000
Supervision labor	45,000	0	0	45,000	12,000	57,000
Materials-handling labor	30,000	0	0	30,000	32,000	62,000
Maintenance labor	45,000	0	0	45,000	32,000	77,000
Depreciation	95,000	5	4,750	99,750	0	99,750
Rent, property taxes, admin.	100,000	7	7,000	107,000	0	107,000
Total	$315,000		$11,750	$326,750	$716,000	$1,042,750

Total manufacturing costs for 2010 = $1,042,750

2. Total cost per unit, 2009 $= \dfrac{\$948,750}{75,000} = \$12.65$

   Total cost per unit, 2010 $= \dfrac{\$1,042,750}{80,000} = \$13.03$

3. How good the classifications are depends on the knowledge of individual managers who classify the costs. Gower may want to undertake *quantitative* analysis of costs, using regression analysis on time-series or cross-sectional data to better estimate the fixed and variable components of costs. Better knowledge of fixed and variable costs will help Gower to *better price* his products, to know when he is getting a positive contribution margin, and to *better manage costs*.

10-24   (20 min.)   **Estimating a cost function, high-low method.**

1.   There is a positive relationship between the number of service reports (a cost driver) and the customer-service department costs. This relationship is economically plausible, i.e. it makes sense that having to produce more reports will lead to increased costs.

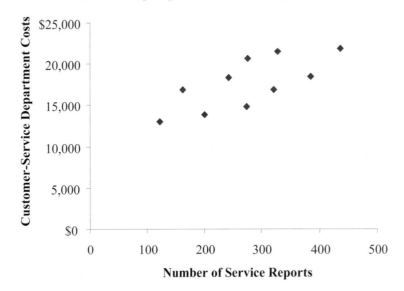

2.

	Number of Service Reports	Customer-Service Department Costs
Highest observation of cost driver	436	$21,890
Lowest observation of cost driver	122	12,941
Difference	314	$ 8,949

Customer-service department costs = constant + slope × (number of service reports)

$$\text{Slope coefficient} \quad = \frac{\$8,949}{314} = \$28.50 \text{ per service report}$$

Substitute either point into the equation to find the constant:

Constant   = $21,890 – $28.50 × 436 = $9,464
            = $12,941 – $28.50 × 122 = $9,464

Customer-service department costs = $9,464 + $28.50 (number of service reports)

3.   Other possible cost drivers of customer-service department costs are:
    a.   Number of products replaced with a new product (and the dollar value of the new products charged to the customer-service department).
    b.   Number of products repaired and the time and cost of repairs.

10-26 (20 min.) **Cost-volume-profit and regression analysis.**

1a. Average cost of manufacturing $= \dfrac{\text{Total manufacturing costs}}{\text{Number of bicycle frames}}$

$\qquad\qquad\qquad\qquad\qquad\qquad = \dfrac{\$900,000}{30,000} = \$30$ per frame

This cost is greater than the $28.50 per frame that Ryan has quoted.

1b. Garvin cannot take the average manufacturing cost in 2009 of $30 per frame and multiply it by 36,000 bicycle frames to determine the total cost of manufacturing 36,000 bicycle frames. The reason is that some of the $900,000 (or equivalently the $30 cost per frame) are fixed costs and some are variable costs, some are unit level and some are batch costs. Without distinguishing they types of costs, Garvin cannot determine the cost of manufacturing 36,000 frames.

2. $\dfrac{\text{Expected cost to make}}{\text{36,000 bicycle frames}}$ $= \$432,000 + \$15 \times 36,000$

$\qquad\qquad\qquad\qquad\qquad\quad = \$432,000 + \$540,000 = \$972,000$

Purchasing bicycle frames from Ryan will cost $28.50 \times 36,000 = \$1,026,000$. Hence, it will cost Garvin $1,026,000 - \$972,000 = \underline{\mathit{\$54,000\ more\ to\ purchase}}$ the frames from Ryan rather than manufacture them in-house.

3. Garvin would need to **consider several factors** before being confident that the equation in requirement 2 accurately predicts the cost of manufacturing bicycle frames.
   a. Is the relationship between total manufacturing costs and quantity of bicycle frames *economically plausible*?
   b. How good is the *goodness of fit*? That is, how well does the estimated line fit the data?
   c. Is the relationship between the number of bicycle frames produced and total manufacturing costs *linear*?
   d. Does the slope of the regression line indicate that a *strong relationship* exists between manufacturing costs and the number of bicycle frames produced?
   e. Are there any *data problems*
      o errors in measuring costs
      o trends in prices of materials, labor or overhead
      o extreme values of observations
      o nonstationary relationship between costs and the quantity of bicycles produced
   f. How is *inflation* expected to affect costs?
   g. Will Ryan supply *high-quality* bicycle frames *on time*?

10-28 High-low, regression

1. Pat will pick the highest point of activity, 3,400 parts (August) at $20,500 of cost, and the lowest point of activity, 1,910 parts (March) at $11,560.

	Cost driver: Quantity Purchased	Cost
Highest observation of cost driver	3,400	$20,500
Lowest observation of cost driver	1,910	11,560
Difference	1,490	$ 8,940

Purchase costs = constant + slope $\times$ Quantity purchased

Slope coefficient $(b) = \dfrac{\$8,940}{1,490} = \$6$ per part

Constant = $20,500 - (\$6 \times 3,400) = \$100$

The equation Pat gets is:

$\qquad$ Purchase costs = $100 + (\$6 \times$ Quantity purchased)

2. Using the equation above, the expected purchase costs for each month will be:

Month	Purchase Quantity Expected	Calculation of Expected cost	Expected cost
October	3,000 parts	$100 + (\$6 \times 3,000)$	$18,100
November	3,200	$100 + (\$6 \times 3,200)$	19,300
December	2,500	$100 + (\$6 \times 2,500)$	15,100

3. $\qquad$ *Economic Plausibility*: Clearly, the cost of purchasing a part is associated with the quantity purchased.

$\qquad$ *Goodness of Fit*: As seen in the graph, the regression line fits the data well. The vertical distance between the regression line and observations is small.

$\qquad$ *Significance of the Independent Variable*: The relatively steep slope of the regression line suggests that the quantity purchased is correlated with purchasing cost for part #4599.

$\qquad$ The *regression is the more accurate* estimate because it uses all available data (all nine data points) while the high-low method only relies on two data points and may therefore miss some important information contained in the other data.

$\qquad$ According to the regression, Pat's *original estimate* of fixed cost is too low given all the data points. The original slope is too steep, but only by 16 cents. So, the variable rate is lower but the fixed cost is higher for the regression line than for the high-low cost equation.

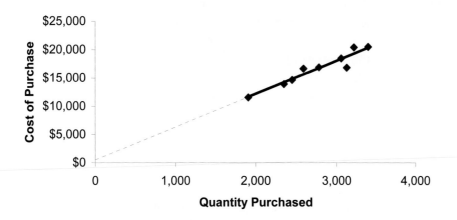

Serth Manufacturing
Purchase Costs for Part #4599

4. Using the regression equation, the purchase costs for each month will be:

Month	Purchase Quantity Expected	Calculation of Expected cost	Expected cost
October	3,000 parts	$501.54 + ($5.84 × 3,000)	$18,022
November	3,200	$501.54 + ($5.84 × 3,200)	19,190
December	2,500	$501.54 + ($5.84 × 2,500)	15,102

Month	High Low	Regression	Difference
October	18,100	18,022	78
November	19,300	19,190	110
December	15,100	15,102	(2)

Although the two equations are different in both fixed element and variable rate, within the relevant range they give similar expected costs. This implies that the high and low points of the data are a reasonable representation of the total set of points within the relevant range.

10-30 (20 min.) **Learning curve, incremental unit-time learning model.**

1.   The direct manufacturing labor-hours (DMLH) required to produce the first 2, 3, and 4 units, given the assumption of an incremental unit-time learning curve of 90%, is as follows:

Cumulative Number of Units (X) (1)	90% Learning Curve Individual Unit Time for Xth Unit (y): Labor Hours (2)	Cumulative Total Time: Labor-Hours (3)
1	3,000	3,000
2	2,700	5,700
3	2,539	8,239
4	2,430	10,669

Values in column (2) are calculated using the formula $y = aX^b$ where $a = 3,000$, $X = 2$, 3, or 4, and $b = -0.152004$, which gives

when $X = 2$, $y = 3,000 \times 2^{-0.152004} = 2,700$

when $X = 3$, $y = 3,000 \times 3^{-0.152004} = 2,539$

when $X = 4$, $y = 3,000 \times 4^{-0.152004} = 2,430$

	Variable Costs of Producing		
	2 Units	3 Units	4 Units
Direct materials $80,000 \times 2$; 3; 4	$160,000	$240,000	$ 320,000
Direct manufacturing labor $25 \times$ Cumulative labor hours	142,500	205,975	266,725
Variable manufacturing overhead $15 \times$ Cumulative labor hours	85,500	123,585	160,035
Total variable costs	$388,000	$569,560	$746,760

2.

	Variable Costs of Producing	
	2 Units	4 Units
Incremental unit-time learning model (from requirement 1)	$388,000	$746,760
Cumulative average-time learning model (from Exercise 10-29)	376,000	708,800
Difference	$ 12,000	$ 37,960

Total variable costs for manufacturing 2 and 4 units are lower under the cumulative average-time learning curve relative to the incremental unit-time learning curve. Hours required to make additional units decline more slowly in the incremental unit-time learning curve when the same 90% factor is used for both curves. In the incremental unit-time learning curve, only the last unit produced has a cost of 90% of the initial cost. In the cumulative average-time learning model, the average cost of *all* the additional units produced (not just the last unit) is 90% of the initial cost.

10-32 (30min.) **High-low method and regression analysis.**

1. Plot, High-low Line, and Regression Line for Number of Customers per Week versus Weekly Total Costs for Happy Business College Restaurant

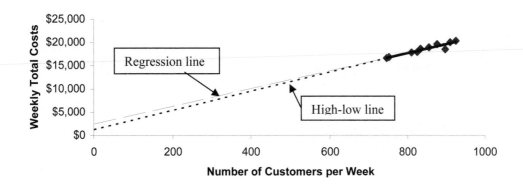

2.

	Number of Customers per week	Weekly Total Costs
Highest observation of cost driver (Week 9)	925	$20,305
Lowest observation of cost driver (Week 2)	745	16,597
Difference	180	$ 3,708

Weekly total costs = *constant* + *slope* × (number of customers per week)

$$\text{Slope coefficient} = \frac{\$3,708}{180} = \$20.60 \text{ per customer}$$

$$\text{Constant} = \$20,305 - (\$20.60 \times 925) = \$1,250$$
$$= \$16,597 - (\$20.60 \times 745) = \$1,250$$

Weekly total costs = $1,250 + $20.60 (number of customers per week)

3. *Economic Plausibility*. The cost function shows a positive economically plausible relationship between number of customers per week and weekly total restaurant costs. Number of customers is a plausible cost driver since both cost of food served and amount of time the waiters must work (and hence their wages) increase with the number of customers served.

Goodness of fit. The regression line appears to fit the data well. The vertical differences between the actual costs and the regression line appear to be quite small.

Significance of independent variable. The regression line has a steep positive slope and increases by more than $19 for each additional customer. Because the slope is not flat, there is a strong relationship between number of customers and total restaurant costs.

The regression line is the more accurate estimate of the relationship between number of customers and total restaurant costs because it uses all available data points while the high-low method relies only on two data points and may therefore miss some information contained in the other data points. Nevertheless, the graphs of the two lines are fairly close to each other, so the cost function estimated using the high-low method appears to be a good approximation of the cost function estimated using the regression method.

4. The cost estimate by the two methods will be equal where the two lines intersect. You can find the number of customers by setting the two equations to be equal and solving for x. That is,

$$\$1,250 + \$20.60x = \$2,453 + \$19.04x$$
$$\$20.60\,x - \$19.04\,x = \$2,453 - \$1,250$$
$$1.56\,x = 1,203$$
$$x = 771.15 \text{ or} \approx 771\text{customers.}$$

10-34 (30 min.) Regression, activity-based costing, choosing cost drivers.

1. **Both** number of units inspected and inspection labor-hours are **plausible cost drivers** for inspection costs. The number of units inspected is likely related to test-kit usage, which is a significant component of inspection costs. Inspection labor-hours are a plausible cost driver if labor hours vary per unit inspected, because costs would be a function of how much time the inspectors spend on each unit. This is particularly true if the inspectors are paid a wage, and if they use electric or electronic machinery to test the units of product (cost of operating equipment increases with time spent).

2.
Plot and Regression Line for **Units Inspected** versus Inspection Costs for Newroute Manufacturing

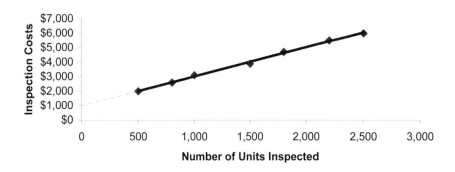

188

Plot and Regression Line for **Inspection Labor-Hours** and Inspection Costs for Newroute Manufacturing

Newroute Manufacturing
Inspection Costs and Inspection Labor-Hours

Goodness of Fit. As you can see from the two graphs, the regression line based on number of units inspected better fits the data (has *smaller vertical distances from the points to the line*) than the regression line based on inspection labor-hours. Hence number of units inspected is a better cost driver.

Significance of independent variable. It is hard to visually compare the slopes because the graphs are not the same size, but both graphs have steep positive slopes indicating a strong relationship between number of units inspected and inspection costs, and inspection labor-hours and inspection costs. Indeed, if labor-hours per inspection do not vary much, number of units inspected and inspection labor-hours will be closely related.

3. At 150 inspection labor hours and 1,200 units inspected, both solutions are presented:

Inspection costs using units inspected = $1,004 + ($2.02 × 1200) = $3,428

Inspection costs using inspection labor-hours = $626 + ($19.51 × 150) = $3,552.50

If Neela uses inspection-labor-hours she will estimate inspection costs to be $3,552.50, $124.50 ($3,552.50 −$3,428) higher than if she had used number of units inspected. If actual costs equaled, say, $3,500, Neela would conclude that Newroute has performed efficiently in its inspection activity because actual inspection costs would be lower than budgeted amounts. In fact, based on the more accurate cost function, actual costs of $3,500 exceeded the budgeted amount of $3,428. Neela should find ways to improve inspection efficiency rather than mistakenly conclude that the inspection activity has been performing well.

10-36 (30–40 min.) **Cost estimation, cumulative average-time learning curve.**

1. Cost to produce the 2nd through the 8th troop deployment boats:

Direct materials, 7 × $100,000	$ 700,000
Direct manufacturing labor (DML), 39,130[1] × $30	1,173,900
Variable manufacturing overhead, 39,130 × $20	782,600
Other manufacturing overhead, 25% of DML costs	293,475
Total costs	$2,949,975

[1]The direct manufacturing labor-hours to produce the second to eighth boats can be calculated in several ways, given the assumption of a cumulative average-time learning curve of 85%:

Use of table format:

Cumulative Number of Units (X) (1)	85% Learning Curve Cumulative Average Time per Unit (y): Labor Hours (2)	Cumulative Total Time: Labor-Hours (3) = (1) × (2)
1	10,000.00	10,000
2	8,500.00 = (10,000 × 0.85)	17,000
3	7,729.00	23,187
4	7,225.00 = (8,500 × 0.85)	28,900
5	6,856.71	34,284
6	6,569.78	39,419
7	6,336.56	44,356
8	6,141.25 = (7,225 × 0.85)	49,130

Use of formula: $y = aX^b$

where $a = 10,000$, $X = 8$, and $b = -0.234465$
$$y = 10,000 \times 8^{-0.234465} = 6,141.25 \text{ hours}$$

The total direct labor-hours for 8 units is $6,141.25 \times 8 = 49,130$ hours

The direct labor-hours required to produce the second through the eighth boats is $49,130 - 10,000 = 39,130$ hours.

2. Cost to produce the 2nd through the 8th boats assuming linear function for direct labor-hours and units produced:

Direct materials, 7 × $100,000	$ 700,000
Direct manufacturing labor (DML), 7 × 10,000 hrs. × $30	2,100,000
Variable manufacturing overhead, 7 × 10,000 hrs. × $20	1,400,000
Other manufacturing overhead, 25% of DML costs	525,000
Total costs	$4,725,000

The difference in predicted costs is:

Predicted cost in requirement 2 (based on linear cost function)	$4,725,000
Predicted cost in requirement 1 (based on 85% learning curve)	2,949,975
Difference in favor of learning-curve based costs	$1,775,025

Note that the linear cost function assumption leads to a total cost that is 60% higher than the cost predicted by the learning curve model. Learning curve effects are most prevalent in large manufacturing industries such as airplanes and boats where costs can run into the millions or hundreds of millions of dollars, resulting in very large and monetarily significant differences between the two models.

10-38 Regression; choosing among models. (chapter appendix)

1. Regression Output for (a) Setup Costs and **Number of Setups** and (b) Setup Costs and **Number of Setup-Hours**

SUMMARY OUTPUT

Regression Statistics	
Multiple R	0.5807364
R Square	0.3372548
Adjusted R Square	0.2425769
Standard Error	28720.995
Observations	9

ANOVA

	df	SS	MS	F	Significance F
Regression	1	2938383589	2938383589	3.562128	0.101066787
Residual	7	5774269011	824895573		
Total	8	8712652600			

	Coefficients	Standard Error	t Stat	P-value	Lower 95%	Upper 95%	Lower 95.0%	Upper 95.0%
Intercept	3905.3482	41439.10166	0.09424307	0.927557	-94082.55656	101893.25	-94082.5566	101893.2529
Number of Setups	410.09094	217.2828325	1.887360052	0.1010668	-103.701317	923.88319	-103.701317	923.883193

Multiple R	0.923210231
R Square	0.85231713
Adjusted R Square	0.831219577
Standard Error	13557.86298
Observations	9

ANOVA

	df	SS	MS	F	Significance F
Regression	1	7425943061	7425943061	40.39886224	0.00038302
Residual	7	1286709539	183815648.5		
Total	8	8712652600			

	Coefficients	Standard Error	t Stat	P-value	Lower 95%	Upper 95%	Lower 95.0%	Upper 95.0%
Intercept	3348.71803	12878.63428	0.260021207	0.80232966	-27104.4129	33801.849	-27104.41289	33801.849
Number of Setup Hours	56.2692934	8.85292724	6.35600993	0.00038302	35.33544701	77.20314	35.33544701	77.2031399

2. Plots and Regression Lines for (a) **Number of Setups** versus Setup Costs and (b) **Number of Setup-Hours** versus Setup Costs

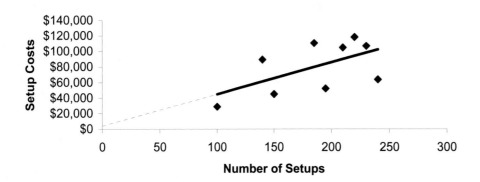

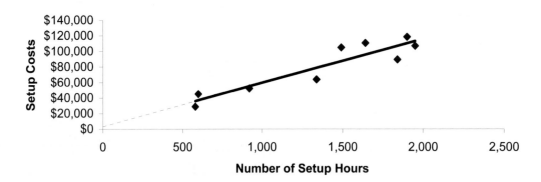

3.

	Number of Setups	Number of Setup Hours
Economic plausibility	A positive relationship between setup costs and the number of setups is economically plausible.	A positive relationship between setup costs and the number of setup-hours economically plausible. The longer it takes to setup, the greater the setup costs.
Goodness of fit	$r^2 = 34\%$ standard error of regression =\$28,721 Poor goodness of fit.	$r^2 = 85\%$ standard error of regression =\$13,558 Excellent goodness of fit.
Significance of Independent Variables	The t-value of 1.89 is not significant at the 0.05 level.	The t-value of 6.36 is significant at the 0.05 level.
Specification analysis of estimation assumptions	Based on a plot of the data, the linearity assumption holds, but the constant variance assumption may be violated. The Durbin-Watson statistic of 1.12 suggests the residuals are independent. The normality of residuals assumption appears to hold. However, inferences drawn from only 9 observations are not reliable.	Based on a plot of the data, the assumptions of linearity, constant variance, independence of residuals (Durbin-Watson = 1.50), and normality of residuals hold. However, inferences drawn from only 9 observations are not reliable.

4. The regression model using **number of setup-hours** should be used to estimate set up costs because number of setup-hours is a *more economically plausible* cost driver of setup costs (compared to number of setups). The setup time is different for different products and the longer it takes to setup, the greater the setup costs such as costs of setup-labor and setup equipment. The regression of number of setup-hours and setup costs also has a better fit, a significant independent variable, and better satisfies the assumptions of the estimation technique.

10-40 (40–50 min.) **Purchasing Department cost drivers, activity-based costing, simple regression analysis.**

1.

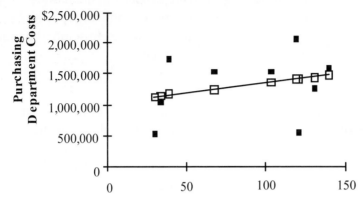

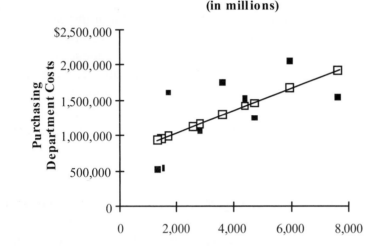

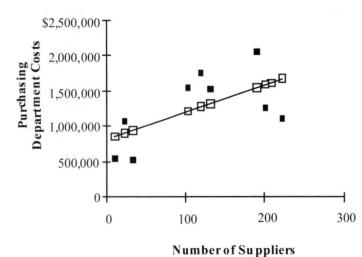

Criterion	Regression 1 PDC = a + (b × MP\$)	Regression 2 PDC = a + (b × # of POs)	Regression 3 PDC = a + (b × # of Ss)
1. Economic Plausibility	Result presented at seminar by Couture Fabrics found little support for MP\$ as a driver. Purchasing personnel at the Miami store believe MP\$ is not a significant cost driver.	Economically plausible. The higher the number of purchase orders, the more tasks undertaken.	Economically plausible. Increasing the number of suppliers increases the costs of certifying vendors and managing the Fashion Flair-supplier relationship.
2. Goodness of fit	$r^2 = 0.08$. Poor goodness of fit.	$r^2 = 0.42$. Reasonable goodness of fit.	$r^2 = 0.39$. Reasonable goodness of fit.
3. Significance of Independent Variables	t-value on MP\$ of 0.84 is insignificant.	t-value on # of POs of 2.43 is significant.	t-value on # of Ss of 2.28 is significant.
4. Specification Analysis			
A. Linearity within the relevant range	Appears questionable but no strong evidence against linearity.	Appears reasonable.	Appears reasonable.
B. Constant variance of residuals	Appears questionable, but no strong evidence against constant variance.	Appears reasonable.	Appears reasonable.
C. Independence of residuals	Durbin-Watson Statistic = 2.41 Assumption of independence is not rejected.	Durbin-Watson Statistic = 1.98 Assumption of independence is not rejected.	Durbin-Watson Statistic = 1.97 Assumption of independence is not rejected.
D. Normality of residuals	Data base too small to make reliable inferences.	Data base too small to make reliable inferences.	Data base too small to make reliable inferences.

2. *Both Regressions 2 and 3 are well-specified regression models*. The slope coefficients on their respective independent variables are significantly different from zero. These results support the Couture Fabrics' presentation in which the number of purchase orders and the number of suppliers were reported to be drivers of purchasing department costs.

In designing an activity-based cost system, Fashion Flair should use number of purchase orders and number of suppliers as cost drivers of purchasing department costs. Fashion Flair can either (a) estimate a multiple regression equation for purchasing department costs with number of purchase orders and number of suppliers as cost drivers, or (b) divide purchasing department costs into two separate cost pools, one for costs related to purchase orders and another for costs related to suppliers, and estimate a separate relationship for each cost pool.

3. Guidelines presented in the chapter could be used to gain additional evidence on cost drivers of purchasing department costs.

   1. Use physical relationships or engineering relationships to establish cause-and-effect links. Lee could observe the purchasing department operations to gain insight into how costs are driven.

   2. Use knowledge of operations. Lee could interview operating personnel in the purchasing department to obtain their insight on cost drivers.

10-42 (40 min.) **High-low method, alternative regression functions, accrual accounting adjustments, ethics.**

1. The plot of engineering support reported costs and machine-hours shows two separate groups of data, each of which may be approximated by a separate cost function. The problem arises because the plant records materials and parts costs on an "as purchased" rather than an "as used" basis. The plot of engineering support restated costs and machine-hours shows a high positive correlation between the two variables (the coefficient of determination is 0.94); a single linear cost function provides a good fit to the data. Better estimates of the cost relation result because Kennedy adjusts the materials and parts costs to an accrual accounting basis.

Plots and Regression Lines for Engineering Support Reported Costs and Engineering Support Restated Costs

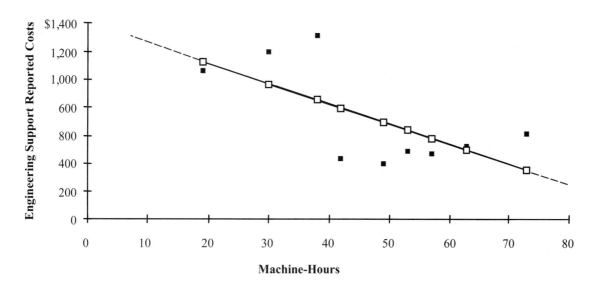

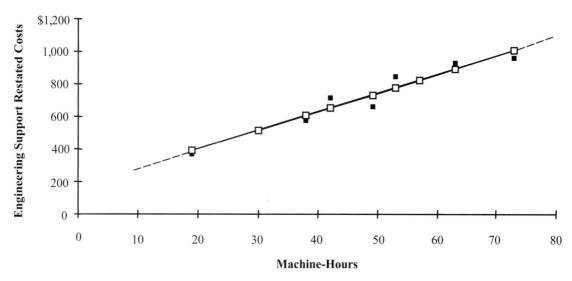

2.

	Cost Driver Machine-Hours	Reported Engineering Support Costs
Highest observation of cost driver (August)	73	$ 617
Lowest observation of cost driver (September)	19	1,066
Difference	54	$ (449)

$$\text{Slope coefficient, } b = \frac{\text{Difference between costs associated with highest and lowest observations of the cost driver}}{\text{Difference between highest and lowest observations of the cost driver}}$$

$$= \frac{-\$449}{54} = -\$8.31 \text{ per machine-hour}$$

Constant (at highest observation of cost driver) = $ 617 – (–$8.31 × 73) = $1,224
Constant (at lowest observation of cost driver) = $1,066 – (–$8.31 × 19) = $1,224
The estimated cost function is $y = \$1,224 – \$8.31X$

	Cost Driver Machine-Hours	Restated Engineering Support Costs
Highest observation of cost driver (August)	73	$966
Lowest observation of cost driver (September)	19	370
Difference	54	$596

$$\text{Slope coefficient, } b = \frac{\text{Difference between costs associated with highest and lowest observations of the cost driver}}{\text{Difference between highest and lowest observations of the cost driver}}$$

$$= \frac{\$596}{54} = \$11.04 \text{ per machine-hour}$$

Constant (at highest observation of cost driver) = $ 966 – ($11.04 × 73) = $160
Constant (at lowest observation of cost driver) = $ 370 – ($11.04 × 19) = $160
The estimated cost function is $y = \$160 + \$11.04\,X$

3. The cost function estimated with engineering support restated costs better approximates the regression analysis assumptions.

Comparison of Alternative Cost Functions for Engineering Support Costs at United Packaging

Criterion	Regression 1 Dependent Variable: Engineering Support Reported Costs	Regression 2 Dependent Variable: Engineering Support Restated Costs
1. Economic Plausibility	Negative slope relationship is economically implausible over the long run.	Positive slope relationship is economically plausible.
2. Goodness of Fit	$r^2 = 0.43$. Moderate goodness of fit.	$r^2 = 0.94$. Excellent goodness of fit.
3. Significance of Independent Variables	t-statistic on machine-hours is statistically significant ($t = -2.31$), albeit economically implausible.	t-statistic on machine-hours is highly statistically significant ($t=10.59$).
4. Specification Analysis: A. Linearity	Linearity does not describe data very well.	Linearity describes data very well.
B. Constant variance of residuals	Appears questionable, although 12 observations do not facilitate the drawing of reliable inferences.	Appears reasonable, although 12 observations do not facilitate the drawing of reliable inferences.
C. Independence of residuals	Durbin-Watson = 2.26. Residuals serially uncorrelated.	Durbin-Watson = 1.31. Some evidence of serial correlation in the residuals.
D. Normality of residuals	Database too small to make reliable inferences.	Database too small to make reliable inferences.

4. Kennedy should choose Regression 2, restated costs, as best representing the relationship between engineering costs and machine-hours. The cost functions estimated using engineering reported costs are mis-specified and not-economically plausible because materials and parts costs are reported on an "as-purchased" rather than on an "as-used" basis. With respect to engineering restated costs, the high-low and regression approaches yield roughly similar estimates. The regression approach is superior because it determines the line that best fits all observations. In contrast, the high-low method considers only two points when estimating the cost function.

5. Problems Kennedy might encounter include
    a. A *perpetual inventory system* may not be used in this case; the amounts requisitioned likely will not permit an accurate matching of costs with the independent variable on a month-by-month basis.
    b. *Quality of the source records* for usage by engineers may be relatively low; e.g., engineers may requisition materials and parts in batches, but not use them immediately.
    c. *Records may not distinguish materials and parts* for maintenance from materials and parts used for repairs and breakdowns; separate cost functions may be appropriate for the two categories of materials and parts.
    d. *Year-end accounting adjustments* to inventory may mask errors that gradually accumulate month-by-month.

6. **Picking the correct cost function** is important for *cost prediction*, *cost management*, and *performance evaluation*. Two problems if they selected regression 1, the wrong model could be:
    a. *Underestimation of costs*: In a month with 60 machine-hours, Regression 1 would predict costs of $1,393.20 – ($14.23 × 60) = $539.40. If actual costs turn out to be $800, management would conclude that changes should be made to reduce costs. In fact, on the basis of the preferred Regression 2, support overhead costs are lower than the predicted amount of $176.38 + ($11.44 × 60) = $862.78—a performance that management should seek to replicate, not change.
    b. *Overestimation of costs*: If machine-hours worked in a month were low, say 25 hours, Regression 1 would erroneously predict support overhead costs of $1,393.20 – ($14.23 × 25) = $1,037.45. If actual costs are $700, management would conclude that its performance has been very good. In fact, compared to the costs predicted by the preferred Regression 2 of $176.38 + ($11.44 × 25) = $462.38, the actual performance is rather poor. Using Regression 1, management may feel costs are being managed very well when in fact they are much higher than what they should be and need to be managed "down."

7. Because Kennedy is confident that the restated numbers are correct, he cannot change them just to please Mason. If he does, he is violating the standards of integrity and objectivity for management accountants. Kennedy should establish the correctness of the numbers with Mason, point out that he cannot change them, and also reason that this is a problem that could crop up each year and they should take a firm, ethical stand right away. If Mason continues to apply pressure, Kennedy has no option but to escalate the problem to higher levels in the organization. He should be prepared to resign, if necessary, rather than compromise his professional ethics.

CHAPTER 11
DECISION MAKING AND RELEVANT INFORMATION

11-2 **Relevant costs** are expected *future* costs that *differ among the alternative* courses of action being considered. Historical costs are irrelevant because they are past costs and, therefore, cannot differ among alternative future courses of action.

11-4 **Quantitative** factors are outcomes that are *measured in numerical terms*. Some quantitative factors are financial—that is, they can be easily expressed in monetary terms. **Qualitative** factors are outcomes that are *difficult to measure* accurately in numerical terms.

11-6 **No**. Some variable costs may not *differ among the alternatives* under consideration and, hence, will be irrelevant. Some fixed costs may differ among the alternatives and, hence, will be relevant.

11-8 **Opportunity cost** is the contribution to income that is *given up* by not using a limited resource in its *next-best alternative use*.

11-10 **No**. Managers should aim to get the highest contribution margin per unit of the constraint.

11-12 Cost written off as depreciation is irrelevant when it pertains to a *past* cost such as equipment already purchased. But the purchase cost of new equipment to be *acquired in the future* that will then be written off as depreciation is often relevant.

11-14 The **three steps** in solving a linear programming problem are
(i) Determine the *objective function*.
(ii) Specify the *constraints*.
(iii) Compute the *optimal* solution.

11-16 (20 min.) **Disposal of assets.**

1. The $75,000 is irrelevant to the decision to remachine or scrap. The only relevant factors are the *future revenues and future costs*. The difference in favor of remachining is $2,000:

	(a) Remachine	(b) Scrap
Future revenues	$30,000	$3,000
Deduct future costs	25,000	–
Operating income	$ 5,000	$3,000

2. The $100,000 original cost is irrelevant to this decision. The difference in relevant costs in favor of rebuilding is $5,000 as follows:

	(a) Replace	(b) Rebuild
New truck	$105,000	–
Deduct current disposal price of existing truck	15,000	–
Rebuild existing truck	–	$85,000
	$ 90,000	$85,000

11-18 (15 min.) **Multiple choice.**

1.

Special order price per unit	$6.00
Variable manufacturing cost per unit	4.50
Contribution margin per unit	$1.50

Effect on operating income = $1.50 × 20,000 units
  = $30,000 increase **Answer (b)**

2.

Cost	Purchase outside	Make	Difference
$60 per unit × 20,000 units	$1,200,000		
Variable manufacturing cost $48 per unit × 20,000 units		$960,000	
Fixed costs that go away $9 × 20,000 units	(180,000)		
Cost under each alternative	1,020,000	960,000	
Difference			$60,000
Minimum required cost savings			25,000
Total required to be saved in Part 575			$85,000
			Answer (b)

11-20 (30 min.) **Make versus buy, activity-based costing.**

1.   The expected manufacturing cost per unit of CMCBs in 2009 is as follows:

	Total Manufacturing Costs of CMCB (1)	Manufacturing Cost per Unit (2) = (1) ÷ 10,000
Direct materials, $170 × 10,000	$1,700,000	$170
Direct manufacturing labor, $45 × 10,000	450,000	45
Variable batch manufacturing costs, $1,500 × 80	120,000	12
Fixed manufacturing costs		
Avoidable fixed manufacturing costs	320,000	32
Unavoidable fixed manufacturing costs	800,000	80
Total manufacturing costs	$3,390,000	$339

2.   The following table identifies the incremental costs in 2009 if Svenson (a) made CMCBs and (b) purchased CMCBs from Minton.

	Total Incremental Costs		Per-Unit Incremental Costs	
Incremental Items	**Make**	**Buy**	**Make**	**Buy**
Cost of purchasing CMCBs from Minton		$3,000,000		$300
Direct materials	$1,700,000		$170	
Direct manufacturing labor	450,000		45	
Variable batch manufacturing costs	120,000		12	
Avoidable fixed manufacturing costs	320,000		32	
Total incremental costs	$2,590,000	$3,000,000	$259	$300
Difference in favor of making	$410,000		$41	

Note that the opportunity cost of using capacity to make CMCBs is zero since Svenson would keep this capacity idle if it purchases CMCBs from Minton.

Svenson should _continue to manufacture the CMCBs internally_ since the incremental costs to manufacture are $259 per unit compared to the $300 per unit that Minton has quoted. Note that the unavoidable fixed manufacturing costs of $800,000 ($80 per unit) will continue to be incurred whether Svenson makes or buys CMCBs. These are not incremental costs under either the make or the buy alternative and hence, are irrelevant.

3. Svenson should continue to make CMCBs. Expected incremental future revenues from CB3s, $2,000,000, are *less* than expected incremental future costs, $2,150,000. This is a financially bad opportunity. Therefore, they will keep the facility idle, and the answer is the same as in requirement 2. Svenson should make CMCBs rather than buy them.

Relevant Items	Make CMCBs and Do Not Make CB3s	Buy CMCBs and Do Not Make CB3s	Buy CMCBs and Make CB3s
Choices for Svenson			
TOTAL-ALTERNATIVES APPROACH TO MAKE-OR-BUY DECISIONS			
Total incremental costs of making/buying CMCBs (from requirement 2)	$2,590,000	$3,000,000	$3,000,000
Excess of future costs over future revenues from CB3s	0	0	150,000
Total relevant costs	$2,590,000	$3,000,000	$3,150,000

11-22 (20–25 min.) **Relevant costs, contribution margin, product emphasis.**

1.

	Cola	Lemonade	Punch	Natural Orange Juice
Selling price	$18.80	$20.00	$27.10	$39.20
Deduct variable cost per case	14.20	16.10	20.70	30.20
Contribution margin per case	$ 4.60	$ 3.90	$ 6.40	$ 9.00

2.   The argument fails to recognize that shelf space is the constraining factor. There are only 12 feet of front shelf space to be devoted to drinks. Sexton should aim to get the highest daily contribution margin per foot of front shelf space:

	Cola	Lemonade	Punch	Natural Orange Juice
Contribution margin per case	$ 4.60	$ 3.90	$ 6.40	$ 9.00
Sales (number of cases) per foot of shelf space per day	× 25	× 24	× 4	× 5
Daily contribution per foot of front shelf space	$115.00	$93.60	$25.60	$45.00

3.	The allocation that maximizes the daily contribution from soft drink sales (subject to max of 6 feet and minimum of 1 foot for each product line) is:

	Feet of Shelf Space	Daily Contribution per Foot of Front Shelf Space	Total Contribution Margin per Day
Cola	6	$115.00	$ 690.00
Lemonade	4	93.60	374.40
Natural Orange Juice	1	45.00	45.00
Punch	1	25.60	25.60
			$1,135.00

The maximum of six feet of front shelf space will be devoted to Cola because it has the highest contribution margin per unit of the constraining factor. Four feet of front shelf space will be devoted to Lemonade, which has the second highest contribution margin per unit of the constraining factor. No more shelf space can be devoted to Lemonade since each of the remaining two products, Natural Orange Juice and Punch must be given at least one foot of front shelf space.

11-24 (20 min.) **Which base to close, relevant-cost analysis, opportunity costs.**

The future outlay operating costs will be $400 million regardless of which base is closed, given the additional $100 million in costs at Everett if Alameda is closed. Further, one of the bases will permanently remain open while the other will be shut down. The only relevant revenue and cost comparisons are

a.	$500 million from sale of the Alameda base. Note that the historical cost of building the Alameda base ($100 million) is irrelevant. Note also that future increases in the value of the land at the Alameda base are also irrelevant. One of the bases must be kept open, so if it is decided to keep the Alameda base open, the Defense Department will not be able to sell this land at a future date.

b.	$60 million which would need to be put into savings in fixed income note if the Everett base is open, which would not happen if the Alameda base was closed. Again, the historical cost of building the Everett base ($150 million) is irrelevant.

The relevant costs and benefits analysis favors closing the Alameda base despite the objections raised by the California delegation in Congress. The net benefit equals $440 ($500 – $60) million.

11-26 (20 min.) **Choosing customers.**

If Broadway accepts the additional business from Kelly, it would take an additional 500 machine-hours. If Broadway accepts all of Kelly's and Taylor's business for February, it would require 2,500 machine-hours (1,500 hours for Taylor and 1,000 hours for Kelly). Broadway has only 2,000 hours of machine capacity. It must, therefore, *choose how much* of the Taylor or Kelly *business to accept*.

To maximize operating income, Broadway should *maximize contribution margin per unit of the constrained resource*. (Fixed costs will remain unchanged at $100,000 regardless of the business Broadway chooses to accept in February, and is, therefore, irrelevant.) The contribution margin per unit of the constrained resource for each customer in January is:

	Taylor Corporation	Kelly Corporation
Contribution margin per machine-hour	$\dfrac{\$78,000}{1,500} = \$52$	$\dfrac{\$32,000}{500} = \$64$

Since the $80,000 of additional Kelly business in February is identical to jobs done in January, it will also have a contribution margin of $64 per machine-hour, which is greater than the contribution margin of $52 per machine-hour from Taylor. To maximize operating income, Broadway should first allocate all the capacity needed to take the Kelly Corporation business (1,000 machine-hours) and then allocate the remaining 1,000 (2,000 – 1,000) machine-hours to Taylor.

	Taylor Corporation	Kelly Corporation	Total
Contribution margin per machine-hour	$52	$64	
Machine-hours to be worked	× 1,000	× 1,000	
Contribution margin	$52,000	$64,000	$116,000
Fixed costs			100,000
Operating income			$ 16,000

11-28 (30 min.) **Equipment upgrade versus replacement.**

1. Based on the analysis in the table below, TechMech will be better off by $180,000 over three years if it replaces the current equipment.

Comparing Relevant Costs of Upgrade and Replace Alternatives	Over 3 years		Difference in favor of Replace (3) = (1) – (2)
	Upgrade (1)	Replace (2)	
Cash operating costs			
$140; $80 per desk × 6,000 desks per yr. × 3 yrs.	$2,520,000	$1,440,000	$1,080,000
Current disposal price		(600,000)	600,000
One time capital costs, written off periodically as depreciation	2,700,000	4,200,000	(1,500,000)
Total relevant costs	$5,220,000	$5,040,000	$ 180,000

Note that the book value of the current machine ($900,000) would either be written off as depreciation over three years under the upgrade option, or, all at once in the current year under the replace option. Its net effect would be the same in both alternatives: to increase costs by $900,000 over three years, hence it is irrelevant in this analysis.

2. Suppose the capital expenditure to replace the equipment is $X. From requirement 1, column (2), substituting for the one-time capital cost of replacement, the relevant cost of replacing is $1,440,000 − $600,000 + $X. From column (1), the relevant cost of upgrading is $5,220,000.

We want to find X such that $1,440,000 − $600,000 + $X < $5,220,000
(i.e., the cost of replacing is less than the cost of upgrading)

Solving the above inequality gives us $X < $5,220,000 − $840,000$
$X < $4,380,000.$

TechMech would prefer to replace, rather than upgrade, if the replacement cost of the new equipment does not exceed $4,380,000. Note that this result can also be obtained by taking the original replacement cost of $4,200,000 and adding to it the $180,000 difference in favor of replacement calculated in requirement 1.

3.   Suppose the units produced and sold over 3 years equal y. Using data from requirement 1, column (1), the relevant cost of upgrade would be $140y + $2,700,000, and from column (2), the relevant cost of replacing the equipment would be $80y − $600,000 + $4,200,000. TechMech would want to upgrade if

$$\$140y + \$2,700,000 < \$80y - \$600,000 + \$4,200,000$$
$$\$60y < \$900,000$$
$$y < \$900,000 \div \$60$$
$$y < 15,000 \text{ units}$$

and replace when y > 15,000 units over 3 years.

4.   Operating income for the first year under the upgrade and replace alternatives are shown below:

	Year 1	
	Upgrade (1)	Replace (2)
Revenues (6,000 × $500)	$3,000,000	$3,000,000
Cash operating costs		
$140; $80 per desk × 6,000 desks per year	840,000	480,000
Depreciation ($900,000[a] + $2,700,000) ÷ 3; $4,200,000 ÷ 3	1,200,000	1,400,000
Loss on disposal of old equipment (0; $900,000 − $600,000)	0	300,000
Total costs	2,040,000	2,180,000
Operating Income	$ 960,000	$ 820,000

[a]The book value of the current production equipment is $1,500,000 × 3 ÷ 5 = $900,000; it has a remaining useful life of 3 years.

First-year operating income is higher by $140,000 under the upgrade alternative, and Dan Doria, with his one-year horizon and operating income-based bonus, will choose the upgrade alternative, even though, as seen in requirement 1, the replace alternative is better in the long run for TechMech. This exercise illustrates the possible conflict between the decision model and the performance evaluation model.

11-30 (30 min.)   **Contribution approach, relevant costs**.

1.

Average one-way fare per passenger	$	500
Commission at 8% of $500		(40)
Net cash to Air Frisco per ticket	$	460
Average number of passengers per flight	×	200
Revenues per flight ($460 × 200)	$	92,000
Food and beverage cost per flight ($20 × 200)		4,000
Total contribution margin from passengers per flight	$	88,000

2.

If fare is	$	480.00
Commission at 8% of $480		(38.40)
Net cash per ticket		441.60
Food and beverage cost per ticket		20.00
Contribution margin per passenger	$	421.60
Total contribution margin from passengers per flight ($421.60 × 212)		$89,379.20

On the basis of quantitative factors alone, Air Frisco should decrease its fare to $480 because reducing the fare gives Air Frisco a higher contribution margin from passengers ($89,379.20 versus $88,000). What they lose in revenue, they more than make up for in volume.

3.   In evaluating whether Air Frisco should charter its plane to Travel International, we compare the charter alternative to the solution in requirement 2 because requirement 2 is preferred to requirement 1.

Under requirement 2, contribution from passengers	$89,379.20
Deduct fuel costs	14,000.00
Total contribution per flight	$75,379.20

Air Frisco gets $74,500 per flight from chartering the plane to Travel International. On the basis of quantitative financial factors, Air Frisco is better off not chartering the plane and, instead, lowering its own fares.

Other qualitative factors that Air Frisco should consider in coming to a decision are
   a. The *lower risk* from chartering its plane relative to the uncertainties regarding the number of passengers it might get on its scheduled flights.
   b. The *stability of the relationship* between Air Frisco and Travel International. If this is not a long-term arrangement, Air Frisco may lose current market share and not benefit from sustained charter revenues.

11-32 (20 min.) **Opportunity costs.**

1. The opportunity cost to Wolverine of producing the 2,000 units of Orangebo is the contribution margin lost on the 2,000 units of Rosebo that would have to be forgone, as computed below:

Selling price		$20
Variable costs per unit:		
Direct materials	$ 2	
Direct manufacturing labor	3	
Variable manufacturing overhead	2	
Variable marketing costs	4	11
Contribution margin per unit		$ 9
Contribution margin for 2,000 units		$ 18,000

The opportunity cost is $18,000. Opportunity cost is the maximum contribution to operating income that is given up by not using a limited resource in its next-best alternative use.

2. Contribution margin from manufacturing 2,000 units of Orangebo and purchasing 2,000 units of Rosebo from Buckeye is $16,000, as follows:

	Manufacture Orangebo	Purchase Rosebo	Total
Selling price	$15	$20	
Variable costs per unit:			
Purchase costs	–	14	
Direct materials	2		
Direct manufacturing labor	3		
Variable manufacturing costs	2		
Variable marketing overhead	2	4	
Variable costs per unit	9	18	
Contribution margin per unit	$ 6	$ 2	
Contribution margin from selling 2,000 units of Orangebo and 2,000 units of Rosebo	$12,000	$4,000	$16,000

As calculated in requirement 1, Wolverine's contribution margin from continuing to manufacture 2,000 units of Rosebo is $18,000. Accepting the Miami Company and Buckeye offer will cost Wolverine $2,000 ($16,000 – $18,000). Hence, Wolverine should refuse the Miami Company and Buckeye Corporation's offers.

3. The minimum price would be $9, the sum of the incremental costs as computed in requirement 2. This follows because, if Wolverine has surplus capacity, the opportunity cost = $0. For the short-run decision of whether to accept Orangebo's offer, fixed costs of Wolverine are irrelevant. Only the incremental costs need to be covered for it to be worthwhile for Wolverine to accept the Orangebo offer.

11-34 (35–40 min.) **Dropping a product line, selling more units.**

1.   The incremental revenue losses and incremental savings in cost by discontinuing the Tables product line follows:

	Difference: Incremental (Loss in Revenues) and Savings in Costs from Dropping Tables Line
Revenues	$(500,000)
Direct materials and direct manufacturing labor	300,000
Depreciation on equipment	0
Marketing and distribution	70,000
General administration	0
Corporate office costs	0
Total costs	370,000
Operating income (loss)	$(130,000)

Dropping the Tables product line results in revenue losses of $500,000 and cost savings of $370,000. Hence, Grossman Corporation's operating income will be $130,000 lower if it drops the Tables line.

Note that, by dropping the Tables product line, Home Furnishings will save none of the depreciation on equipment, general administration costs, and corporate office costs, but it will save variable manufacturing costs and all marketing and distribution costs on the Tables product line.

2.   Grossman's will generate incremental operating income of $128,000 from selling 4,000 additional tables and, hence, should try to increase table sales. The calculations follow:

	Incremental Revenues (Costs) and Operating Income
Revenues	$500,000
Direct materials and direct manufacturing labor	(300,000)
Cost of equipment written off as depreciation	(42,000)[*]
Marketing and distribution costs	(30,000)[†]
General administration costs	0[**]
Corporate office costs	0[**]
Operating income	$128,000

[*]Note that the additional costs of equipment are relevant future costs for the "selling more tables decision" because they represent incremental future costs that differ between the alternatives of selling and not selling additional tables.

[†]Current marketing and distribution costs which varies with number of shipments = $70,000 – $40,000 = $30,000. As the sales of tables double, the number of shipments will double, resulting in incremental marketing and distribution costs of (2 × $30,000) – $30,000 = $30,000.

[**]General administration and corporate office costs will be unaffected if Grossman decides to sell more tables. Hence, these costs are irrelevant for the decision.

3. Relevant-Revenue and Relevant-Cost Analysis for Closing Northern Division and Opening Southern Division

	(Loss in Revenues) and Savings in Costs from Closing Northern Division (1)	Incremental Revenues and (Incremental Costs) from Opening Southern Division (2)
Revenues	$(1,500,000)	$1,500,000
Variable direct materials and direct manufacturing labor costs	825,000	(825,000)
Equipment cost written off as depreciation	0	(100,000)
Marketing and distribution costs	205,000	(205,000)
Division general administration costs	330,000	(330,000)
Corporate office costs	0	0
Total costs	1,360,000	(1,460,000)
Effect on operating income (loss)	$ (140,000)	$ 40,000

Column 1, presents the relevant loss of revenues and the relevant savings in costs from closing the Northern Division. As the calculations show, Grossman's operating income would decrease by $140,000 if it shut down the Northern Division (loss in revenues of $1,500,000 versus savings in costs of $1,360,000).

Grossman will save variable manufacturing costs, marketing and distribution costs, and division general administration costs by closing the Northern Division but equipment-related depreciation and corporate office allocations are irrelevant to the decision. Equipment-related costs are irrelevant because they are past costs (and the equipment has zero disposal price). Corporate office costs are irrelevant because Grossman will not save any actual corporate office costs by closing the Northern Division. The corporate office costs that used to be allocated to the Northern Division will be allocated to other divisions.

4.   Column 2, presents the relevant revenues and relevant costs of opening the Southern Division. Grossman should open the Southern Division because it would increase operating income by $40,000. The cost of equipment written off as depreciation is relevant because it is an expected future cost that Grossman will incur only if it opens the Southern Division.

11-36 (30 min.)   **Make versus buy, activity-based costing, opportunity costs.**

1.   Relevant costs under buy alternative:
     Purchases, 10,000 × $8.20   __$82,000__

Relevant costs under make alternative:

Direct materials	$40,000
Direct manufacturing labor	20,000
Variable manufacturing overhead	15,000
Inspection, setup, materials handling	2,000
Machine rent	3,000
Total relevant costs under make alternative	__$80,000__

The allocated fixed plant administration, taxes, and insurance will not change if Ace makes or buys the chains. Hence, these costs are irrelevant to the make-or-buy decision. The analysis indicates that Ace should make and not buy the chains from the outside supplier.

2.   Relevant costs under the make alternative:
     Relevant costs (as computed in requirement 1)   __$80,000__

Relevant costs under the buy alternative:

Costs of purchases (10,000 × $8.20)	$82,000
Additional fixed costs	16,000
Additional contribution margin from using the space where the chains were made to upgrade the bicycles by adding mud flaps and reflector bars, 10,000 × ($20 – $18)	(20,000)
Total relevant costs under the buy alternative	__$78,000__

Ace should now buy the chains from an outside vendor and use its own capacity to upgrade its own bicycles.

3.   In this requirement, the decision on mud flaps and reflectors is irrelevant to the analysis.

Cost of manufacturing chains:

Variable costs, ($4 + $2 + $1.50 = $7.50) × 6,200	$46,500
Batch costs, $200/batch[a] × 8 batches	1,600
Machine rent	3,000
	__$51,100__

Cost of buying chains, $8.20 × 6,200   __$50,840__

[a]$2,000 ÷ 10 batches

In this case, Ace should buy the chains from the outside vendor.

11-38 (25 min.) **Closing down divisions**.

1.

	Division A	Division D
Sales	$530,000	$450,000
Variable costs of goods sold ($450,000×0.90; $390,000×0.95)	405,000	370,500
Variable S,G & A ($100,000×0.60; $120,000×0.80)	60,000	96,000
Total variable costs	465,000	466,500
Contribution margin	$ 65,000	$(16,500)

2.

	Division A	Division D
Fixed costs of goods sold ($450,000 − $405,000; $390,000 − $370,500)	$45,000	$19,500
Fixed S,G & A ($100,000 − $60,000; $120,000 − $96,000)	40,000	24,000
Total fixed costs	$85,000	$43,500
Fixed costs savings if shutdown ($85,000×0.60; $43,500×0.60)	$51,000	$26,100

Division A's contribution margin of $65,000 more than covers its avoidable fixed costs of $51,000. The difference of $14,000 helps cover the company's unavoidable fixed costs. Since $51,000 of Division A's fixed costs are avoidable, the remaining $34,000 is unavoidable and will be incurred regardless of whether Division A continues to operate. Division A's $20,000 loss is the rest of the unavoidable fixed costs ($34,000 − $14,000). If Division A is closed, the remaining divisions will need to generate sufficient profits to cover the entire $34,000 unavoidable fixed cost. Consequently, Division A should not be closed since it helps defray $14,000 of this cost.

In contrast, Division D earns a negative contribution margin, which means its revenues are less than its variable costs. Division D also generates $26,100 of avoidable fixed costs. Based strictly on financial considerations, Division D should be closed because the company will save $42,600 ($26,100 + $16,500).

An alternative set of calculations is as follows:

	Division A	Division D
Total variable costs	$465,000	$466,500
Avoidable fixed costs if shutdown	51,000	26,100
Total cost savings if shutdown	516,000	492,600
Loss of revenues if shutdown	530,000	450,000
Cost savings minus loss of revenues	$ (14,000)	$ 42,600

3. Before deciding to close Division D, management should consider
    o the *role* that the Division's product line plays relative to other product lines.
      o If it *attracts customers* to the company, then dropping Division D may have a detrimental effect on the revenues of the remaining divisions.
    o the impact on the *morale* of the remaining employees if Division D is closed.
      o Talented employees may *leave*.

11-40 (30–40 min.) **Optimal product mix.**

1. Let D represent the batches of Della's Delight made and sold.
    Let B represent the batches of Bonny's Bourbon made and sold.
    The contribution margin per batch of Della's Delight is $300.
    The contribution margin per batch of Bonny's Bourbon is $250.

    The LP formulation for the decision is:

    Maximize $300D + $250 B
    Subject to   30D + 15B   ≤ 660 (Mixing Department constraint)
                 15B   ≤ 270 (Filling Department constraint)
                 10D + 15B   ≤ 300 (Baking Department constraint)

2. The graph shows the optimal corner is the point (18, 8) i.e., 18 batches of Della's Delights and 8 of Bonny's Bourbons.

Graphic Solution to Find Optimal Mix, Della Simpson, Inc.

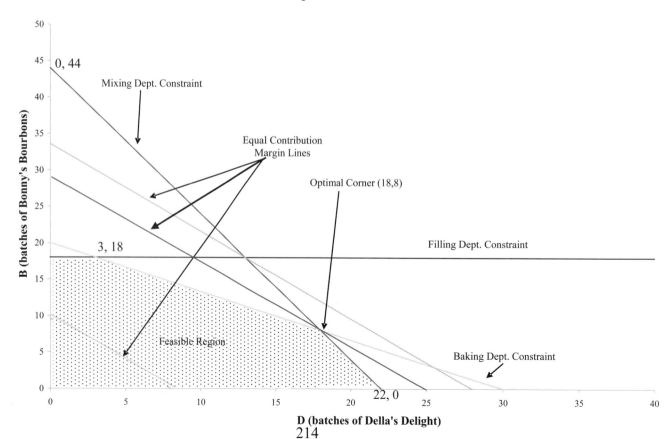

Della Simpson Production Model

We next calculate the optimal production mix using the trial-and-error method.

The corner point where the Mixing Dept. and Baking Dept. constraints intersect can be calculated as (18, 8) by solving:

$$30D + 15B = 660 \text{ (1) Mixing Dept. constraint}$$
$$10D + 15B = 300 \text{ (2) Baking Dept. constraint}$$

Subtracting (2) from (1), we have
$$20D = 360$$
$$\text{or } D = 18$$

Substituting in (2)
$$(10 \times 18) + 15B = 300$$
that is,
$$15B = 300 - 180 = 120$$
or
$$B = 8$$

The corner point where the Filling and Baking Department constraints intersect can be calculated as (3,18) by substituting B = 18 (Filling Department constraint) into the Baking Department constraint:

$$10 D + (15 \times 18) = 300$$
$$10 D = 300 - 270 = 30$$
$$D = 3$$

The feasible region, defined by 5 corner points, is shaded in the graph. We next use the trial-and-error method to check the contribution margins at each of the five corner points of the area of feasible solutions.

Trial	Corner (D,B)	Total Contribution Margin
1	(0,0)	($300 × 0) + ($250 × 0) = $0
2	(22,0)	($300 × 22) + ($250 × 0) = $6,600
3	*(18,8)*	*($300 × 18) + ($250 × 8) = $7,400*
4	(3,18)	($300 × 3) + ($250 × 18) = $5,400
5	(0,18)	($300 × 0) + ($250 × 18) = $4,500

The optimal solution that maximizes contribution margin and operating income is 18 batches of Della's Delights and 8 batches of Bonny's Bourbons.

11-42 (30 min.) **Product mix, constrained resource.**

1.

	Units (1)	Machine Hrs Per Unit (2) = Var. Mach. Cost/Unit ÷ $200/Hour	Machine Hrs Demanded (3) = (1) × (2)
Nealy	1,800	$600 ÷ $200 = 3	5,400
Tersa	4,500	$500 ÷ $200 = 2.5	11,250
Pelta	39,000	$200 ÷ $200 = 1	39,000
Total			55,650

2.

	Nealy	Tersa	Pelta
Selling price	$3,000	$2,100	$800
Variable costs:			
Direct materials	750	500	100
Variable machining	600	500	200
Sales commissions (5%, 5%, 10%)	150	105	80
Total variable costs	1,500	1,105	380
Contribution margin per unit	$1,500	$ 995	$420

3. Total machine hours needed to satisfy demand exceed the machine hours available (55,650 needed > 50,000 available). Consequently Marion Taylor needs to evaluate these products based on the contribution margin per machine hour.

	Nealy	Tersa	Pelta
Unit contribution margin	$1,500	$995	$420
Machine-hours (MH) per unit	÷3 MH	÷2.5 MH	÷1 MH
Unit contribution margin per MH	$ 500	$398	$420

Based on this analysis, Marion Taylor should produce to meet the demand for products with the highest unit contribution margin per machine hour, first Nealy, then Pelta, and finally Tersa. The optimal product mix will be as follows:

Nealy	1,800 units	=	5,400 MH
Pelta	39,000 units	=	39,000 MH
Tersa	2,240 (5,600 MH ÷ 2.5 MH/unit) units	=	5,600 MH (50,000 — 5,400 — 39,000)
Total			50,000 MH

4. The optimal product mix in Part 3 satisfies the demand for Nealy and Pelta and leaves only 2,260 units (4,500 − 2,240) of Tersa unfilled. These remaining units of Tersa require 5,650 machine hours (2,260 units × 2.5 MH per unit). The maximum price Marion Taylor is willing to pay for extra machine hours is $398, which is the unit contribution per machine hour for additional units of Tersa. That is, total cost per machine-hour for these units will be $398 + $200 (variable cost per machine-hour) = $598 per machine-hour.

CHAPTER 12
PRICING DECISIONS AND COST MANAGEMENT

12-2 **Not necessarily**. For a one-time-only special order, the relevant costs are only those costs that will change as a result of accepting the order. In this case, full product costs will rarely be relevant. It is more likely that *full product costs will be relevant costs for long-run pricing decisions*.

12-4 **Activity-based costing** helps managers in pricing decisions in two ways.
1. It gives managers *more accurate* product-cost information for making pricing decisions.
2. It helps managers to *manage costs* during value engineering by identifying the cost impact of eliminating, reducing, or changing various activities.

12-6 A **target cost per unit** is the *estimated long-run cost per unit of a product* (or service) that, when sold at the target price, enables the company to achieve the targeted operating income per unit.

12-8 A **value-added cost** is a cost that customers are willing to pay more for:
o materials,
o direct labor,
o tools,
o machinery.

A **nonvalue-added cost** is a cost that customers do not want to pay for:
o transporting goods around the facility
o rework,
o scrap,
o expediting (sometimes)
o breakdown maintenance.

12-10 **Cost-plus pricing** is a pricing approach in which managers *add a markup to cost* in order to determine price.

12-12 Two examples where the **difference in the costs** of two products or services is much **smaller** than the **differences in their prices** follow:
1. The difference in prices charged for a telephone call, hotel room, or car rental during *busy versus slack periods* is often much greater than the difference in costs to provide these services.
2. The difference in *costs for an airplane seat* sold to a passenger traveling on business or a passenger traveling for pleasure is roughly the same. However, airline companies price discriminate.

12-14 Three benefits of using a **product life-cycle reporting** format are:
1. The *full set of revenues and costs* associated with each product becomes more visible.
2. Differences among products in the *percentage of total costs committed at early stages in* the life cycle are highlighted.
3. *Interrelationships* among business function cost categories are highlighted.

12-16 (20–30 min.) Relevant-cost approach to pricing decisions, special order.

1.	Relevant revenues, $4.00 × 1,000		$4,000
	Relevant costs		
	Direct materials, $1.60 × 1,000	$1,600	
	Direct manufacturing labor, $0.90 × 1,000	900	
	Variable manufacturing overhead, $0.70 × 1,000	700	
	Variable selling costs, 0.05 × $4,000	200	
	Total relevant costs		3,400
	Increase in operating income		$ 600

This calculation assumes that:

   a. *The monthly fixed manufacturing overhead of $150,000 and $65,000 of monthly <u>fixed</u> marketing costs will be <u>unchanged</u> by acceptance of the 1,000 unit order.*
   b. *The price charged and the volumes sold to <u>other customers are not affected</u> by the special order.*

2. The president's reasoning is defective on at least two counts:
   a. The <u>*inclusion of irrelevant costs*</u>—assuming the monthly fixed manufacturing overhead of $150,000 will be unchanged; it is irrelevant to the decision.
   b. The <u>*exclusion of relevant costs*</u>—variable selling costs (5% of the selling price) are excluded.

3. Key issues are:
   a. Will the existing customer base demand price reductions? If this 1,000-tape order is not independent of other sales, cutting the price from $5.00 to $4.00 can have a large negative effect on total revenues.
   b. Is the 1,000-tape order a one-time-only order, or is there the possibility of sales in subsequent months? The fact that the customer is not in Dill Company's "normal marketing channels" does not necessarily mean it is a one-time-only order. Indeed, the sale could well open a new marketing channel. Dill Company should be reluctant to consider only short-run variable costs for pricing long-run business.

12-18 (15-20 min.) Short-run pricing, capacity constraints.

1. Per kilogram of hard cheese:

Milk (10 liters × $1.50 per liter)	$15
Direct manufacturing labor	5
Variable manufacturing overhead	3
Total manufacturing cost	$23

If Vermont Hills can get all the Holstein milk it needs, and has sufficient production capacity, then, the minimum price it should charge for the hard cheese is the variable cost per kilo $23.

2. If milk is in short supply, then each kilo of hard cheese displaces 2.5 kilos of soft cheese (10 liters of milk per kilo of hard cheese versus 4 liters of milk per kilo of soft cheese). Then, for the hard cheese, the minimum price Vermont should charge is the variable cost per kilo of hard cheese plus the contribution margin from 2.5 kilos of soft cheese, or,

$$\$23 + (2.5 \times \$8 \text{ per kilo}) = \$43 \text{ per kilo}$$

That is, if milk is in short supply, Vermont should not agree to produce any hard cheese unless the buyer is willing to pay at least $43 per kilo.

12-20 (25–30 min.) **Target operating income, value-added costs, service company.**

1. The classification of total costs in 2009 into value-added, nonvalue-added, or in the gray area in between follows:

	Value Added (1)	Gray Area (2)	Nonvalue-added (3)	Total (4) = (1)+(2)+(3)
Doing calculations and preparing drawings 75% × $400,000	$300,000			$300,000
Checking calculations and drawings 4% × $400,000		$16,000		16,000
Correcting errors found in drawings 7% × $400,000			$28,000	28,000
Making changes in response to client requests 6% × $400,000	24,000			24,000
Correcting errors to meet government building code, 8% × $400,000			32,000	32,000
Total professional labor costs	324,000	16,000	60,000	400,000
Administrative and support costs at 40% ($160,000 ÷ $400,000) of professional labor costs	129,600	6,400	24,000	160,000
Travel	18,000		—	18,000
Total	$471,600	$22,400	$84,000	$578,000

Doing calculations and responding to client requests for changes are value-added costs because customers perceive these costs as necessary for the service of preparing architectural drawings. Costs incurred on correcting errors in drawings and making changes because they were inconsistent with building codes are nonvalue-added costs. Customers do not perceive these costs as necessary and would be unwilling to pay for them. Carasco should seek to *eliminate these costs by making sure that all associates are well-informed regarding building code requirements and by training associates to improve the quality of their drawings*. Checking calculations and drawings is in the gray area (some, but not all, checking may be needed). There is room for disagreement on these classifications. For example, checking calculations may be regarded as value added.

2.   Reduction in professional labor-hours by
        a. Correcting errors in drawings (7% × 8,000)   560 hours
        b. Correcting errors to conform to building code (8% × 8,000)   640 hours
           Total   1,200 hours
        Cost savings in professional labor costs (1,200 hours × $50) $ 60,000
        Cost savings in variable administrative and support
           costs (40% × $60,000)   24,000
        Total cost savings $ 84,000
        Current operating income in 2009 $102,000
        Add cost savings from eliminating errors   84,000
        Operating income in 2009 if errors eliminated $186,000

This solution assumes that the administrative support costs can also be proportionately reduced.

3.   Currently 85% × 8,000 hours = 6,800 hours are billed to clients generating revenues of
        $680,000. The remaining 15% of professional labor-hours (15% × 8,000 = 1,200 hours) is
        lost in making corrections. Carasco bills clients at the rate of $680,000 ÷ 6,800 = $100 per
        professional labor-hour. If the 1,200 professional labor-hours currently not being billed to
        clients were billed to clients, Carasco's revenues would increase by 1,200 hours × $100 =
        $120,000 from $680,000 to $800,000.

Costs remain unchanged
   Professional labor costs $400,000
   Administrative and support (40% × $400,000)   160,000
   Travel   18,000
   Total costs $578,000
Carasco's operating income would be
   Revenues $800,000
   Total costs   578,000
   Operating income $222,000

12-22 (20 min.)   **Target costs, effect of product-design changes on product costs**.

1. and 2. Manufacturing costs of HJ6 in 2008 and 2009 are as follows:

	2008		2009	
	Total **(1)**	**Per Unit** **(2) =** **(1) ÷ 3,500**	**Total** **(3)**	**Per Unit** **(4) =** **(3) ÷ 4,000**
Direct materials, $1,200 × 3,500; $1,100 × 4,000	$4,200,000	$1,200	$4,400,000	$1,100
Batch-level costs, $8,000 × 70; $7,500 × 80	560,000	160	600,000	150
Manuf. operations costs, $55 × 21,000; $50 × 22,000	1,155,000	330	1,100,000	275
Engineering change costs, $12,000 × 14; $10,000 × 10	168,000	48	100,000	25
Total	$6,083,000	$1,738	$6,200,000	$1,550

3. $$\begin{array}{l}\text{Target manufacturing cost}\\ \text{per unit of HJ6 in 2009}\end{array} = \begin{array}{l}\text{Manufacturing cost}\\ \text{per unit in 2008}\end{array} \times 90\%$$

$$= \$1,738 \times 0.90 = \$1,564.20$$

Actual manufacturing cost per unit of HJ6 in 2009 was $1,550. Hence, Medical Instruments did achieve its target manufacturing cost reduction of 10%.

4.   To **reduce the manufacturing cost per unit** in 2009, Medical Instruments reduced the cost per unit in each of the four cost categories—direct materials costs, batch-level costs, manufacturing operations costs, and engineering change costs. It also reduced machine-hours and number of engineering changes made—the quantities of the cost drivers. In 2008, Medical Instruments used 6 machine-hours per unit of HJ6 (21,000 machine-hours ÷3,500 units). In 2009, Medical Instruments used 5.5 machine-hours per unit of HJ6 (22,000 machine-hours ÷ 4,000 units). Medical Instruments reduced engineering changes from 14 in 2008 to 10 in 2009. Medical Instruments achieved these gains through value engineering activities that retained only those product features that customers wanted while eliminating nonvalue-added activities and costs.

12-24 (20–25 min.) **Cost-plus, target pricing, working backwards.**

1. For this question, the missing pieces are not obvious. Given the information that you have, the easiest way to solve the problem is to _find profit_, work backwards to _selling price_, and use the markup to find _variable costs_. To find profit, you need to calculate income from return on investment. Once you have profit, since you know full cost, you can compute selling price and then the percent markup on full cost. Once you know selling price, since you are given the markup percentage on variable costs, you can back into the variable costs.

Investment	$2,400,000
Return on investment	20%
Operating income (20% × $2,400,000)	$480,000
Operating income per unit of RF17 ($480,000 ÷ 20,000)	$24
Full cost per unit of RF17	$300
Selling price ($300 + $24)	$324
Markup percentage on full cost ($24 ÷ $300)	8%

With a 50% markup on variable costs,
Selling price of RF17 = Variable cost per unit of RF17 × 1.50, so:

$$\text{Variable costs per unit of RF17} = \frac{\text{Selling price of RF17}}{1.50} = \frac{\$324}{1.50} = \$216$$

2.
Fixed cost per unit = $300 − $216 =	$84
Total fixed costs = $84 per unit × 20,000 units =	$1,680,000
At a price of $348, sales = 20,000 units × 0.90	18,000
Revenues ($348 × 18,000)	$6,264,000
Variable costs ($216 × 18,000)	3,888,000
Contribution margin ($132 × 18,000)	2,376,000
Fixed costs	1,680,000
Operating income	$ 696,000

If Waterbuy increases the selling price of RF17 to $348, its operating income will be $696,000. This would be more than the $480,000 operating income Waterbury earns by selling 20,000 units at a price of $324, so, if its forecast is accurate, and based on financial considerations alone, Waterbury should increase the selling price to $348.

3.
Target investment in 2009	$2,100,000
Target return on investment	20%
Target operating income in 2009, 20% × $2,100,000	$420,000
Anticipated revenues in 2009, $315 × 20,000	$6,300,000
Less target operating income in 2009	420,000
Target full costs in 2009	5,880,000
Less: total target fixed costs	1,680,000
Total target variable costs in 2009	$4,200,000

Target variable cost per unit in 2009, $4,200,000 ÷ 20,000 = $210

12-26 (30 min.)   **Relevant-cost approach to pricing decisions.**

1.

Revenues (1,000 crates at $100 per crate)		$100,000
Variable costs:		
Manufacturing	$40,000	
Marketing	14,000	
Total variable costs		54,000
Contribution margin		46,000
Fixed costs:		
Manufacturing	$20,000	
Marketing	16,000	
Total fixed costs		36,000
Operating income		$ 10,000

Normal markup percentage: $46,000 ÷ $54,000 = 85.19% of total variable costs.

2. *Only the manufacturing-cost category is relevant* to considering this special order; no additional marketing costs will be incurred. The relevant manufacturing costs for the 200-crate special order are:

Variable manufacturing cost per unit	
$40 × 200 crates	$ 8,000
Special packaging	2,000
Relevant manufacturing costs	$10,000

Any price *above $50 per crate* ($10,000 ÷ 200) will make a *positive contribution* to operating income. We do need to consider the relevant range. The relevant range for the fixed manufacturing costs is from 500 to 1,500 crates per month; the special order will increase production from 1,000 to 1,200 crates per month, inside the range. Therefore, based on financial considerations, Stardom should *accept* the 200-crate special order at $55 per crate that will generate revenues of $11,000 ($55 × 200) and relevant (incremental) costs of $10,000.

3. If the new customer is likely to remain in business, Stardom should consider whether a strictly short-run focus is appropriate. For example, what is the likelihood of demand from other customers increasing over time? If Stardom accepts the 200-crate special offer for more than one month, it may preclude accepting other customers at prices exceeding $55 per crate. Moreover, the existing customers may learn about Stardom's willingness to set a price based on variable cost plus a small contribution margin. The longer the time frame over which Stardom keeps selling 200 crates of canned peaches at $55 a crate, the more likely it is that existing customers will approach Stardom for their own special price reductions. If the new customer wants the contract to extend over a longer time period, Stardom should negotiate a higher price.

12-28 (25 min.) **Cost-plus, target pricing, working backward**.

1. In the following table, work backwards from operating income to calculate the selling price

Selling price	$	9.45 (plug)
Less: Variable cost per unit		2.50
Unit contribution margin	$	6.95
Number of units produced and sold		×500,000 units
Contribution margin	$3,475,000	
Less: Fixed costs	3,250,000	
Operating income	$ 225,000	

a) Total sales revenue = $9.45×500,000 units = $4,725,000
b) Selling price = $9.45 (from above)
Alternatively,

Operating income	$ 225,000
Add fixed costs	3,250,000
Contribution margin	3,475,000
Add variable costs ($2.50 × 500,000 units)	1,250,000
Sales revenue	$4,725,000

$$\text{Selling price} = \frac{\text{Sales revenue}}{\text{Units sold}} = \frac{\$4,725,000}{500,000} = \$9.45$$

c) $$\text{Rate of return on investment} = \frac{\text{Operating income}}{\text{Total investment in assets}} = \frac{\$225,000}{2,500,000} = 9\%$$

d) Markup % on full cost
Total cost = ($2.50×500,000 units) + $3,250,000 = $4,500,000

$$\text{Unit cost} = \frac{\$4,500,000}{500,000 \text{ units}} = \$9$$

$$\text{Markup \%} = \frac{\$9.45 - \$9}{\$9} = 5\%$$

$$\text{Or} \quad \frac{\$4,725,000 - \$4,500,000}{\$4,500,000} = 5\%$$

2.

New fixed costs	= $3,250,000 − $250,000 = $3,000,000
New variable costs	= $2.50 − $0.50 = $2
New total costs	= ($2×500,000 units) + $3,000,000 = $4,000,000
New total revenue (5% markup)	= $4,000,000×1.05 = $4,200,000
New selling price	= $4,200,000 ÷ 500,000 units = $8.40
Alternatively,	
New unit cost	= $4,000,000 ÷ 500,000 units = $8
New selling price	= $8×1.05 = $8.40

3.   New units sold = $500,000 × 90% = $450,000 units

Budgeted Operating Income
For the year ending December 31, 20xx

Revenues ($8.40×450,000 units)	$3,780,000
Variable costs ($2.00×450,000 units)	900,000
Contribution margin	2,880,000
Fixed costs	3,000,000
Operating income (loss)	$ (120,000)

12-30 (25 min.) **Cost-plus, target return on investment pricing.**

1. Target operating income = Return on capital in dollars = $13,000,000 × 10% = $1,300,000

2.

Revenues*	$6,000,000
Variable costs [($3.50 + $1.50)×500,000 cases	2,500,000
Contribution margin	3,500,000
Fixed costs ($1,000,000 + $700,000 + $500,000)	2,200,000
Operating income (from requirement 1)	$1,300,000

 * solve backwards for revenues

$$\text{Selling price} = \frac{\$6,000,000}{500,000 \text{ cases}} = \$12 \text{ per case.}$$

Markup % on full cost
    Full cost = $2,500,000 + $2,200,000 = $4,700,000
    Unit cost = $4,700,000 ÷ 500,000 cases = $9.40 per case

$$\text{Markup \% on full cost} = \frac{\$12 - \$9.40}{\$9.40} = 27.66\%$$

3.

Budgeted Operating Income
For the year ending December 31, 20xx

Revenues ($14×475,000 cases*)	$6,650,000
Variable costs ($5×475,000 cases)	2,375,000
Contribution margin	4,275,000
Fixed costs	2,200,000
Operating income	$2,075,000

 * New units = 500,000 cases×95% = 475,000 cases

$$\text{Return on investment} = \frac{\$2,075,000}{\$13,000,000} = 15.96\%$$

Yes, increasing the selling price is a good idea because operating income increases without increasing invested capital, which results in a higher return on investment. The new return on investment exceeds the 10% target return on investment.

12-32 (25 min.) **Cost-plus and market-based pricing.**

1.   California Temps' full cost per hour of supplying contract labor is

Variable costs	$12
Fixed costs ($240,000 ÷ 80,000 hours)	3
Full cost per hour	$15

Price per hour at full cost plus 20% = $15 × 1.20 = $18 per hour.

2.   Contribution margins for different prices and demand realizations are as follows:

Price per Hour (1)	Variable Cost per Hour (2)	Contribution Margin per Hour (3) = (1) – (2)	Demand in Hours (4)	Total Contribution (5) = (3) × (4)
$16	$12	$4	120,000	$480,000
17	**12**	**5**	100,000	**500,000**
18	12	6	80,000	480,000
19	12	7	70,000	490,000
20	12	8	60,000	480,000

Fixed costs will remain the same regardless of the demand realizations. Fixed costs are, therefore, *irrelevant* since they do not differ among the alternatives.

The table above indicates that California Temps can maximize contribution margin and operating income by charging a price of $17 per hour.

3.   The *cost-plus approach* to pricing in requirement 1 *does not consider the effect of prices on demand*. The approach in requirement 2 models the interaction between price and demand and determines the optimal level of profitability using concepts of relevant costs. The two different approaches lead to two different prices. As the chapter describes, *pricing decisions should consider both demand or market considerations and supply or cost factors*.

12-34 (25–30 min.)   **Life-cycle costing.**

1.

Projected Life Cycle Income Statement

Revenues [$500×(16,000 + 4,800)]	$10,400,000
Variable costs:	
Production [$225×(16,000 + 4,800)]	4,680,000
Distribution [($20×16,000) + ($22×4,800)]	425,600
Contribution margin	5,294,400
Fixed costs:	
Design costs	700,000
Production ($9,000×48 mos.)	432,000
Marketing [($3,000×32 mos.) + ($1,000×16 mos.)]	112,000
Distribution [($2,000×32 mos.) + ($1,000×16 mos.)]	80,000
Life cycle operating income	$ 3,970,400

$$\text{Average profit per desk} = \frac{\$3,970,400}{(16,000+4,800)} = \$190.88$$

2.

Projected Life Cycle Income Statement

Revenues ($400×16,000)	$6,400,000
Variable costs:	
Production ($225×16,000)	3,600,000
Distribution ($20×16,000)	320,000
Contribution margin	2,480,000
Fixed costs:	
Design costs	700,000
Production ($9,000×32 mos.)	288,000
Marketing ($3,000×32 mos.)	96,000
Distribution ($2,000×32 mos.)	64,000
Life cycle operating income	$1,332,000

The new desk design is still profitable even if FFM drops the product after only 32 months of production. However, the operating income per unit falls to only $83.25 ($\frac{\$1,332,000}{16,000 \text{ desks}}$) per desk.

3.

Life cycle operating income (requirement 2)	$1,332,000
Additional fixed production costs ($9,000×16 mos.)	144,000
Revised life cycle operating income	$1,188,000

No, the answer does not change even if FFM continues to incur the fixed production costs for the full 48 months. The revised operating income for the new executive desk becomes $1,188,000, which translates into $74.25 ($\frac{\$1,188,000}{16,000 \text{ desks}}$) operating income per desk.

12-36 (25 min.) **Ethics and pricing.**

1. Baker prices at full product costs plus a mark-up of 10% = $80,000 + 10% of $80,000 = $80,000 + $8,000 = $88,000.

2.   The incremental costs of the order are as follows:

Direct materials	$40,000
Direct manufacturing labor	10,000
30% of overhead costs (30% × $30,000)	9,000
Incremental costs	$59,000

Any bid above $59,000 will generate a positive contribution margin for Baker. *Baker may prefer to use full product costs because it regards the new ball-bearings order as a long-term business relationship rather than a special order.* For a business to be profitable in the long run, it needs to recover *both* its variable and its fixed product costs. Using only variable costs may tempt the manager to engage in excessive long-run price cutting as long as prices give a positive contribution margin.

3. Not using full product costs (including an allocation of fixed overhead) to price the order, particularly if it is in *direct contradiction of company policy*, may be unethical. In assessing the situation, the specific "Standards of Ethical Conduct for Management Accountants," described in Chapter 1 (p. 16), that the management accountant should consider are listed below.

Competence
Clear reports using relevant and reliable information should be prepared. Reports prepared on the basis of excluding certain fixed costs that should be included would violate the management accountant's responsibility for competence. It is unethical for Lazarus to suggest that Decker change the cost numbers that were prepared for the bearings order and for Decker to change the numbers in order to make Lazarus's performance look good.

Integrity
The management accountant has a responsibility to avoid actual or apparent conflicts of interest and advise all appropriate parties of any potential conflict. Lazarus's motivation for wanting Decker to reduce costs was precisely to earn a larger bonus. This action could be viewed as violating the standard for integrity. The Standards of Ethical Conduct require the management accountant to communicate favorable as well as unfavorable information. In this regard, both Lazarus's and Decker's behavior (if Decker agrees to reduce the cost of the order) could be viewed as unethical.

Credibility
The Standards of Ethical Conduct for Management Accountants require that information should be fairly and objectively communicated and that all relevant information should be disclosed. From a management accountant's standpoint, reducing fixed overhead costs in deciding on the price to bid are clearly violating both of these precepts. For the reasons cited above, the behavior described by Lazarus and Decker (if he goes along with Lazarus's wishes) is unethical.

Decker should indicate to Lazarus that the costs were correctly computed and that determining prices on the basis of full product costs plus a mark-up of 10% are required by company policy. If Lazarus still insists on making the changes and reducing the costs of the order, Decker should raise the matter with Lazarus's superior. If, after taking all these steps, there is continued pressure to understate the costs, Decker should consider resigning from the company, rather than engaging in unethical behavior.

CHAPTER 13
STRATEGY, BALANCED SCORECARD, AND
STRATEGIC PROFITABILITY ANALYSIS

13-2 The **five key forces** to consider in industry analysis are:
(a) *competitors*,
(b) potential *entrants* into the market,
(c) equivalent *products*,
(d) bargaining power of *customers*,
(e) bargaining power of input *suppliers*.

13-4 A **customer preference map** describes how different *competitors perform* across various *product attributes* desired by customers, such as price, quality, customer service and product features.

13-6 The four key perspectives in the **balanced scorecard** are:
(1) *Financial* perspective—the *profitability* of the strategy,
(2) *Customer* perspective—the success in the targeted customer and market segments,
(3) *Internal business process* perspective—focuses on internal operations to increase value to customers and shareholders
(4) *Learning and growth* perspective—the capabilities the organization must excel at to achieve superior internal processes.

13-8 A good balanced **scorecard design** has several features:
1. It tells the story of a company's *strategy* by articulating a sequence of *cause-and-effect* relationships.
2. It helps to *communicate the strategy* to all members of the organization by translating the strategy into a coherent and linked set of understandable and measurable operational targets.
3. It places *strong emphasis on financial objectives and measures* in for-profit companies. Nonfinancial measures are regarded as part of a program to achieve future financial performance.
4. It *limits* the *measures* to only those that are *critical* to the implementation of strategy.
5. It *highlights tradeoffs* that managers may make when they fail to consider operational and financial measures together.

13-10 Three key components in doing a **strategic analysis of operating income** are:
1. The *growth* component which measures the change in operating income attributable solely to the change in quantity of output sold from one year to the next.
2. The *price-recovery* component which measures the change in operating income attributable solely to changes in the prices of inputs and outputs from one year to the next.
3. The *productivity* component which measures the change in costs attributable to a change in the quantity and mix of inputs used in the current year relative to the quantity and mix of inputs that would have been used in the previous year to produce current year output.

13-12 **Engineered costs** result from a cause-and-effect relationship between the cost driver, output, and the (direct or indirect) resources used to produce that output. **Discretionary costs** arise from periodic (usually annual) decisions regarding the maximum amount to be incurred. There is no measurable cause-and-effect relationship between output and resources used.

13-14 A **partial productivity measure** is the quantity of output produced divided by the quantity of an individual input used (e.g., direct materials or direct manufacturing labor).

13-16 (15 min.) **Balanced scorecard.**

1.   La Quinta's 2009 strategy is a *cost leadership* strategy. La Quinta plans to grow by producing high-quality boxes at a low cost delivered to customers in a timely manner. La Quinta's boxes are not differentiated, and there are many other manufacturers who produce similar boxes.

2.
Customer Preference Map for Corrugated Boxes

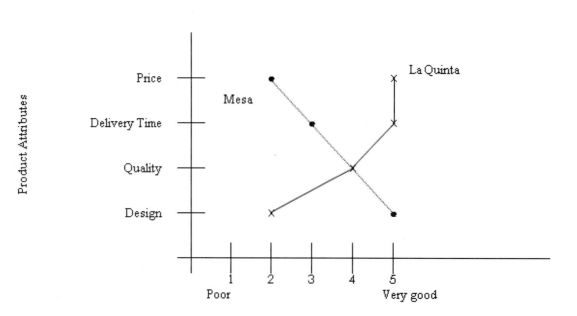

3. Measures that we would expect to see on a La Quinta's balanced scorecard for 2009 are

Financial Perspective
(1) Operating income from productivity gain,
(2) operating income from growth,
(3) cost reductions in key areas.
These measures evaluate whether La Quinta has successfully reduced costs and generated growth through cost leadership.

Customer Perspective
(1) Market share in corrugated boxes market,
(2) new customers,
(3) customer satisfaction index.
The logic is that improvements in these customer measures are leading indicators of whether La Quinta's cost leadership strategy is succeeding with its customers and helping it to achieve superior financial performance.

Internal Business Process Perspective
(1) Productivity,
(2) order delivery time,
(3) on-time delivery,
(4) number of major process improvements.
Improvements in these measures are key drivers of achieving cost leadership and are expected to lead to more satisfied customers and in turn to superior financial performance

Learning and Growth Perspective
(1) Percentage of employees trained in process and quality management,
(2) employee satisfaction.
Improvements in these measures aim to improve La Quinta's ability to achieve cost leadership and have a cause-and-effect relationship with improvements in internal business processes, which in turn lead to customer satisfaction and financial performance.

Strategy Map for La Quinta for 2009

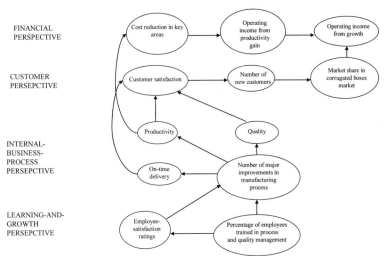

231

13-18 (20 min.)   **Strategy, balanced scorecard, merchandising operation.**

1.   Oceano & Sons follows a _product differentiation strategy_. Oceano's designs are "trendsetting," its T-shirts are distinctive, and it aims to make its T-shirts a "must have" for each and every teenager. These are all clear signs of a product differentiation strategy, and, to succeed, Oceano must continue to innovate and be able to charge a premium price for its product.

2.   Possible key elements of Oceano's balance scorecard, given its product differentiation strategy:

Financial Perspective

(1) Increase in operating income from charging higher margins,

(2) price premium earned on products.

These measures will indicate whether Oceano has been able to charge premium prices and achieve operating income increases through product differentiation.

Customer Perspective

(1) Market share in distinctive, name-brand T-shirts,

(2) customer satisfaction,

(3) new customers,

(4) number of mentions of Oceano's T-shirts in the leading fashion magazines

Oceano's strategy should result in improvements in these customer measures that help evaluate whether Oceano's product differentiation strategy is succeeding with its customers. These measures are, in turn, leading indicators of superior financial performance.

Internal Business Process Perspective

(1) Quality of silk-screening (number of colors, use of glitter, durability of the design),

(2) frequency of new designs,

(3) time between concept and delivery of design

Improvements in these measures are expected to result in more distinctive and trendsetting designs delivered to its customers and in turn, superior financial performance.

Learning and Growth Perspective

(1) Ability to attract and retain talented designers

(2) improvements in silk-screening processes,

(3) continuous education and skill levels of marketing and sales staff,

(4) employee satisfaction.

Improvements in these measures are expected to improve Oceano's capabilities to produce distinctive designs that have a cause-and-effect relationship with improvements in internal business processes, which in turn lead to customer satisfaction and financial performance.

13-20 (20 min.)   **Analysis of growth, price-recovery, and productivity components (continuation of 13-19).**

Effect of the industry-market-size factor on operating income
Of the 48,700-unit (246,700 – 198,000) increase in sales between 2008 and 2009, 19,800 (10% × 198,000) units are due to growth in market size, and 28,900 units are due to an increase in market share.
The change in Oceano's operating income from the industry-market size factor rather than from specific strategic actions is:

$$\$725{,}580 \text{ (the growth component in Exercise 13-19)} \times \frac{19{,}800}{48{,}700} \qquad \underline{\$295{,}000} \text{ F}$$

Effect of product differentiation on operating income
The change in operating income due to:

Increase in the selling price (revenue effect of price recovery)	$246,700 F
Increase in price of inputs (cost effect of price recovery)	308,788 F

Growth in market share due to product differentiation

$$\$725{,}580 \text{ (the growth component in Exercise 13-19)} \times \frac{28{,}900}{48{,}700} \qquad \underline{430{,}580} \text{ F}$$

Change in operating income due to product differentiation	$986,068 F

Effect of cost leadership on operating income
The change in operating income from cost leadership is:

Productivity component	$ 70,632 F

The change in operating income between 2008 and 2009 can be summarized as follows:

Change due to industry-market-size	$ 295,000 F
Change due to product differentiation	986,068 F
Change due to cost leadership	70,632 F
Change in operating income	$1,351,700 F

Oceano has been very successful in implementing its product differentiation strategy. Nearly 73% ($986,068 ÷ $1,351,700) of the increase in operating income during 2009 was due to product differentiation, i.e., the distinctiveness of its T-shirts. It was able to raise prices of its products despite a decline in the cost of the T-shirts purchased. Oceano's operating income increase in 2009 was also helped by a growth in the overall market and a small productivity improvement, which it did not pass on to its customers in the form of lower prices.

13-22 (15 min.)   **Strategy, balanced scorecard.**

1.   Meredith Corporation follows a *product differentiation strategy* in 2009. Meredith's D4H machine is distinct from its competitors and generally regarded as superior to competitors' products. To succeed, Meredith must continue to differentiate its product and charge a premium price.

2.   Possible Balanced Scorecard measures for 2009:

Financial Perspective
(1) Increase in operating income from charging higher margins,
(2) price premium earned on products.
These measures indicate whether Meredith has been able to charge premium prices and achieve operating income increases through product differentiation.

Customer Perspective
(1) Market share in high-end special-purpose textile machines,
(2) customer satisfaction,
(3) new customers.
Meredith's strategy should result in improvements in these customer measures that help evaluate whether Meredith's product differentiation strategy is succeeding with its customers. These measures are leading indicators of superior financial performance.

Internal Business Process Perspective
(1) Manufacturing quality,
(2) new product features added,
(3) order delivery time.
Improvements in these measures are expected to result in more distinctive products delivered to its customers and in turn superior financial performance.

Learning and Growth Perspective
(1) Development time for designing new machines,
(2) improvements in manufacturing processes,
(3) employee education and skill levels,
(4) employee satisfaction.
Improvements in these measures are likely to improve Meredith's capabilities to produce distinctive products that have a cause-and-effect relationship with improvements in internal business processes, which in turn lead to customer satisfaction and financial performance.

13-24 (20 min.)Analysis of growth, price-recovery, and productivity components (continuation of 13-23).

Effect of the industry-market-size factor on operating income
Of the 10-unit increase in sales from 200 to 210 units, 6units (3%) are due to growth in market size, and 4 (10 − 6) units are due to an increase in market share.

The change in Meredith's operating income from the industry-market size factor rather than from specific strategic actions is:

$280,000 (the growth component in Exercise 13-23) $\times \dfrac{6}{10}$ $168,000 F

Effect of product differentiation on operating income
The change in operating income due to:
Increase in the selling price of D4H (revenue effect of price recovery) $420,000 F
Increase in price of inputs (cost effect of price recovery)   184,500 U

Growth in market share due to product differentiation

$280,000 (the growth component in Exercise 13-23) $\times \dfrac{4}{10}$ 112,000 F

Change in operating income due to product differentiation $347,500 F

Effect of cost leadership on operating income
The change in operating income from cost leadership is:
Productivity component $ 92,000 F

The change in operating income between 2008 and 2009 can be summarized as follows:

Change due to industry-market-size	$168,000 F
Change due to product differentiation	347,500 F
Change due to cost leadership	92,000 F
Change in operating income	$607,500 F

Meredith has been successful in implementing its product differentiation strategy. More than 57% ($347,500 ÷ $607,500) of the increase in operating income during 2009 was due to product differentiation, i.e., the distinctiveness of its machines. It was able to raise the prices of its machines faster than the costs of its inputs and still grow market share. Meredith's operating income increase in 2009 was also helped by a growth in the overall market and some productivity improvements.

13-26 (15 min.) **Strategy, balanced scorecard, service company.**

1.   Snyder Corporation's strategy in 2009 is _cost leadership_. Snyder's consulting services for implementing sales management software is not distinct from its competitors. The market for these services is very competitive. To succeed, Snyder must deliver quality service at low cost. Improving productivity while maintaining quality is key.

2.   Possible Balanced Scorecard measures for 2009:

Financial Perspective
(1) Increase operating income from productivity gains and growth,
(2) revenues per employee,
(3) cost reductions in key areas, for example, software implementation and overhead costs.
These measures indicate whether Snyder has been able to reduce costs and achieve operating income increases through cost leadership.

Customer Perspective
(1) Market share,
(2) new customers,
(3) customer responsiveness,
(4) customer satisfaction.
Snyder's strategy should result in improvements in these customer measures that help evaluate whether Snyder's cost leadership strategy is succeeding with its customers. These measures are leading indicators of superior financial performance.

Internal Business Process Perspective
(1) Time to complete customer jobs,
(2) time lost due to errors,
(3) quality of job (Is system running smoothly after job is completed?)
Improvements in these measures are key drivers of achieving cost leadership and are expected to lead to more satisfied customers, lower costs, and superior financial performance.

Learning and Growth Perspective
(1) Time required to analyze and design implementation steps,
(2) time taken to perform key steps implementing the software,
(3) skill levels of employees,
(4) hours of employee training,
(5) employee satisfaction and motivation.
Improvements in these measures are likely to improve Snyder's ability to achieve cost leadership and have a cause-and-effect relationship with improvements in internal business processes, customer satisfaction, and financial performance.

13-28 (25 min.) **Analysis of growth, price-recovery, and productivity components (continuation of 13-27).**

Effect of industry-market-size factor on operating income
Of the 10-unit increase in sales from 60 to 70 units, 5% or 3 units (5% × 60) are due to growth in market size, and 7 (10 – 3) units are due to an increase in market share.

The change in Snyder's operating income from the industry market-size factor rather than from specific strategic actions is:

$$\$200{,}000 \text{ (the growth component in Exercise 13-27)} \times \frac{3}{10} \qquad \underline{\$\ 60{,}000}\ F$$

Effect of product differentiation on operating income
Of the $2,000 decrease in selling price, 1% or $500 (1% × $50,000) is due to a general decline in prices, and the remaining decrease of $1,500 ($2,000 – $500) is due to a strategic decision by Snyder's management to implement its cost leadership strategy of lowering prices to stimulate demand.

The change in operating income due to a decline in selling price (other than the strategic reduction in price included in the cost leadership component) $500 × 70 units	$ 35,000 U
Increase in prices of inputs (cost effect of price recovery)	129,000 U
Change in operating income due to product differentiation	$164,000 U

Effect of cost leadership on operating income

Productivity component	$189,000 F
Effect of strategic decision to reduce selling price, $1,500 × 70	105,000 U
Growth in market share due to productivity improvement and strategic decision to reduce selling price	

$$\$200{,}000 \text{ (the growth component in Exercise 13-27)} \times \frac{7}{10} \qquad \underline{140{,}000}\ F$$

Change in operating income due to cost leadership	$224,000 F

The change in operating income between 2008 and 2009 can then be summarized as

Change due to industry-market-size	$ 60,000 F
Change due to product differentiation	164,000 U
Change due to cost leadership	224,000 F
Change in operating income	$120,000 F

Snyder has been very successful in implementing its cost leadership strategy. Due to a lack of product differentiation, Snyder was unable to pass along increases in labor costs by increasing the selling price—in fact, the selling price declined by $2,000 per work unit. However, Snyder was able to take advantage of its productivity gains to reduce price, gain market share, and increase operating income.

13-30 (30 min.) **Balanced scorecard and strategy.**

1.

Customer Preference Map for ZP98-type Electronic Components

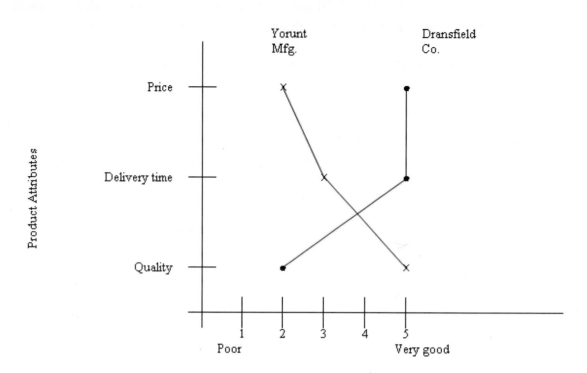

2.   Dransfield currently follows a _cost leadership strategy_, which is reflected in its lower price compared to Yorunt Manufacturing. The electronic component ZP98 is similar to products offered by competitors.

3.   To improve quality without increasing costs or time, Dransfield needs to concentrate on eliminating waste. The following measures in the balanced scorecard could help Dransfield ensure that they were meeting their goals:

Financial Perspective	Operating income from productivity and quality improvement Operating income from growth Revenue growth
Customer Perspective	Market share in electronic components Number of additional customers Customer-satisfaction ratings
Internal-Business-Process Perspective	Percentage of defective products sold Order delivery time On-time delivery Number of major improvements in manufacturing process
Learning-and-Growth Perspective	Employee-satisfaction ratings Percentage of employees trained in quality management Percentage of line workers empowered to manage processes Percentage of manufacturing processes with real-time feedback

4.

Strategy Map for Dransfield Company for 2009

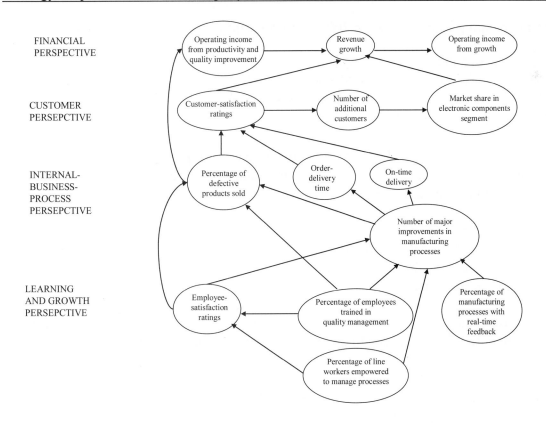

13-32 (20 min.) **Analysis of growth, price-recovery, and productivity components (continuation of 13-31)**

Effect of the industry-market-size factor on operating income
Of the 1,525 increase in sales from 4,500 to 6,025 units, 8% or 360 units (8% × 4,500) are due to growth in market size, and 1,165 (1,525 − 360) units are due to an increase in market share.

The change in Dransfield's operating income from the industry-market size factor rather than from specific strategic actions is:

$$\$58,628 \text{ (the growth component in Exercise 13-31)} \times \frac{360}{1,525} \qquad \underline{\$13,840} \text{ F}$$

Effect of product differentiation on operating income
The change in operating income due to:

Increase in the selling price of ZP98 (revenue effect of price recovery)	$36,150 F
Increase in price of inputs (cost effect of price recovery)	60,180 U
Change in operating income due to product differentiation	$24,030 U

Effect of cost leadership on operating income
The change in operating income from cost leadership is:

Productivity component	$ 2,222 F
Growth in market share due to cost leadership	

$$\$58,628 \text{ (the growth component in Exercise 13-31)} \times \frac{1,165}{1,525} \qquad \underline{44,788} \text{ F}$$

Change in operating income due to cost leadership	$47,010 F

The change in operating income between 2008 and 2009 can be summarized as follows:

Change due to industry market-size	$13,840 F
Change due to product differentiation	24,030 U
Change due to cost leadership	47,010 F
Change in operating income	$36,820 F

One might argue that the $24,030 U price-recovery variance could also be thought of as part of the productivity variance. Under this assumption, the change in operating income between 2008 and 2009 can be summarized as follows:

Change due to market industry size	$13,840 F
Change due to product differentiation	0
Change due to cost leadership ($47,010 − $24,030)	22,980 F
Change in operating income	$36,820 F

Dransfield has been successful in implementing its cost leadership strategy. The increase in operating income during 2009 was due to quality improvements and market size growth.

13-34 (20–30 min.)   **Balanced scorecard.**

Perspectives	Strategic Objectives	Performance Measures
▪ Financial	▪ Increase shareholder value	▪ Earnings per share ▪ Net income ▪ Return on assets ▪ Return on sales ▪ Return on equity ▪ Product cost per unit ▪ Customer cost per unit
	▪ Increase profit generated by each salesperson	▪ Profit per salesperson
▪ Customer	▪ Acquire new customers ▪ Retain customers ▪ Develop profitable customers	▪ Number of new customers ▪ Percentage of customers retained ▪ Customer profitability
▪ Internal Business Processs	▪ Improve manufacturing quality ▪ Introduce new products	▪ Percentage of defective product units
	▪ Minimize invoice error rate ▪ On-time delivery by suppliers ▪ Increase proprietary products	▪ Percentage of error-free invoices ▪ Percentage of on-time deliveries by suppliers ▪ Number of patents
▪ Learning and Growth	▪ Increase information system capabilities ▪ Enhance employee skills	▪ Percentage of processes with real-time feedback ▪ Employee turnover rate ▪ Average job-related training hours per employee

13-36 (30 min.) **Balanced scorecard**.

1. It appears from the scorecard that _Lee was not successful_ in implementing its strategy in 2009. Although it achieved targeted performance in the learning and growth and internal business process perspectives, it significantly missed its targets in the customer and financial perspectives. Lee has not had the success it targeted in the market and has not been able to reduce fixed costs.

The market for color laser printers is competitive. Lee's strategy is to produce and sell high quality laser printers at a low cost. The key to achieving higher quality is reducing defects in its manufacturing operations. The key to managing costs is dealing with the high fixed costs of Lee's automated manufacturing facility. To reduce costs per unit, Lee would have to either produce more units or eliminate excess capacity.

2. Lee's scorecard *does not provide any explanation of why the target market share was not met in 2009*. Was it due to poor quality? Higher prices? Poor post-sales service? Inadequate supply of products? Poor distribution? Aggressive competitors? The scorecard is not helpful for understanding the reasons underlying the poor market share.

   Lee may want to include some measures in the customer perspective (and internal business process perspective). These measures would then serve as leading indicators for lower market share. For example, Lee should measure customer satisfaction with its printers on various dimensions of product features, quality, price, service, and availability to see how they compare to competitors. This is critical information for Lee to successfully implement its strategy.

3. Lee considers training and empowering workers as important for implementing its high-quality, low-cost strategy. Therefore *employee training and employee satisfaction should appear in the learning and growth perspective of the scorecard*. Lee can then evaluate if improving employee-related measures results in improved internal-business process measures, market share and financial performance.

   Adding new product development measures to internal business processes is also important. A reduction of defects leads to excess capacity for new products. Hence, the scorecard should contain some measure to monitor progress in new product development. Improving quality without developing and selling new products (or downsizing) will result in weak financial performance.

4. Improving quality and significantly downsizing to eliminate unused capacity is difficult. Recall that the key to improving quality at Lee Corporation is training and empowering workers. But, reducing costs will require selling equipment and laying off employees. How can management lay off the very employees whose hard work and skills led to improved quality? Lee's management should first focus on using the newly available capacity to sell more product. If it cannot do so and must downsize, management should try to downsize in a way that would not hurt employee morale, such as through retirements and voluntary severance.

13-38 (25 min.) **Total factor productivity (continuation of 13-37)**

1. $$\text{Total factor productivity for 2009 using 2009 prices} = \frac{\text{Quantity of output produced in 2009}}{\text{Costs of inputs used in 2009 based on 2009 prices}}$$

$$= \frac{2,650,000}{(1,669,500 \times \$4) + (8,680,000)}$$

$$= \frac{2,650,000}{\$6,678,000 + \$8,680,00} = \frac{2,650,000}{\$15,358,000}$$

$$= 0.1725 \text{ units of output per dollar of input}$$

2. By itself, the 2009 TFP of 0.1725 units per dollar of input is not particularly helpful. We need something to compare the 2009 TFP against. We use, as a benchmark, TFP calculated using the inputs that Berkshire would have used in 2008 to produce 2,650,000 units of output calculated in requirement 1 at 2009 prices. Using the current year's (2009) prices in both calculations controls for input price differences and focuses the analysis on the adjustments the manager made in the quantities of inputs in response to changes in prices.

$$\text{2009 price of capacity} = \frac{\text{Cost of capacity in 2009}}{\text{Capacity in 2009}} = \frac{\$8,680,000}{2,800,000 \text{ units}} = \$3.10 \text{ per unit of capacity}$$

$$\begin{aligned}\text{Benchmark TFP} &= \frac{\text{Quantity of output produced in 2009}}{\begin{array}{c}\text{Costs of inputs that would have been used in 2008}\\\text{to produce 2009 output at year 2009 input prices}\end{array}}\\[2mm]
&= \frac{2,650,000}{(1,987,500 \times \$4)+(3,000,000 \times \$3.10)}\\[2mm]
&= \frac{2,650,000}{\$7,950,000 + \$9,300,000}\\[2mm]
&= \frac{2,650,000}{\$17,250,000}\\[2mm]
&= 0.1536 \text{ units of output per dollar of input}\end{aligned}$$

Using year 2009 prices, total factor productivity increased 12.3% [(0.1725 – 0.1536) ÷ 0.1536] from 2008 to 2009.

3. Total factor productivity increased because Guble produced more output per dollar of input in 2009 relative to 2008, measured in both years using 2009 prices. The change in partial productivity of direct materials and conversion costs tells us that Guble used fewer materials and less capacity in 2009 relative to output, than in 2008.

A major advantage of TFP over partial productivity measures is that TFP combines the productivity of all inputs and so measures gains from using fewer physical inputs *and* substitution among inputs.

Partial productivities cannot be combined to indicate the overall effect on cost as a result of these individual improvements. The TFP measure allows managers to evaluate the change in overall productivity by simultaneously combining all inputs to measure gains from using fewer physical inputs as well as substitution among inputs.

CHAPTER 14
COST ALLOCATION, CUSTOMER-PROFITABILITY
ANALYSIS, AND SALES-VARIANCE ANALYSIS

14-2 Exhibit 14-1 outlines **four purposes for allocating costs**:
1. To provide information for economic *decisions*.
2. To *motivate* managers and other employees.
3. To *justify* costs or compute reimbursement amounts.
4. To *measure* income and assets.

14-4 **Disagree**. In general, companies have three choices regarding the allocation of corporate costs to divisions: allocate all corporate costs, allocate some corporate costs (those "controllable" by the divisions), and allocate none of the corporate costs. Which one of these is appropriate depends on several factors: the composition of corporate costs, the purpose of the costing exercise, and the time horizon, to name a few. For example, one can easily justify allocating all corporate costs when they are closely related to the running of the divisions and when the purpose of costing is, say, pricing products or motivating managers to consume corporate resources judiciously.

14-6 **Customer profitability** analysis highlights to managers how individual customers differentially contribute to total profitability. It helps managers to see whether *customers who contribute sizably* to total profitability are *receiving* a comparable level of *attention* from the organization.

14-8 **No**. A customer-profitability profile highlights differences in current period's profitability across customers. *Dropping customers should be the last resort*. The company can work with customers to improve profitability. Also, if costs aren't purely variable, when customers are dropped, costs assigned to those customers may not disappear in the short run.

14-10 By computing the sales-mix and sales-quantity variances, market-size, and market-share variances, managers can gain insight into the causes of a specific sales-volume variance caused by changes in the mix and quantity of the products sold as well as changes in market size and market share.

14-12 A **favorable sales-quantity variance** arises because the *actual* units of all products *sold exceed* the *budgeted* units of all products sold.

14-14 Some companies believe that *reliable information on total market size is not available* and therefore they choose not to compute market-size and market-share variances.

14-16 (15-20 min.) **Cost allocation in hospitals, alternative allocation criteria.**

1. Direct costs   = $2.40
    Indirect costs ($11.52 – $2.40) = $9.12

$$\text{Overhead rate} \quad = \frac{\$9.12}{\$2.40} = 380\%$$

2. The answers here are less than clear-cut in some cases.

Overhead Cost Item	Allocation Criteria
Processing of paperwork for purchase	Cause and effect
Supplies room management fee	Benefits received
Operating-room and patient-room handling costs	Cause and effect
Administrative hospital costs	Benefits received
University teaching-related costs	Ability to bear
Malpractice insurance costs	Ability to bear or benefits received
Cost of treating uninsured patients	Ability to bear
Profit component	None. This is not a cost.

3. Assuming that Meltzer's insurance company is responsible for paying the $4,800 bill, Meltzer probably can only express outrage at the amount of the bill. Insurance companies, not individual patients, have considerable power and may decide that certain costs are not reimbursable—for example, the costs of treating uninsured patients.

14-18 (30 min.) **Cost allocation to divisions.**

1.

	Hotel	Restaurant	Casino	Rembrandt
Revenue	$16,425,000	$5,256,000	$12,340,000	$34,021,000
Direct costs	9,819,260	3,749,172	4,248,768	17,817,200
Segment margin	$ 6,605,740	$1,506,828	$ 8,091,232	16,203,800
Fixed overhead costs				14,550,000
Income before taxes				$ 1,653,800
Segment margin %	40.22%	28.67%	65.57%	

2.

	Hotel	Restaurant	Casino	Rembrandt
Direct costs	$9,819,260	$3,749,172	$4,248,768	$17,817,200
Direct cost %	55.11%	21.04%	23.85%	100.00%
Square footage	80,000	16,000	64,000	160,000
Square footage %	50.00%	10.00%	40.00%	100.00%
Number of employees	200	50	250	500
Number of employees %	40.00%	10.00%	50.00%	100.00%

A: Cost allocation based on direct costs:

	Hotel	Restaurant	Casino	Rembrandt
Revenue	$16,425,000	$ 5,256,000	$12,340,000	$34,021,000
Direct costs	9,819,260	3,749,172	4,248,768	17,817,200
Segment margin	6,605,740	1,506,828	8,091,232	16,203,800
Allocated fixed overhead costs	8,018,505	3,061,320	3,470,175	14,550,000
Segment pre-tax income	$ (1,412,765)	$ (1,554,492)	$ 4,621,057	$ 1,653,800
Segment pre-tax income % of rev.	-8.60%	-29.58%	37.45%	

B: Cost allocation based on floor space:

	Hotel	Restaurant	Casino	Rembrandt
Allocated fixed overhead costs	$7,275,000	$1,455,000	$5,820,000	$14,550,000
Segment pre-tax income	$ (669,260)	$ 51,828	$2,271,232	$ 1,653,800
Segment pre-tax income % of rev.	-4.07%	0.99%	18.41%	

C: Cost allocation based on number of employees

	Hotel	Restaurant	Casino	Rembrandt
Allocated fixed overhead costs	$5,820,000	$1,455,000	$7,275,000	$14,550,000
Segment pre-tax income	$ 785,740	$ 51,828	$ 816,232	$ 1,653,800
Segment pre-tax income % of rev.	4.78%	0.99%	6.61%	

3.   Requirement 2 shows the dramatic effect of choice of cost allocation base on segment pre-tax income as a percentage of revenues:

	Pre-tax Income Percentage		
Allocation Base	Hotel	Restaurant	Casino
Direct costs	-8.60%	-29.58%	37.45%
Floor space	-4.07	0.99	18.41
Number of employees	4.78	0.99	6.61

The *decision context* should guide (a) whether costs should be allocated, and (b) the preferred cost allocation base. Decisions about, say, performance measurement, may be made on a combination of financial and nonfinancial measures. It may well be that Rembrandt may prefer to exclude allocated costs from the financial measures to reduce areas of dispute.

4.   Allocation of indirect costs *should not guide the decision on whether to shut down any of the divisions*. The overhead costs are fixed costs in the short run. It is not clear how these costs would be affected in the long run if Rembrandt shut down one of the divisions. Also, each division is *not independent* of the other two. A decision to shut down, say, the restaurant, likely would negatively affect the attendance at the casino and possibly the hotel. Rembrandt should examine the future revenue and future cost implications of different resource investments in the three divisions. This is a future-oriented exercise, whereas the analysis in requirement 2 is an analysis of past costs.

14-20 (30 min.) **Customer profitability, customer cost hierarchy.**

1.

	Wholesale		Retail	
	North America Wholesaler	**South America Wholesaler**	**Big Sam Stereo**	**World Market**
Revenues at list prices	$420,000	$580,000	$130,000	$100,000
Price discounts	30,000	40,000	7,000	500
Revenues (at actual prices)	390,000	540,000	123,000	99,500
Cost of goods sold	325,000	455,000	118,000	90,000
Gross margin	65,000	85,000	5,000	9,500
Customer-level operating costs				
Delivery	450	650	200	125
Order processing	800	1,000	200	130
Sales visit	5,600	5,500	2,300	1,350
Total cust.-level optg.costs	6,850	7,150	2,700	1,605
Customer-level operating income	$ 58,150	$ 77,850	$ 2,300	$ 7,895

All amounts in thousands of U.S. dollars

2.

Customer Distribution Channels
(all amounts in $000s)

	Total (all customers) (1) = (2) + (5)	Wholesale Customers			Retail Customers		
		Total Wholesale (2) = (3) + (4)	North America Wholesaler (3)	South America Wholesaler (4)	Total Retail (5) = (6) + (7)	Big Sam Stereo (6)	World Market (7)
Revenues (at actual prices)	$1,152,500	$930,000	$390,000	$540,000	$222,500	$123,000	$99,500
Customer-level costs	1,006,305	794,000	331,850 [a]	462,150 [a]	212,305	120,700 [a]	91,605 [a]
Customer-level operating income	146,195	136,000	$ 58,150	$ 77,850	10,195	$ 2,300	$ 7,895
Distribution-channel costs	45,000	38,000			7,000		
Distribution-channel-level oper. income	101,195	$ 98,000			$ 3,195		
Corporate-sustaining costs	65,000						
Operating income	$ 36,195						

[a] Cost of goods sold + Total customer-level operating costs from Requirement 1

3. If corporate costs are allocated to the channels, the retail channel will show an operating loss of $10,805,000 ($3,195,000 – $14,000,000), and the wholesale channel will show an operating profit of $47,000,000 ($98,000,000 – $51,000,000). The overall operating profit, of course, is still $36,195,000, as in requirement 2. There is, however, no cause-and-effect or benefits-received relationship between corporate costs and any allocation base, i.e., the allocation of $51,000,000 to the wholesale channel and of $14,000,000 to the retail channel is arbitrary and not useful for decision-making. Therefore, the management of Ramish Electronics should not base any performance evaluations or investment/disinvestment decisions based on these channel-level operating income numbers. They may want to take corporate costs into account, however, when making pricing decisions.

248

14-22 (20–25 min.) **Customer profitability, distribution.**

1.   The activity-based costing for each customer is:

		Charleston Pharmacy	Chapel Hill Pharmacy
1.	Order processing, $40 × 13; $40 × 10	$ 520	$ 400
2.	Line-item ordering, $3 × (13 × 9; 10 × 18)	351	540
3.	Store deliveries, $50 × 7; $50 ×10	350	500
4.	Carton deliveries, $1 × (7 × 22; 10 × 20)	154	200
5.	Shelf-stocking, $16 × (7 × 0; 10 × 0.5)	0	80
	Operating costs	$1,375	$1,720

The operating income of each customer is:

	Charleston Pharmacy	Chapel Hill Pharmacy
Revenues, $2,400 × 7; $1,800 × 10	$16,800	$18,000
Cost of goods sold, $2,100 × 7; $1,650 × 10	14,700	16,500
Gross margin	2,100	1,500
Operating costs	1,375	1,720
Operating income	$ 725	$ (220)

Chapel Hill Pharmacy has a lower gross margin percentage than Charleston (8.33% vs. 12.50%) and consumes more resources to obtain this lower margin.

2.   Ways Figure Four could use this information include:
   a.   Pay *increased attention to the top 20% of the customers*: ask what they want; ensure that employees deliver for these customers, especially.
   b.   *Reduce the rate per cost driver*: lower ordering costs through automation, or delivery costs through routing or fuel efficiency.
   c.   *Reduce customer costs* by working with customers: make fewer orders, fewer line items. There are several options here:
   • Verbal persuasion by showing customers cost drivers at Figure Four.
   • Explicitly pricing out activities like cartons delivered and shelf-stocking so that customers pay for the costs they cause.
   • Restricting options available to certain customers, e.g., customers with low revenues could be restricted to one free delivery per week.
   • Working with customers so that deliveries are easier to make and shelf-stocking can be done faster.

d. Offer salespeople bonuses based on the operating income of each customer rather than the gross margin of each customer.

Dropping should be only a last resort after all other avenues have been explored. Moreover, an unprofitable customer today may well be a profitable customer tomorrow, and it is myopic to focus on only a 1-month customer-profitability analysis to classify a customer as unprofitable.

14-24 (30 min.) **Variance analysis, working backward.**

Columnar Presentation of Sales-Volume, Sales-Quantity and Sales-Mix Variances for Jinwa Corporation *(explanation follows)*

	Flexible Budget: Actual Units of All Glasses Sold × Actual Sales Mix × Budgeted Contribution Margin per Unit	**Actual Units of All Glasses Sold × Budgeted Sales Mix × Budgeted Contribution Margin per Unit**	**Static Budget: Budgeted Units of All Glasses Sold × Budgeted Sales Mix × Budgeted Contribution Margin per Unit**
Panel A: Plain	(1,500 × 0.6) × $2	(1,500 × 0.8) × $2	(2,000 × 0.8) × $2
	900 × $2	1,200 × $2	1,600 × $2
	$1,800	$2,400	$3,200
	$600 U Sales-mix variance		$800 U Sales-quantity variance
	$1,400 U Sales-volume variance		
Panel B: Chic	(1,500 × 0.4) × $6	(1,500 × 0.2) × $6	(2,000 × 0.2) × $6
	600 × $6	300 × $6	400 × $6
	$3,600	$1,800	$2,400
	$1,800 F Sales-mix variance		$600 U Sales-quantity variance
	$1,200 F Sales-volume variance		
Panel C: All Glasses	$5,400	$4,200	$5,600
	$1,200 F Total sales-mix variance		$1,400 U Total sales-quantity variance
	$200 U Total sales-volume variance		

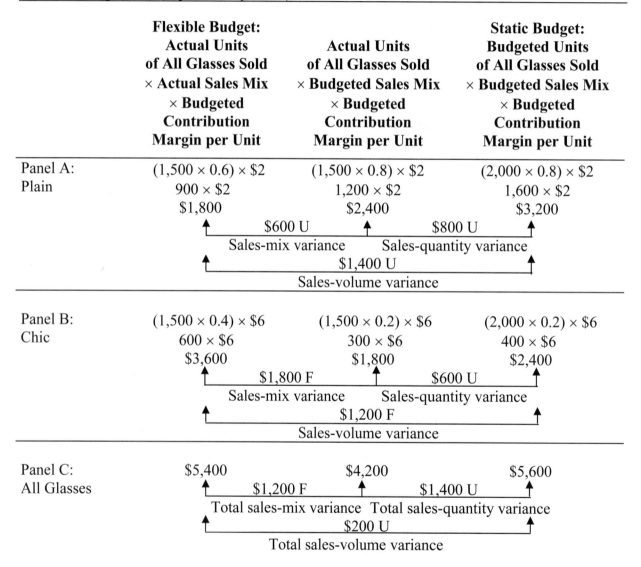

F = favorable effect on operating income; U = unfavorable effect on operating income.

Step 1

Consider the static budget column (Column 3):

Static budget total contribution margin	$5,600
Budgeted units of all glasses to be sold	2,000
Budgeted contribution margin per unit of Plain	$2
Budgeted contribution margin per unit of Chic	$6

Suppose that the budgeted sales-mix percentage of Plain is y. Then the budgeted sales-mix percentage of Chic is $(1 - y)$. Therefore,

$$
\begin{aligned}
(2,000y \times \$2) + (2,000 \times (1 - y) \times \$6) &= \$5,600 \\
\$4000y + \$12,000 - \$12,000y &= \$5,600 \\
\$8,000y &= \$6,400 \\
y &= 0.8 \text{ or } 80\% \\
1 - y &= 20\%
\end{aligned}
$$

Jinwa's budgeted sales mix is 80% of Plain and 20% of Chic. We can then fill in all the numbers in Column 3.

Step 2

Next, consider Column 2

The total of Column 2 in Panel C is $4,200 (the static budget total contribution margin of $5,600 – the total sales-quantity variance of $1,400 U which was given in the problem).

We need to find the actual units sold of all glasses, which we denote by q. From Column 2, we know that

$$
\begin{aligned}
(q \times 0.8 \times \$2) + (q \times 0.2 \times \$6) &= \$4,200 \\
\$1.6q + \$1.2q &= \$4,200 \\
\$2.8q &= \$4,200 \\
q &= 1,500 \text{ units}
\end{aligned}
$$

So, the total quantity of all glasses sold is 1,500 units. This computation allows us to fill in all the numbers in Column 2.

Step 3

Next, consider Column 1. We know actual units sold of all glasses (1,500 units), the actual sales-mix percentage (given in the problem information as Plain, 60%; Chic, 40%), and the budgeted unit contribution margin of each product (Plain, $2; Chic, $6). We can therefore determine all the numbers in Column 1.

3. Jinwa Corporation shows an _unfavorable sales-quantity variance_ because it sold fewer wine glasses in total than was budgeted. This unfavorable sales-quantity variance is _partially offset by a favorable sales-mix variance_ because the actual mix of wine glasses sold has shifted in _favor of the higher contribution margin_ Chic wine glasses.

14-26 (20 min.)   Market-share and market-size variances (continuation of 14-25).

	Actual	**Budgeted**
Western region	24 million	25 million
Soda King	3 million	2.5 million
Market share	12.5%	10%

Average budgeted contribution margin per unit = $2.108 ($5,270,000 ÷ 2,500,000)

Market-Share and Market-Size Variance Analysis of Soda King for 2009

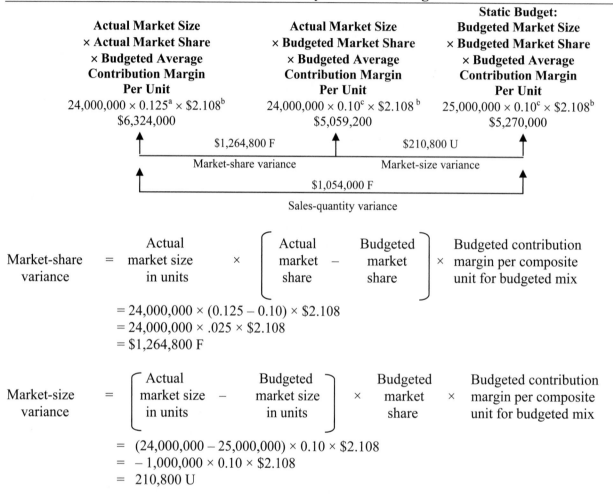

The *market share variance is favorable* because the actual 12.5% market share was higher than the budgeted 10% market share. The *market size variance is unfavorable* because the market size decreased 4% [(25,000,000 − 24,000,000) ÷ 25,000,000].

While the overall total market size declined (from 25 million to 24 million), the increase in market share meant a favorable sales-quantity variance.

14-28 Cost allocation to divisions.

1.

	Bread	Cake	Doughnuts	Total
Segment margin	$6,400,000	$1,300,000	$6,150,000	$13,850,000
Allocated headquarter costs ($5,100,000 ÷ 3)	1,700,000	1,700,000	1,700,000	5,100,000
Operating income	$4,700,000	$ (400,000)	$4,450,000	$ 8,750,000

2.

	Bread	Cake	Doughnuts	Total
Segment margin	$6,400,000	$1,300,000	$6,150,000	$13,850,000
Allocated headquarter costs, Human resources[1] (50%; 12.5%; 37.5% × $1,900,000)	950,000	237,500	712,500	1,900,000
Accounting department[2] (53.9%; 11.6%; 34.5% × $1,400,000)	754,600	162,400	483,000	1,400,000
Rent and depreciation[3] (50%; 20%; 30% × $1,200,000)	600,000	240,000	360,000	1,200,000
Other ($\frac{1}{3}$ × $600,000)	200,000	200,000	200,000	600,000
Total	2,504,600	839,900	1,755,500	5,100,000
Operating income	$3,895,400	$ 460,100	$4,394,500	$ 8,750,000

[1]HR costs: For each division, # employees ÷ by total # employees. 400 ÷ 800 = 50%;
100 ÷ 800 = 12.5%;
300 ÷ 800 = 37.5%

[2]Accounting: For each division, Revenue ÷ Total Revenue. $20,900,000 ÷ $38,800,000 = 53.9%;
$4,500,000 ÷ $38,800,000 = 11.6%;
$13,400,000 ÷ $38,800,000 = 34.5%

[3] Rent and depreciation: For each division, Square feet ÷ Total Square feet. 10,000 ÷ 20,000 = 50%;
4,000 ÷ 20,000 = 20%;
6,000 ÷ 20,000 = 30%

A cause-and-effect relationship may exist between Human Resources costs and the number of employees at each division. Rent and depreciation costs may be related to square feet. The Accounting Department costs are probably related to the revenues earned by each division – higher revenues mean more transactions and more accounting. Other overhead costs are allocated arbitrarily.

3. The Cake Division manager probably suggested the new allocation bases. Originally, the Cake Division showed an operating loss after allocation. It is smaller, yet was charged an equal share of headquarter costs. In the new allocation The Cake Division shows an operating profit after allocating headquarter costs. The ABC method is a better way to allocate headquarter costs because it uses cost allocation bases that, by and large, represent cause-and-effect relationships between various categories of headquarter costs and the demands that different divisions place on these costs.

14-30 (40 min.) **Customer profitability, distribution.**

1.

	Customer				
	P	**Q**	**R**	**S**	**T**
Revenues at list prices[a]	$29,952	$126,000	$875,520	$457,920	$56,160
Discount[b]	0	2,100	72,960	15,264	5,616
Revenues (at actual prices)	29,952	123,900	802,560	442,656	50,544
Cost of goods sold[c]	24,960	105,000	729,600	381,600	46,800
Gross margin	4,992	18,900	72,960	61,056	3,744
Customer-level operating costs					
Order taking[d]	1,500	2,500	3,000	2,500	3,000
Customer visits[e]	160	240	480	160	240
Delivery vehicles[f]	280	240	360	640	1,600
Product handling[g]	1,040	4,375	30,400	15,900	1,950
Expedited runs[h]	0	0	0	0	300
Total	2,980	7,355	34,240	19,200	7,090
Customer-level operating income	$ 2,012	$ 11,545	$ 38,720	$ 41,856	$ (3,346)

[a] $14.40 × 2,080; 8,750; 60,800; 31,800; 3,900

[b] ($14.40 – $14.40) × 50,000; ($14.40 – $14.16) × 8,750; ($14.40 – $13.20) × 60,800; ($14.40 – $13.92) × 31,800; ($14.40 – $12.96) × 3,900

[c] $12 × 2,080; 8,750; 60,800; 31,800; 3,900

[d] $100 × 15; 25; 30; 25; 30

[e] $80 × 2; 3; 6; 2; 3

[f] $2 × (10 × 14); (30 × 4); (60 × 3); (40 × 8); (20 × 40)

[g] $0.50 × 2,080; 8,750; 60,800; 31,800; 3,900

[h] $300 × 0; 0; 0; 0; 1

Customer S is the most profitable customer, despite having only 52% (31,800 ÷ 60,800) of the unit volume of Customer R. A major explanation is that Customer R receives a $1.20 discount per case while Customer S receives only a $0.48 discount per case. Customer T is unprofitable, while the smaller customer P is profitable. Customer T receives a $1.44 discount per case, makes more frequent orders, requires more customer visits, and requires more delivery miles than Customer P.

2.   Separate reporting of both the list selling price and the actual selling price enables Spring Distribution to examine which customers receive different discounts and how salespeople may differ in the discounts they grant. There is a size pattern in the discounts across the five customers, except for Customer T, larger volume customers get larger discounts:

Sales Volume	Discount per case
R (60,800 cases)	$1.20
S (31,800 cases)	$0.48
Q (8,750 cases)	$0.24
T (3,900 cases)	**$1.44**
P (2,080 cases)	$0.00

The reasons for the $1.44 discount for T should be explored.

3. Dropping customers should be the last resort taken by Spring Distribution. Factors to consider include the following:
   a. What is the expected future profitability of each customer? Are the currently unprofitable (T) or low-profit (P) customers likely to be highly profitable in the future?
   b. Are there externalities from having some customers, even if they are unprofitable in the short run? For example, some customers have a marquee-value that is "in effect" advertising that benefits the business.
   c. What costs are avoidable if one or more customers are dropped?
   d. Can the relationship with the "problem" customers be restructured so that there is a "win-win" situation? For example, could Customer T get by with fewer deliveries per month?

14-32 (60 min.)   **Variance analysis, sales-mix and sales-quantity variances.**

1.   Actual Contribution Margins

Product	Actual Selling Price	Actual Variable Cost per Unit	Actual Contribution Margin per Unit	Actual Sales Volume in Units	Actual Contribution Dollars	Actual Contribution Percent
Palm Pro	$349	$178	$171	11,000	$ 1,881,000	16%
Palm CE	285	92	193	44,000	8,492,000	71%
PalmKid	102	73	29	55,000	1,595,000	13%
				110,000	$11,968,000	100%

The actual average contribution margin per unit is $108.80 ($11,968,000 ÷ 110,000 units).

Budgeted Contribution Margins

Product	Budgeted Selling Price	Budgeted Variable Cost per Unit	Budgeted Contribution Margin per Unit	Budgeted Sales Volume in Units	Budgeted Contribution Dollars	Budgeted Contribution Percent
Palm Pro	$379	$182	$197	12,500	$ 2,462,500	19%
Palm CE	269	98	171	37,500	6,412,500	49%
Palm Kid	149	65	84	50,000	4,200,000	32%
				100,000	$13,075,000	100%

The budgeted average contribution margin per unit is $130.75 ($13,075,000 ÷ 100,000 units).

2.   Actual Sales Mix

Product	Actual Sales Volume in Units	Actual Sales Mix
Palm Pro	11,000	10.0% (11,000 ÷ 110,000)
Palm CE	44,000	40.0% (44,000 ÷ 110,000)
Palm Kid	55,000	50.0% (55,000 ÷ 110,000)
	110,000	100.0%

Budgeted Sales Mix

Product	Budgeted Sales Volume in Units	Budgeted Sales Mix
Palm Pro	12,500	12.5% (12,500 ÷ 100,000)
Palm CE	37,500	37.5% (37,500 ÷ 100,000)
Palm Kid	50,000	50.0% (50,000 ÷ 100,000)
	100,000	100.0%

3. Sales-volume variance:

$$= \left(\begin{array}{c} \text{Actual} \\ \text{quantity of} \\ \text{units sold} \end{array} - \begin{array}{c} \text{Budgeted} \\ \text{quantity of} \\ \text{units sold} \end{array} \right) \times \begin{array}{c} \text{Budgeted} \\ \text{contribution margin} \\ \text{per unit} \end{array}$$

PalmPro	(11,000	–	12,500)	×	$197	$ 295,500	U
PalmCE	(44,000	–	37,500)	×	$171	1,111,500	F
PalmKid	(55,000	–	50,000)	×	$ 84	420,000	F
Total sales-volume variance						$1,236,000	F

Sales-mix variance:

$$= \begin{array}{c} \text{Actual units} \\ \text{of all} \\ \text{products sold} \end{array} \times \left(\begin{array}{c} \text{Actual} \\ \text{sales mix} \\ \text{percentage} \end{array} - \begin{array}{c} \text{Budgeted} \\ \text{sales mix} \\ \text{percentage} \end{array} \right) \times \begin{array}{c} \text{Budgeted} \\ \text{contrib. margin} \\ \text{per unit} \end{array}$$

PalmPro	=	110,000	×	(0.10	–	0.125)	×	$197	$541,750 U
PalmCE	=	110,000	×	(0.40	–	0.375)	×	$171	470,250 F
PalmKid	=	110,000	×	(0.50	–	0.50)	×	$ 84	0 F
Total sales-mix variance									$ 71,500 U

Sales-quantity variance:

$$= \left(\begin{array}{c} \text{Actual units} \\ \text{of all} \\ \text{products sold} \end{array} - \begin{array}{c} \text{Budgeted units} \\ \text{of all} \\ \text{products sold} \end{array} \right) \times \begin{array}{c} \text{Budgeted} \\ \text{sales mix} \\ \text{percentage} \end{array} \times \begin{array}{c} \text{Budgeted} \\ \text{contrib. margin} \\ \text{per unit} \end{array}$$

PalmPro	(110,000	–	100,000)	×	0.125	×	$197	$ 246,250	F
PalmCE	(110,000	–	100,000)	×	0.375	×	$171	641,250	F
PalmKid	(110,000	–	100,000)	×	0.50	×	$ 84	420,000	F
Total sales-quantity variance								$1,307,500	F

Sales-Mix and Sales-Quantity Variance Analysis of Aussie Infonautics for the Third Quarter 2010.

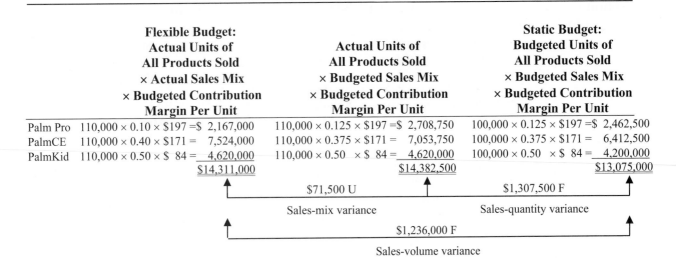

	Flexible Budget: Actual Units of All Products Sold × Actual Sales Mix × Budgeted Contribution Margin Per Unit	Actual Units of All Products Sold × Budgeted Sales Mix × Budgeted Contribution Margin Per Unit	Static Budget: Budgeted Units of All Products Sold × Budgeted Sales Mix × Budgeted Contribution Margin Per Unit
Palm Pro	$110,000 \times 0.10 \times \$197 = \$ 2,167,000$	$110,000 \times 0.125 \times \$197 = \$ 2,708,750$	$100,000 \times 0.125 \times \$197 = \$ 2,462,500$
PalmCE	$110,000 \times 0.40 \times \$171 = 7,524,000$	$110,000 \times 0.375 \times \$171 = 7,053,750$	$100,000 \times 0.375 \times \$171 = 6,412,500$
PalmKid	$110,000 \times 0.50 \times \$\ 84 = \underline{4,620,000}$	$110,000 \times 0.50 \ \times \$\ 84 = \underline{4,620,000}$	$100,000 \times 0.50 \ \times \$\ 84 = \underline{4,200,000}$
	$\underline{\$14,311,000}$	$\underline{\$14,382,500}$	$\underline{\$13,075,000}$

$71,500 U

Sales-mix variance

$1,307,500 F

Sales-quantity variance

$1,236,000 F

Sales-volume variance

F = favorable effect on operating income; U= unfavorable effect on operating income

4.   The following factors help us understand the differences between actual and budgeted amounts:

- The difference in actual versus budgeted contribution margins was $1,107,000 unfavorable ($11,968,000 – $13,075,000). However, the contribution margin from the PalmCE exceeded budget by $2,079,500 ($8,492,000 – $6,412,500) while the contributions from the PalmPro and the PalmKid were lower than expected and offset this gain. This is attributable to lower unit sales in the case of PalmPro and lower contribution margins in the case of PalmKid.
- In percentage terms, the PalmCE accounted for 71% of actual contribution margin versus a planned 49% contribution margin. However, the PalmPro accounted for 16% versus planned 19% and the PalmKid accounted for only 13% versus a planned 32%.
- In unit terms (rather than in contribution terms), the PalmKid accounted for 50% of the sales mix as planned. However, the PalmPro accounted for only 10% versus a budgeted 12.5% and the PalmCE accounted for 40% versus a planned 37.5%.
- Variance analysis for the PalmPro shows an unfavorable sales-mix variance outweighing a favorable sales-quantity variance and producing an unfavorable sales-volume variance. The drop in sales-mix share was far larger than the gain from an overall greater quantity sold.
- The PalmCE gained both from an increase in share of the sales mix as well as from the increase in the overall number of units sold.
- The PalmKid maintained sales-mix share at 50%—as a result, the sales-mix variance is zero. However, PalmKid sales gained from the overall increase in units sold.
- Overall, there was a favorable total sales-volume variance. However, the large drop in PalmKid's contribution margin per unit combined with a decrease in the actual number of PalmPro units sold as well as a drop in the actual contribution margin per unit below budget, led to the total contribution margin being much lower than budgeted.

14-34 (40 min.) **Variance analysis, multiple products.**

Columnar Presentation of Sales-Volume, Sales-Quantity, and Sales-Mix Variances for Debbie's Delight, Inc.

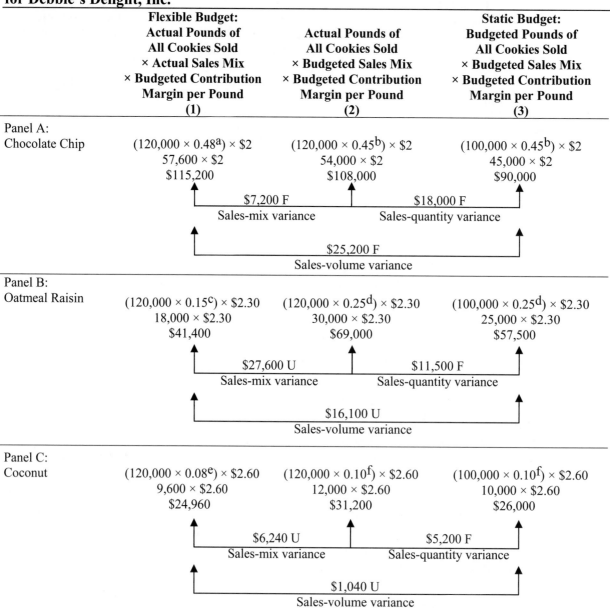

F = favorable effect on operating income; U = unfavorable effect on operating income.

Actual Sales Mix:

[a]Chocolate Chip   = 57,600 ÷ 120,000 = 48%

[c]Oatmeal Raisin   = 18,000 ÷ 120,000 = 15%

[e]Coconut   =   9,600 ÷ 120,000 =   8%

Budgeted Sales Mix:

[b]Chocolate Chip   =   45,000 ÷ 100,000 = 45%

[d]Oatmeal Raisin   =   25,000 ÷ 100,000 = 25%

[f]Coconut   =   10,000 ÷ 100,000 = 10%

Columnar Presentation of Sales-Volume, Sales-Quantity, and Sales-Mix Variances for Debbie's Delight, Inc. (Con't)

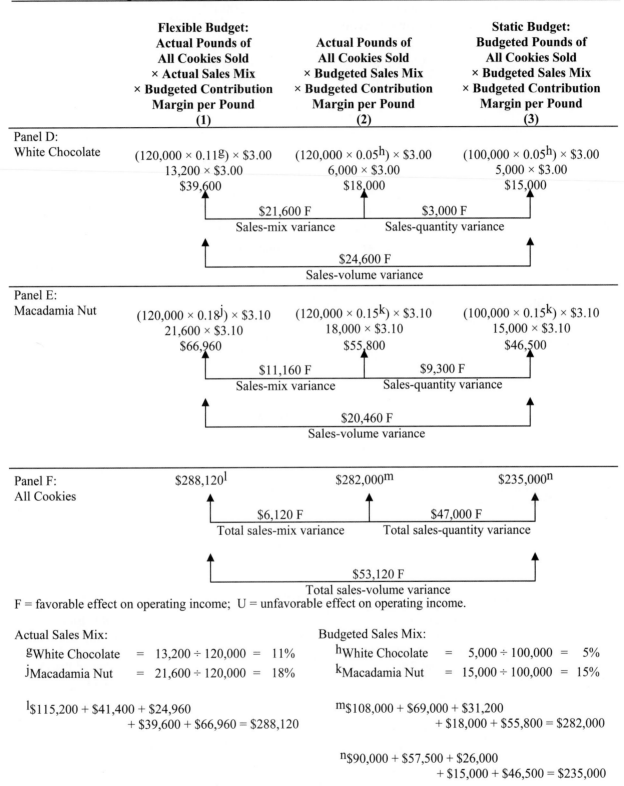

	Flexible Budget: Actual Pounds of All Cookies Sold × Actual Sales Mix × Budgeted Contribution Margin per Pound (1)	Actual Pounds of All Cookies Sold × Budgeted Sales Mix × Budgeted Contribution Margin per Pound (2)	Static Budget: Budgeted Pounds of All Cookies Sold × Budgeted Sales Mix × Budgeted Contribution Margin per Pound (3)
Panel D: White Chocolate	$(120{,}000 \times 0.11^g) \times \$3.00$ $13{,}200 \times \$3.00$ $\$39{,}600$	$(120{,}000 \times 0.05^h) \times \$3.00$ $6{,}000 \times \$3.00$ $\$18{,}000$	$(100{,}000 \times 0.05^h) \times \$3.00$ $5{,}000 \times \$3.00$ $\$15{,}000$

$\$21{,}600$ F — Sales-mix variance $\$3{,}000$ F — Sales-quantity variance

$\$24{,}600$ F — Sales-volume variance

Panel E: Macadamia Nut	$(120{,}000 \times 0.18^j) \times \$3.10$ $21{,}600 \times \$3.10$ $\$66{,}960$	$(120{,}000 \times 0.15^k) \times \$3.10$ $18{,}000 \times \$3.10$ $\$55{,}800$	$(100{,}000 \times 0.15^k) \times \$3.10$ $15{,}000 \times \$3.10$ $\$46{,}500$

$\$11{,}160$ F — Sales-mix variance $\$9{,}300$ F — Sales-quantity variance

$\$20{,}460$ F — Sales-volume variance

Panel F: All Cookies	$\$288{,}120^l$	$\$282{,}000^m$	$\$235{,}000^n$

$\$6{,}120$ F — Total sales-mix variance $\$47{,}000$ F — Total sales-quantity variance

$\$53{,}120$ F — Total sales-volume variance

F = favorable effect on operating income; U = unfavorable effect on operating income.

Actual Sales Mix:
  [g]White Chocolate = $13{,}200 \div 120{,}000$ = 11%
  [j]Macadamia Nut = $21{,}600 \div 120{,}000$ = 18%

Budgeted Sales Mix:
  [h]White Chocolate = $5{,}000 \div 100{,}000$ = 5%
  [k]Macadamia Nut = $15{,}000 \div 100{,}000$ = 15%

[l]$115{,}200 + \$41{,}400 + \$24{,}960$
     $+ \$39{,}600 + \$66{,}960 = \$288{,}120$

[m]$108{,}000 + \$69{,}000 + \$31{,}200$
     $+ \$18{,}000 + \$55{,}800 = \$282{,}000$

[n]$90{,}000 + \$57{,}500 + \$26{,}000$
     $+ \$15{,}000 + \$46{,}500 = \$235{,}000$

A summary of the variances is:

Sales-Volume Variance	
Chocolate chip	$25,200 F
Oatmeal raisin	16,100 U
Coconut	1,040 U
White chocolate	24,600 F
Macadamia nut	20,460 F
All cookies	$53,120 F

Sales-Mix Variance		Sales-Quantity Variance	
Chocolate chip	$ 7,200 F	Chocolate chip	$18,000 F
Oatmeal raisin	27,600 U	Oatmeal raisin	11,500 F
Coconut	6,240 U	Coconut	5,200 F
White chocolate	21,600 F	White chocolate	3,000 F
Macadamia nut	11,160 F	Macadamia nut	9,300 F
All cookies	$ 6,120 F	All cookies	$47,000 F

4. Debbie's Delight shows a *favorable sales-quantity variance* because it sold more cookies in total than was budgeted. Together with the higher quantities, Debbie's also *sold more of the high-contribution margin* white chocolate and macadamia nut cookies relative to the budgeted mix—as a result, Debbie's also showed a *favorable total sales-mix variance*.

14-36 (35 min.) Direct materials efficiency, mix, and yield variances (Chapter Appendix).

1.

Sugar ($1 × 7 cups)	$ 7
Flavoring ($3 × 2 cups)	6
Coloring ($2 × 1 cup)	2
Cost per batch	$ 15
Number of batches	×23
Budgeted Cost	$345

2.
Columnar Presentation of Direct Materials Price and Efficiency Variances for Flavr-Wave Company.

	Actual Costs Incurred (Actual Input Quantity × Actual Price) (1)	Actual Input Quantity × Budgeted Price (2)	Flexible Budget (Budgeted Input Quantity Allowed for Actual Output × Budgeted Price) (3)
Sugar	165× $1= $165	165 × $1 = $165	23 × 7 × $1 = $161
Flavoring	45 × $3 = 135	45 × $3 = 135	23 × 2 × $3 = 138
Coloring	25 × $2 = 50	25 × $2 = 50	23 × 1 × $2 = 46
	$350	$350	$345

$0 $5 U
Total price variance   Total efficiency variance

$5 U
Total flexible-budget variance

F = favorable effect on operating income; U = unfavorable effect on operating income

260

3. Actual price per cup:

Sugar	$165 ÷ 165 cups = $1 per cup
Flavoring	$135 ÷ 45 cups = $3 per cup
Coloring	$50 ÷ 25 cups = $2 per cup

The total direct materials price variance equals zero because for all three inputs, actual price per cup equals the budgeted price per cup.

4.   Columnar Presentation of Direct Materials Yield and Mix Variances for Flavr-Wave Company.

	Actual Total Quantity of All Inputs Used × Actual Input Mix × Budgeted Price (1)	Actual Total Quantity of All Inputs Used × Budgeted Input Mix × Budgeted Price (2)	Flexible Budget: Budgeted Total Quantity of All Inputs Allowed for Actual Output × Budgeted Input Mix × Budgeted Price (3)
Sugar	235 × 0.7021 × $1 = $165	235 × 0.70 × $1 = $164.50	230 × 0.70 × $1 = $161
Flavoring	235 × 0.1915 × $3 = 135	235 × 0.20 × $3 = 141.00	230 × 0.20 × $3 = 138
Coloring	235 × 0.1064 × $2 = 50	235 × 0.10 × $2 = 47.00	230 × 0.10 × $2 = 46
	$350	$352.50	$345

$2.50 F
Total mix variance

$7.50 U
Total yield variance

$5 U
Total efficiency variance

F = favorable effect on operating income; U = unfavorable effect on operating income.

The total direct materials yield variance can also be computed as the sum of the direct materials yield variances for each input:

$$\begin{array}{l} \text{Direct} \\ \text{materials} \\ \text{yield variance} \\ \text{for each input} \end{array} = \left(\begin{array}{l} \text{Actual total} \\ \text{quantity of all} \\ \text{direct materials} \\ \text{inputs used} \end{array} - \begin{array}{l} \text{Budgeted total quantity} \\ \text{of all direct materials inputs} \\ \text{allowed for actual output} \end{array} \right) \times \begin{array}{l} \text{Budgeted} \\ \text{direct materials} \\ \text{input mix} \\ \text{percentage} \end{array} \times \begin{array}{l} \text{Budgeted} \\ \text{price of} \\ \text{direct materials} \\ \text{inputs} \end{array}$$

Sugar	= (235 − 230) × 0.70[a] × $1 = 5 × 0.70 × $1 = $3.50
Flavoring	= (235 − 230) × 0.20[b] × $3 = 5 × 0.20 × $3 = 3.00 U
Coloring	= (235 − 230) × 0.10[c] × $2 = 5 × 0.10 × $2 = 1.00 U
Total direct materials yield variance	$7.50 U

[a] 7 ÷ 10; [b] 2 ÷ 10; [c] 1 ÷ 10

The direct materials mix variance of $2.50 F indicates that actual product mix uses relatively more of less expensive ingredients than planned. In this case, the actual mix contains slightly more coloring and slightly less flavoring.

The direct materials yield variance of $7.50 U occurs because the amount of total inputs needed (235 cups) exceeded the budgeted amount (230 cups) expected to produce 2,300 pops.

The variances are very small relative to the budgeted cost to produce 2,300 pops. The company should not spend resources investigating them, especially since changing the standard mix slightly does not significantly affect product quality.

14-38 (40 min.) Customer profitability and ethics.

1. Customer-level operating income based on expected cost of orders:

	Customers					
	IHoG	**GRU**	**GM**	**GC**	**GG**	**Gmart**
Revenues at list price $40 × 200; 540; 300; 100; 400; 1,000	$8,000	$21,600	$12,000	$4,000	$16,000	$40,000
Price discounts GRU: 5% × $21,600; Gmart: 5% × $40,000	0	1,080	0	0	0	2,000
Revenues (actual price)	8,000	20,520	12,000	4,000	16,000	38,000
Cost of good sold $30 × 200; 540; 300; 100; 400; 1,000	6,000	16,200	9,000	3,000	12,000	30,000
Gross margin	2,000	4,320	3,000	1,000	4,000	8,000
Customer-level operating costs:						
Order taking $28 × 4; 12; 6; 4; 16; 20	112	336	168	112	448	560
Product handling $1 × 200; 540; 300; 100; 400; 1,000	200	540	300	100	400	1,000
Delivery $1 × 80; 120; 72; 28; 304; 100	80	120	72	28	304	100
Expedited delivery $300 × 0; 4; 0; 0; 1; 3	0	1,200	0	0	300	900
Sales commissions $20 × 4; 12; 6; 4; 16; 20)	80	240	120	80	320	400
Total customer-level operating costs	472	2,436	660	320	1,772	2,960
Customer-level operating income	$1,528	$1,884	$2,340	$680	$2,228	$5,040

2. Customer level operating income based on actual order costs:

	Customer					
	IHoG	**GRU**	**GM**	**GC**	**GG**	**Gmart**
Revenues at list price $40 × 200; 540; 300; 100; 400; 1,000	$8,000	$21,600	$12,000	$4,000	$16,000	$40,000
Price discounts GRU: 5% × $21,600; Gmart: 5% × $40,000	0	1,080	0	0	0	2,000
Revenues (actual price)	8,000	20,520	12,000	4,000	16,000	38,000
Cost of good sold $30 × 200; 540; 300; 100; 400; 1,000	6,000	16,200	9,000	3,000	12,000	30,000
Gross margin	2,000	4,320	3,000	1,000	4,000	8,000
Customer-level operating costs:						
Order taking $12 × 4; $28 × 12; $12 × 6; $12 × 4; $12 × 16; $12 × 20	48	336	72	48	192	240
Product handling $1 × 200; 540; 300; 100; 400; 1,000	200	540	300	100	400	1,000
Delivery $1 × 80; 120; 72; 28; 304; 100	80	120	72	28	304	100
Expedited delivery $300 × 0; 4; 0; 0; 1; 3	0	1,200	0	0	300	900
Sales commissions $20 × 4; 12; 6; 4; 16; 20	80	240	120	80	320	400
Total customer-level operating costs	408	2,436	564	256	1,516	2,640
Customer-level operating income	$1,592	$1,884	$2,436	$744	$2,484	$5,360

Comparing the answers in requirements 1 and 2, it appears that operating income is higher than expected, so the management of Glat Corporation would be very pleased with the performance of the salespeople for reducing order costs. Except for GRU, all of the customers are more profitable than originally reported.

3. Customer-level operating

	Customer					
	IHoG	GRU	GM	GC	GG	Gmart
Revenues at list price $40 × 200; 540; 300; 100; 400; 1,000	$8,000	$21,600	$12,000	$4,000	$16,000	$40,000
Price discounts GRU: 5% × $21,600; Gmart: 5% × $40,000	0	1,080	0	0	0	2,000
Revenues (actual price)	8,000	20,520	12,000	4,000	16,000	38,000
Cost of good sold $30 × 200; 540; 300; 100; 400; 1,000	6,000	16,200	9,000	3,000	12,000	30,000
Gross margin	2,000	4,320	3,000	1,000	4,000	8,000
Customer-level operating costs:						
Order taking $28 × 2; 12; 2; 2; 4; 10	56	336	56	56	112	280
Product handling $1 × 200; 540; 300; 100; 400; 1,000	200	540	300	100	400	1,000
Delivery $1 × 80; 120; 72; 28; 304; 100	80	120	72	28	304	100
Expedited delivery $300 × 0; 4; 0; 0; 1; 3	0	1,200	0	0	300	900
Sales commissions $20 × 2; 12; 2; 2; 4; 10	40	240	40	40	80	200
Total customer-level operating costs	376	2,436	468	224	1,196	2,480
Customer-level operating income	$1,624	$1,884	$2,532	$776	$2,804	$5,520

4. The behavior of the salespeople is costing Glat Corporation $640 in profit (the difference between the incomes in requirements 2 and 3.) Although management thinks the salespeople are saving money based on the budgeted order costs, in reality they are costing the firm money by increasing the costs of orders ($936 in requirement 2 versus $896 in requirement 3) and at the same time increasing their sales commissions ($1,240 in requirement 2 versus $640 in requirement 3). This is not ethical.

Glat Corporation needs to *change the structure of the sales commission*, possibly linking commissions to the overall units sold rather than on number of orders. They could also base commissions on total revenues, which will discourage salespeople from offering discounts unless they are needed to close the sale. A negative consequence of greater reluctance to offer discounts is that salespeople will not seek larger orders but instead focus on smaller orders that do not require discounts to be offered. This behavior will, in turn, increase order-taking costs.

CHAPTER 15
ALLOCATION OF SUPPORT-DEPARTMENT COSTS,
COMMON COSTS, AND REVENUES

15-2 The **dual-rate** method provides information to division managers about cost behavior. Knowing *how fixed costs and variable costs behave differently* is useful in decision making.

15-3 Examples of **bases** used to allocate support department cost pools to operating departments include
- the number of employees
- square feet of space
- number of hours
- machine-hours

15-6 **Disagree.** Allocating costs on "the basis of estimated long-run use by user department managers" means department managers can lower their cost allocations by deliberately underestimating their long-run use (assuming all other managers do not similarly underestimate their usage).

15-8 The *reciprocal* method is theoretically the most defensible method because it fully recognizes the mutual services provided among all departments, irrespective of whether those departments are operating or support departments.

15-10 *All contracts with U.S. government agencies must comply* with cost accounting standards issued by the Cost Accounting Standards Board (CASB).

15-12 Companies *increasingly are selling packages of products or services for a single price*. Revenue allocation is required when managers in charge of developing or marketing individual products in a bundle are evaluated using product-specific revenues.

15-14 To support higher revenue allocation to their product, managers typically will argue that their product is the prime reason why consumers buy a bundle of products. They might cite:
- sales of the products when sold as individual products
- surveys of users of each product
- surveys of people who purchase the bundle of products.

15-16 (20 min.)   **Single-rate versus dual-rate methods, support department.**

Bases available (kilowatt hours):

	Rockford	Peoria	Hammond	Kankakee	Total
Practical capacity	10,000	20,000	12,000	8,000	50,000
Expected monthly usage	8,000	9,000	7,000	6,000	30,000

1a.   Single-rate method based on practical capacity:

Total costs in pool	=	$6,000 + $9,000	= $15,000
Practical capacity	=	50,000 kilowatt hours	
Allocation rate	=	$15,000 ÷ 50,000	= $0.30 per hour of capacity

	Rockford	Peoria	Hammond	Kankakee	Total
Practical capacity in hours	10,000	20,000	12,000	8,000	50,000
Costs allocated at $0.30 per hour	$3,000	$6,000	$3,600	$2,400	$15,000

1b.   Single-rate method based on expected monthly usage:

Total costs in pool	= $6,000 + $9,000	= $15,000
Expected usage	= 30,000 kilowatt hours	
Allocation rate	= $15,000 ÷ 30,000	= $0.50 per hour of expected usage

	Rockford	Peoria	Hammond	Kankakee	Total
Expected monthly usage in hours	8,000	9,000	7,000	6,000	30,000
Costs allocated at $0.50 per hour	$4,000	$4,500	$3,500	$3,000	$15,000

2.   Variable-Cost Pool:

Total costs in pool	=	$6,000
Expected usage	=	30,000 kilowatt hours
Allocation rate	=	$6,000 ÷ 30,000 = $0.20 per hour of expected usage

Fixed-Cost Pool:

Total costs in pool	=	$9,000
Practical capacity	=	50,000 kilowatt hours
Allocation rate	=	$9,000 ÷ 50,000 = $0.18 per hour of capacity

	Rockford	Peoria	Hammond	Kankakee	Total
Variable-cost pool $0.20 × 8,000; 9,000; 7,000, 6,000	$1,600	$1,800	$1,400	$1,200	$ 6,000
Fixed-cost pool $0.18 × 10,000; 20,000; 12,000, 8,000	1,800	3,600	2,160	1,440	9,000
Total	$3,400	$5,400	$3,560	$2,640	$15,000

The **dual-rate method** permits a *more refined allocation* of the power department costs; it permits the use of different allocation bases for different cost pools. The fixed costs result from decisions most likely associated with the practical capacity level. The variable costs result from decisions most likely associated with monthly usage.

15-18 (20 min.) **Dual-rate method, budgeted versus actual costs, and practical capacity versus actual quantities (continuation of 15-17).**

1. Charges with dual rate method.

Variable indirect cost rate	=	$1,500 per trip
Fixed indirect cost rate	=	$40,000 budgeted costs/ 50 round trips budgeted
	=	$800 per trip

Dark Chocolate Division
Variable indirect costs, $1,500 × 30 $45,000
Fixed indirect costs, $800 × 30   24,000
                                            $69,000

Milk Chocolate Division
Variable indirect costs, $1,500 × 15 $22,500
Fixed indirect costs, $800 × 20   16,000
                                            $38,500

2. The <u>dual rate</u> changes how the fixed indirect cost component is treated. By using *budgeted* trips made, the Dark Chocolate Division is *unaffected by changes from its own budgeted usage or that of other divisions*. When budgeted rates and actual trips are used for allocation, the Dark Chocolate Division is assigned the same $24,000 for fixed costs as under the dual-rate method because it made the same number of trips as budgeted. However, note that the Milk Chocolate Division is allocated $16,000 in fixed trucking costs under the dual-rate system, compared to $800 × 15 actual trips = $12,000 when actual trips are used for allocation. As such, the Dark Chocolate Division is not made to appear disproportionately more expensive than the Milk Chocolate Division simply because the latter did not make the number of trips it budgeted at the start of the year.

15-20 (50 min.) **Support-department cost allocation, reciprocal method (continuation of 15-19).**

1a.

	Support Departments		Operating Departments	
	AS	I S	Govt.	Corp.
Costs	$600,000	$2,400,000		
Alloc. of AS costs				
(0.25, 0.40, 0.35)	(861,538)	215,385	$ 344,615	$ 301,538
Alloc. of IS costs				
(0.10, 0.30, 0.60)	261,538	(2,615,385)	784,616	1,569,231
	$ 0	$ 0	$1,129,231	$1,870,769

Reciprocal Method Computation

$$
\begin{aligned}
AS &= \$600,000 + 0.10\ IS \\
IS &= \$2,400,000 + 0.25AS \\
IS &= \$2,400,000 + 0.25\ (\$600,000 + 0.10\ IS) \\
&= \$2,400,000 + \$150,000 + 0.025\ IS \\
0.975IS &= \$2,550,000 \\
IS &= \$2,550,000 \div 0.975 \\
&= \$2,615,385 \\
AS &= \$600,000 + 0.10\ (\$2,615,385) \\
&= \$600,000 + \$261,538 \\
&= \$861,538
\end{aligned}
$$

1b.

	Support Departments		Operating Departments	
	AS	I S	Govt.	Corp.
Costs	$600,000	$2,400,000		
1st Allocation of AS				
(0.25, 0.40, 0.35)	(600,000)	150,000	$ 240,000	$ 210,000
		2,550,000		
1st Allocation of IS				
(0.10, 0.30, 0.60)	255,000	(2,550,000)	765,000	1,530,000
2nd Allocation of AS				
(0.25, 0.40, 0.35)	(255,000)	63,750	102,000	89,250
2nd Allocation of IS				
(0.10, 0.30, 0.60)	6,375	(63,750)	19,125	38,250
3rd Allocation of AS				
(0.25, 0.40, 0.35)	(6,375)	1,594	2,550	2,231
3rd Allocation of IS				
(0.10, 0.30, 0.60)	160	(1,594)	478	956
4th Allocation of AS				
(0.25, 0.40, 0.35)	(160)	40	64	56
4th Allocation of IS				
(0.10, 0.30, 0.60)	4	(40)	12	24
5th Allocation of AS				
(0.25, 0.40, 0.35)	(4)	1	2	1
5th Allocation of IS				
(0.10, 0.30, 0.60)	0	(1)	0	1
Total allocation	$ 0	$ 0	$1,129,231	$1,870,769

2.

	Govt. Consulting	Corp. Consulting
a. Direct	$1,120,000	$1,880,000
b. Step-Down (AS first)	1,090,000	1,910,000
c. Step-Down (IS first)	1,168,000	1,832,080
d. Reciprocal (linear equations)	1,129,231	1,870,769
e. Reciprocal (repeated iterations)	1,129,231	1,870,769

The four methods differ in the level of support department cost allocation across support departments. The level of reciprocal service by support departments is material. Administrative Services supplies 25% of its services to Information Systems. Information Systems supplies 10% of its services to Administrative Services. The Information Department has a budget of $2,400,000 that is 400% higher than Administrative Services.

The reciprocal method recognizes all the interactions and is thus the most accurate. This is especially clear from looking at the repeated iterations calculations.

15-22 (30 min.) **Reciprocal cost allocation (continuation of 15-21).**

1. The reciprocal allocation method explicitly includes the mutual services provided among all support departments. Interdepartmental relationships are fully incorporated into the support department cost allocations.

2. $\quad$ HR $= \$72,700 + .08333\text{IS}$
    $\quad$ IS $\;\;= \$234,400 + .23077\text{HR}$
    $\quad$ HR $= \$72,700 + [.08333(\$234,400 + .23077\text{HR})]$
    $\qquad\quad = \$72,700 + [\$19,532.55 + 0.01923\text{HR}]$
    $0.98077\text{HR} = \$92,232.55$
    $\quad$ HR $= \$92,232.55 \div 0.98077$
    $\qquad\quad = \$94,041$
    $\quad$ IS $\;\;= \$234,400 + (0.23077 \times \$94,041)$
    $\qquad\quad = \$256,102$

	Support Depts.		Operating Depts.		
	HR	Info. Systems	Corporate	Consumer	Total
Costs Incurred	$72,700	$234,400	$ 998,270	$489,860	$1,795,230
Alloc. of HR costs					
(21/91, 42/91, 28/91)	(94,041)	21,702	43,404	28,935	
Alloc. of Info. Syst. costs					
(320/3,840, 1,920/3,840,					
1,600/3,840)	21,341	(256,102)	128,051	106,710	
	$ 0	$ 0	$1,169,725	$625,505	$1,795,230

268

Reciprocal Method of Allocating Support Department Costs for September 2009 at E-books Using Repeated Iterations

	Support Departments		Operating Departments		
	Human Resources	Information Systems	Corporate Sales	Consumer Sales	Total
Budgeted manufacturing overhead costs before any interdepartmental cost allocation	$72,700	$234,400	$ 998,270	$489,860	$1,795,230
1st Allocation of HR (21/91, 42/91, 28/91)[a]	(72,700)	16,777	33,554	22,369	
		251,177			
1st Allocation of Information Systems (320/3,840, 1,920/3,840, 1,600/3,840)[b]	20,931	(251,177)	125,589	104,657	
2nd Allocation of HR (21/91, 42/91, 28/91)[a]	(20,931)	4,830	9,661	6,440	
2nd Allocation of Information Systems (320/3,840, 1,920/3,840, 1,600/3,840)[b]	402	(4,830)	2,415	2,013	
3rd Allocation of HR (21/91, 42/91, 28/91)[a]	(402)	93	185	124	
3rd Allocation of Information Systems (320/3,840, 1,920/3,840, 1,600/3,840)[b]	8	(93)	46	39	
4th Allocation of HR (21/91, 42/91, 28/91)[a]	(8)	2	4	2	
4th Allocation of Information Systems: (320/3,840, 1,920/3,840, 1,600/3,840)[b]	0	(2)	1	1	
Total budgeted manufacturing overhead of operating departments	$ 0	$ 0	$1,169,725	$625,505	$1,795,230

Total accounts allocated and reallocated (the numbers in parentheses in first two columns)
HR $72,700 + $20,931 + $402 + $8 = $94,041
Information Systems $251,177 + $4,830 + $93 + $2 = $256,102

[a]Base is (21 + 42 + 28) or 91 employees
[b]Base is (320 + 1,920 + 1,600) or 3,840 minutes

3.   The reciprocal method is more accurate than the direct and step-down methods when there are reciprocal relationships among support departments.

A summary of the alternatives is:

	Corporate Sales	Consumer Sales
Direct method	$1,169,745	$625,485
Step-down method (HR first)	1,168,830	626,400
Reciprocal method	1,169,725	625,505

The reciprocal method is the preferred method, although for September 2009 the numbers do not appear materially different across the alternatives.

15-24 (20 min.) **Allocation of common costs.**

1.   Alternative approaches for the allocation of the $1,800 airfare include the following:

   a. *The stand-alone cost allocation method*. This method would allocate the air fare on the basis of each client's percentage of the total of the individual stand-alone costs.

   Baltimore client $\dfrac{\$1,400}{(\$1,400+\$1,100)} \times \$1,800 = \$1,008$

   Chicago client $\dfrac{\$1,100}{(\$1,400+\$1,100)} \times \$1,800 = \underline{792}$

   $\underline{\underline{\$1,800}}$

   Advocates of this method often emphasize an equity or **fairness** rationale.

   b. *The incremental cost allocation method*. This requires the choice of a primary party and an incremental party.

   If the Baltimore client is the primary party, the allocation would be:

Baltimore client	$1,400
Chicago client	400
	$1,800

   One rationale is that Gunn was *planning to make the Baltimore trip*, and the Chicago stop was added subsequently. Some students have suggested allocating as much as possible to the Baltimore client since Gunn had decided not to work for them.

   If the Chicago client is the primary party, the allocation would be:

Chicago client	$1,100
Baltimore client	700
	$1,800

   One rationale is that the *Chicago* client is the one who is going to use Gunn's services, and presumably *receives more benefits* from the travel expenditures.

   c. Gunn could calculate the *Shapley value* that considers each client in turn as the primary party: The Baltimore client is allocated $1,400 as the primary party and $700 as the incremental party for an **average** of ($1,400 + $700) ÷ 2 = $1,050. The Chicago client is allocated $1,100 as the primary party and $400 as the incremental party for an **average** of ($1,100 + 400) ÷ 2 = $750. The Shapley value approach would allocate $1,050 to the Baltimore client and $750 to the Chicago client.

2.   I would **recommend** Gunn use the *Shapley value*. It is fairer than the incremental method because it avoids considering one party as the primary party and allocating more of the common costs to that party. It also avoids disputes about who is the primary party. It allocates costs in a manner that is close to the costs allocated under the stand-alone method but takes a more comprehensive view of the common cost allocation problem by considering primary and incremental users, which the stand-alone method ignores.

The Shapley value (or the stand-alone cost allocation method) would be the preferred methods if Gunn was to send the travel expenses to the Baltimore and Chicago clients before deciding which engagement to accept. Other factors such as whether to charge the Chicago client more because Gunn is accepting the Chicago engagement or the Baltimore client more because Gunn is not going to work for them can be considered if Gunn sends in her travel expenses after making her decision. However, each company would not want to be considered as the primary party and so is likely to object to these arguments.

3.   A simple approach is to split the $60 equally between the two clients. The limousine costs at the Sacramento end are not a function of distance traveled on the plane.

An alternative approach is to add the $60 to the $1,800 and repeat requirement 1:

a. Stand-alone cost allocation method.

Baltimore client $\dfrac{\$1,460}{(\$1,460+\$1,160)} \times \$1,860 = \$1,036$

Chicago client $\dfrac{\$1,160}{(\$1,460+\$1,160)} \times \$1,860 = \$\ 824$

b. Incremental cost allocation method.

With Baltimore client as the primary party:
Baltimore client	$1,460
Chicago client	400
	$1,860

With Chicago client as the primary party:
Chicago client	$1,160
Baltimore client	700
	$1,860

c. Shapley value.
Baltimore client: ($1,460 + $700) ÷ 2 = $1,080
Chicago client: ($400 + $1,160) ÷ 2 = $ 780

As discussed in requirement 2, the Shapley value or the stand-alone cost allocation method would probably be the preferred approaches.

15-26 (10-15 min.) **Allocation of Common Costs**

1. a. Stand-alone method (costs are in thousands):

City	Separate Cost	Percentage	Joint Cost	Allocation
Albany	$2,100	$2,100 ÷ $7,000=0.3	$5,000	$1,500
Troy	1,400	$1,400 ÷ $7,000=0.2	5,000	1,000
Schenectady	3,500	$3,500 ÷ $7,000=0.5	5,000	2,500
	$7,000			$5,000

1. b. Incremental method (cities ranked in order of most waste to least waste):

	Allocated Cost	Cost Remaining to Allocate
Schenectady	$3,500	$1,500 ($5,000 – $3,500)
Albany	1,500	0 ($1,500 – $1,500)
Troy	0	0

2. In this situation, the *stand-alone method is the better method* because the weights it uses for allocation are based on the cost for each user as a separate entity. The citizens of Schenectady would not consider the incremental method fair because they would be subsidizing the other cities (especially Troy). Albany is indifferent across the two methods; its citizens save $600,000 over the stand-alone cost in either case. While the citizens of Troy would clearly prefer the incremental allocation method and might seek to justify it because they generate the least amount of waste, they should understand that citizens of the other cities would believe it is not fair.

15-28 (20 min.) **Revenue allocation**

1. a. Stand-alone method for the BegM + RCC package

DVD	Separate Revenue	Percentage	Joint Revenue	Allocation
BegM	$ 60	$60 ÷ $100=0.6	$90	$54
RCC	40	$40 ÷ $100=0.4	90	36
	$100			$90

1. b. Incremental method

i)

	Allocated Revenue (BegM first)	Revenue Remaining To Allocate
BegM	$60	$30 ($90 – $60)
RCC	30	

ii)

	Allocated Revenue (RCC first)	Revenue Remaining To Allocate
RCC	$40	$50 ($90 – $40)
BegM	50	

272

1. c. Shapley method. (assuming each DVD is demanded in equal proportion)

      i) BegM   ($60 + $50) ÷ 2 = $55
      ii) RCC   ($30 + $40) ÷ 2 = $35

2. a. Stand-alone method for the ConM + RCC package

DVD	Separate Revenue	Percentage	Joint Revenue	Allocation
ConM	$50	$50 ÷ $90=0.556	$72	$40
RCC	40	$40 ÷ $90=0.444	72	32
	$90			$72

2. b. Incremental method

  i)

	Allocated Revenue (ConM first)	Revenue Remaining To Allocate
ConM	$50	$22 ($72 − $50)
RCC	22	

  ii)

	Allocated Revenue (RCC first)	Revenue Remaining To Allocate
RCC	$40	$32 ($72 − $40)
ConM	32	

2. c. Shapley method. (assuming each DVD is demanded in equal proportion)

      i) BegM   (50+32) ÷ 2 = 41
      ii) RCC   (22+40) ÷ 2 = 31

3.   For each DVD package, the *stand-alone method and the Shapley method give approximately the same allocation to each DVD*. These methods are fair if the *demand for the DVDs is approximately equal*. The stand-alone method might be slightly preferable here since it is simpler and easier to explain.

The *incremental* method would be appropriate if *one DVD has a higher level of demand* than the other DVD. In this situation, the dominant DVD would be sold anyway so it should receive its stand-alone revenue, and the other DVD should receive the remainder.

15-30 (45 min.)   Allocating costs of support departments; step-down and direct methods.

	Building & Grounds	Personnel	General Plant Admin.	Cafeteria Operating Loss	Storeroom	Machining	Assembly
1. Step-down Method:							
(1) Building & grounds at $0.10/sq.ft. ($10,000 ÷ 100,000)	$ 10,000	$ 1,000	$ 26,090	$ 1,640	$ 2,670	$34,700	$48,900
(2) Personnel at $6/employee ($1,200 ÷ 200)	$(10,000)	200	700	400	700	3,000	5,000
(3) General plant administration at $1/labor-hour ($27,000 ÷ 27,000)		$(1,200)	210	60	30	300	600
(4) Cafeteria at $20/empoloyee ($3,100 ÷ 155)			$(27,000)	1,000	1,000	8,000	17,000
(5) Storeroom at $1.50/requisition ($4,500 ÷ 3,000)				$(3,100)	100	1,000	2,000
(6) Costs allocated to operating depts.					$(4,500)	3,000	1,500
(7) Divide (6) by dir. manuf. labor-hrs.						$50,000	$75,000
(8) Overhead rate per direct manuf. labor-hour						÷ 5,000	÷15,000
						$ 10	$ 5
2. Direct method:							
(1) Building & grounds, 30,000/80,000: 50,000/80,000	$10,000	$1,000	$26,090	$1,640	$2,670	$34,700	$48,900
(2) Personnel, 50/150; 100/150	(10,000)					3,750	6,250
(3) General plant administration, 8,000/25,000; 17,000/25,000		(1,000)				333	667
(4) Cafeteria, 50/150; 100/150			(26,090)			8,349	17,741
(5) Storeroom: 2,000/3,000; 1,000/3,000				(1,640)		547	1,093
(6) Costs allocated to operating depts.					(2,670)	1,780	890
(7) Divide (6) by direct manufacturing labor-hours						$49,459	$75,541
(8) Overhead rate per direct manufacturing labor-hour						÷ 5,000	÷15,000
						$ 9,892	$ 5,036

274

3.   Comparison of Methods:

Step-down method:	Job 88:	18 × $10	$180	
		2 × $ 5	10	$190.00
	Job 89:	3 × $10	$ 30	
		17 × $ 5	85	115.00
Direct method:	Job 88:	18 × $9.892	$178.06	
		2 × $5.036	10.07	$188.13
	Job 89:	3 × $9.892	$ 29.68	
		17 × $5.036	85.61	115.29

4.   The manager of _Machining Department would prefer the direct method_. The direct method results in a lower amount of support departments' costs being allocated to the Machining Department than the step-down method. This is clear from a comparison of the overhead rate, per direct manufacturing labor-hour, for the Machining Department under the two methods.

15-32 (25 min.) **Common costs.**

1.   Stand-alone cost-allocation method.

Wright, Inc. $= \dfrac{(900 \times \$40)}{(900 \times \$40) + (600 \times \$40)} \times (1,500 \times \$32)$

$= \dfrac{\$36,000}{(\$36,000 + \$24,000)} \times \$48,000 = \$28,800$

Brown, Inc. $= \dfrac{(600 \times \$40)}{(900 \times \$40) + (600 \times \$40)} \times (1,500 \times \$32)$

$= \dfrac{\$24,000}{(\$36,000 + \$24,000)} \times \$48,000 = \$19,200$

2.   With Wright, Inc. as the primary party:

Party	Costs Allocated	Cumulative Costs Allocated
Wright	$36,000	$36,000
Brown	12,000 ($48,000 – $36,000)	$48,000
Total	$48,000	

With Brown, Inc. as the primary party:

Party	Costs Allocated	Cumulative Costs Allocated
Brown	$24,000	$24,000
Wright	24,000 ($48,000 – $24,000)	$48,000
Total	$48,000	

3.   To use the Shapley value method, consider each party as first the primary party and then the incremental party. Compute the average of the two to determine the allocation.

Wright, Inc.:
Allocation as the primary party	$36,000
Allocation as the incremental party	24,000
Total	$60,000
Allocation ($60,000 ÷ 2)	$30,000

Brown, Inc.:
Allocation as the primary party	$24,000
Allocation as the incremental party	12,000
Total	$36,000
Allocation ($36,000 ÷ 2)	$18,000

Using this approach, Wright, Inc. is allocated $30,000 and Brown, Inc. is allocated $18,000 of the total costs of $48,000.

4.   The results of the four cost-allocation methods are shown below.

	Wright, Inc.	**Brown, Inc.**
Stand-alone method	$28,800	$19,200
Incremental (Wright primary)	36,000	12,000
Incremental (Brown primary)	24,000	24,000
Shapley value	30,000	18,000

The *allocations are very sensitive to the method used*. The stand-alone method is simple and fair since it allocates the common cost of the dyeing machine in proportion to the individual costs of leasing the machine. The Shapley values are also fair. They result in very similar allocations and any one of them can be chosen. In this case, the stand-alone method is likely more acceptable. If they used the incremental cost-allocation method, Wright, Inc. and Brown, Inc. would probably have disputes over who is the primary party because the primary party gets allocated all of the primary party's costs.

15-34 (10-15 min.) **Effect of demand (continuation of 15-33)**

1.   If the Water park receives its full ticket price of $40, then the remaining proceeds from the sale of the three day ticket, $90 – 40 = $50, would be divided between the two remaining parks. Using ticket price as the basis of allocation, each park would receive:

Park	**Ticket Price**	**Percentage of Total Price**	**Allocation % × $50**
Superhero Theme	$60	0.750	$37.50
Animal	20	0.250	12.50
Total	$80		$50.00

The same process would be used for the other two allocation bases. Under the cost basis, the Superhero Theme park receives $\frac{25}{25+10} \times \$50 = \$35.71$, while Animal park gets the other $14.29.

If revenue is assigned based on the number of tickets received, then the Superhero Theme and Animal Parks would each receive $25.

2.   If the Superhero Theme park also demanded its full ticket price then it would want to receive $60. The two parks, Water and Superhero Theme, would then receive a combined amount of $40 + 60 = $100. Since the three-day ticket sells for only $90, this would not be possible. In addition, the Animal park director would not be pleased because he would incur a $10 cost for each entrant but receive no proceeds from the ticket.

3.   If both the Water and the Superhero Theme parks are really operating at capacity then Funland is losing money by selling the three-day ticket for $90. Kent Clark should either raise the price or decide not to sell the three-day ticket. Alternatively, if he wishes to persist with the current arrangement, he should use a more sophisticated arrangement for allocating revenue, such as the Shapley method or even the weighted Shapley method. In the latter case, Kent could assign the number of months each park is considered the primary park as the weighting scheme. For example, while the Water Park may drive sales of the three-day ticket during summer months, customers may be more interested in one of the other parks during cooler periods.

CHAPTER 16
COST ALLOCATION: JOINT PRODUCTS AND BYPRODUCTS

16-2 A **joint cost** is a cost of a production _process that yields multiple products simultaneously_. A **_separable cost_** is a _cost incurred beyond the splitoff point_ that is assignable to each of the specific products identified at the splitoff point.

16-4 A **product** is any output that has a _positive sales value_. In some joint-cost settings, **outputs** can occur that _do not have a positive sales value_. The offshore processing of hydrocarbons yields the output water that is recycled back into the ocean as well as yielding the products oil and gas. The processing of mineral ore to yield the products gold and silver also yields dirt as an output, which is recycled back into the ground.

16-6 The joint production process yields individual products that are either sold this period or held as inventory to be sold in subsequent periods. _Proper matching_ requires the joint costs to be allocated between all production rather than just those sold this period.

16-8 Both methods use _market selling-price data in allocating joint costs_, but they differ in _which sales-price data they use_.
  - The **sales value at splitoff method** allocates joint costs on the basis of the relative _revenue_ that could be obtained immediately after they cease being joint.
  - The **net realizable value method** allocates joint costs to joint products on the basis of the relative _revenue less separable costs_. This is removed from the split off point by further processing.

16-10 The **NRV** method can be **simplified** by assuming
       (a) a standard set of post-splitoff point processing steps, and
       (b) a standard set of selling prices.

16-12 **No**. Any method used to allocate joint costs to individual products _should not be used for management decisions_ regarding whether a product should be sold or processed further. Joint costs are irrelevant for these decisions. The _only_ relevant items for these decisions are the _incremental revenue and the incremental costs_ beyond the splitoff point.

16-14 Two methods to account for **byproducts** are:
    a. _Production method_—recognizes byproducts in the financial statements at the time production is completed.
    b. _Sales method_—delays recognition of byproducts until the time of sale.

16-16 (20-30 min.) **Joint-cost allocation, insurance settlement.** Note: This problem assumes that all products are main products. You could make a different determination about the bones and/or feathers. See problem 16-17 for more detail on that issue. There are other problems in the solution manual that deal with byproducts as well.

1. (a) Sales value at splitoff method:

	Pounds of Product	Wholesale Selling Price per Pound	Sales Value at Splitoff	Weighting: Sales Value at Splitoff	Joint Costs Allocated	Allocated Costs per Pound
Breasts	100	$0.55	$55.00	0.675	$33.75	0.3375
Wings	20	0.20	4.00	0.049	2.45	0.1225
Thighs	40	0.35	14.00	0.172	8.60	0.2150
Bones	80	0.10	8.00	0.098	4.90	0.0613
Feathers	10	0.05	0.50	0.006	0.30	0.0300
	250		$81.50	1.000	$50.00	

Costs of Destroyed Product

Breasts: $0.3375 per pound × 40 pounds = $13.50
Wings: $0.1225 per pound × 15 pounds = 1.84
$15.34

b. Physical measure method:

	Pounds of Product	Weighting: Physical Measures	Joint Costs Allocated	Allocated Costs per Pound
Breasts	100	0.400	$20.00	$0.200
Wings	20	0.080	4.00	0.200
Thighs	40	0.160	8.00	0.200
Bones	80	0.320	16.00	0.200
Feathers	10	0.040	2.00	0.200
	250	1.000	$50.00	

Costs of Destroyed Product

Breast: $0.20 per pound × 40 pounds = $ 8
Wings: $0.20 per pound × 15 pounds = 3
$11

2. The *sales-value at splitoff method* captures the benefits-received criterion of cost allocation and is the preferred method. Quality Chicken's decision to process chicken is heavily influenced by the revenues from breasts and thighs. The bones provide relatively few benefits to Quality Chicken despite their high physical volume.

    The *physical measures* method shows profits on breasts and thighs and losses on bones and feathers. Quality Chicken is processing chicken mainly for breasts and thighs and not for wings, bones, and feathers, while the physical measure method allocates a disproportionate amount of costs to wings, bones and feathers.

280

16-18 (10 min.) **Net realizable value method.**

	Corn Syrup	Corn Starch	Total
Final sales value of total production, 12,500 × $50; 6,250 × $25	$625,000	$156,250	$781,250
Deduct separable costs	375,000	93,750	468,750
Net realizable value at splitoff point	$250,000	$ 62,500	$312,500
Weighting, $250,000; $62,500 ÷ $312,500	0.8	0.2	
Joint costs allocated, 0.8; 0.2 × $325,000	$260,000	$ 65,000	$325,000

CONVAD COMPANY – JOINT PRODUCTS

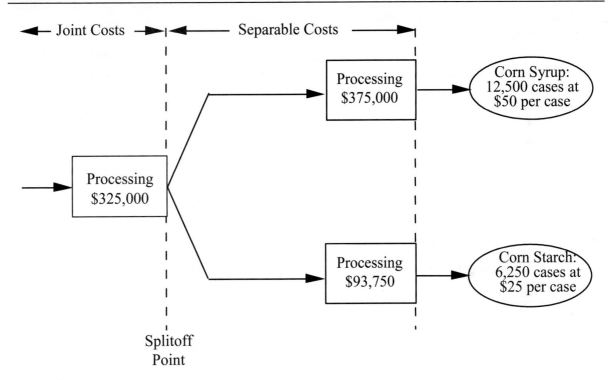

16-20 (40 min.)   **Alternative methods of joint-cost allocation, ending inventories.**

Total production for the year was:

	Sold	Ending Inventories	Total Production
X	120	180	300
Y	340	60	400
Z	475	25	500

1.   a. Net realizable value (NRV) method:

	X	Y	Z	Total
Final sales value of total production,				
300 × $1,500; 400 × $1,000; 500 × $700	$450,000	$400,000	$350,000	$1,200,000
Deduct separable costs	—	—	200,000	200,000
Net realizable value at splitoff point	$450,000	$400,000	$150,000	$1,000,000
Weighting, $450; $400; $150 ÷ $1,000	0.45	0.40	0.15	
Joint costs allocated,				
0.45, 0.40, 0.15 × $400,000	$180,000	$160,000	$ 60,000	$ 400,000

Ending Inventory Percentages:

	X	Y	Z
Ending inventory	180	60	25
Total production	300	400	500
Ending inventory percentage	60%	15%	5%

Income Statement

	X	Y	Z	Total
Revenues,				
120 × $1,500; 340 × $1,000; 475 × $700	$180,000	$340,000	$332,500	$852,500
Cost of goods sold:				
Joint costs allocated	180,000	160,000	60,000	400,000
Separable costs	—	—	200,000	200,000
Production costs	180,000	160,000	260,000	600,000
Deduct ending inventory,				
60%; 15%; 5% of production costs	108,000	24,000	13,000	145,000
Cost of goods sold	72,000	136,000	247,000	455,000
Gross margin	$108,000	$204,000	$ 85,500	$397,500
Gross-margin percentage	60%	60%	25.71%	

b.   Constant gross-margin percentage NRV method:

Step 1:

Final sales value of prodn., (300 × $1,500) + (400 × $1,000) + (500 × $700)	$1,200,000
Deduct joint and separable costs, $400,000 + $200,000	600,000
Gross margin	$ 600,000
Gross-margin percentage, $600,000 ÷ $1,200,000	50%

Step 2:

	X	Y	Z	Total
Final sales value of total production,				
300 × $1,500; 400 × $1,000; 500 × $700	$450,000	$400,000	$350,000	$1,200,000
Deduct gross margin, using overall				
gross-margin percentage of sales, 50%	225,000	200,000	175,000	600,000
Total production costs	225,000	200,000	175,000	600,000
Step 3: Deduct separable costs	—	—	200,000	200,000
Joint costs allocated	$225,000	$200,000	$(25,000)	$ 400,000

The negative joint-cost allocation to Product Z illustrates one "unusual" feature of the constant gross-margin percentage NRV method: some products may receive negative cost allocations so that all individual products have the same gross-margin percentage.

Income Statement

	X	Y	Z	Total
Revenues, 120 × $1,500;				
340 × $1,000; 475 × $700	$180,000	$340,000	$332,500	$852,500
Cost of goods sold:				
Joint costs allocated	225,000	200,000	(25,000)	400,000
Separable costs	-	-	200,000	200,000
Production costs	225,000	200,000	175,000	600,000
Deduct ending inventory,				
60%; 15%; 5% of production costs	135,000	30,000	8,750	173,750
Cost of goods sold	90,000	170,000	166,250	426,250
Gross margin	$ 90,000	$170,000	$166,250	$426,250
Gross-margin percentage	50%	50%	50%	50%

Summary

	X	Y	Z	Total
a. NRV method:				
Inventories on balance sheet	$108,000	$ 24,000	$ 13,000	$145,000
Cost of goods sold on income statement	72,000	136,000	247,000	455,000
				$600,000
b. Constant gross-margin percentage NRV method				
Inventories on balance sheet	$135,000	$ 30,000	$ 8,750	$173,750
Cost of goods sold on income statement	90,000	170,000	166,250	426,250
				$600,000

2. Gross-margin percentages:

	X	Y	Z
NRV method	60%	60%	25.71%
Constant gross-margin percentage NRV	50%	50%	50.00%

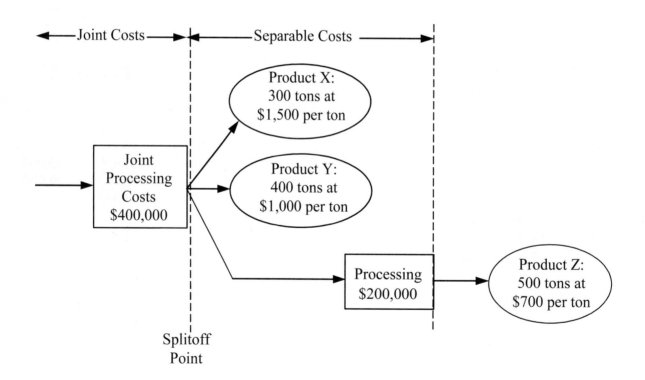

← Joint Costs → | ← Separable Costs →

Joint Processing Costs $400,000

Product X: 300 tons at $1,500 per ton

Product Y: 400 tons at $1,000 per ton

Processing $200,000

Product Z: 500 tons at $700 per ton

Splitoff Point

16-22 (30 min.) **Joint-cost allocation, sales value, physical measure, NRV methods.**

1a.

PANEL A: Allocation of Joint Costs using Sales Value at Splitoff Method	Special B/ Beef Ramen	Special S/ Shrimp Ramen	Total
Sales value of total production at splitoff point (10,000 tons × $10 per ton; 20,000 × $15 per ton)	$100,000	$300,000	$400,000
Weighting ($100,000; $300,000 ÷ $400,000)	0.25	0.75	
Joint costs allocated (0.25; 0.75 × $240,000)	$60,000	$180,000	$240,000

PANEL B: Product-Line Income Statement for June 2009	Special B	Special S	Total
Revenues (12,000 tons × $18 per ton; 24,000 × $25 per ton)	$216,000	$600,000	$816,000
Deduct joint costs allocated (from Panel A)	60,000	180,000	240,000
Deduct separable costs	48,000	168,000	216,000
Gross margin	$108,000	$252,000	$360,000
Gross margin percentage	50%	42%	44%

1b.

PANEL A: Allocation of Joint Costs using Physical-Measure Method	Special B/ Beef Ramen	Special S/ Shrimp Ramen	Total
Physical measure of total production (tons)	10,000	20,000	30,000
Weighting (10,000 tons; 20,000 tons ÷ 30,000 tons)	33%	67%	
Joint costs allocated (0.33; 0.67 × $240,000)	$80,000	$160,000	$240,000

PANEL B: Product-Line Income Statement for June 2009	Special B	Special S	Total
Revenues (12,000 tons × $18 per ton; 24,000 × $25 per ton)	$216,000	$600,000	$816,000
Deduct joint costs allocated (from Panel A)	80,000	160,000	240,000
Deduct separable costs	48,000	168,000	216,000
Gross margin	$ 88,000	$272,000	$360,000
Gross margin percentage	41%	45%	44%

1c.

PANEL A: Allocation of Joint Costs using Net Realizable Value Method	Special B	Special S	Total
Final sales value of total production during accounting period (12,000 tons × $18 per ton; 24,000 tons × $25 per ton)	$216,000	$600,000	$816,000
Deduct separable costs	48,000	168,000	216,000
Net realizable value at splitoff point	$168,000	$432,000	$600,000
Weighting ($168,000; $432,000 ÷ $600,000)	28%	72%	
Joint costs allocated (0.28; 0.72 × $240,000)	$67,200	$172,800	$240,000

PANEL B: Product-Line Income Statement for June 2009	Special B	Special S	Total
Revenues (12,000 tons × $18 per ton; 24,000 tons × $25 per ton)	$216,000	$600,000	$816,000
Deduct joint costs allocated (from Panel A)	67,200	172,800	240,000
Deduct separable costs	48,000	168,000	216,000
Gross margin	$100,800	$259,200	$360,000
Gross margin percentage	46.7%	43.2%	44.1%

2.   Sherrie Dong probably performed the analysis shown below to arrive at the net loss of $2,228 from marketing the stock:

PANEL A: Allocation of Joint Costs using Sales Value at Splitoff	Special B/ Beef Ramen	Special S/ Shrimp Ramen	Stock	Total
Sales value of total production at splitoff point (10,000 tons × $10 per ton; 20,000 × $15 per ton; 4,000 × $5 per ton)	$100,000	$300,000	$20,000	$420,000
Weighting ($100,000; $300,000; $20,000 ÷ $420,000)	23.8095%	71.4286%	4.7619%	100%
Joint costs allocated (0.238095; 0.714286; 0.047619 × $240,000)	$57,143	$171,429	$11,428	$240,000

PANEL B: Product-Line Income Statement for June 2009	Special B	Special S	Stock	Total
Revenues (12,000 tons × $18 per ton; 24,000 × $25 per ton; 4,000 × $5 per ton)	$216,000	$600,000	$20,000	$836,000
Separable processing costs	48,000	168,000	0	216,000
Joint costs allocated (from Panel A)	57,143	171,429	11,428	240,000
Gross margin	$110,857	$260,571	8,572	380,000
Deduct marketing costs			10,800	10,800
Operating income			$ (2,228)	$369,200

In this (misleading) analysis, the $240,000 of joint costs are re-allocated between Special B, Special S, and the stock. Irrespective of the method of allocation, this analysis is wrong. **Joint costs are always irrelevant in a process-further decision**. Only incremental costs and revenues past the splitoff point are relevant. In this case, the correct analysis is much simpler: the *incremental revenues from selling the stock are $20,000*, and the *incremental costs are the marketing costs of $10,800*. So, Instant Foods should sell the stock—this will increase its operating income by $9,200 ($20,000 – $10,800).

16-24 (30 min.)   **Accounting for a main product and a byproduct.**

		Production Method	Sales Method
1.	Revenues		
	Main product	$640,000[a]	$640,000
	Byproduct	—	28,000[d]
	Total revenues	640,000	668,000
	Cost of goods sold		
	Total manufacturing costs	480,000	480,000
	Deduct value of byproduct production	40,000[b]	0
	Net manufacturing costs	440,000	480,000
	Deduct main product inventory	88,000[c]	96,000[e]
	Cost of goods sold	352,000	384,000
	Gross margin	$288,000	$284,000

Joint costs are reduced by the revenue from by-products under the production method.

[a] $32,000 \times \$20.00$
[b] $8,000 \times \$5.00$
[c] $(8,000/40,000) \times \$440,000 = \$88,000$

[d] $5,600 \times \$5.00$
[e] $(8,000/40,000) \times \$480,000 = \$96,000$

		Production Method	Sales Method
2.	Main Product	$88,000	$96,000
	Byproduct	12,000[a]	0[b]

[a] Under the production method, Ending inventory is shown at *unrealized selling price*.
   BI + Production – Sales = EI
   0 + 8,000 – 5,600 = 2,400 pounds
   Ending inventory = 2,400 pounds × $5 per pound = $12,000

[b] Under the sales method, the ending inventory is not valued. It is recorded as revenue once sold.

16-26 (25 min.) **Accounting for a byproduct.**

1. Byproduct recognized at time of production:
   Joint cost = $1,500
   Joint cost to be charged to main product = Joint Cost − NRV of Byproduct = $1,500 − (50 lbs. × $1.20)
   $$= \$1,440$$

   Inventoriable cost of main product $= \dfrac{\$1440}{400 \text{ containers}} = \$3.60$ per container

   Inventoriable cost of byproduct = NRV = $1.20 per pound

   Gross Margin Calculation under Production Method

Revenues	
Main product: Water (600/2 containers × $8)	$2,400
Byproduct: Sea Salt	0
	2,400
Cost of goods sold	
Main product: Water (300 containers × $3.60)	1,080
Gross margin	$1,320
Gross-margin percentage ($1,320 ÷ $2,400)	55.00%

   Inventoriable costs (end of period):
   Main product: Water (100 containers × $3.60) = $360
   Byproduct: Sea Salt (10 pounds × $1.20) = $12

2. Byproduct recognized at time of sale:
   Joint cost to be charged to main product = Total joint cost = $1,500

   Inventoriable cost of main product $= \dfrac{\$1500}{400 \text{ containers}} = \$3.75$ per container

   Inventoriable cost of byproduct = $0

   Gross Margin Calculation under Sales Method

Revenues	
Main product: Water (600/2 containers × $8)	$2,400
Byproduct: Sea Salt (40 pounds × $1.20)	48
	2,448
Cost of goods sold	
Main product: Water (300 containers × $3.75)	1,125
Gross margin	$1,323
Gross-margin percentage ($1,323 ÷ $2,448)	54.04%

   Inventoriable costs (end of period):
   Main product: Water (100 containers × $3.75) = $375
   Byproduct: Sea Salt (10 pounds × $0) = $0

3. The **production method** recognizes the byproduct cost as inventory (and a reduction in joint costs) in the period it is produced. Any cash received reduces the inventory value. This method sets the cost of the byproduct inventory equal to its net realizable value until it is sold. The **sales method** associates all of the production cost with the main product. Under this method, the byproduct has no inventoriable cost and is recognized only when it is sold.

16-28 (40–60 min.) **Comparison of alternative joint-cost allocation methods, further-processing decision, chocolate products.**

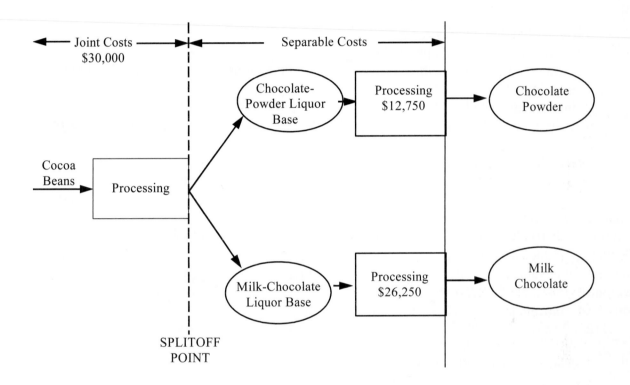

1a. Sales value at splitoff method:

	Chocolate-Powder/ Liquor Base	Milk-Chocolate/ Liquor Base	Total
Sales value of total production at splitoff, 600 × $21; 900 × $26	$12,600	$23,400	$36,000
Weighting, $12,600; $23,400 ÷ $36,000	0.35	0.65	
Joint costs allocated, 0.35; 0.65 × $30,000	$10,500	$19,500	$30,000

1b.

Physical-measure method:

	Chocolate-Powder/ Liquor Base	Milk-Chocolate/ Liquor Base	Total
Physical measure of total production (15,000 ÷ 1,500) × 60; 90	600 gallons	900 gallons	1,500 gallons
Weighting, 600; 900 ÷ 1,500	0.40	0.60	
Joint costs allocated, 0.40; 0.60 × $30,000	$12,000	$18,000	$30,000

1c. Net realizable value method:

	Chocolate-Powder	Milk-Chocolate	Total
Final sales value of total production, 6,000 × $4; 10,200 × $5	$24,000	$51,000	$75,000
Deduct separable costs	12,750	26,250	39,000
Net realizable value at splitoff point	$11,250	$24,750	$36,000
Weighting, $11,250; $24,750 ÷ $36,000	0.3125	0.6875	
Joint costs allocated, 0.3125; 0.6875 × $30,000	$ 9,375	$20,625	$30,000

1d. Constant gross-margin percentage NRV method:

Step 1:

Final sales value of total production, (6,000 × $4) + (10,200 × $5)	$75,000
Deduct joint and separable costs, ($30,000 + $12,750 + $26,250)	69,000
Gross margin	$ 6,000
Gross-margin percentage ($6,000 ÷ $75,000)	8%

Step 2:

	Chocolate-Powder	Milk-Chocolate	Total
Final sales value of total production, 6,000 × $4; 10,200 × $5	$24,000	$51,000	$75,000
Deduct gross margin, using overall gross-margin percentage of sales (8%)	1,920	4,080	6,000
Total production costs	22,080	46,920	69,000

Step 3:

	Chocolate-Powder	Milk-Chocolate	Total
Deduct separable costs	12,750	26,250	39,000
Joint costs allocated	$ 9,330	$20,670	$30,000

2.		Chocolate-Powder	Milk-Chocolate	Total
a.	Revenues	$24,000	$51,000	$75,000
	Joint costs	10,500	19,500	30,000
	Separable costs	12,750	26,250	39,000
	Total cost of goods sold	23,250	45,750	69,000
	Gross margin	$ 750	$ 5,250	$ 6,000
	Gross-margin percentage	3.125%	10.294%	8%
b.	Revenues	$24,000	$51,000	$75,000
	Joint costs	12,000	18,000	30,000
	Separable costs	12,750	26,250	39,000
	Total cost of goods sold	24,750	44,250	69,000
	Gross margin	$ (750)	$ 6,750	$ 6,000
	Gross-margin percentage	(3.125)%	13.235%	8%
c.	Revenues	$24,000	$51,000	$75,000
	Joint costs	9,375	20,625	30,000
	Separable costs	12,750	26,250	39,000
	Total cost of goods sold	22,125	46,875	69,000
	Gross margin	$ 1,875	$ 4,125	$ 6,000
	Gross-margin percentage	7.812%	8.088%	8%
d.	Revenues	$24,000	$51,000	$75,000
	Joint costs	9,330	20,670	30,000
	Separable costs	12,750	26,250	39,000
	Total cost of goods sold	22,080	46,920	69,000
	Gross margin	$ 1,920	$ 4,080	$ 6,000
	Gross-margin percentage	8%	8%	8%

3.   Further processing of chocolate-powder liquor base into chocolate powder:

Incremental revenue, $24,000 – $12,600	$11,400
Incremental costs	12,750
Incremental operating income from further processing	$ (1,350)

Further processing of milk-chocolate liquor base into milk chocolate:

Incremental revenue, $51,000 – $23,400	$27,600
Incremental costs	26,250
Incremental operating income from further processing	$ 1,350

Chocolate Factory could increase operating income by $1,350 (to $7,350) if chocolate-powder liquor base is sold at the splitoff point. They would continue to process the milk-chocolate liquor into milk chocolate.

16-30 (40 min.) **Joint-cost allocation.**

1.

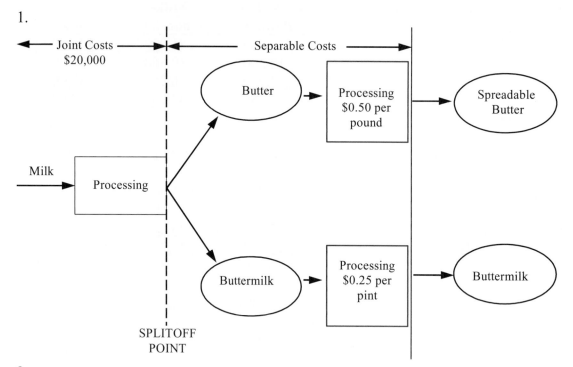

a.
Physical-measure method:

	Butter	**Buttermilk**	**Total**
Physical measure of total production (10,000 lbs × 2; 20,000 qts × 4)	20,000 cups	80,000 cups	100,000 cups
Weighting, 20,000; 80,000 ÷ 100,000	0.20	0.80	
Joint costs allocated, 0.20; 0.80 × $20,000	$4,000	$16,000	$20,000

b.   Sales value at splitoff method:

	Butter	**Buttermilk**	**Total**
Sales value of total production at splitoff, 10,000 × $2; 20,000 × $1.5	$20,000	$30,000	$50,000
Weighting, $20,000; $30,000 ÷ $50,000	0.40	0.60	
Joint costs allocated, 0.40; 0.60 × $20,000	$ 8,000	$12,000	$20,000

c.   Net realizable value method:

	Butter	**Buttermilk**	**Total**
Final sales value of total production, 20,000 × $2.50; 20,000 × $1.50	$50,000	$30,000	$80,000
Deduct separable costs	5,000	0	5,000
Net realizable value	$45,000	$30,000	$75,000
Weighting, $45,000; $30,000 ÷ $75,000	0.60	0.40	
Joint costs allocated, 0.60; 0.40 × $20,000	$12,000	$ 8,000	$20,000

d.   Constant gross-margin percentage NRV method:

Step 1:

Final sales value of total production,	$80,000
Deduct joint and separable costs, ($20,000 + $5,000)	25,000
Gross margin	$55,000
Gross-margin percentage ($55,000 ÷ $80,000)	68.75%

Step 2:

	Butter	Buttermilk	Total
Final sales value of total production (see 1c.)	$50,000	$30,000	$80,000
Deduct gross margin, using overall gross-margin percentage of sales (68.75%)	34,375	20,625	55,000
Total production costs	15,625	9,375	25,000

Step 3:

	Butter	Buttermilk	Total
Deduct separable costs	5,000	0	5,000
Joint costs allocated	$10,625	$ 9,375	$20,000

2.   Advantages and disadvantages:

Physical-Measure

Advantage: Low information needs. Only knowledge of joint cost and physical distribution is needed.

Disadvantage: Allocation is unrelated to the revenue-generating ability of products.

Sales Value at Splitoff

Advantage: Considers market value of products as basis for allocating joint cost. Relative sales value serves as a proxy for relative benefit received by each product from the joint cost.

Disadvantage: Uses selling price at the time of splitoff even if product is not sold by the firm in that form. Selling price may not exist for product at splitoff.

Net Realizable Value

Advantage: Allocates joint costs using ultimate net value of each product.

Disadvantage: High information needs; Makes assumptions about expected outcomes of future processing decisions

Constant Gross-Margin percentage method

Advantage: Since it is necessary to produce all joint products, they all look equally profitable.

Disadvantage: High information needs. All products are not necessarily equally profitable; method may lead to negative cost allocations so that unprofitable products are subsidized by profitable ones.

3. When *selling prices for all products exist* at splitoff, the **sales value at split off method is the preferred technique**. It is a relatively *simple* technique that depends on a common basis for cost allocation – revenues. It is better than the physical method because it considers the relative market values of the products generated by the joint cost when seeking to allocate it. Further, the sales value at splitoff method has advantages over the NRV method and the constant gross margin percentage method because it requires no assumptions about future processing activities and selling prices.

16-32 (20 min.) **Joint-cost allocation with a byproduct.**

1. Sales value at splitoff method: Byproduct recognized at time of production method

Joint cost to be charged to joint products = Joint Cost – NRV of Byproduct
$$= \$10,000 - 1000 \text{ tons} \times 20\% \times 0.25 \text{ vats} \times \$60$$
$$= \$10,000 - 50 \text{ vats} \times \$60$$
$$= \$7,000$$

	Grade A Coal	Grade B Coal	Total
Sales value of coal at splitoff,			
1,000 tons × 0.4 × $100; 1,000 tons × 0.4 × $60	$40,000	$24,000	$64,000
Weighting, $40,000; $24,000 ÷ $64,000	0.625	0.375	
Joint costs allocated (inventoriable cost),			
0.625; 0.375 × $7,000	$ 4,375	$ 2,625	$ 7,000
Gross margin (Sales revenue – Allocated cost)	$35,625	$21,375	$57,000

2. Sales value at splitoff method: Byproduct recognized at time of sale method

Joint cost to be charged to joint products = Total Joint Cost = $10,000

	Grade A Coal	Grade B Coal	Total
Sales value of coal splitoff,			
1,000 tons × .4 × $100; 1,000 tons × .4 × $60	$40,000	$24,000	$64,000
Weighting, $40,000; $24,000 ÷ $64,000	0.625	0.375	
Joint costs allocated (inventoriable cost),			
0.625; 0.375 × $10,000	$ 6,250	$ 3,750	$10,000
Gross margin (Sales revenue – Allocated cost)	$33,750	$20,250	$54,000

Since the entire production is sold during the period, the overall gross margin is the same under the production and sales methods. Under the sales method, the $3,000 received from the sale of the coal tar is added to the overall revenues, so that Cumberland's overall gross margin is $57,000.

3. The **production** method of accounting for the byproduct is appropriate if Cumberland is positive they can sell the byproduct and positive of the selling price. The **sales** method is appropriate if either the disposition of the byproduct is unsure or the selling price is unknown, or if the amounts involved are so negligible as to make it economically infeasible for Cumberland to keep track of byproduct inventories.

16-34 (40 min.) Process further or sell, byproduct.

1. The analysis shown below indicates that it would be more profitable for Newcastle Mining Company to *continue to sell bulk raw coal* without further processing. This analysis ignores any value related to coal fines. It also assumes that the costs of loading and shipping the bulk raw coal on river barges will be the same whether Newcastle sells the bulk raw coal directly or processes it further.

Incremental sales revenues:	
Sales revenue after further processing (9,400,000[a] tons × $36)	$338,400,000
Sales revenue from bulk raw coal (10,000,000 tons × $27)	270,000,000
Incremental sales revenue	68,400,000
Incremental costs:	
Direct labor	800,000
Supervisory personnel	200,000
Heavy equipment costs ($25,000 × 12 months)	300,000
Sizing and cleaning (10,000,000 tons × $3.50)	35,000,000
Outbound rail freight (9,400,000 tons ÷ 60 tons) × $240 per car	37,600,000
Incremental costs	73,900,000
Incremental gain (loss)	$ (5,500,000)

[a]10,000,000 tons × (1− 0.06)

2. The *cost of producing the raw coal is irrelevant to the decision to process further* or not. The answer would be the same as in requirement 1.

3. The potential revenue from the coal fines byproduct would result in additional revenue, ranging between $4,950,000 and $9,900,000, depending on the market price of the fines.

Coal fines	=	75% of 6% of raw bulk tonnage
	=	0.75 × (10,000,000 × .06)
	=	450,000 tons

Potential incremental income from preparing and selling the coal fines:

	Minimum	Maximum
Incremental income per ton	$11 ($15 − $4)	$22 ($24 − $2)
(Market price − Incremental costs)		
Incremental income ($11; $22 × 450,000)	$4,950,000	$9,900,000

The incremental loss from sizing and cleaning the raw coal is $5,500,000, as calculated in requirement 1. Analysis indicates that relative to selling bulk raw coal, the effect of further processing and selling coal fines is only slightly negative at the minimum incremental gain ($4,950,000 − $5,500,000 = − $550,000) and very beneficial at the maximum incremental gain ($9,900,000 − $5,500,000 = $4,400,000). *NMC will benefit from further processing and selling the coal fines as long as its incremental income per ton of coal fines is at least $12.22* ($5,500,000 ÷ 450,000 tons). Hence, further processing is preferred.

Note that other than the financial implications, some factors that should be considered in evaluating a sell-or-process-further decision include:
- Stability of the current customer market for raw coal and how it compares to the market for sized and cleaned coal.
- Storage space needed for the coal fines until they are sold and the handling costs of coal fines.
- Reliability of cost (e.g., rail freight rates) and revenue estimates, and the risk of depending on these estimates.
- Timing of the revenue stream from coal fines and impact on the need for liquidity.
- Possible environmental problems, i.e., dumping of waste and smoke from unprocessed coal.

Collaborative Learning Problem

16-36 (60 min.) Joint Cost Allocation

1.   (a) Net Realizable Value Method

	Deluxe Module	Standard Module	Total
Final sales value of total production	$25,000	$ 8,500	$33,500
Deduct separable costs	1,500	1,000	2,500
Net realizable value at splitoff point	$23,500	$ 7,500	$31,000
Weighting ($23,500; $7,500 ÷ $31,000)	0.7581	0.2419	
Joint costs allocated (0.7581; 0.2419 × $24,000)	$18,194	$ 5,806	$24,000
Total production costs			
($18,194 + $1,500; $5,806 + $1,000)	$19,694	$ 6,806	$26,500
Production costs per unit			
($19,694; $6,806 ÷ 500 units)	$ 39.39	$ 13.61	

296

(b) Constant Gross Margin Method

Step 1

Final sales value of total production:	
(Deluxe, $25,000; Standard, $8,500)	$33,500
Deduct joint and separable costs (Joint, $24,000 +	
Separable Deluxe, $1,500 + Separable Standard, $1,000)	26,500
Gross margin	$ 7,000
Gross-margin percentage ($7,000 ÷ $33,500)	20.8955%

Step 2

	Deluxe Module	Standard Module	Total
Final sales value of total production	$25,000	$8,500	$33,500
Deduct gross margin using overall gross margin percentage (20.8955%)	5,224	1,776	7,000
Total production costs	19,776	6,724	26,500

Step 3

	Deluxe Module	Standard Module	Total
Deduct separable costs	1,500	1,000	2,500
Joint costs allocated	$18,276	$5,724	$24,000
Production costs per unit ($19,776; $6,724 ÷ 500 units)	$ 39.55	$13.45	

(c)   Physical Measure Method

	Deluxe Module/ Chips	Standard Module/ Chips	Total
Physical measure of total production (bits)	500,000	250,000	750,000
Weighting (500,000; 250,000 ÷ 750,000)	0.6667	0.3333	
Joint costs allocated (0.6667; 0.3333 × $24,000)	$16,000	$ 8,000	$24,000
Total production costs ($16,000 + $1,500; $8,000 + $1,000)	$17,500	$ 9,000	$26,500
Production costs per unit ($17,500; $9,000 ÷ 500 units)	$ 35.00	$18.00	

Each of the methods for allocating joint costs has weaknesses. *Because the costs are joint in nature, managers cannot use the cause-and-effect criterion in making this choice.* Managers cannot be sure what causes the joint costs attributable to individual products.

The net realizable value (NRV) method (or sales value at splitoff method) is widely used when selling price data are available. The NRV method provides a meaningful common denominator to compute the weighting factors. It allocates costs on the ability-to-pay principle. It is probably preferred to the constant gross-margin percentage method which also uses sales values to allocate costs to products, because the constant gross-margin percentage method makes the assumption that all products have the same ratio of cost to sales value.

The physical measure method bears little relationship to the revenue-producing power of the individual products. Several physical measures could be used such as the number of chips and the number of good bits. In each case, the physical measure only relates to one aspect of the chip that contributes to its value. The value of the module as determined by the marketplace is a function of multiple physical features. Another key question is whether the physical measure chosen portrays the amount of joint resources used by each product. It is possible that the resources required by each type of module depend on the number of good bits produced during chip manufacturing. But this cause-and-effect relationship is hard to establish.

MMC should use the NRV method. But the choice of method should have no effect on their current control and measurement systems.

2.   The correct approach in deciding whether to process further and make DRAM modules from the standard modules is to compare the incremental revenue with the incremental costs:

Incremental revenue from making DRAMs ($26 × 400) – ($17 × 500)	$1,900
Incremental costs of DRAMs, further processing	1,600
Incremental operating income from converting standard modules into DRAMs	$ 300

A total income computation of each alternative follows:

	Alternative 1: Sell Deluxe and Standard	Alternative 2: Sell Deluxe and DRAM	Difference
Total revenues	($25,000 + $8,500) $33,500	($25,000 + $10,400) $35,400	$1,900
Total costs	26,500	($26,500 + $1,600) 28,100	1,600
Operating income	$ 7,000	$ 7,300	$ 300

It is profitable to extend processing and to incur additional costs on the standard module to convert it into a DRAM module as long as the incremental revenue exceeds incremental costs. It doesn't matter which method is used to allocate joint costs, they are irrelevant to the sell/process further decision.

CHAPTER 17
PROCESS COSTING

17-2 **Process costing systems** separate costs into cost categories according to the *timing of when costs are introduced* into the process. Direct materials are frequently added at one point in time, often the start or the end of the process, and all conversion costs are usually added throughout the process.

17-4 The **accuracy of the estimates** of completion depends on the care and skill of the estimator and the nature of the process. Semiconductor chips may differ substantially in the finishing necessary to obtain a final product. The amount of work necessary to finish a product may not always be easy to ascertain in advance.

17-6 Three inventory methods associated with process costing are:
- Weighted average.
- First-in, first-out.
- Standard costing.

17-8 **FIFO** computations are distinctive because they assign the cost of the previous accounting period's equivalent units in beginning work-in-process inventory to the first units completed and transferred out of the process and assigns the cost of equivalent units worked on during the current period first to complete beginning inventory, next to start and complete new units, and finally to units in ending work-in-process inventory.

17-10 A **major advantage of FIFO** is that managers can *judge the performance in the current period* independently from the performance in the preceding period.

17-12 **Standard-cost** procedures are particularly appropriate to process-costing systems where there are various combinations of materials and operations used to make a wide variety of similar products as in the textiles, paints, and ceramics industries. Standard-cost procedures also *avoid the intricacies involved in detailed tracking* with weighted-average or FIFO methods when there are frequent price variations over time.

17-14 **No**. Transferred-in costs or previous department costs are costs incurred in a *previous department* that have been charged to a subsequent department. These costs may be costs incurred in that previous department during this accounting period or a preceding accounting period.

17-16 (25 min.) **Equivalent units, zero beginning inventory.**

1.

Direct materials cost per unit ($750,000 ÷ 10,000)	$ 75.00
Conversion cost per unit ($798,000 ÷ 10,000)	79.80
Assembly Department cost per unit	$154.80

2a. Steps 1 and 2: Summarize Output in Physical Units and Compute Output in Equivalent Units;
Assembly Department of Nihon, Inc. for February 2009.

| | (Step 1) | (Step 2) Equivalent Units | |
Flow of Production	Physical Units	Direct Materials	Conversion Costs
Work in process, beginning (given)	0		
Started during current period (given)	10,000		
To account for	10,000		
Completed and transferred out during current period	9,000	9,000	9,000
Work in process, ending* (given)	1,000		
1,000 × 100%; 1,000 × 50%	_____	1,000	500
Accounted for	10,000		
Work done in current period		10,000	9,500

*Degree of completion in this department: direct materials, 100%; conversion costs, 50%.

Compute Cost per Equivalent Unit,
Assembly Department of Nihon, Inc. for February 2009.

	Total Production Costs	Direct Materials	Conversion Costs
(Step 3) Costs added during February	$1,548,000	$750,000	$798,000
Divide by equivalent units of work done in current period (above)		÷ 10,000	÷ 9,500
Cost per equivalent unit		$ 75	$ 84

2b. Direct materials cost per unit $ 75
     Conversion cost per unit   84
     Assembly Department cost per unit $159

3.   The difference in the Assembly Department cost per unit calculated in requirements 1 and 2 arises because the costs incurred in January and February are the same but fewer equivalent units of work are done in February. In January, all 10,000 units introduced are fully completed. In February, of the 10,000 units introduced, 10,000 equivalent units of work is done with respect to direct materials but only 9,500 equivalent units of work is done with respect to conversion costs.

300

17-18 (25 min.) **Zero beginning inventory, materials introduced in middle of process.**

1.Steps 1 and 2: Summarize Output in Physical Units and Compute Output in Equivalent Units; Mixing Department of Roary Chemicals for July 2009.

	(Step 1)	(Step 2) Equivalent Units		
Flow of Production	Physical Units	Chemical P	Chemical Q	Conversion Costs
Work in process, beginning (given)	0			
Started during current period (given)	50,000			
To account for	50,000			
Completed and transferred out during current period	35,000	35,000	35,000	35,000
Work in process, ending* (given)	15,000			
15,000 × 100%; 15,000 × 0%; 15,000 × 66 2/3%		15,000	0	10,000
Accounted for	50,000			
Work done in current period only		50,000	35,000	45,000

*Degree of completion in this department: Chemical P, 100%; Chemical Q, 0%; conversion costs, 66 2/3%.

2.Steps 3, 4, and 5: Summarize Total Costs to Account For, Compute Cost per Equivalent Unit, and Assign Total Costs to Units Completed and to Units in Ending Work in Process; Mixing Department of Roary Chemicals for July 2009.

	Total Production Costs	Chemical P	Chemical Q	Conversion Costs
(Step 3) Costs added during July	$455,000	$250,000	$70,000	$135,000
Total costs to account for	$455,000	$250,000	$70,000	$135,000
(Step 4) Costs added in current period		$250,000	$70,000	$135,000
Divide by equivalent units of work done in current period (Requirement 1)		÷ 50,000	÷35,000	÷ 45,000
Cost per equivalent unit		$ 5	$ 2	$ 3
(Step 5) Assignment of costs:				
Completed and transferred out (35,000 units)	$350,000	(35,000* × $5) + (35,000* × $2) + (35,000* × $3)		
Work in process, ending (15,000 units)	105,000	(15,000‡ × $5) + (0‡ × $2) + (10,000‡× $3)		
Total costs accounted for	$455,000	$250,000 + $70,000 + 135,000		

*Equivalent units completed and transferred out from Requirement 1, Step 2.
‡Equivalent units in ending work in process from Requirement 1, Step 2.

17-20 (20 min.) **Weighted-average method, assigning costs (continuation of 17-19).**

Steps 3, 4, and 5: Summarize Total Costs to Account For, Compute Cost per Equivalent Unit, and Assign Total Costs to Units Completed and to Units in Ending Work in Process; Weighted-Average Method of Process Costing, Assembly Division of Fenton Watches, Inc., for May 2009.

		Total Production Costs	Direct Materials	Conversion Costs
(Step 3)	Work in process, beginning (given)	$ 584,400	$ 493,360	$ 91,040
	Costs added in current period (given)	4,612,000	3,220,000	1,392,000
	Total costs to account for	$5,196,400	$3,713,360	$1,483,040
(Step 4)	Costs incurred to date		$3,713,360	$1,483,040
	Divide by equivalent units of work done to date (Problem 17-19)		÷ 532	÷ 496
	Cost per equivalent unit of work done to date		$ 6,980	$ 2,990
(Step 5)	Assignment of costs:			
	Completed and transferred out (460 units)	$4,586,200	(460* × $6,980) + (460* × $2,990)	
	Work in process, ending (120 units)	610,200	(72‡ × $6,980) + (36‡× $2,990)	
	Total costs accounted for	$5,196,400	$3,713,360 + $1,483,040	

*Equivalent units completed and transferred out from Problem 17-19, Step 2.
†Equivalent units in work in process, ending from Problem 17-19, Step 2.

17-22 (20 min.)   **FIFO method, assigning costs (continuation of 17-21).**

Steps 3, 4, and 5: Summarize Total Costs to Account For, Compute Cost per Equivalent Unit, and Assign Total Costs to Units Completed and to Units in Ending Work in Process; FIFO Method of Process Costing, Assembly Division of Fenton Watches, Inc., for May 2009.

	Total Production Costs	Direct Materials	Conversion Costs
(Step 3) Work in process, beginning (given)	$ 584,400	$ 493,360	$ 91,040
Costs added in current period (given)	4,612,000	3,220,000	1,392,000
Total costs to account for	$5,196,400		$1,483,040
		$3,713,360	
(Step 4) Costs added in current period		$3,220,000	$1,392,000
Divide by equivalent units of work done in current period (Problem 17-21)		÷ 460	÷ 464
Cost per equiv. unit of work done in current period		$ 7,000	$ 3,000
(Step 5) Assignment of costs:			
Completed and transferred out (460 units):			
Work in process, beginning (80 units)	$ 584,400	$493,360 +	$91,040
Costs added to beginning work in process in current period	200,000	(8* × $7,000) +	(48* × $3,000)
Total from beginning inventory	784,400		
Started and completed (380 units)	3,800,000	(380† × $7,000) +	(380† × $3,000)
Total costs of units completed and transferred out	4,584,400		
Work in process, ending (120 units)	612,000	(72# × $7,000) +	(36# × $3,000)
Total costs accounted for	$5,196,400	$3,713,360 +	$1,483,040

*Equivalent units used to complete beginning work in process from Problem 17-21, Step 2.
†Equivalent units started and completed from Problem 17-21, Step 2.
#Equivalent units in work in process, ending from Problem 17-21, Step 2.

303

17-24 (25 min.) Weighted-average method, assigning costs.

1. Steps 1 and 2: Summarize Output in Physical Units and Compute Output in Equivalent Units; Weighted-Average Method of Process Costing, Bio Doc Corporation for July 2008.

Flow of Production	(Step 1) Physical Units	(Step 2) Equivalent Units	
		Direct Materials	Conversion Costs
Work in process, beginning (given)	12,500		
Started during current period (given)	50,000		
To account for	62,500		
Completed and transferred out during current period	42,500	42,500	42,500
Work in process, ending* (given)	20,000		
20,000 × 100%; 20,000 × 50%		20,000	10,000
Accounted for	62,500		
Work done to date		62,500	52,500

*Degree of completion: direct materials, 100%; conversion costs, 50%.

2. Steps 3, 4, and 5: Summarize Total Costs to Account For, Compute Cost per Equivalent Unit, and Assign Total Costs to Units Completed and to Units in Ending Work in Process; Weighted-Average Method of Process Costing, Bio Doc Corporation for July 2008.

		Total Production Costs	Direct Materials	Conversion Costs
(Step 3)	Work in process, beginning (given)	$162,500	$ 75,000	$ 87,500
	Costs added in current period (given)	813,750	350,000	463,750
	Total costs to account for	$976,250	$425,000	$551,250
(Step 4)	Costs incurred to date		$425,000	$551,250
	Divide by equivalent units of work done to date (Requirement 1)		÷ 62,500	÷ 52,500
	Cost per equivalent unit of work done to date		$ 6.80	$ 10.50
(Step 5)	Assignment of costs:			
	Completed and transferred out (42,500 units)	$735,250	(42,500* × $6.80) + (42,500* × $10.50)	
	Work in process, ending (20,000 units)	241,000	(20,000‡ × $6.80) + (10,000‡ × $10.50)	
	Total costs accounted for	$976,250	$425,000 + $551,250	

*Equivalent units completed and transferred out (given).
‡Equivalent units in ending work in process (given).

17-26 (30 min.) **Standard-costing method, assigning costs.**

1. Steps 1 and 2: Summarize Output in Physical Units and Compute Output in Equivalent Units; Bio Doc Corporation for July 2008.

	(Step 1)	(Step 2) Equivalent Units	
Flow of Production	**Physical Units**	**Direct Materials**	**Conversion Costs**
Work in process, beginning (given)	12,500	(work done before current period)	
Started during current period (given)	50,000		
To account for	62,500		
Completed and transferred out during current period:			
From beginning work in process[§]			
12,500 × (100% − 100%); 12,500 × (100% − 70%)	12,500	0	3,750
Started and completed			
30,000 × 100%, 30,000 × 100%	30,000[†]	30,000	30,000
Work in process, ending (given)			
20,000 × 100%; 20,000 × 50%	20,000	20,000	10,000
Accounted for	62,500		
Work done in current period only		50,000	43,750

[§]Degree of completion in this department: direct materials, 100%; conversion costs, 70%.
[†]42,500 physical units completed and transferred out minus 12,500 physical units completed and transferred out from beginning work-in-process inventory.

Steps 3, 4, and 5: Summarize Total Costs to Account For, Compute Cost per Equivalent Unit, and Assign Total Costs to Units Completed and to Units in Ending Work in Process; Standard Costing Method of Process Costing, Bio Doc Corporation for July 2008.

	Total Production Costs	**Direct Materials**	**Conversion Costs**
(Step 3) Work in process, beginning (given)	$173,500	(12,500 × $6.60) +	(8,750 × $10.40)
Costs added in current period at standard costs	785,000	(50,000 × $6.60) +	(43,750 × $10.40)
Total costs to account for	$958,500	$412,500 +	$546,000
(Step 4) Standard cost per equivalent unit (given)		$ 6.60	$ 10.40
(Step 5) Assignment of costs at standard costs:			
Completed and transferred out (42,500 units):			
Work in process, beginning (12,500 units)	$173,500	(12,500 × $6.60) +	(8,750 × $10.40)
Costs added to beg. work in process in current period	39,000	(0 × $6.60) +	(3,750 × $10.40)
Total from beginning inventory	212,500		
Started and completed (30,000 units)	510,000	(30,000 × $6.60) +	(30,000 × $10.40)
Total costs of units transferred out	722,500		
Work in process, ending (20,000 units)	236,000	(20,000 × $6.60) +	(10,000 × $10.40)
Total costs accounted for	$958,500	$412,500 +	$546,000
Summary of variances for current performance:			
Costs added in current period at standard costs (see Step 3 above)		$330,000	$455,000
Actual costs incurred (given)		350,000	463,750
Variance		**$ 20,000** U	**$ 8,750** U

17-28 (35–40 min.) **Transferred-in costs, FIFO method.**

1. Steps 1 and 2: Summarize Output in Physical Units and Compute Output in Equivalent Units
FIFO Method of Process Costing;
Finishing Department of Asaya Clothing for June 2009.

| | (Step 1) | (Step 2) Equivalent Units | | |
| | | | | |
Flow of Production	Physical Units	Transferred-in Costs	Direct Materials	Conversion Costs
Work in process, beginning (given)	75	(work done before current period)		
Transferred-in during current period (given)	135			
To account for	210			
Completed and transferred out during current period:				
From beginning work in process[a]	75			
[75 × (100% – 100%); 75 × (100% – 0%); 75 × (100% – 60%)]		0	75	30
Started and completed	75[b]			
(75 × 100%; 75 × 100%; 75 × 100%)		75	75	75
Work in process, ending[c] (given)	60			
(60 × 100%; 60 × 0%; 60 × 75%)		60	0	45
Accounted for	210			
Work done in current period only		135	150	150

[a]Degree of completion in this department: Transferred-in costs, 100%; direct materials, 0%; conversion costs, 60%.

[b]150 physical units completed and transferred out minus 75 physical units completed and transferred out from beginning work-in-process inventory.

[c]Degree of completion in this department: transferred-in costs, 100%; direct materials, 0%; conversion costs, 75%.

2. and 3. Steps 3, 4, and 5: Summarize Total Costs to Account For, Compute Cost per Equivalent Unit, and Assign Total Costs to Units Completed and to Units in Ending Work in Process;
FIFO Method of Process Costing,
Finishing Department of Asaya Clothing for June 2009.

		Total Production Costs	Transferred-in Costs	Direct Materials	Conversion Costs
(Step 3)	Work in process, beginning (given)	$ 90,000	$ 60,000	$ 0	$ 30,000
	Costs added in current period (given)	246,300	130,800	37,500	78,000
	Total costs to account for	$336,300	$190,800	$37,500	$108,000
(Step 4)	Costs added in current period		$130,800	$37,500	$ 78,000
	Divide by equivalent units of work done in current period (Requirement 1)		÷ 135	÷ 150	÷ 150
	Cost per equivalent unit of work done in current period		$ 968.89	$ 250	$ 520
(Step 5)	Assignment of costs:				
	Completed and transferred out (150 units)				
	Work in process, beginning (75 units)	$ 90,000	$ 60,000	$ 0	$ 30,000
	Costs added to beginning work in process in current period	34,350	$(0^a \times \$968.89)$	$+ (75^a \times \$250)$	$+ (30^a \times \$520)$
	Total from beginning inventory	124,350			
	Started and completed (75 units)	130,416	$(75^b \times \$968.89)$	$+ (75^b \times \$250)$	$+ (75^b \times \$520)$
	Total costs of units completed and transferred out	254,766			
	Work in process, ending (60 units):	81,534	$(60^c \times \$968.89)$	$+ (0^c \times \$250)$	$+ (45^c \times \$520)$
	Total costs accounted for	$336,300	$190,800	$37,500	$108,000

[a] Equivalent units used to complete beginning work in process from Requirement 1, step 2.
[b] Equivalent units started and completed from Requirement 1, step 2.
[c] Equivalent units in ending work in process from Requirement 1, step 2.

17-30 (25 min.) **Weighted-average method.**

1.   Since direct materials are added at the beginning of the assembly process, the units in this department must be 100% complete with respect to direct materials.

Steps 1 and 2: Summarize Output in Physical Units and Compute Output in Equivalent Units; Weighted-Average Method of Process Costing, Assembly Department of Larsen Company, for October 2009.

Flow of Production	(Step 1) Physical Units	(Step 2) Equivalent Units Direct Materials	Conversion Costs
Work in process, beginning (given)	5,000		
Started during current period (given)	20,000		
To account for	25,000		
Completed and transferred out during current period	22,500	22,500	22,500
Work in process, ending* (given)	2,500		
2,500 × 100%; 2,500 × 70%		2,500	1,750
Accounted for	25,000		
Work done to date		25,000	24,250

*Degree of completion in this department: direct materials, 100%; conversion costs, 70%.

2. & 3.
Steps 3, 4, and 5: Summarize Total Costs to Account For, Compute Cost per Equivalent Unit, and Assign Total Costs to Units Completed and to Units in Ending Work in Process; Weighted-Average Method of Process Costing, Assembly Department of Larsen Company, for October 2009.

		Total Production Costs	Direct Materials	Conversion Costs
(Step 3)	Work in process, beginning (given)	$1,652,750	$1,250,000	$ 402,750
	Costs added in current period (given)	6,837,500	4,500,000	2,337,500
	Total costs to account for	$8,490,250	$5,750,000	$2,740,250
(Step 4)	Costs incurred to date		$5,750,000	$2,740,250
	Divide by equivalent units of work done to date (Requirement 1)		÷ 25,000	÷ 24,250
	Cost per equivalent unit of work done to date		$ 230	$ 113
(Step 5)	Assignment of costs:			
	Completed and transferred out (22,500 units)	$7,717,500	(22,500* × $230) +	(22,500* × $113)
	Work in process, ending (2,500 units)	772,750	(2,500‡ × $230) +	(1,750‡ × $113)
	Total costs accounted for	$8,490,250	$6,150,000 +	$2,619,000

*Equivalent units completed and transferred out from Requirement 1, Step 2.
†Equivalent units in work in process, ending from Requirement, Step 2.

17-32 (20 min.) **FIFO method (continuation of 17-30).**

1. Steps 1 and 2: Summarize Output in Physical Units and Compute Output in Equivalent Units;
    FIFO Method of Process Costing,
    Assembly Department of Larsen Company for October 2009.

| | (Step 1) | (Step 2) Equivalent Units | |
Flow of Production	Physical Units	Direct Materials	Conversion Costs
Work in process, beginning (given)	5,000	(work done before current period)	
Started during current period (given)	20,000		
To account for	25,000		
Completed and transferred out during current period:			
From beginning work in process[§]			
5,000 × (100% − 100%); 5,000 × (100% − 60%)	5,000	0	2,000
Started and completed			
17,500 ×100%, 17,500 × 100%	17,000[†]	17,500	17,500
Work in process, ending* (given)	2,500		
2,500 × 100%; 2,500 × 70%		2,500	1,750
Accounted for	25,000		
Work done in current period only		20,000	21,250

[§]Degree of completion in this department: direct materials, 100%; conversion costs, 60%.

[†]22,500 physical units completed and transferred out minus 5,000 physical units completed and transferred out from
   beginning work-in-process inventory.

*Degree of completion in this department: direct materials, 100%; conversion costs, 70%.

2. & 3. Steps 3, 4, and 5: Summarize Total Costs to Account For, Compute Cost per Equivalent Unit, and Assign Total Costs to Units Completed and to Units in Ending Work in Process; FIFO Method of Process Costing, Assembly Department of Larsen Company for October 2009.

	Total Production Costs	Direct Materials	Conversion Costs
(Step 3) Work in process, beginning (given)	$1,652,750	$1,250,000	$ 402,750
Costs added in current period (given)	6,837,500	4,500,000	2,337,500
Total costs to account for	$8,490,250	$5,750,000	$2,740,250
(Step 4) Costs added in current period		$4,500,000	$2,337,500
Divide by equivalent units of work done in current period (Requirement 1)		÷ 20,000	÷ 21,250
Cost per equivalent unit of work done in current period		$ 225	$ 110
(Step 5) Assignment of costs:			
Completed and transferred out (22,500 units):			
Work in process, beginning (5,000 units)	$1,652,750	$1,250,000	$ 402,750
Costs added to beg. work in process in current period	220,000	(0* × $225) +	(2,000* × $110)
Total from beginning inventory	1,872,750		
Started and completed (17,500 units)	5,862,500	(17,500† × $225) +	(17,500† × $110)
Total costs of units completed & transferred out	7,735,250		
Work in process, ending (2,500 units)	755,000	(2,500# × $225) +	(1,750# × $110)
Total costs accounted for	$8,490,250	$5,750,000 +	$2,740,250

*Equivalent units used to complete beginning work in process from Requirement 1, Step 2.
†Equivalent units started and completed from Requirement 1, Step 2.
#Equivalent units in ending work in process from Requirement 1, Step 2.

The cost per equivalent unit of beginning inventory and of work done in the current period differ:

	Beginning Inventory	Work Done in Current Period
Direct materials	$250.00 ($1,250,000 ÷ 5,000 equiv. units)	$225.00
Conversion costs	134.25 ($ 402,750 ÷ 3,000 equiv. units)	110.00
Total cost per unit	$384.25	$335.00

	Direct Materials	Conversion Costs
Cost per equivalent unit (weighted-average)	$230*	$113*
Cost per equivalent unit (FIFO)	$225**	$110**

* from Problem 17-30
** from Requirement 2 & 3

The cost per equivalent unit differs between the two methods because each method uses different costs as the numerator of the calculation. FIFO uses only the costs added during the current period whereas weighted-average uses the costs from the beginning work-in-process as well as costs added during the current period. Both methods also use different equivalent units in the denominator.

The following table summarizes the costs assigned to units completed and those still in process under the weighted-average and FIFO process-costing methods for our example.

	Weighted Average (Problem 17-30)	FIFO (Requirement 2 & 3)	Difference
Cost of units completed and transferred out	$7,717,500	$7,735,250	+ $17,750
Work in process, ending	772,750	755,000	– $17,750
Total costs accounted for	$8,490,250	$8,490,250	

The FIFO ending inventory is lower than the weighted-average ending inventory by $17,750. This is because FIFO assumes that all the higher-cost prior-period units in work in process are the first to be completed and transferred out while ending work in process consists of only the lower-cost current-period units. The weighted-average method, however, smoothes out cost per equivalent unit by assuming that more of the lower-cost units are completed and transferred out, while some of the higher-cost units in beginning work in process are placed in ending work in process. So, the weighted-average method results in a lower cost of units completed and transferred out and a higher ending work-in-process inventory relative to the FIFO method **in this case.**

17-34 (30 min.)   **Transferred-in costs, FIFO method (continuation of 17-33).**

1.   Transferred-in costs are 100% complete and direct materials are 0% complete in both beginning and ending work-in-process inventory.

2.   Steps 1 and 2: Summarize Output in Physical Units and Compute Output in Equivalent Units; FIFO Method of Process Costing,
Testing Department of Larsen Company for October 2009.

| | (Step 1) | (Step 2) Equivalent Units | | |
| | | | | |
Flow of Production	Physical Units	Transferred-in Costs	Direct Materials	Conversion Costs
Work in process, beginning (given)	7,500	(work done before current period)		
Transferred-in during current period (given)	22,500			
To account for	30,000			
Completed and transferred out during current period:				
From beginning work in process[§]	7,500			
7,500 × (100% − 100%); 7,500 × (100% − 0%);				
7,500 × (100% − 70%)		0	7,500	2,250
Started and completed	18,800[†]			
18,800 × 100%; 18,800 × 100%; 18,800 × 100%		18,800	18,800	18,800
Work in process, ending* (given)	3,700			
3,700 × 100%; 3,700 × 0%; 3,700 × 60%		3,700	0	2,220
Accounted for	30,000			
Work done in current period only		22,500	26,300	23,270

[§] Degree of completion in this department: Transferred-in costs, 100%; direct materials, 0%; conversion costs, 70%.
[†] 26,300 physical units completed and transferred out minus 7,500 physical units completed and transferred out from beginning work-in-process inventory.
*Degree of completion in this department: transferred-in costs, 100%; direct materials, 0%; conversion costs, 60%.

3. Steps 3, 4, and 5: Summarize Total Costs to Account For, Compute Cost per Equivalent Unit, and Assign Total Costs to Units Completed and to Units in Ending Work in Process; FIFO Method of Process Costing, Testing Department of Larsen Company for October 2009.

	Total Production Costs	Transferred-in Costs	Direct Materials	Conversion Costs
(Step 3) Work in process, beginning (given)	$ 3,717,335	$ 2,881,875	$ 0	$ 835,460
Costs added in current period (given)	21,395,850	7,735,250	9,704,700	3,955,900
Total costs to account for	$25,113,185	$10,617,125	$9,704,700	$4,791,360
(Step 4) Costs added in current period		$ 7,735,250	$9,704,700	$3,955,900
Divide by equivalent units of work done in current period (Requirement 2)		÷ 22,500	÷ 26,300	÷ 23,270
Cost per equiv. unit of work done in current period		$ 343.79	$ 369.00	$ 170.00
(Step 5) Assignment of costs:				
Completed and transferred out (26,300 units):				
Work in process, beginning (7,500 units)	$ 3,717,335	$2,881,875	$0	+ $835,460
Costs added to beg. work in process in current period	3,150,000	(0* × $343.79) +	(7,500* × $369.00) +	(2,250* × $170.00)
Total from beginning inventory	6,867,335			
Started and completed (18,800 units)	16,596,431	(18,800† × $343.79)+	(18,800† × $369.00)+	(18,800† ×$170.00)
Total costs of units completed & transferred out	23,463,766			
Work in process, ending (3,700 units)	1,649,419	(3,700# × $343.79) +	(0# × $369.00) +	(2,220# × $170.00)
Total costs accounted for	$25,113,185	$ 10,617,125	$9,704,700	+ $4,791,360

*Equivalent units used to complete beginning work in process from Requirement 2, Step 2.
†Equivalent units started and completed from Requirement 2, Step 2.
#Equivalent units in ending work in process from Requirement 2, Step 2.

4. Journal entries:
a. Work in Process—Testing Department 7,735,250
    Work in Process—Assembly Department 7,735,250
    Cost of goods completed and transferred out during October from the Assembly Dept. to the Testing Dept.

b. Finished Goods 23,463,766
    Work in Process—Testing Department 23,463,766
    Cost of goods completed and transferred out during October from the Testing Department to Finished Goods inventory.

17-36 (5–10 min.)   **Journal entries (continuation of 17-35).**

1. Work in Process— Assembly Department   17,600
       Accounts Payable   17,600
   To record direct materials purchased and used in production during April

2. Work in Process— Assembly Department   10,890
       Various Accounts   10,890
   To record Assembly Department conversion costs for April

3. Work in Process—Finishing Department   26,000
       Work in Process— Assembly Department   26,000
   To record cost of goods completed and transferred out in April from the Assembly
   Department to the Finishing Department

Work in Process — Assembly Department

Beginning inventory, April 1	1,910	3. Transferred out to	
1. Direct materials	17,600	Work in Process—Finishing	26,000
2. Conversion costs	10,890		
Ending inventory, April 30	4,400		

17-38 (30 min.) **Transferred-in costs, weighted average.**

1. Steps 1 and 2: Summarize Output in Physical Units and Compute Output in Equivalent Units;
Weighted-Average Method of Process Costing,
Binding Department of Publish, Inc. for April 2009.

	(Step 1)	(Step 2) Equivalent Units		
Flow of Production	**Physical Units**	**Transferred-in Costs**	**Direct Materials**	**Conversion Costs**
Work in process, beginning (given)	900			
Transferred-in during current period (given)	2,700			
To account for	3,600			
Completed and transferred out during current period:	3,000	3,000	3,000	3,000
Work in process, ending[a] (given)	600			
(600 × 100%; 600 × 0%; 600 × 60%)		600	0	360
Accounted for	3,600			
Work done to date		3,600	3,000	3,360

[a]Degree of completion in this department: transferred-in costs, 100%; direct materials, 0%; conversion costs, 60%.

Steps 3, 4, and 5: Summarize Total Costs to Account For, Compute Cost per Equivalent Unit, and Assign Total Costs to Units Completed and to Units in Ending Work in Process; Weighted-Average Method of Process Costing, Binding Department of Publish, Inc. for April 2009.

	Total Production Costs	Transferred-in Costs	Direct Materials	Conversion Costs
(Step 3)				
Work in process, beginning (given)	$ 47,775	$ 32,775	$ 0	$15,000
Costs added in current period (given)	239,700	144,000	26,700	69,000
Total costs to account for	$287,475	$176,775	$26,700	$84,000
(Step 4)				
Costs incurred to date		$176,775	$26,700	$84,000
Divide by equivalent units of work done to date (Requirement 1)		÷ 3,600	÷ 3,000	÷ 3,360
Cost per equivalent unit of work done to date		$ 49.104	$ 8.90	$ 25
(Step 5) Assignment of costs:				
Completed and transferred out (3,000 units):	$249,012	$(3,000^a \times \$49.104) +$	$(3,000^a \times \$8.90) +$	$(3,000^a \times \$25)$
Work in process, ending (600 units):	38,463	$(600^b \times \$49.104) +$	$(0^b \times \$8.90) +$	$(360^b \times \$25)$
Total costs accounted for	$287,475	$176,775	+ $26,700	+ $84,000

^{a} Equivalent units completed and transferred out Requirement 1, step 2.
^{b} Equivalent units in ending work in process from Requirement 1, step 2.

2. Journal entries:

a. Work in Process— Binding Department   144,000
          Work in Process—Printing Department   144,000
   Cost of goods completed and transferred out during April from the Printing Department to the Binding Department

b. Finished Goods   249,012
          Work in Process— Binding Department   249,012
   Cost of goods completed and transferred out during April from the Binding Department to Finished Goods inventory

17-40 (45 min.) **Transferred-in costs, weighted-average and FIFO methods.**

1. Steps 1 and 2: Summarize Output in Physical Units and Compute Output in Equivalent Units;
Weighted-Average Method of Process Costing,
Drying and Packaging Department of Frito-Lay Inc. for Week 37.

	(Step 1)	(Step 2) Equivalent Units		
Flow of Production	**Physical Units**	**Transferred-in Costs**	**Direct Materials**	**Conversion Costs**
Work in process, beginning (given)	1,250			
Transferred in during current period (given)	5,000			
To account for	6,250			
Completed and transferred out during current period	5,250	5,250	5,250	5,250
Work in process, ending* (given)	1,000			
1,000 × 100%; 1,000 × 0%; 1,000 × 40%		1,000	0	400
Accounted for	6,250			
Work done to date		6,250	5,250	5,650

*Degree of completion in this department: transferred-in costs, 100%; direct materials, 0%; conversion costs, 40%.

Steps 3, 4, and 5: Summarize Total Costs to Account For, Compute Cost per Equivalent Unit, and Assign Total Costs to Units Completed and to Units in Ending Work in Process;
Weighted-Average Method of Process Costing,
Drying and Packaging Department of Frito-Lay Inc. for Week 37.

		Total Production Costs	Transferred -in Costs	Direct Materials	Conversion Costs
(Step 3)	Work in process, beginning (given)	$ 38,060	$ 29,000	$ 0	$ 9,060
	Costs added in current period (given)	159,600	96,000	25,200	38,400
	Total costs to account for	$197,660	$125,000	$25,200	$47,460
(Step 4)	Costs incurred to date		$125,000	$25,200	$47,460
	Divide by equivalent units of work done to date (Requirement 1)		÷ 6,250	÷ 5,250	÷ 5,650
	Equivalent unit costs of work done to date		$ 20	$ 4.80	$ 8.40
(Step 5)	Assignment of costs:				
	Completed and transferred out (5,250 units)	$174,300	(5,250* × $20)	+ (5,250* × $4.80)	+ (5,250* × $8.40)
	Work in process, ending (1,000 units)	23,360	(1,000† × $20)	+ (0† × $4.80)	+ (400† × $8.40)
	Total costs accounted for	$197,660	$125,000	+ $25,200	+ $47,460

*Equivalent units completed and transferred out from Requirement 1, Step 2.
†Equivalent units in ending work in process from Requirement 1, Step 2.

317

2. Steps 1 and 2: Summarize Output in Physical Units and Compute Output in Equivalent Units; FIFO Method of Process Costing,
Drying and Packaging Department of Frito-Lay Inc. for Week 37.

| | (Step 1) | (Step 2) Equivalent Units | | |
| | Physical | Transferred- | Direct | Conversion |
Flow of Production	**Units**	**in Costs**	**Materials**	**Costs**
Work in process, beginning (given)	1,250	(work done before current period)		
Transferred-in during current period (given)	5,000			
To account for	6,250			
Completed and transferred out during current period:				
From beginning work in process[§]	1,250			
$1,250 \times (100\% - 100\%)$; $1,250 \times (100\% - 0\%)$;				
$1,250 \times (100\% - 80\%)$		0	1,250	250
Started and completed	4,000[†]			
$4,000 \times 100\%$; $4,000 \times 100\%$; $4,000 \times 100\%$		4,000	4,000	4,000
Work in process, ending* (given)	1,000			
$1,000 \times 100\%$; $1,000 \times 0\%$; $1,000 \times 40\%$		1,000	0	400
Accounted for	6,250			
Work done in current period only		5,000	5,250	4,650

[§]Degree of completion in this department: Transferred-in costs, 100%; direct materials, 0%; conversion costs, 80%.
[†]5,250 physical units completed and transferred out minus 1,250 physical units completed and transferred out from beginning work-in-process inventory.
*Degree of completion in this department: transferred-in costs, 100%; direct materials, 0%; conversion costs, 40%.

Steps 3, 4, and 5: Summarize Total Costs to Account For, Compute Cost per Equivalent Unit, and Assign Total Costs to Units Completed and to Units in Ending Work in Process;

FIFO Method of Process Costing,

Drying and Packaging Department of Frito-Lay Inc. for Week 37.

	Total Production Costs	Transferred-in Costs	Direct Materials	Conversion Costs
(Step 3) Work in process, beginning (given)	$ 37,980	$ 28,920	$ 0	$ 9,060
Costs added in current period (given)	157,600	94,000	25,200	38,400
Total costs to account for	$195,580	$122,920	$25,200	$47,460
(Step 4) Costs added in current period		$ 94,000	$25,200	$38,400
Divide by equivalent units of work done in current period (Requirement 2)		÷ 5,000	÷ 5,250	÷ 4,650
Cost per equivalent unit of work done in current period		$ 18.80	$ 4.80	$ 8.258
(Step 5) Assignment of costs:				
Completed and transferred out (5,250 units):				
Work in process, beginning (1,250 units)	$ 37,980			
Costs added to beg. work in process in current period	8,065	$28,920 +	$0 +	$9,060
		$(0^* \times \$18.80) + (1,250^* \times \$4.80) + (250^* \times \$8.258)$		
Total from beginning inventory	46,045			
Started and completed (4,000 units)	127,432	$(4,000^{\dagger} \times \$18.80) + (4,000^{\dagger} \times \$4.80) + (4,000^{\dagger} \times \$8.258)$		
Total costs of units completed & transferred out	173,477			
Work in process, ending (1,000 units)	22,103	$(1,000^{\#} \times \$18.80) + (0^{\#} \times \$4.80) + (400^{\#} \times \$8.258)$		
Total costs accounted for	$195,580	$122,920	$25,200	$47,460

(Step 3)

* Equivalent units used to complete beginning work in process from Requirement 2, Step 2.

† Equivalent units started and completed from Requirement 2, Step 2.

Equivalent units in ending work in process from Requirement 2, Step 2.

17-42 (25-30 min.) **Operation costing**

1. To obtain the overhead rates, divide the budgeted cost of each operation by the pairs of shoes that are expected to go through that operation.

	Budgeted Conversion Cost	Budgeted Pairs of Shoes	Conversion Cost per Pair of Shoes
Operation 1	$145,125	32,250	$4.50
Operation 2	58,050	32,250	1.80
Operation 3	4,275	2,250	1.90
Operation 4	67,725	32,250	2.10
Operation 5	13,500	30,000	0.45
Operation 6	2,025	2,250	0.90

2.

	Work Order 10399	Work Order 10400
Shoe type:	Basic	Elaborate
Quantity:	1,000	150
Direct Materials	$13,000	$4,200
Operation 1	4,500	675
Operation 2	1,800	270
Operation 3	0	285
Operation 4	2,100	315
Operation 5	450	0
Operation 6	0	135
Total	$21,850	$5,880

The direct materials costs per unit vary based on the type of shoe ($390,000 ÷ 30,000 = $13 for the Basic, and $63,000 ÷ 2,250 = $28 for the Elaborate). Conversion costs are charged using the rates computed in part (1), taking into account the specific operations that each type of shoe actually goes through.

3. Work order 10399 (Basic shoes):

Total cost	$21,850
Divided by number of pairs of shoes:	÷ 1,000
Cost per pair of plain shoes:	$ 21.85

Work order 10400 (Elaborate shoes):

Total cost:	$5,880
Divided by number of pairs of shoes:	÷ 150
Cost per pair of fancy shoes:	$39.20

CHAPTER 18
SPOILAGE, REWORK, AND SCRAP

18-2 **Spoilage**: units of production that *do not meet the standards* required by customers for good units and that are *discarded or sold at reduced prices*.

  Rework: units of production that *do not meet the specifications* required by customers but which are *subsequently repaired and sold as good* finished units.

  Scrap: *residual material* that results from manufacturing a product. It has low total sales value compared to the total sales value of the product.

18-4 **Abnormal spoilage** is spoilage that is not inherent in a particular production process and would not arise under efficient operating conditions. Costs of abnormal spoilage are "lost costs," measures of inefficiency that should be written off directly as losses for the accounting period.

18-6 **Normal spoilage** typically is expressed as a percentage of good units passing the inspection point. Given actual spoiled units, we infer abnormal spoilage as follows:
Abnormal spoilage = Actual spoilage – Normal spoilage.

18-8 **Yes**. Normal spoilage rates should be computed from the good output or from the *normal* input, not the *total* input. Normal spoilage is a given percentage of a certain output base. This base should never include abnormal spoilage, which is included in total input. Abnormal spoilage does not vary in direct proportion to units produced, and to include it would cause the normal spoilage count to fluctuate irregularly and not vary in direct proportion to the output base.

18-10 **Not necessarily**. If abnormal spoilage is *detected at a different point* in the production cycle than normal spoilage, then unit costs would differ. If, however normal and abnormal spoilage are detected at the same point in the production cycle, their unit costs would be the same.

18-12 **No**. Unless there are special reasons for charging normal rework to jobs that contained the bad units, the costs of extra materials, labor, and so on are usually charged to manufacturing overhead and allocated to all jobs.

18-14 A company is justified in inventorying scrap when its estimated *net realizable value is significant* and the time between storing it and selling or reusing it is quite long.

18-16 (5–10 min.) **Normal and abnormal spoilage in units.**

1. | | |
    |---|---:|
    | Total spoiled units | 12,000 |
    | Normal spoilage in units, 5% × 132,000 | 6,600 |
    | Abnormal spoilage in units | 5,400 |

2. | | |
    |---|---:|
    | Abnormal spoilage, 5,400 × $10 | $ 54,000 |
    | Normal spoilage, 6,600 × $10 | 66,000 |
    | Potential savings, 12,000 × $10 | $120,000 |

Zero spoilage usually means higher-quality products, more customer satisfaction, more employee satisfaction, and various beneficial effects on nonmanufacturing (for example, purchasing) costs of direct materials. Arriving at zero spoilage can be costly, however, and the costs and benefits need to be understood.

18-18 (20–25 min.) **Weighted-average method, assigning costs (continuation of 18-17).**

Summarize Total Costs to Account For, Compute Cost per Equivalent Unit, and Assign Total Costs to Units Completed, to Spoiled Units, and to Units in Ending Work in Process;
Weighted-Average Method of Process Costing,
Gray Manufacturing Company, November 2009.

		Total Production Costs	Direct Materials	Conversion Costs
(Step 3)	Work in process, beginning (given)	$ 2,533	$ 1,423	$ 1,110
	Costs added in current period (given)	39,930	12,180	27,750
	Total costs to account for	$42,463	$13,603	$28,860
(Step 4)	Costs incurred to date		$13,603	$28,860
	Divided by equivalent units of work done to date		÷11,150	÷ 9,750
	Cost per equivalent unit		$ 1.22	$ 2.96
(Step 5)	Assignment of costs			
	Good units completed and transferred out (9,000 units)			
	Costs before adding normal spoilage	$37,620	(9,000# × $1.22) + (9,000# × $2.96)	
	Normal spoilage (100 units)	418	(100# × $1.22) + (100# × $2.96)	
(A)	Total cost of good units completed & transf. out	38,038		
(B)	Abnormal spoilage (50 units)	209	(50# × $1.22) + (50# × $2.96)	
(C)	Work in process, ending (2,000 units)	4,216	(2,000# × $1.22) + (600# × $2.96)	
(A)+(B)+(C)	Total costs accounted for	$42,463	$13,603 + $28,860	

#Equivalent units of direct materials and conversion costs calculated in Problem 18-17, Step 2.

18-20 (20–25 min.) **FIFO method, assigning costs (continuation of 18-19).**

Summarize Total Costs to Account For, Compute Cost per Equivalent Unit, and Assign Total Costs to Units Completed, to Spoiled Units, and to Units in Ending Work in Process;
FIFO Method of Process Costing,
Gray Manufacturing Company, November 2009.

		Total Production Costs	Direct Materials	Conversion Costs
(Step 3)	Work in process, beginning (given)	$ 2,533	$ 1,423	$ 1,110
	Costs added in current period (given)	39,930	12,180	27,750
	Total costs to account for	$42,463	$13,603	$28,860
(Step 4)	Costs added in current period		$12,180	$27,750
	Divided by equivalent units of work done in current period		÷10,150	÷ 9,250
	Cost per equivalent unit		$ 1.20	$ 3
(Step 5)	Assignment of costs:			
	Good units completed and transferred out (9,000 units)			
	Work in process, beginning (1,000 units)	$ 2,533	$1,423 +	$1,110
	Costs added to beg. work in process in current period	1,500	$(0^a \times \$1.20)$ +	$(500^a \times \$3)$
	Total from beginning inventory before normal spoilage	4,033		
	Started and completed before normal spoilage (8,000 units)	33,600	$(8,000^a \times \$1.20)$ +	$(8,000^a \times \$3)$
	Normal spoilage (100 units)	420	$(100^a \times \$1.20)$ +	$(100^a \times \$3)$
(A)	Total costs of good units completed and transferred out	38,053		
(B)	Abnormal spoilage (50 units)	210	$(50^a \times \$1.20)$ +	$(50^a \times \$3)$
(C)	Work in process, ending (2,000 units)	4,200	$(2,000^a \times \$1.20)$ +	$(600^a \times \$3)$
(A)+(B)+(C)	Total costs accounted for	$42,463	$13,603 +	$28,860

^{a} Equivalent units of direct materials and conversion costs from Problem 18-19, Step 2.

18-22 (10 min.) **Standard costing method, spoilage, journal entries.**

Spoilage represents the amount of resources that go into the process, but do not result in finished product. A simple way to account for spoilage in process costing is to calculate the amount of direct material that was spoiled. The journal entry to record the spoilage incurred in Aaron's production process is:

Manufacturing overhead control (normal spoilage)	250	
Work-in-process inventory (cost of spoiled sheet metal)		250

18-24 (25 min.) **Weighted-average method, spoilage.**

1. Weighted-Average Method of Process Costing with Spoilage;
Chipcity, September 2008.

PANEL A: Steps 1 and 2—Summarize Output in Physical Units and Compute Output in Equivalent Units

Flow of Production	(Step 1) Physical Units	(Step 2) Equivalent Units	
		Direct Materials	Conversion Costs
Work in process, beginning (given)	600		
Started during current period (given)	2,550		
To account for	3,150		
Good units completed and transferred out during current period:	2,100	2,100	2,100
Normal spoilage*	315		
315 × 100%; 315 × 100%		315	315
Abnormal spoilage†	285		
285 × 100%; 285 × 100%		285	285
Work in process, ending‡ (given)	450		
450 × 100%; 450 × 40%		450	180
Accounted for	3,150		
Work done to date		3,150	2,880

*Normal spoilage is 15% of good units transferred out: 15% × 2,100 = 315 units. Degree of completion of normal spoilage in this department: direct materials, 100%; conversion costs, 100%.

†Total spoilage = 600 + 2,550 − 2,100 − 450 = 600 units; Abnormal spoilage = Total spoilage − Normal spoilage = 600 − 315 = 285 units. Degree of completion of abnormal spoilage in this department: direct materials, 100%; conversion costs, 100%.

‡Degree of completion in this department: direct materials, 100%; conversion costs, 40%.

2.
___

PANEL B: Steps 3, 4, and 5— Summarize Total Costs to Account For, Compute Cost per Equivalent Unit, and Assign Total Costs to Units Completed, to Spoiled Units, and to Units in Ending Work in Process

		Total Production Costs	Direct Materials	Conversion Costs
(Step 3)	Work in process, beginning (given)	$111,300	$ 96,000	$ 15,300
	Costs added in current period (given)	797,400	567,000	230,400
	Total costs to account for	$908,700	$663,000	$245,700
(Step 4)	Costs incurred to date		$663,000	$245,700
	Divided by equivalent units of work done to date		÷ 3,150	÷ 2,880
	Cost per equivalent unit		$210.476	$85.3125
(Step 5)	Assignment of costs			
	Good units completed and transferred out (2,100 units)			
	Costs before adding normal spoilage	$621,156	$(2,100^\#\times\$210.476) + (2,100^\#\times\$85.3125)$	
	Normal spoilage (315 units)	93,173	$(315^\# \times \$210.476) + (315^\# \times \$85.3125)$	
(A)	Total cost of good units completed and transferred out	714,329		
(B)	Abnormal spoilage (285 units)	84,300	$(285^\# \times \$210.476) + (285^\# \times \$85.3125)$	
(C)	Work-in-process, ending (450 units)	110,071	$(450^\# \times \$210.476) + (180^\# \times \$85.3125)$	
(A)+(B)+(C)	Total costs accounted for	$908,700	$663,000	$245,700

$^\#$ Equivalent units of direct materials and conversion costs calculated in Step 2 in Panel A.

18-26 (30 min.) **Standard-costing method, spoilage.**

1. The computation is the same for FIFO and standard-costing, so this is the same as the solution to 18-25.

Standard Cost Method of Process Costing with Spoilage;
Chipcity, September 2008.

PANEL A: Steps 1 and 2—Summarize Output in Physical Units and Compute Output in Equivalent Units

	(Step 1)	(Step 2) Equivalent Units	
Flow of Production	**Physical Units**	**Direct Materials**	**Conversion Costs**
Work in process, beginning (given)	600		
Started during current period (given)	2,550		
To account for	3,150		
Good units completed and transferred out during current period:			
From beginning work in process$^{\|}$	600		
$600 \times (100\% - 100\%)$; $600 \times (100\% - 30\%)$		0	420
Started and completed	1,500$^{\#}$		
$1,500 \times 100\%$; $1,500 \times 100\%$		1,500	1,500
Normal spoilage*	315		
$315 \times 100\%$; $315 \times 100\%$		315	315
Abnormal spoilage†	285		
$285 \times 100\%$; $285 \times 100\%$		285	285
Work in process, ending‡	450		
$450 \times 100\%$; $450 \times 40\%$		450	180
Accounted for	3,150		
Work done in current period only		2,550	2,700

$^{\|}$Degree of completion in this department: direct materials, 100%; conversion costs, 30%.

$^{\#}$2,100 physical units completed and transferred out minus 600 physical units completed and transferred out from beginning work in process inventory.

*Normal spoilage is 15% of good units transferred out: $15\% \times 2,100 = 315$ units. Degree of completion of normal spoilage in this department: direct materials, 100%; conversion costs, 100%.

†Abnormal spoilage = Actual spoilage – Normal spoilage = $600 - 315 = 285$ units. Degree of completion of abnormal spoilage in this department: direct materials, 100%; conversion costs, 100%.

‡Degree of completion in this department: direct materials, 100%; conversion costs, 40%.

2. Direct materials cost per equivalent unit: $200 given.
   The conversion cost per equivalent unit: $75 given.

Standard Costing Method of Process Costing with Spoilage;
Chipcity, September 2008.

___

Steps 3, 4, and 5—Summarize Total Costs to Account For, Compute Cost per Equivalent Unit, and Assign Total Costs to Units Completed, to Spoiled Units, and to Units in Ending Work in Process

		Total Production Costs	Direct Materials		Conversion Costs
(Step 3)	Work in process, beginning*	$133,500	(600 × $200)		(180 × $75)
	Costs added in current period at standard prices	712,500	(2,550 × $200)		(2,700 × $75)
	Costs to account for	$846,000	$630,000		$216,000
(Step 4)	Standard costs per equivalent unit (given)	$ 275	$ 200		$ 75
(Step 5)	Assignment of costs at standard costs:				
	Good units completed and transferred out (2,100 units)				
	Work in process, beginning (600 units)*	$133,500	(600 × $200)	+	(180 × $75)
	Costs added to beg. work in process in current period	31,500	(0§ × $200)	+	(420§ × $75)
	Total from beginning inventory before normal spoilage	165,000			
	Started and completed before normal spoilage (1,500 units)	412,500	(1,500§ × $200)	+	(1,500§ × $75)
	Normal spoilage (315 units)	86,625	(315§ × $200)	+	(315§ × $75)
(A)	Total costs of good units completed and transferred out	664,125			
(B)	Abnormal spoilage (285 units)	78,375	(285§ × $200)	+	(285§ × $75)
(C)	Work in process, ending (450 units)	103,500	(450§ × $200)	+	(180§ × $75)
(A)+(B)+(C)	Total costs accounted for	$846,000	$630,000	+	$216,000

*Work in process, beginning has 600 equivalent units (600 physical units ×100%) of direct materials and 180 equivalent units (600 physical units × 30%) of conversion costs.

§Equivalent units of direct materials and conversion costs calculated in Requirement 1, Step 2.

18-28 (15 min.)   **Reworked units, costs of rework.**

1.   The **two alternative approaches** to account for the materials costs of reworked units are:
   a.   To charge the costs of rework to the *current period as a separate expense* item as *abnormal* rework. This approach would highlight to White Goods the costs of the supplier problem.
   b.   To charge the costs of the rework to *manufacturing overhead* as *normal* rework.

2.   The **$50 tumbler cost** is the cost of the actual tumblers included in the washing machines. The $44 tumbler units from the first supplier were eventually never used in any washing machine.

3.   The **total costs of rework** due to the defective tumbler units include the following:
   a.   the *labor and other conversion costs* spent on substituting the new tumbler units;
   b.   the costs of any *extra negotiations* to obtain the replacement tumbler units;
   c.   any higher price the existing supplier may have *charged to do a rush order* for the replacement tumbler units; and
   d.   *ordering costs* for the replacement tumbler units.

18-30 (30 min.) **Weighted-average method, spoilage.**

Weighted-Average Method of Process Costing with Spoilage;Cleaning Department of the Boston Company for May.

PANEL A: Steps 1 and 2—Summarize Output in Physical Units and Compute Output in Equivalent Units

Flow of Production	(Step 1) Physical Units	(Step 2) Equivalent Units Direct Materials	Conversion Costs
Work in process, beginning (given)	2,500		
Started during current period (given)	22,500		
To account for	25,000		
Good units completed and transferred out during current period:	18,500	18,500	18,500
Normal spoilage* 1,850 × 100%; 1,850 × 100%	1,850	1,850	1,850
Abnormal spoilage[†] 650 × 100%; 650 ×100%	650	650	650
Work in process, ending[‡] (given) 4,000 × 100%; 4,000 × 25%	4,000	4,000	1,000
Accounted for			
Work done to date	25,000	25,000	22,000

*Normal spoilage is 10% of good units transferred out: 10% × 18,500 = 1,850 units. Degree of completion of normal spoilage in this department: direct materials, 100%; conversion costs, 100%.

[†]Total spoilage = 2,500 + 22,500 – 18,500 – 4,000 = 2,500 units; Abnormal spoilage = 2,500 – 1,850 = 650 units. Degree of completion of abnormal spoilage in this department: direct materials, 100%; conversion costs, 100%.

[‡]Degree of completion in this department: direct materials, 100%; conversion costs, 25%.

PANEL B: Steps 3, 4, and 5— Summarize Total Costs to Account For, Compute Cost per Equivalent Unit, and Assign Total Costs to Units Completed, to Spoiled Units, and to Units in Ending Work in Process

		Total Production Costs	Direct Materials	Conversion Costs
(Step 3)	Work in process, beginning (given)	$ 4,500	$ 2,500	$ 2,000
	Costs added in current period (given)	42,500	22,500	20,000
	Total costs to account for	$47,000	$25,000	$22,000
(Step 4)	Costs incurred to date		$25,000	$22,000
	Divided by equivalent units of work done to date		÷25,000	÷22,000
	Cost per equivalent unit		$ 1	$ 1
(Step 5)	Assignment of costs			
	Good units completed and transferred out (18,500 units)			
	Costs before adding normal spoilage	$37,000	$(18,500[#] × $1) +	(18,500[#] × $1)
	Normal spoilage (1,850 units)	3,700	(1,850[#] × $1) +	(1,850[#] × $1)
(A)	Total costs of good units completed and transferred out	40,700		
(B)	Abnormal spoilage (650 units)	1,300	(650[#] × $1) +	(650[#] × $1)
(C)	Work in process, ending (4,000 units)	5,000	(4,000[#] × $1) +	(1,000[#] × $1)
(A)+(B)+(C)	Total costs accounted for	$47,000	$25,000 +	$22,000

[#]Equivalent units of direct materials and conversion costs calculated in Step 2 in Panel A above.

18-32 (35 min.) **Weighted-average method, Packaging Department (continuation of 18-30).**

Weighted-Average Method of Process Costing with Spoilage;
Packaging Department of the Boston Company for May.

PANEL A: Steps 1 and 2—Summarize Output in Physical Units and Compute Output in Equivalent Units

	(Step 1)	(Step 2) Equivalent Units		
Flow of Production	Physical Units	Transferred-in Costs	Direct Materials	Conversion Costs
Work in process, beginning (given)	7,500			
Started during current period (given)	18,500			
To account for	26,000			
Good units completed and transferred out during current period:	15,000	15,000	15,000	15,000
Normal spoilage*	750			
750 × 100%; 750 × 100%; 750 × 100%		750	750	750
Abnormal spoilage†	250			
250 × 100%; 250 ×100%, 250 × 100%		250	250	250
Work in process, ending‡ (given)	10,000			
10,000 ×100%; 10,000×0%; 10,000×25%	_____	10,000	0	2,500
Accounted for	26,000			
Work done to date		26,000	16,000	18,500

*Normal spoilage is 5% of good units transferred out: 5% × 15,000 = 750 units. Degree of completion of normal spoilage in this department: transferred-in costs, 100%; direct materials, 100%; conversion costs, 100%.

†Total spoilage =7,500 + 18,500 – 15,000 – 10,000 = 1,000 units. Abnormal spoilage = 1,000 – 750 = 250 units. Degree of completion of abnormal spoilage in this department: transferred-in costs, 100%; direct materials, 100%; conversion costs, 100%.

‡Degree of completion in this department: transferred-in costs, 100%; direct materials, 0%; conversion costs, 25%.

PANEL B: Steps 3, 4, and 5— Summarize Total Costs to Account For, Compute Cost per Equivalent Unit, and Assign Total Costs to Units Completed, to Spoiled Units, and to Units in Ending Work in Process

		Total Production Costs	Transferred-in costs	Direct Materials	Conversion Costs
(Step 3)	Work in process, beginning (given)	$22,250	$16,125	$ 0	$ 6,125
	Costs added in current period (given)	54,675	40,700*	1,600	12,375
	Total costs to account for	$76,925	$56,825	$1,600	$18,500
(Step 4)	Costs incurred to date		56,825	1,600	18,500
	Divided by equivalent units of work done to date		÷26,000	÷ 16,000	÷18,500
	Cost per equivalent unit		$2.1856	$ 0.10	$ 1
(Step 5)	Assignment of costs				
	Good units completed and transferred out (15,000 units)				
	Costs before adding normal spoilage	$49,284	15,000# × ($2.1856 + $0.10 + $1)		
	Normal spoilage (750 units)	2,464	750# × ($2.1856 + $0.10 + $1)		
(A)	Total cost of good units completed and transferred out	51,748			
(B)	Abnormal spoilage (250 units)	821	250# × ($2.1856 + $0.10 + $1)		
(C)	Work in process, ending (10,000 units)	24,356	(10,000# × $2.1856)+(0# × $0.10)+(2,500#× $1)		
(A)+(B)+(C)	Total costs accounted for	$76,925	$56,825 + $1,600 + $18,500		

*Total costs of good units completed and transferred out in Problem 18-30, Step 5.

#Equivalent units of direct materials and conversion costs calculated in Step above.

330

18-34 (20–25 min.) **Job-costing spoilage and scrap.**

1. a. Materials Control   800

           Manufacturing Overhead Control   1,075

                 Work-in-Process Control   1,875

                 (975 + 600 + 300 = 1,875)

           To record the return of spoiled materials and reduce the cost of the job.

      b. Accounts Receivable or Cash   1,995

                 Work-in-Process Control   1,995

           To record the sale of scrap and reduce the cost of the job.

2. a. The clause does not specify whether the 1% calculation is to be based on the input cost ($40,400 + $22,600 + $11,300) or the cost of the good output before the "1% normal spoilage" is added.

      b. **If the inputs are used to determine the 1%:**

$$\$40,400 + \$22,600 + \$11,300 = \$74,300$$

1% of $74,300 = $743. Then, the entry to leave the $743 "normal spoilage" cost on the job, remove the salvageable material, and charge manufacturing overhead would be:

Materials Control   800

Manufacturing Overhead Control   332

                 Work-in-Process Control   1,132

($1,075 spoilage minus $743 = $332 spoilage
cost that is taken out of the job;
$800 salvage value plus $332 = $1,132; or
$1,875 minus $743 = $1,132)

      If the outputs are used to determine the 1%:

$$\$40,400 - \$975 = \$39,425$$
$$22,600 - \ \ 600 = \ 22,000$$
$$\underline{11,300} - \ \ 300 = \underline{\ 11,000}$$
$$\underline{\$74,300} \qquad\qquad \underline{\$72,425}$$

Then, $72,425 × 1% = $724.25 or $724, rounded. The journal entry would be:

Materials Control   800

Manufacturing Overhead Control   351

                 Work-in-Process Control   1,151

18-36 (10 min.) **Rework in job costing, journal entry (continuation of 18-35)**

a) Journal entry for rework related to a specific job:

Work-in-Process Control (Job #10)	1,800	
Various Accounts		1,800
(To charge rework costs to the job)		

b) Journal entry for rework common to all jobs:

Manufacturing Overhead Control (rework costs)	1,800	
Various Accounts		1,800

c) Journal entry for abnormal rework:

Loss from Abnormal Rework	1,800	
Various Accounts		1,800

18-38 (20–25 min.) **Physical units, inspection at various stages of completion (chapter appendix).**

	Inspection at 15%	Inspection at 40%	Inspection at 100%
Work in process, beginning (20%)*	14,000	14,000	14,000
Started during March	120,000	120,000	120,000
To account for	134,000	134,000	134,000
Good units completed and transferred out	113,000[a]	113,000[a]	113,000[a]
Normal spoilage	6,600[b]	7,440[c]	6,780[d]
Abnormal spoilage (10,000 – normal spoilage)	3,400	2,560	3,220
Work in process, ending (70%)*	11,000	11,000	11,000
Accounted for	134,000	134,000	134,000

*Degree of completion for conversion costs of the forging process at the dates of the work-in-process inventories
[a] 14,000 beginning inventory +120,000 –10,000 spoiled – 11,000 ending inventory = 113,000.
[b] 6% × (120,000 units started – 10,000 units spoiled) = 6% × 110,000 = 6,600; beginning work-in-process inventory is excluded because it was already 20% complete at March 1 and past the inspection point.
[c] 6% × (134,000 units – 10,000) = 6% × 124,000 = 7,440, because all units passed the 40% completion inspection point in March.
[d] 6% × 113,000 = 6,780, because 113,000 units are fully completed and inspected during March.

18-40 (30 min.)   **Job costing, rework.**

1.   Work-in-Process Control (CS1 chips) ($110 × 80)   8,800
         Materials Control ($60 × 80)   4,800
         Wages Payable ($12 × 80)   960
         Manufacturing Overhead Allocated ($38 × 80)   3,040
     Total costs assigned to 80 spoiled units of CS1 chips before considering rework costs.

     Manufacturing Department Overhead Control (rework)   1,800
         Materials Control ($12 × 50)   600
         Wages Payable ($9 × 50)   450
         Manufacturing Overhead Allocated ($15 × 50)   750
     Normal rework on 50 units, but not attributable specifically to the CS1 chip batches or jobs.

     Loss from Abnormal Rework ($36 × 30)   1,080
         Materials Control ($12 × 30)   360
         Wages Payable ($9 × 30)   270
         Manufacturing Overhead Allocated ($15 × 30)   450
     Total costs of abnormal rework on 30 units
         Abnormal rework   = Actual rework – Normal rework
                                         = 80 – 50 = 30 units of CS1 chips.

     Work-in-Process Control (CS1 chips)   1,200
     Work-in-Process Control (CS2 chips)   600
         Manufacturing Department Overhead Allocated (rework)   1,800
     (Allocating manufacturing department rework costs to CS1 and CS2 in the proportion 1,000:500
     since each calculator requires the same number of machine-hours.)

2.   Total rework costs for CS1 chips in August 2008 are as follows:

         Normal rework costs allocated to CS1 $1,200
         Abnormal rework costs for CS1   1,080
         Total rework costs $2,280

We emphasize two points:

a.   Only $1,200 of the normal rework costs are allocated to CS1 even though the normal rework costs of the 50 CS1 calculators reworked equal $1,800. The reason is that the normal rework costs are not specifically attributable to CS1. For example, the machines happened to malfunction when CS1 was being made, but the rework was not caused by the specific requirements of CS1. If it were, then all $1,800 would be charged to CS1.

b.   Abnormal rework costs of $1,080 are linked to CS1 in the management control system even though for financial reporting purposes the abnormal rework costs are written off to the income statement.

CHAPTER 19
BALANCED SCORECARD: QUALITY, TIME, AND THE THEORY OF CONSTRAINTS

19-2 **Design quality** refers to how closely the characteristics of a product or service meet the needs and wants of customers. **Conformance quality** refers to the performance of a product or service relative to its design and product specifications.

19-4 An **internal failure cost** is detected *before a product is shipped* to a customer, whereas an **external failure** is detected after a product is shipped to a customer.

19-6 **No**. Companies should emphasize financial as well as nonfinancial measures of quality, such as yield and defect rates. Nonfinancial measures are not directly linked to bottom-line performance but they indicate and direct attention to the specific areas that need improvement to improve the bottom line.

19-8 Examples of **nonfinancial measures of internal-business-process** quality:
1. the *percentage of defects* for each product line;
2. *yield* (rates of good output to total output);
3. *manufacturing lead time* (time between order receipt and finished good);
4. number of product and process *design changes*

19-10 **No**. There is a trade-off between customer-response time and on-time performance. Simply *scheduling longer customer-response time makes achieving on-time performance easier*.

19-12 **No**. Adding a product when capacity is constrained and the timing of customer orders is uncertain causes delays in delivering all existing products. If the revenue losses from delays on existing products exceed the positive contribution earned by the product that was added, then the new product is not worthwhile.

19-14 The four key steps in **managing bottleneck resources** are:
Step 1: *Recognize* that the bottleneck operation determines *throughput contribution* of the entire system.
Step 2: Search for, and *identify* the bottleneck operation.
Step 3: *Keep the bottleneck operation busy*, and subordinate planning of all nonbottleneck operations to plans for the bottleneck operation.
Step 4: *Increase bottleneck efficiency and capacity*.

19-16 (30 min.) **Costs of quality.**

1. The ratios of each COQ category to revenues and to total quality costs for each period are as follows:

Costen, Inc.: Semi-annual Costs of Quality Report
(in thousands)

	6/30/2009			12/31/2009			6/30/2010			12/31/2010		
	Actual	% of Revenues	% of Total Quality Costs	Actual	% of Revenues	% of Total Quality Costs	Actual	% of Revenues	% of Total Quality Costs	Actual	% of Revenues	% of Total Quality Costs
		(2) = (1) ÷ $8,240	(3) = (1) ÷ $2,040		(5) = (4) ÷ $9,080	(6) = (4) ÷ $2,159		(8) = (7) ÷ $9,300	(9) = (7) ÷ $1,605		(11) = (10) ÷ $9,020	(12) = (10) ÷ $1,271
	(1)	(2)	(3)	(4)	(5)	(6)	(7)	(8)	(9)	(10)	(11)	(12)
Prevention costs												
Machine maintenance	$ 440			$ 440			$ 390			$ 330		
Supplier training	20			100			50			40		
Design reviews	50			214			210			200		
Total prevention costs	510	6.2%	25.0%	754	8.3%	34.9%	650	7.0%	40.5%	570	6.3%	44.9%
Appraisal costs												
Incoming inspection	108			123			90			63		
Final testing	332			332			293			203		
Total appraisal costs	440	5.3%	21.6%	455	5.0%	21.1%	383	4.1%	23.9%	266	3.0%	20.9%
Internal failure costs												
Rework	231			202			165			112		
Scrap	124			116			71			67		
Total internal failure costs	355	4.3%	17.4%	318	3.5%	14.7%	236	2.5%	14.7%	179	2.0%	14.1%
External failure costs												
Warranty repairs	165			85			72			68		
Customer returns	570			547			264			188		
Total external failure costs	735	8.9%	36.0%	632	7.0%	29.3%	336	3.6%	20.9%	256	2.8%	20.1%
Total quality costs	$2,040	24.7%	100.0%	$2,159	23.8%	100.0%	$1,605	17.2%	100.0%	$1,271	14.1%	100.0%
Total production and revenues	$8,240			$9,080			$9,300			$9,020		

2. From an analysis of the Cost of Quality Report, it would appear that Costen, Inc.'s program **has been successful** because:

- Total *quality costs as a percentage of total revenues have declined* from 24.7% to 14.1%.
- *External failure costs* have declined from 8.9% of total revenues to 2.8% of total revenues and from 36% of all quality costs to 20.1% of all quality costs.
- *Internal failure costs* as a percentage of revenues have been *halved* from 4.3% to 2%.
- *Appraisal costs have decreased* from 5.3% to 3% of revenues.
- *Quality costs have shifted to prevention* where problems are solved before production starts: total prevention costs (maintenance, supplier training, and design reviews) have risen from 25% to 44.9% of total quality costs. The $60,000 increase in these costs is more than offset by decreases in other quality costs.
- Because of improved designs, quality training, and additional pre-production inspections, *scrap and rework costs have almost been halved*
- *Sales have increased* by 9.5%.
- Production does not have to spend an inordinate amount of time with customer service since they are now making the product right the first time and warranty repairs and customer returns have decreased.

3. To estimate the **opportunity cost of not implementing the quality program** and to help her make her case, Jessica Tolmy could have assumed that:

- *Sales and market share would continue to decline* if the quality program was not implemented and then calculated the loss in revenue and contribution margin.
- *The company would have to compete on price* rather than quality and calculated the impact of having to lower product prices.

19-18 (15 min.)   **Cost of quality analysis, ethical considerations (continuation of 19-17).**

1. Cost of improving quality of plastic = $25 \times 100,000 = \$2,500,000$

2. Total cost of lawsuits = $2 \times \$750,000 = \$1,500,000$

3. While economically this may seem like a good decision, qualitative factors should be more important than quantitative factors when it comes to protecting customers from harm and injury. *If a product can cause a customer serious harm and injury, an ethical and moral company should take steps to prevent that harm and injury*. The company's code of ethics should guide this decision.

4. In addition to ethical considerations, the company should consider the societal cost of this decision, reputation effects if word of these problems leaks out at a later date, and governmental intervention and regulation.

19-20 (25 min.) **Quality improvement, relevant costs, and relevant revenues.**

1. Relevant costs over the next year of choosing the new lens
    = $55 × 20,000 copiers
    = $1,100,000

	Relevant Benefits over the Next Year of Choosing the New Lens
Costs of quality items	
Savings in rework costs	
$80 × 12,875 rework hours	$1,030,000
Savings in customer-support costs	
$40 × 900 customer-support-hours	36,000
Savings in transportation costs for parts	
$360 × 200 fewer loads	72,000
Savings in warranty repair costs	
$90 × 7,000 repair-hours	630,000
Opportunity costs	
Contribution margin from increased sales	1,800,000
Cost savings and additional contribution margin	$3,568,000

Because the expected relevant benefits of $3,568,000 exceed the expected relevant costs of the new lens of $1,100,000, Photon should introduce the new lens. Note that the opportunity cost benefits in the form of higher contribution margin from increased sales is an important component for justifying the investment in the new lens.

2. The incremental cost of the new lens of $1,100,000 is less than the incremental savings in rework and repair costs of $1,768,000 ($1,030,000 + $36,000 + $72,000 + $630,000). Thus, it is beneficial for TechnoPrint to invest in the new lens even without making any additional sales.

19-22 (30 min.) Waiting time, service industry.

1. If SMU's advisors expect to see 300 students each day and it takes an average of 12 minutes to advise each student, then the average time that a student will wait can be calculated using the following formula:

$$\text{Wait time} = \frac{\left(\begin{array}{c}\text{Average number}\\\text{of students per day}\end{array}\right) \times \left(\begin{array}{c}\text{Time taken to}\\\text{advise a student}\end{array}\right)^2}{2 \times \left[\begin{array}{c}\text{Maximum amount}\\\text{of time available}\end{array} - \left[\left(\begin{array}{c}\text{Average number}\\\text{of students per day}\end{array}\right) \times \left(\begin{array}{c}\text{Time taken to}\\\text{advise a student}\end{array}\right)\right]\right]}$$

$$= \frac{300 \times (12)^2}{2 \times \left[10 \text{ advisors} \times 10 \text{ hours} \times 60 \text{ minutes} - \left[300 \times 12\right]\right]}$$

$$= \frac{43,200}{2 \times \left[6,000 - 3,600\right]} = 9 \text{ minutes}$$

2. At 400 students seen a day,

$$\text{Wait time} = \frac{\left(\begin{array}{c}\text{Average number}\\\text{of students per day}\end{array}\right) \times \left(\begin{array}{c}\text{Time taken to}\\\text{advise a student}\end{array}\right)^2}{2 \times \left[\begin{array}{c}\text{Maximum amount}\\\text{of time available}\end{array} - \left[\left(\begin{array}{c}\text{Average amount}\\\text{of students per day}\end{array}\right) \times \left(\begin{array}{c}\text{Time taken to}\\\text{advise a student}\end{array}\right)\right]\right]}$$

$$= \frac{400 \times (12)^2}{2 \times \left[10 \text{ advisors} \times 10 \text{ hours} \times 60 \text{ minutes} - \left[400 \times 12\right]\right]}$$

$$= \frac{57,600}{2 \times \left[6,000 - 4,800\right]} = 24 \text{ minutes}$$

3. If the average time to advise a student is reduced to 10 minutes, then the average wait time would be

$$= \frac{\left(\begin{array}{c}\text{Average number}\\\text{of students per day}\end{array}\right) \times \left(\begin{array}{c}\text{Time taken to}\\\text{advise a student}\end{array}\right)^2}{2 \times \left[\begin{array}{c}\text{Maximum amount}\\\text{of time available}\end{array} - \left[\left(\begin{array}{c}\text{Average amount}\\\text{of students per day}\end{array}\right) \times \left(\begin{array}{c}\text{Time taken to}\\\text{advise a student}\end{array}\right)\right]\right]}$$

$$= \frac{400 \times (10)^2}{2 \times \left[10 \text{ advisors} \times 10 \text{ hours} \times 60 \text{ minutes} - \left[400 \times 10\right]\right]}$$

$$= \frac{40,000}{2 \times \left[6,000 - 4,000\right]}$$

$$= 10 \text{ minutes}$$

19-24 (15 min.) **Manufacturing cycle time, manufacturing cycle efficiency.**

1. Manufacturing cycle efficiency (MCE) is defined as follows:

$$MCE = \text{Value-added manufacturing time} \div \text{Total manufacturing time}$$

So MCE in Torrance Manufacturing is:

$$MCE = 4 \text{ days of processing time} \div 22 \text{ days total manufacturing time} = 0.18$$

2. Manufacturing cycle time = Total time from receipt of an order by production until its completion.

So Manufacturing cycle time in Torrance Manufacturing is:

$$MCT = (8 + 6 + 2 + 4 + 2) \text{ days} = 22 \text{ days}$$

19-26 (15 min.) **Theory of constraints, throughput contribution, quality.**

1. Cost of defective unit at machining operation which is not a bottleneck operation is the loss in direct materials (variable costs) of $32 per unit. Producing 2,000 units of defectives does not result in loss of throughput contribution. Despite the defective production, machining can produce and transfer 80,000 units to finishing. Therefore, cost of 2,000 defective units at the machining operation is $32 × 2,000 = $64,000.

2. A defective unit produced at the bottleneck finishing operation costs Mayfield materials costs plus the opportunity cost of lost throughput contribution. Bottleneck capacity not wasted in producing defective units could be used to generate additional sales and throughput contribution. Cost of 2,000 defective units at the finishing operation is:

Loss of direct materials $32 × 2,000	$ 64,000
Forgone throughput contribution ($72 – $32) × 2,000	80,000
Total cost of 2,000 defective units	$144,000

Alternatively, the cost of 2,000 defective units at the finishing operation can be calculated as the lost revenue of $72 × 2,000 = $144,000. This line of reasoning takes the position that direct materials costs of $32 × 2,000 = $64,000 and all fixed operating costs in the machining and finishing operations would be incurred anyway whether a defective or good unit is produced. The cost of producing a defective unit is the revenue lost of $144,000.

19-28 (30 min.) **Quality improvement, relevant costs, and relevant revenues.**

1. By implementing the new method, Tan would incur additional direct materials costs on all the 200,000 units started at the molding operation.

    Incremental Costs
    Additional direct materials costs = $4 per lamp × 200,000 lamps $800,000
    Incremental Benefits
    Increased revenue from selling 30,000 more lamps
    $40 per lamp × 30,000 lamps $1,200,000

    Tan Corporation continues to incur the same total manufacturing costs that it is currently incurring, even when it improves quality. Since these costs do not differ among the alternatives, they are excluded from the analysis.

    On the basis of quantitative considerations alone, Tan should use the new material. Relevant benefits of $1,200,000 exceed the relevant costs of $800,000 by $400,000.

2. Other **nonfinancial and qualitative factors** that Tan should consider in making a decision include the effects of quality improvement on:
    a. gaining manufacturing *expertise* that could lead to further cost reductions in the future;
    b. enhanced *reputation* and increased *customer goodwill* which could lead to higher future revenues through greater unit sales and higher sales prices; and
    c. higher *employee morale* as a result of higher quality.

19-30 (30–40 min.) **Compensation linked with profitability, on-time delivery, and external quality-performance measures.**

1.

	Jan.-June	July-Dec.
Philadelphia		
Add: Profitability 1% of operating income	$106,500	$106,000
Add: Average waiting time $50,000 if < 15 minutes	50,000	0
Deduct: Patient satisfaction $50,000 if < 70	0	0
Total: Bonus paid	$156,500	$106,000
Baltimore		
Add: Profitability 1% of operating income	$90,000	$ 9,500
Add: Average waiting time $50,000 if < 15 minutes	0	50,000
Deduct: Patient satisfaction $50,000 if < 70	(50,000)	0
Total: Bonus paid	$40,000	$59,500

2.

Operating income as a measure of profitability

Operating income captures revenue and cost-related factors. However, there is no recognition of investment differences between the two groups. If one group is substantially bigger than the other, differences in size alone give the president of the larger group the opportunity to earn a bigger bonus. An alternative approach would be to use return on investment (perhaps relative to the budgeted ROI).

15 minute benchmark as a measure of patient response time

This measure reflects the ability of Mid-Atlantic Healthcare to meet a benchmark for patient response time. Several concerns arise with this specific measure:

a. It is a yes-or-no cut-off. A 16 minute waiting time earns no bonus, but neither does a two hour wait. Moreover, no extra bonus is paid for additional waiting time reductions below 15 minutes. An alternative is to have the bonus that increases with greater waiting time improvements.
b. It can be manipulated. Doctors might quickly make initial contact with a patient to meet the benchmark, but then leave the patient sitting in the examination room for a more detailed examination or procedure to take place.
c. It reflects performance relative only to the initial waiting time. It does not consider other time-related issues such as the wait for an appointment or the time needed to fill out forms.

Problems in (b) and (c) can be overcome by measuring total patient response time (such as how long it takes from the time a patient makes an appointment to the time the actual appointment is concluded), in addition to average waiting time to meet the doctor.

Patient satisfaction as a measure of quality

This measure represents a common method for assessing quality. However, there are several concerns with its use:

a. Patient satisfaction is likely to be influenced by a number of factors that are outside the groups' control, such as how sick the patients are when coming in or the extent to which they follow doctors' orders.
b. It is influenced by the questions asked in the survey and the survey methodology. As a result, is likely to be "noisy" or very sensitive to assumptions.
c. Patient satisfaction is not the same as patient health outcomes, an important measure of healthcare quality.

A combination of measures may work well as a composite measure of quality.

3. Most companies **use both financial and nonfinancial measures to evaluate performance**. Using multiple measures of performance enables top management to evaluate whether lower-level managers have improved one area at the expense of others. If waiting time is not used for performance evaluation, managers will concentrate on increasing operating income and give less attention to waiting time, even if waiting time has a significant influence on whether customers choose Mid-Atlantic.

19-32 (60 min.) **Waiting times, relevant revenues, and relevant costs (continuation of 19-31).**

1. The direct approach is to look at incremental revenues and incremental costs.

Selling price per order of Y28, which has	
an average manufacturing lead time of 350 hours	$ 8,000
Variable cost per order	5,000
Additional contribution per order of Y28	3,000
Multiply by expected number of orders	× 25
Increase in expected contribution from Y28	$75,000

Expected loss in revenues and increase in costs from introducing Y28

Product (1)	Expected Loss in Revenues from Increasing Average Manufacturing Lead Times for All Products (2)	Expected Increase in Carrying Costs from Increasing Average Manufacturing Lead Times for All Products (3)	Expected Loss in Revenues Plus Expected Increases in Carrying Costs of Introducing Y28 (4) = (2) + (3)
Z39	$25,000.00[a]	$6,375.00[b]	$31,375.00
Y28	–	2,187.50[c]	2,187.50
Total	$25,000.00	$8,562.50	$33,562.50

[a] 50 orders × ($27,000 – $26,500)
[b] (410 hours – 240 hours) × $0.75 × 50 orders
[c] (350 hours – 0) × $0.25 × 25

Increase in expected contribution from Y28 of $75,000 is greater than increase in expected costs of $33,562.50 by $41,437.50. Therefore, SRG should introduce Y28.

2.

Selling price per order of Y28, which has an average	
manufacturing lead time of more than 320 hours	$ 6,000
Variable cost per order	5,000
Additional contribution per order of Y28	$ 1,000
Multiply by expected number of orders	× 25
Increase in expected contribution from Y28	$25,000

Expected loss in revenues and increase in costs from introducing Y28:

Product (1)	Expected Loss in Revenues from Increasing Average Manufacturing Lead Times for All Products (2)	Expected Increase in Carrying Costs from Increasing Average Manufacturing Lead Times for All Products (3)	Expected Loss in Revenues Plus Expected Increases in Carrying Costs of Introducing Y28 (4) = (2) + (3)
Z39	$25,000.00[a]	$6,375.00[b]	$31,375.00
Y28	–	2,187.50[c]	2,187.50
Total	$25,000.00	$8,562.50	$33,562.50

[a] 50 orders × ($27,000 – $26,500)
[b] (410 hours – 240 hours) × $0.75 × 50 orders
[c] (350 hours – 0) × $0.25 × 25

Increase in expected contribution from Y28 of $25,000 is less than increase in expected costs of $33,562.50 by $8,562.50. Therefore, SRG should not introduce Y28.

19-34 (20 min.) **Theory of constraints, throughput contribution, relevant costs.**

1. It will cost Colorado $50 per unit to reduce manufacturing time. But manufacturing is not a bottleneck operation; installation is. Therefore, manufacturing more equipment will not increase sales and throughput contribution. Colorado Industries should not implement the new manufacturing method.

2. Incremental costs of new direct materials, $2,000 × 320 units, $640,000
    Incremental throughput contribution, $25,000 × 20 units, $500,000

    The additional incremental costs exceed the benefits from higher throughput contribution by $140,000, so Colorado Industries should not implement the new design.

3. Incremental throughput contribution, $25,000 × 10 units $250,000
    Incremental costs $ 50,000

    The additional throughput contribution exceeds incremental costs by $200,000, so Colorado Industries should implement the new installation technique.

4. *Motivating installation workers to increase productivity is worthwhile* because installation is a bottleneck operation, and any increase in productivity at the bottleneck will increase throughput contribution. On the other hand, *motivating workers in the manufacturing department to increase productivity is not worthwhile*. Manufacturing is not a bottleneck operation, so any increase in output will result only in extra inventory of equipment.

19-36 (30-35 min.) **Theory of constraints, contribution margin, sensitivity analysis.**

1.   Assuming only one type of doll is produced, the maximum production in each department given their resource constraints is:

	Molding Department	Assembly Department	Contribution Margin
Chatty Chelsey	$\dfrac{30,000 \text{ lbs}}{1.5 \text{ lbs}} = 20,000$	$\dfrac{8,400 \text{ hours}}{1/3 \text{ hours}} = 25,200$	$\$35 - 1.5 \times \$10 - 1/3 \times \$12$ $= \$16$
Talking Tanya	$\dfrac{30,000 \text{ lbs}}{2 \text{lbs}} = 15,000$	$\dfrac{8,400 \text{ hours}}{1/2 \text{hours}} = 16,800$	$\$45 - 2 \times \$10 - \frac{1}{2} \times \$12$ $= \$19$

For both types of dolls, the constraining resource is the availability of material since this constraint causes the lowest maximum production.

If only Chatty Chelsey is produced, LTT can produce 20,000 dolls with a contribution margin of 20,000 × $16 = $320,000

If only Talking Tanya is produced, LTT can produce 15,000 dolls with a contribution margin of 15,000 × $19 = $285,000.

LTT should produce Chatty Chelseys.

2.   As shown in Requirement 1, available material in the Molding department is the limiting constraint.

If LTT sells two Chatty Chelseys for each Talking Tanya, then the maximum number of Talking Tanya dolls the Molding Department can produce (where the number of Talking Tanya dolls is denoted as T) is:

$$(\text{T} \times 2 \text{ lbs.}) + ([2 \times \text{T}] \times 1.5 \text{ lbs.}) = 30,000 \text{ lbs.}$$
$$2\text{T} + 3\text{T} = 30,000$$
$$5\text{T} = 30,000$$
$$\text{T} = 6,000$$

      The Molding Department can produce 6,000 Talking Tanya dolls, and 2 × 6,000 (or 12,000) Chatty Chelsey dolls.

Since LTT can only produce 6,000 Talking Tanyas and 12,000 Chatty Chelseys before it runs out of ingredients, the maximum contribution margin (CM) is:

$$\text{CM} = 12,000 \times \$16 + 6,000 \times \$19$$
$$= \$306,000$$

3.   With 10 more pounds of materials, LTT would produce more dolls. Using the same technique as in Requirement 2, the increase in production is:

$$(T \times 2 \text{ lbs.}) + ([2 \times T] \times 1.5 \text{ lbs.}) = 10 \text{ lbs.}$$
$$2T + 3T = 10$$
$$T = 2$$

LTT would produce 2 extra Talking Tanya dolls and 4 extra Chatty Chelsey dolls.

Contribution margin would increase by

$$4 \times \$16 + 2 \times \$19 = \$102$$

4.   With 10 more labor hours, production would not change. The limiting constraint is pounds of material, not labor hours. LTT already has more labor hours available than it needs.

19-38 (30–35 min.)   **Ethics and quality.**

1.

	2009
Revenues	$10,000,000

Costs of Quality	Cost (1)	Percentage of Revenues (2) = (1) ÷ $10,000,000
Prevention costs		
Design engineering	$200,000	2.0%
Appraisal costs		
Inspection of production	90,000	
Product testing	210,000	
Total appraisal costs	300,000	3.0%
Internal failure costs		
Scrap	230,000	2.3%
External failure costs		
Warranty liability	260,000	2.6%
Total costs of quality	$990,000	9.9%

The total costs of quality are less than 10% of revenues.

2.   Evans is obviously concerned because he expected the customer complaints calculation to be based on the number of customers who *actually complained*, not on Williams's survey. However, Williams's approach has the advantage of being thorough and systematic.

Having done the survey, it would be unethical for Williams to modify her analysis and incorrectly report the costs of quality and various nonfinancial measures of quality. In assessing the situation, the specific "Standards of Ethical Conduct for Management Accountants" (described in Exhibit 1-7) that Lindsey Williams should consider are listed below.

Competence

Clear reports using relevant and reliable information should be prepared. Preparing reports on the basis of incorrect numbers violates competence standards.

Integrity

Integrity requires that Williams report the numbers she collected. The standards of ethical conduct require the management accountant to communicate favorable as well as unfavorable information. Williams also has a responsibility to avoid actual or apparent conflicts of interest and advise all appropriate parties of any potential conflict. If Williams revises the customer complaints numbers, her action could be interpreted as being motivated by her desire to please her bosses. This would violate the responsibility for integrity.

Credibility

The management accountant's standards of ethical conduct require that information should be fairly and objectively communicated and that all relevant information should be disclosed. From a management accountant's standpoint, adjusting the customer complaints numbers to make performance look good would violate the standard of objectivity.

Williams should indicate to Roche that the costs of quality and nonfinancial measures of quality presented in the reports are, indeed, appropriate. She could propose that she add another line item indicating the number of unsolicited complaints she received, that is, complaints she received independent of the survey. She should not, however, change the numbers she obtained in the survey. If Roche still insists on modifying the customer complaints numbers, Williams should raise the matter with one of Roche's superiors, other than Evans, who has a vested interest in this dispute. If, after taking all these steps, there is continued pressure to change survey results, Williams should consider resigning from the company and not engage in unethical behavior.

CHAPTER 20
INVENTORY MANAGEMENT, JUST-IN-TIME,
AND SIMPLIFIED COSTING METHODS

20-2 Six cost categories important in managing goods for sale in a retail organization are the following:
1. purchasing costs;
2. ordering costs;
3. carrying costs;
4. stockout costs;
5. quality costs;
6. shrinkage costs.

20-4 Costs included in the **carrying costs of inventory** are incremental costs for:
- Insurance
- Rent
- Obsolescence
- Spoilage
- breakage
- opportunity cost of capital

20-6 The steps in computing the **costs of a prediction error** when using the EOQ decision model are:

Step 1: Compute the *monetary outcome from the best action* that could be taken, given the *actual* amount of the cost input.

Step 2: Compute the *monetary outcome from the best action* based on the *incorrect* amount of the predicted cost input.

Step 3: Compute the *difference* between the monetary outcomes from Steps 1 and 2.

20-8 **Just-in-time (JIT) purchasing** is the purchase of materials (or goods) so that they are *delivered just as needed* for production (or sales). **Benefits** include *lower inventory holdings* (reduced warehouse space required and less money tied up in inventory) and *less* risk of inventory *obsolescence and spoilage*.

20-10 **Disagree**. The supplier who offers the lowest price will not necessarily result in the lowest total cost to the buyer. This is because the price of the goods is only one cost associated with purchasing and managing inventories.

Other relevant cost items are:
- ordering costs,
- carrying costs,
- stockout costs
- quality costs.

20-12 **Just-in-time (JIT) production** is a "demand-pull" manufacturing system that has the following features:

- Production organized in *manufacturing cells*,
- *Multi-skilled workers*
- *Total quality management (TQM)* to eliminate defects,
- Emphasis on *reducing setup time and manufacturing lead time*, and
- *Suppliers* who deliver *quality materials* in a *timely* manner.

20-14 Versions of backflush costing differ in the number and placement of trigger points at which journal entries are made in the accounting system:

	Number of Journal Entry Trigger Points	Location in Cycle Where Journal Entries Made
Version 1	3	Stage A. Purchase of direct materials
		Stage C. Completion of good finished units of product
		Stage D. Sale of finished goods
Version 2	2	Stage A. Purchase of direct materials
		Stage D. Sale of finished goods
Version 3	2	Stage C. Completion of good finished units of product
		Stage D. Sale of finished goods

20-16 (20 min.) **Economic order quantity for retailer.**

1. D = 10,000, P = $200, C = $7

$$EOQ = \sqrt{\frac{2\,DP}{C}} = \sqrt{\frac{2 \times 10,000 \times \$200}{7}} = 755.93 \cong 756 \text{ jerseys}$$

2. Number of orders per year $= \dfrac{D}{EOQ} = \dfrac{10,000}{756} = 13.22 \cong 14$ orders

3. Demand each working day $= \dfrac{D}{\text{Number of working days}} = \dfrac{10,000}{365} = 27.40$ jerseys per day

Purchase lead time $= 7$ days

Reorder point $= 27.40 \times 7$

$= 191.80 \cong 192$ jerseys

20-18 (15 min.) **EOQ for a retailer.**

1.   D = 20,000, P = \$160, C = 20% × \$8 = \$1.60

$$EOQ = \sqrt{\frac{2DP}{C}} = \sqrt{\frac{2 \times 20,000 \times \$160}{\$1.60}} = 2,000 \text{ yards}$$

2.   Number of orders per year: $\dfrac{D}{EOQ} = \dfrac{20,000}{2,000} = 10$ orders

3.   Demand each working day $= \dfrac{D}{\text{Number of working days}}$

$$= \frac{20,000}{250}$$

= 80 yards per day

= 400 yards per week

Purchasing lead time = 2 weeks

Reorder point = 400 yards per week × 2 weeks = 800 yards

20-20 (20 min.) **Sensitivity of EOQ to changes in relevant ordering and carrying costs.**

1. $$EOQ = \sqrt{\frac{2DP}{C}}$$

where D = demand in units for a specified period of time

P = relevant ordering costs per purchase order

C = relevant carrying costs of one unit in stock for the time period used for D

Relevant Carrying Costs per Unit per Year	Relevant Ordering Costs per Purchase Order	
	\$300	**\$200**
\$10	$\sqrt{\dfrac{2 \times 10,000 \times \$300}{\$10}} = 775$	$\sqrt{\dfrac{2 \times 10,000 \times \$200}{\$10}} = 632$
15	$\sqrt{\dfrac{2 \times 10,000 \times \$300}{\$15}} = 632$	$\sqrt{\dfrac{2 \times 10,000 \times \$200}{\$15}} = 516$
20	$\sqrt{\dfrac{2 \times 10,000 \times \$300}{\$20}} = 548$	$\sqrt{\dfrac{2 \times 10,000 \times \$200}{\$20}} = 447$

2.   For a given demand level, as relevant carrying costs increase, EOQ becomes smaller. For a given demand level, as relevant order costs increase, EOQ increases.

20-22 (20 min.) **JIT production, relevant benefits, relevant costs.**

1. Annual Relevant Costs of Current Production System and JIT Production System for Champion Hardware Company

Relevant Items	Relevant Costs under Current Production System	Relevant Costs under JIT Production System
Annual tooling costs	–	$100,000
Required return on investment:		
15% per year × $1,000,000 of average inventory per year	$150,000	
15% per year × $200,000[a] of average inventory per year		30,000
Insurance, space, materials handling, and setup costs	300,000	225,000[b]
Rework costs	200,000	140,000[c]
Incremental revenues from higher selling prices	–	(160,000)[d]
Total net incremental costs	$650,000	$335,000
Annual difference in favor of JIT production		$315,000

[a] $1,000,000 × (1 – 80%) = $200,000
[b] $300,000 × (1 – 0.25) = $225,000
[c] $200,000 × (1 – 0.30) = $140,000
[d] $4 × 40,000 units = $160,000

2. **Nonfinancial and qualitative factors** that Champion should consider in deciding whether it should implement a JIT system include:
    a. The possibility of developing and implementing a *revised manufacturing system*.
    b. The ability to *design products that use standardized parts* and reduce manufacturing time.
    c. The ease of obtaining *reliable vendors* who can deliver quality direct materials on time with minimum lead time in smaller and more frequent orders.
    d. The confidence of being able to *deliver quality products on time*.
    e. The skill levels of workers to perform multiple tasks such as minor repairs, maintenance, quality testing and inspection.

3. Personal observation by production line workers and managers is more effective in JIT plants than in traditional plants. A JIT plant's production process layout is streamlined. Operations are not obscured by piles of inventory or rework. As a result, such plants are easier to evaluate by personal observation than cluttered plants where the flow of production is not logically laid out.

Besides personal observation, nonfinancial performance measures are the dominant methods of control. Nonfinancial performance measures provide most timely and easy to understand measures of plant performance. Examples of nonfinancial performance measures of time, inventory, and quality include:

- Manufacturing lead time
- Units produced per hour
- Machine setup time ÷ manufacturing time
- Number of defective units ÷ number of units completed

In addition to personal observation and nonfinancial performance measures, financial performance measures are also used. Examples of financial performance measures include:

- Cost of rework
- Ordering costs
- Stockout costs
- Inventory turnover (cost of goods sold ÷ average inventory)

The success of a JIT system depends on the speed of information flows from customers to manufacturers to suppliers. The Enterprise Resource Planning (ERP) system has a single database, and gives lower-level managers, workers, customers, and suppliers access to operating information. This benefit, accompanied by tight coordination across business functions, enables the ERP system to rapidly transmit information in response to changes in supply and demand so that manufacturing and distribution plans may be revised accordingly.

20-24 (20 min.) **Backflush costing, two trigger points, materials purchase and sale (continuation of 20-23).**

1.

(a) Purchases of direct materials	Inventory Control	2,754,000	
	Accounts Payable Control		2,754,000
(b) Incur conversion costs	Conversion Costs Control	723,600	
	Various Accounts		723,600
(c) Completion of finished goods	No entry		
(d) Sale of finished goods	Cost of Goods Sold	3,432,000	
	Inventory Control		2,692,800
	Conversion Costs Allocated		739,200
(e) Underallocated or overallocated conversion costs	Conversion Costs Allocated	739,200	
	Costs of Goods Sold		15,600
	Conversion Costs Control		723,600

2.

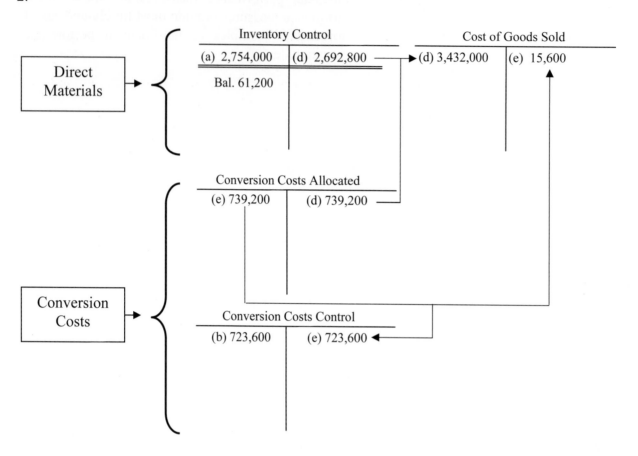

20-26 (30 min.) **Effect of different order quantities on ordering costs and carrying costs, EOQ.**

1.

	Scenario				
	1	2	3	4	5
Demand (units) (D)	234,000	234,000	234,000	234,000	234,000
Cost per purchase order (P)	$ 81.00	$ 81.00	$ 81.00	$ 81.00	$ 81.00
Annual carrying cost per package (C)	$ 11.70	$ 11.70	$ 11.70	$ 11.70	$ 11.70
Order quantity per purchase order (units) (Q)	900	1,500	1,800	2,100	2,700
Number of purchase orders per year (D ÷ Q)	260.00	156.00	130.00	111.43	86.67
Annual ordering costs (D ÷ Q) × P	$21,060	$12,636	$10,530	$ 9,026	$ 7,020
Annual carrying costs (QC ÷ 2)	$ 5,265	$ 8,775	$10,530	$12,285	$15,795
Total relevant costs of ordering and carrying inventory	$26,325	$21,411	$21,060	$21,311	$22,815

The economic order quantity is 1,800 packages. It is the order quantity at which carrying costs equal ordering costs and total relevant ordering and carrying costs are minimized.

2.   When the ordering cost per purchase order is reduced to $49:

$$EOQ = \sqrt{\frac{2 \times 234,000 \times \$49}{\$11.70}} = 1,400 \text{ packages}$$

The EOQ drops from 1,800 packages to 1,400 packages when Koala Blue's ordering cost per purchase order decreases from $81 to $49.

And the new relevant costs of ordering inventory $= \left(\frac{D}{Q} \times P\right) = \left(\frac{234,000}{1,400} \times \$49\right) = \$8,190$

and the new relevant costs or carrying inventory $= \left(\frac{Q}{2} \times C\right) = \left(\frac{1,400}{2} \times \$11.70\right) = \$8,190$

The total new costs of ordering and carrying inventory $= \$8,190 \times 2 = \$16,380$

3.   As summarized below, the new Mona Lisa web-based ordering system, by lowering the EOQ to 1,400 packages, will lower the carrying and ordering costs by $4,680. Koala Blue will spend $2,000 to train its purchasing assistants on the new system. Overall, Koala Blue will still save $2,680 in the first year alone.

Total relevant costs at EOQ (from Requirement 2)	$16,380
Annual cost benefit over old system ($21,060 – $16,380)	$ 4,680
Training costs	2,000
Net benefit in first year alone	$ 2,680

20-28 (25 min.) **MRP, EOQ, and JIT.**

1. Under a MRP system:
    Annual cost of producing and carrying J-Pods in inventory
        = Variable production cost + Setup cost + Carrying cost
        = $50 × 48,000 + ($50,000 × 12 months) + [$20 × (4,000 ÷ 2)]
        = $2,400,000 + 600,000 + 40,000
        = $3,040,000

2. Using an EOQ model to determine batch size:

$$EOQ = \sqrt{\frac{2\ DP}{C}} = \sqrt{\frac{2 \times 48,000 \times \$50,000}{\$20}}$$
$$= 15,492 \text{ J-Pods per batch}$$

Production of 48,000 per year divided by a batch size of 15,492 would imply J-Pods would be produce 3.1 batches per year. Rounding this up to the nearest whole number yields 4 batches per year.

Annual Cost of producing and carrying J-Pods in inventory
    = Variable production cost + Setup cost + Carrying cost
    = $50 × 48,000 + ($50,000 × 4) + [$20 × (15,492 ÷ 2)]
    = $2,400,000 + 200,000 + 154,920
    = $2,754,920

3. Under a JIT system

   Annual Cost of producing and carrying J-Pods in inventory
   = Variable production cost + Setup cost + Carrying cost
   = $50 × 48,000 + ($5,000 × 96[a]) + [$20 × (500 ÷ 2)]
   = $2,400,000 + 480,000 + 5,000
   = $2,885,000

   [a] production of 48,000 per year divided by a batch size of 500 would imply 96 setups per year.

4. The *EOQ system resulted in the lowest costs*, despite the fact that carrying costs were lower for the JIT model. However, the EOQ model, in this case, limits production to only once every four months. This would not allow managers to react quickly to changing market demand or economic conditions. The JIT model provides management with much more flexibility. JIT systems might also lead managers to improve processes, reduce costs and increase quality.

20-30 (25 min.) **Effect of EOQ ordering on supplier costs (continuation of Problem 20-29).**

1.

   i) Set up cost = Cost per setup × annual setups
   Alternative A: $1,000 ×50 setups = $50,000
   Alternative B: $1,000 × 250 setups = $250,000

   ii) Carrying Cost = Average inventory level × carrying cost
   Alternative A: 10,000 ÷ 2 × $50 = $250,000
   Alternative B: $0 (given)

   iii) Total relevant cost
   Alternative A: $50,000 + $250,000 = $300,000
   Alternative B: $250,000 + $0 = $250,000

   Costs would be lower if IMBest produced computers every day.

2. Let C = carrying costs per unit
   Alternative A: Total cost = $50,000 + (10,000 ÷ 2) × C
   Alternative B: Total cost = $250,000 + $0

   Equating these costs, $50,000 + $5,000C = $250,000
   $5,000C = $200,000
   C = $40

   If carrying costs fall below $40 per unit, IMBest would be better off producing the computers once a week.

20-32 (25 min.) **Supply chain effects on total relevant inventory costs.**

1. The relevant costs of purchasing from Maji and Induk are:

Cost Category	Maji	Induk
Purchase costs		
10,000 boards × $93 per board	$930,000	
10,000 boards × $90 per board		900,000
Ordering costs		
50 orders × $10 per order	500	
50 orders × $8 per order		400
Inspection costs		
10,000 boards × 5% × $5 per board	2,500	
10,000 boards × 25% × $5 per board		12,500
Required annual return on investment		
100 boards × $93 per board × 10%	930	
100 boards × $90 per board × 10%		900
Stockout costs		
100 boards × $5 per board	500	
300 boards × $8 per board		2,400
Return costs		
50 boards × $25 per board	1,250	
500 boards × $25 per board		12,500
Other carrying costs		
100 boards × $2.50 per board per year	250	
100 boards × $2.50 per board per year		250
Total Cost	$935,930	$928,950

2. While Induk will save Cow Spot $6,980 ($935,930 − $928,950), Cow Spot may still choose to use Maji for the following reasons:
    a. The *savings are less than 1%* of the total cost of the mother boards.
    b. With *ten times the number of returns*, Induk will probably have a *negative* effect on Cow Spot's *reputation*.
    c. With Induk's higher *stockouts*, Cow Spot's *reputation for availability* and on time delivery will be effected.
    d. The *increased number of inspections* may necessitate the hiring of additional personnel and the need for additional factory space and equipment which would actually increase costs, potentially beyond the $6,980 savings.

20-34 (20 min.) **Backflush, two trigger points, materials purchase and sale (continuation of 20-33).**

1.

(a) Purchases of direct materials

Inventory Control	550,000	
Accounts Payable Control		550,000

(b) Incur conversion costs

Conversion Costs Control	440,000	
Various Accounts (such as Accounts Payable Control and Wages Payable Control)		440,000

(c) Completion of finished goods   No entry

(d) Sale of finished goods

Cost of Goods Sold	900,000	
Inventory Control		500,000
Conversion Costs Allocated		400,000

(e) Underallocated or overallocated conversion costs

Conversion Costs Allocated	400,000	
Cost of Goods Sold	40,000	
Conversion Costs Control		440,000

2.

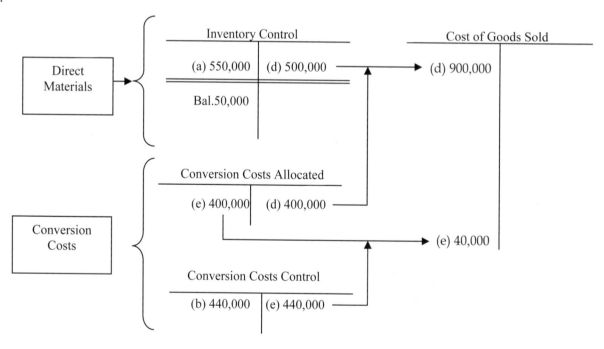

20-36 (20 min.) **Lean accounting.**

1. *The cost object in lean accounting is the value stream, not the individual product.* FSD has identified two distinct value streams: Mechanical Devices and Electronic Devices. All direct costs are traced to the value streams. However, not all plant-level overhead costs are allocated to the value streams when computing operating income. Value streams are only charged for the percentage of space they actually use, only 85% of the $120,000 occupancy costs are charged to the two value streams. The remaining 15%, or $18,000, is not used to compute value stream profits, nor are other plant-level overhead costs.

2. Operating income under lean accounting are the following (in thousands of dollars):

	Mechanical Devices	Electronic Devices
Sales ($700 + $500; $900 + $450)	$1,200	$1,350
Costs		
Direct material **purchased**		
($190 + $125; $250 + $90)	315	340
Direct manufacturing labor		
($150 + $75; $200 + $60)	225	260
Equipment costs		
($90 + $125; $200 + $100)	215	300
Product-line overhead		
($110 + $60; $125 + $50)	170	175
Occupancy costs		
($120,000 × 40%)		
($120,000 × 45%)	48	54
Value stream operating income	$ 227	$ 221

In addition to the differences discussed in Requirement 1, FSD's lean accounting system treats all direct material costs as expenses in the period they are purchased. The following factors explain the differences between traditional operating income and lean accounting income for the two value streams:

	Mechanical Devices	Electronic Devices
Traditional operating income		
($100 + $105; $45 + $140)	$205	$185
Additional cost of direct materials		
($315 − $300; $340 − $325)	(15)	(15)
Decrease in allocated plant-level overhead		
($50 + 30 − $48; $80 + 25 − $54)	37	51
Value stream operating income	$227	$221

CHAPTER 21
CAPITAL BUDGETING AND COST ANALYSIS

21-2 The **five stages in capital budgeting** are the following:
1. An *identification* stage to determine which types of capital investments are available to accomplish organization objectives and strategies.
2. An *information-acquisition* stage to gather data from all parts of the value chain in order to evaluate alternative capital investments.
3. A *forecasting* stage to project the future cash flows attributable to the various capital projects.
4. An *evaluation* stage where capital budgeting methods are used to choose the best alternative for the firm.
5. A *financing, implementation and control* stage to fund projects, get them under way and monitor their performance.

21-4 **No**. Only quantitative outcomes are formally analyzed in capital budgeting decisions. Many effects of capital budgeting decisions, however, are difficult to quantify in financial terms. These nonfinancial or qualitative factors (for example, the number of accidents in a manufacturing plant or employee morale) are important to consider in making capital budgeting decisions.

21-6 The **payback method** measures the time it will take to recoup, in the form of expected future net cash inflows, the net initial investment in a project.
Strengths:
*   The payback method is *simple* and easy to understand.
*   It is a handy method when *screening* many proposals
*   Useful when predicted *cash flows in later years are highly uncertain*.
Weaknesses:
*   Neglect of the *time value of money*
*   Doesn't take account of *cash flows after the payback period*.

21-8 **No**. The discounted cash-flow techniques implicitly consider depreciation in rate of return computations; the compound interest tables automatically allow for recovery of investment. The net initial investment of an asset is usually regarded as a lump-sum outflow at time zero. Where taxes are included in the DCF analysis, depreciation costs are included in the computation of the taxable income number that is used to compute the tax payment cash flow.

21-10 **No.** Overhead costs are relevant only if the capital investment results in a change in total overhead cash flows..

21-12 The categories of cash flow that should be considered in an **equipment-replacement decision** are:

1. a. Initial machine investment,
    b. Initial working-capital investment,
    c. After-tax cash flow from current disposal of old machine,
2. a. Annual after-tax cash flow from operations (excluding the depreciation effect),
    b. Income tax cash savings from annual depreciation deductions,
3. a. After-tax cash flow from terminal disposal of machines, and
    b. After-tax cash flow from terminal recovery of working-capital investment.

21-14 A cellular telephone company manager **responsible for retaining customers** needs to consider the *expected future revenues and the expected future costs* of "different investments" to retain customers. One such investment could be a special price discount. An alternative investment is offering loyalty club benefits to long-time customers.

21-16 Exercises in compound interest, no income taxes.
The answers to these exercises are in your textbook. They are printed after the last problem, at the end of this chapter.

21-18 (30 min.) **Capital budgeting methods, no income taxes.**

The table for the present value of annuities (Appendix B, Table 4) shows:
10 periods at 14% = 5.216

1a. Net present value
$$= \$28,000 \,(5.216) - \$110,000$$
$$= \$146,048 - \$110,000 = \$36,048$$

b. Payback period
$$= \frac{\$110,000}{\$28,000}$$
$$= 3.93 \text{ years}$$

c. Internal rate of return:

$110,000 = Present value of annuity of \$28,000 at R% for 10 years, or what factor (F) in the table of present values of an annuity (Appendix B, Table 4) will satisfy the following equation.

$$\$110,000 = \$28,000F$$

$$F = \frac{\$110,000}{\$28,000} = 3.929$$

On the 10-year line in the table for the present value of annuities (Appendix B, Table 4), find the column closest to 3.929; 3.929 is between a rate of return of 20% and 22%.

Interpolation can be used to determine the exact rate:

	Present Value Factors	
20%	4.192	4.192
IRR rate	—	3.929
22%	3.923	—
Difference	0.269	0.263

$$\text{Internal rate of return} \quad = 20\% + \left[\frac{0.263}{0.269}\right](2\%)$$

$$= 20\% + (0.978)\,(2\%) = 21.96\%$$

d. Accrual accounting rate of return based on net initial investment:

Net initial investment	$= \$110,000$
Estimated useful life	$= 10 \text{ years}$
Annual straight-line depreciation	$= \$110,000 \div 10 = \$11,000$

$$\text{Accrual accounting rate of return} \quad = \frac{\$28,000 - \$11,000}{\$110,000}$$

$$= \frac{\$17,000}{\$110,000} = 15.46\%$$

2. Factors City Hospital should consider include:
   a. Quantitative financial aspects.
   b. Qualitative factors, such as the benefits to its customers of a better eye-testing machine and the employee-morale advantages of having up-to-date equipment.
   c. Financing factors, such as the availability of cash to purchase the new equipment.

21-20 (25 min.) **Capital budgeting with uneven cash flows, no income taxes.**
1. Present value of savings in cash operating costs:

$\$10,000 \times 0.862$	$ 8,620
$8,000 \times 0.743$	5,944
$6,000 \times 0.641$	3,846
$5,000 \times 0.552$	2,760
Present value of savings in cash operating costs	21,170
Net initial investment	(23,000)
Net present value	$(1,830)

2. Payback period:

Year	Cash Savings	Cumulative Cash Savings	Initial Investment Yet to Be Recovered at End of Year
0	—	—	$23,000
1	$10,000	$10,000	13,000
2	8,000	18,000	5,000
3	6,000	24,000	—

$$\text{Payback period} \quad = \quad 2 \text{ years} + \frac{\$5,000}{\$6,000} = 2.83 \text{ years}$$

3. From requirement 1, the net present value is negative with a 16% required rate of return. Therefore, the internal rate of return must be less than 16%.

Year (1)	Cash Savings (2)	P.V. Factor at 14% (3)	P.V. at 14% (4) = (2) × (3)	P.V. Factor at 12% (5)	P.V. at 12% (6) = (2) × (5)	P.V. Factor at 10% (7)	P.V. at 10% (8) = (2) × (7)
1	$10,000	0.877	$ 8,770	0.893	$ 8,930	0.909	$ 9,090
2	8,000	0.769	6,152	0.797	6,376	0.826	6,608
3	6,000	0.675	4,050	0.712	4,272	0.751	4,506
4	5,000	0.592	2,960	0.636	3,180	0.683	3,415
			$21,932		$22,758		$23,619

Net present value at 14% = $21,932 – $23,000 = $(1,068)

Net present value at 12% = $22,758 – $23,000 = $(242)

Net present value at 10% = $23,619 – $23,000 = $619

$$\text{Internal rate of return} = 10\% + \left[\frac{619}{619 + 242}\right](2\%)$$

$$= 10\% + (0.719)(2\%) = 11.44\%$$

4. Accrual accounting rate of return based on net initial investment:

$$\text{Average annual savings in cash operating costs} = \frac{\$29,000}{4 \text{ years}} = \$7,250$$

$$\text{Annual straight-line depreciation} = \frac{\$23,000}{4 \text{ years}} = \$5,750$$

$$\text{Accrual accounting rate of return} = \frac{\$7,250 - \$5,750}{\$23,000}$$

$$= \frac{\$1,500}{\$23,000} = 6.52\%$$

21-22 (30 min.)   **Payback and NPV methods, no income taxes.**

1a.   Payback measures the time it will take to recoup, in the form of expected future cash flows, the net initial investment in a project.

Strengths

- Easy to understand
- One way to capture uncertainty about expected cash flows in later years of a project

Weaknesses

- Fails to incorporate the time value of money
- Does not consider a project's cash flows after the payback period

1b.

Project A
Outflow, $3,000,000
Inflow, $1,000,000 (Year 1) + $1,000,000 (Year 2) + $1,000,000 (Year 3) + $1,000,000 (Year 4)

Payback = 3 years

Project B
Outflow, $1,500,000
Inflow, $400,000 (Year 1) + $900,000 (Year 2) + $800,000 (Year 3)

$$\text{Payback} = 2 \text{ years} + \frac{(\$1,500,000 - \$400,000 - \$900,000)}{\$800,000} = 2.25 \text{ years}$$

Project C
Outflow, $4,000,000
Inflow, $2,000,000 (Year 1) + $2,000,000 (Year 2) + $200,000 (Year 3) + $100,000 (Year 4)
Payback = 2 years

	Payback Period
1. Project C	2 years
2. Project B	2.25 years
3. Project A	3 years

If payback period is the deciding factor, Andrews will choose Project C (payback period = 2 years; investment = $4,000,000) and Project B (payback period = 2.25 years; investment = $1,500,000), for a total capital investment of $5,500,000. Assuming that each of the projects is an all-or-nothing investment, Andrews will have $500,000 left over in the capital budget, not enough to make the $3,000,000 investment in Project A.

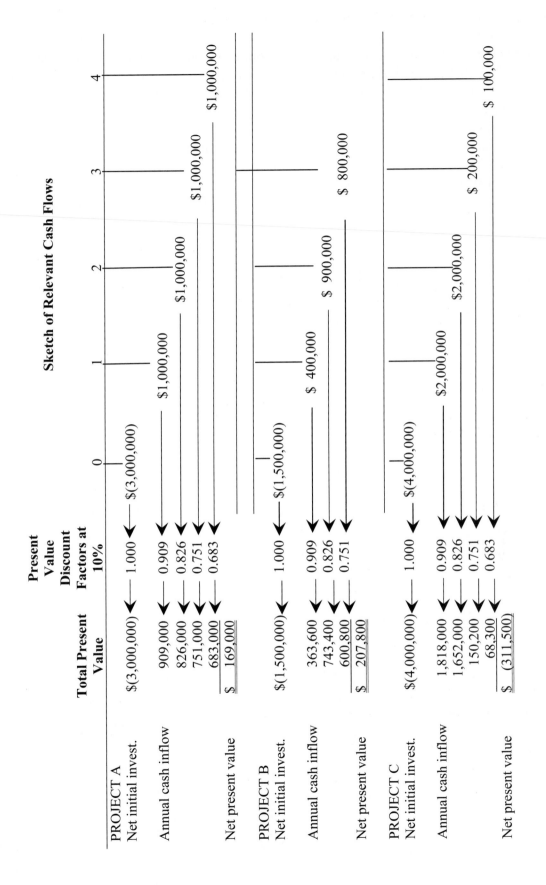

2.

Sketch of Relevant Cash Flows

	Total Present Value	Present Value Discount Factors at 10%	0	1	2	3	4
PROJECT A							
Net initial invest.	$(3,000,000)	1.000	$(3,000,000)				
Annual cash inflow	909,000	0.909		$1,000,000			
	826,000	0.826			$1,000,000		
	751,000	0.751				$1,000,000	
	683,000	0.683					$1,000,000
Net present value	$ 169,000						
PROJECT B							
Net initial invest.	$(1,500,000)	1.000	$(1,500,000)				
Annual cash inflow	363,600	0.909		$ 400,000			
	743,400	0.826			$ 900,000		
	600,800	0.751				$ 800,000	
Net present value	$ 207,800						
PROJECT C							
Net initial invest.	$(4,000,000)	1.000	$(4,000,000)				
Annual cash inflow	1,818,000	0.909		$2,000,000			
	1,652,000	0.826			$2,000,000		
	150,200	0.751				$ 200,000	
	68,300	0.683					$ 100,000
Net present value	$ (311,500)						

363

3.   Using NPV rankings, Projects B and A, which require a total investment of $3,000,000 + $1,500,000 = $4,500,000, which is less than the $6,000,000 capital budget, should be funded. This does not match the rankings based on payback period because Projects B and A have substantial cash flows after the payback period, cash flows that the payback period ignores.

Nonfinancial qualitative factors should also be considered. For example, are there differential worker safety issues across the projects? Are there differences in the extent of learning that can benefit other projects? Are there differences in the customer relationships established with different projects that can benefit Andrews Construction in future projects?

21-24 (40 min.) **New equipment purchase, income taxes.**

1. The after-tax cash inflow per year is **$29,600** ($21,600 + $8,000), as shown below:

Annual cash flow from operations	$ 36,000
Deduct income tax payments (0.40 × $36,000)	14,400
Annual after-tax cash flow from operations	$ 21,600
Annual depreciation on machine [($88,000 − $8,000) ÷ 4]	$ 20,000
Income tax cash savings from annual depreciation deductions (0.40 × $20,000)	$8,000

	Total Present Value	Present Value Discount Factor at 12%	Sketch of Relevant After-Tax Cash Flows				
			0	**1**	**2**	**3**	**4**
1a. Initial machine investment	$(88,000) ←	1.000 ←	$(88,000)				
1b. Initial working capital investment	0 ←	1.000 ←	$0				
2a. Annual after-tax cash flow from operations (excl. depr.)							
Year 1	19,289 ←	0.893 ←		$21,600			
Year 2	17,215 ←	0.797 ←			$21,600		
Year 3	15,379 ←	0.712 ←				$21,600	
Year 4	13,738 ←	0.636 ←					$21,600
2b. Income tax cash savings from annual depreciation deductions							
Year 1	7,144 ←	0.893 ←		$8,000			
Year 2	6,376 ←	0.797 ←			$8,000		
Year 3	5,696 ←	0.712 ←				$8,000	
Year 4	5,088 ←	0.636 ←					$8,000
3. After-tax cash flow from:							
a. Terminal disposal of machine	5,088 ←	0.636 ←					$8,000
b. Recovery of working capital	0 ←	0.636 ←					$0
Net present value if new machine is purchased	$ 7,013						

365

b.   Payback = $88,000 ÷ $29,600 = 2.97 years

c.

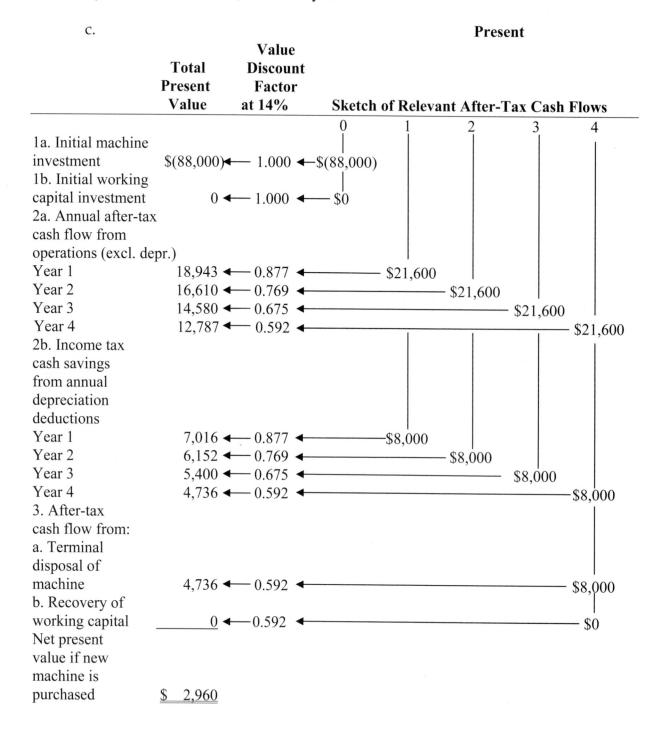

	Total Present Value	Present Value Discount Factor at 14%	Sketch of Relevant After-Tax Cash Flows				
			0	1	2	3	4
1a. Initial machine investment	$(88,000)	1.000	$(88,000)				
1b. Initial working capital investment	0	1.000	$0				
2a. Annual after-tax cash flow from operations (excl. depr.)							
Year 1	18,943	0.877		$21,600			
Year 2	16,610	0.769			$21,600		
Year 3	14,580	0.675				$21,600	
Year 4	12,787	0.592					$21,600
2b. Income tax cash savings from annual depreciation deductions							
Year 1	7,016	0.877		$8,000			
Year 2	6,152	0.769			$8,000		
Year 3	5,400	0.675				$8,000	
Year 4	4,736	0.592					$8,000
3. After-tax cash flow from:							
a. Terminal disposal of machine	4,736	0.592					$8,000
b. Recovery of working capital	0	0.592					$0
Net present value if new machine is purchased	$ 2,960						

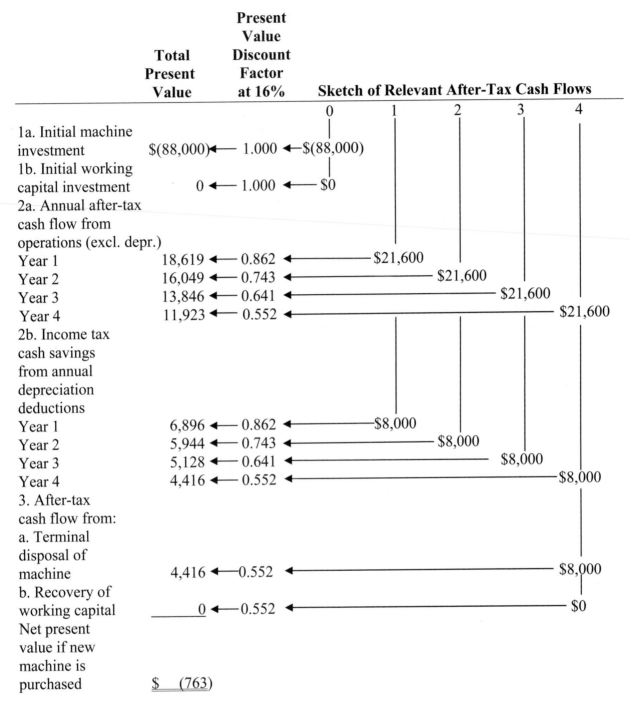

	Total Present Value	Present Value Discount Factor at 16%	Sketch of Relevant After-Tax Cash Flows				
			0	1	2	3	4
1a. Initial machine investment	$(88,000)	← 1.000	←$(88,000)				
1b. Initial working capital investment	0	← 1.000	← $0				
2a. Annual after-tax cash flow from operations (excl. depr.)							
Year 1	18,619	← 0.862		← $21,600			
Year 2	16,049	← 0.743			← $21,600		
Year 3	13,846	← 0.641				← $21,600	
Year 4	11,923	← 0.552					← $21,600
2b. Income tax cash savings from annual depreciation deductions							
Year 1	6,896	← 0.862		←$8,000			
Year 2	5,944	← 0.743			← $8,000		
Year 3	5,128	← 0.641				← $8,000	
Year 4	4,416	← 0.552					←$8,000
3. After-tax cash flow from:							
a. Terminal disposal of machine	4,416	←0.552					← $8,000
b. Recovery of working capital	0	←0.552					← $0
Net present value if new machine is purchased	$ (763)						

The above panels report the net present value of the project using 14% (small positive NPV) and 16% (small negative NPV). The IRR, the discount rate at which the NPV of the cash flows is zero, must lie between 14% and 16%.

By interpolation:

$$\text{Internal rate of return} = 16\% - \left(\frac{\$763}{\$763 + \$2,960} \right) \times 2\%$$

$$= 15.59\%$$

2.   Both the net present value and internal rate of return methods use a discounted cash flow approach in which *all* expected future cash inflows and cash outflows of a project are measured as if they occurred at a single point in time. The payback method considers only cash flows up to the time when the expected future cash inflows recoup the net initial investment in a project. The payback method ignores profitability and the time value of money. However, the payback method is becoming increasingly important in the global economy. When the local environment in an international location is unstable and therefore highly risky for a potential investment, a company would likely pay close attention to the payback period for making its investment decision. In general, the more unstable the environment, the shorter the payback period desired.

21-26 (60 min.)   **Selling a plant, income taxes.**

1.   *Option 1*

Current disposal price	$340,000
Deduct current book value	0
Gain on disposal	340,000
Deduct 40% tax payments	136,000
Net present value	$204,000

Option 2

Crossroad receives three sources of cash inflows:

a. Rent. Four annual payments of $96,000. The after-tax cash inflow is:
    $96,000 × (1 − 0.40) = $57,600 per year

b. Discount on material purchases, payable at year-end for each of the four years: $18,960
    The after-tax cash inflow is: $18,960 × (1 − 0.40) = $11,376

c. Sale of plant at year-end 2012. The after-tax cash inflow is:
    $80,000 × (1 − 0.40) = $48,000

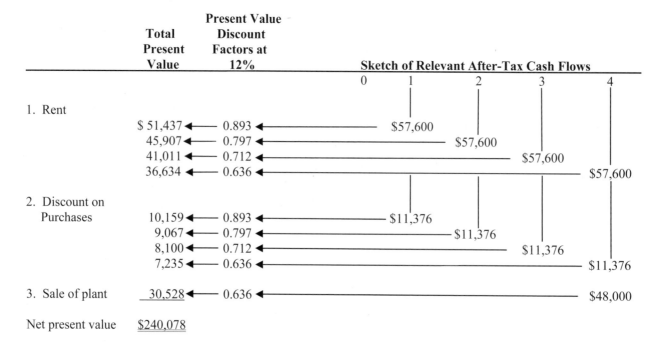

Net present value $240,078

368

Option 3

Contribution margin per jacket:

Selling price	$42.00
Variable costs	33.00
Contribution margin	$ 9.00

	2009	2010	2011	2012
Contribution margin $9.00 × 8,000; 12,000; 16,000; 4,000	$72,000	$108,000	$144,000	$36,000
Fixed overhead (cash) costs	8,000	8,000	8,000	8,000
Annual cash flow from operations	64,000	100,000	136,000	28,000
Income tax payments (40%)	25,600	40,000	54,400	11,200
After-tax cash flow from operations (excl. depcn.)	$38,400	$ 60,000	$ 81,600	$16,800

Depreciation: $60,000 ÷ 4 = $15,000 per year

Income tax cash savings from depreciation deduction: $15,000 × 0.40 = $6,000 per year

Sale of plant at end of 2012: $120,000 × (1 − 0.40) = $72,000

	Total Present Value	Present Value Discount Factors at 12%	Sketch of Relevant After-Tax Cash Flows				
			2008	2009	2010	2011	2012
1a. Initial plant equipment upgrade investment	$(60,000)	1.000	$60,000				
1b. Initial working capital investment	0	1.000	$0				
2a. Annual after-tax cash flow from operations (excluding depreciation effects)							
Year 1	34,291	0.893		$38,400			
Year 2	47,820	0.797			$60,000		
Year 3	58,099	0.712				$81,600	
Year 4	10,685	0.636					$16,800
2b. Income tax cash savings from annual depreciation deductions							
Year 1	5,358	0.893		$6,000			
Year 2	4,782	0.797			$6,000		
Year 3	4,272	0.712				$6,000	
Year 4	3,816	0.636					$6,000
3. After-tax cash flow from							
a. Terminal disposal of plant	45,792	0.636					$72,000
b. Recovery of working capital	0	0.636					$0
Net present value	$154,915						

Option 2 has the highest NPV:

	NPV
Option 1	$204,000
Option 2	$240,078
Option 3	$154,915

2.   **Nonfinancial factors** that Crossroad should consider include the following:
   • Option 1 gives Crossroad immediate *liquidity* which it can use for other projects.
   • Option 2 has the advantage of Crossroad having a *closer relationship with the supplier*. However, it limits Crossroad's flexibility if Austin Corporation's quality is not comparable to competitors.
   • Option 3 has Crossroad entering a *new line of business*. If this line of business is successful, it could be expanded to cover souvenir jackets for other major events. The risks of selling the predicted number of jackets should also be considered.

21-28 (40 min.)   **Equipment replacement, income taxes (continuation of 21-27).**

1. & 2. Income tax rate = 30%
Modernize Alternative
Annual depreciation:
$33,600,000 ÷ 7 years = $4,800,000 a year.

Income tax cash savings from annual depreciation deductions:
$4,800,000 × 0.30 = $1,440,000 a year.

Terminal disposal of equipment = $6,000,000.

After-tax cash flow from terminal disposal of equipment:
       $6,000,000 × 0.70 = $4,200,000.

The NPV components are:

a. Initial investment:

                                                  NPV

    Jan. 1, 2010 $(33,600,000) × 1.000 $(33,600,000)

b. Annual after-tax cash flow from operations
(excluding depreciation):

		NPV
Dec. 31, 2010	9,936,000 × 0.70 × 0.893	6,210,994
2011	11,016,000 × 0.70 × 0.797	6,145,826
2012	12,096,000 × 0.70 × 0.712	6,028,646
2013	13,176,000 × 0.70 × 0.636	5,865,955
2014	14,256,000 × 0.70 × 0.567	5,658,206
2015	15,336,000 × 0.70 × 0.507	5,442,746
2016	16,416,000 × 0.70 × 0.452	5,194,022

c. Income tax cash savings from annual depreciation
deductions ($1,440,000 each year for 7 years):

                              $1,440,000 × 4.564   6,572,160

d. After-tax cash flow from terminal sale of equipment:

                              $4,200,000 × 0.452   <u>1,898,400</u>

    Net present value of modernize alternative   <u>$ 15,416,955</u>

Replace alternative

Initial machine replacement = $58,800,000

Sale on Jan. 1, 2010, of equipment = $3,600,000

After-tax cash flow from sale of old equipment: $3,600,000 × 0.70 = $2,520,000

Net initial investment: $58,800,000 – $2,520,000 = $56,280,000

Annual depreciation: $58,800,000 ÷ 7 years = $8,400,000 a year

Income-tax cash savings from annual depreciation deductions: $8,400,000 × 0.30 = $2,520,000

After-tax cash flow from terminal disposal of equipment: $14,400,000 × 0.70 = $10,080,000

The NPV components of the replace alternative are:

a. Net initial investment $(56,280,000)
Jan. 1, 2010 $(56,280,000) × 1.000

b. Annual after-tax cash flow from operations (excluding depreciation)
Dec. 31,   2010 $13,248,000 × 0.70 × 0.893   8,281,325
           2011   14,688,000 × 0.70 × 0.797   8,194,435
           2012   16,128,000 × 0.70 × 0.712   8,038,195
           2013   17,568,000 × 0.70 × 0.636   7,821,274
           2014   19,008,000 × 0.70 × 0.567   7,544,275
           2015   20,448,000 × 0.70 × 0.507   7,256,995
           2016   21,888,000 × 0.70 × 0.452   6,925,363

c. Income tax cash savings from annual depreciation deductions
   ($2,520,000 each year for 7 years) $2,520,000 × 4.564   11,501,280

d. After-tax cash flow from terminal sale of equipment, $10,080,000 × 0.452   4,556,160

Net present value of replace alternative $13,839,302

On the basis of NPV, Pro Chips should modernize rather than replace the equipment. Note that absent taxes, the replace alternative had a higher NPV than the modernize alternative. In making decisions, companies should always consider after-tax amounts.

3.   Pro Chips would prefer to:
        a. have lower tax rates,
        b. have revenue exempt from taxation,
        c. recognize taxable revenues in later years rather than earlier years,
        d. recognize taxable cost deductions greater than actual outlay costs, and
        e. recognize cost deductions in earlier years rather than later years (including accelerated amounts in earlier years).

21-30 (45 min.)   **NPV, IRR and sensitivity analysis.**

1. Net Present Value of project:

	Period	
	0	**1 - 10**
Cash inflows		$23,000
Cash outflows	$(42,000)	(16,000)
Net cash flows	$(42,000)	$ 7,000

Annual net cash inflows	$ 7,000
Present value factor for annuity, 10 periods, 6%	× 7.36
Present value of net cash inflows	$51,520
Initial investment	(42,000)
Net present value	$ 9,520

To find IRR, first divide the initial investment by the net annual cash inflow:
$42,000 ÷ $7,000 = 6.0.
The 6.0 represents the present value factor for a ten-period project with the given cash flows, so look in Table 4, Appendix B for the present value of an annuity in arrears to find the factor closest to 6.0 along the ten period row. You should find that it is between 10% and 12%.

The internal rate of return can be calculated by interpolation:

	Present Value Factors for	
	Annuity of $1 for 10 years	
10%	6.145	6.145
IRR	–	6.000
12%	5.650	–
Difference	0.495	0.145

Internal rate of return $= 10\% + \left(\dfrac{0.145}{0.495} \right)(2\%) = 10.6\%$.

Note: You can use a calculator or excel to find the IRR, and you will get an answer of approximately 10.56%.

2. If revenues are 10% higher, the new Net Present Value will be:

	Period	
	0	**1 - 10**
Cash inflows		$25,300
Cash outflows	$(42,000)	(16,000)
Net cash inflows	$(42,000)	$ 9,300

Annual net cash inflows	$ 9,300
Present value factor for annuity, 10 periods, 6%	× 7.36
Present value of net cash inflows	$68,448
Initial investment	(42,000)
Net present value	$26,448

And the IRR will be: $42,000 ÷ $9,300 = present value factor of 4.516, yielding a return of 17.87% via interpolation (see below), or using a calculator, a return of 17.86%.

	Present Value Factors for Annuity of $1 for 10 years	
16%	4.833	4.833
IRR	–	4.516
18%	4.494	–
Difference	0.339	0.317

Internal rate of return = $16\% + \left(\dfrac{0.317}{0.339} \right)(2\%) = 17.87\%$.

If revenues are 10% lower, the new net present value will be:

	Period	
	0	**1 - 10**
Cash inflows		$20,700
Cash outflows	$(42,000)	(16,000)
Net cash inflows	$(42,000)	$ 4,700

Annual net cash inflows	$ 4,700
Present value factor for annuity, 10 periods, 6%	× 7.36
Present value of net cash inflows	$ 34,592
Initial investment	(42,000)
Net present value	$ (7,408)

And the IRR will be: $42,000 ÷ $4,700 = present value factor of 8.936, yielding a return of 2.11% using interpolation (see calculations below) or, using a calculator, a return of 2.099%.

	Present Value Factors for Annuity of $1 for 10 years	
2%	8.983	8.983
IRR	–	8.936
4%	8.111	–
Difference	0.872	0.047

Internal rate of return $= 2\% + \left(\dfrac{0.047}{0.872} \right)(2\%) = 2.11\%$.

3. If both revenues and costs are higher, the new Net Present Value will be:

	Period	
	0	**1 - 10**
Cash inflows		$25,300
Cash outflows	$(42,000)	(17,120)
Net cash inflows	$(42,000)	$ 8,180

Annual net cash inflows	$ 8,180
Present value factor for annuity, 10 periods, 6%	× 7.36
Present value of net cash inflows	$60,205
Initial investment	(42,000)
Net present value	$18,205

And the IRR will be: $42,000 ÷ $8,180 = present value factor of 5.134, yielding a return of 14.43% via interpolation, or using a calculator, a return of 14.406%.

	Present Value Factors for Annuity of $1 for 10 years	
14%	5.216	5.216
IRR	–	5.134
16%	4.833	–
Difference	0.383	0.082

Internal rate of return $= 14\% + \left(\dfrac{0.082}{0.383} \right)(2\%) = 14.43\%$.

If both revenues and costs are lower, the new Net Present Value will be:

	Period	
	0	**1 - 10**
Cash inflows		$20,700
Cash outflows	$(42,000)	(14,400)
Net cash inflows	$(42,000)	$ 6,300

Annual net cash inflows	$ 6,300
Present value factor for annuity, 10 periods, 6%	× 7.36
Present value of net cash inflows	$46,368
Initial investment	(42,000)
Net present value	$ 4,368

To compute the IRR, note that the present value factor is $42,000 ÷ $6,300= present value factor of 6.667, yielding a return of 8.15% from interpolation or, using a calculator, a return of 8.144%.

	Present Value Factors for	
	Annuity of $1 for 10 years	
8%	6.710	6.710
IRR	–	6.667
10%	6.145	–
Difference	0.565	0.043

$$\text{Internal rate of return} = 8\% + \left(\frac{0.043}{0.565} \right)(2\%) = 8.15\%.$$

4. To find the NPV with a different rate of return, use the same cash flows but with a different discount rate, this time for ten periods at 8%.

Annual net cash inflows	$ 7,000
Present value factor for annuity, 10 periods, 8%	× 6.71
Present value of net cash inflows	$46,970
Initial investment	(42,000)
Net present value	$ 4,970

The NPV is positive, so they should accept this project. Of course, this result is to be expected since in requirement 1, the IRR was determined to be 10.6%. Therefore, for any discount rate less than 10.6%, the NPV of the stream of cash flows will be positive.

5. The **sensitivity analysis** shows that the *return on the project is sensitive to changes in the projected revenues and costs*. However, *for almost all situations, the NPV has been positive and the IRR has been greater than the required rate of return.* The one exception is the case where the revenues decline by 10%, but the costs do not. Overall, the project appears to be a good one for Crumbly Cookie, provided that the likelihood of the scenario where revenues decline substantially but costs do not is not too high.

21-32 (40 min.) **Replacement of a machine, income taxes, sensitivity**.

1a. Original cost of old machine: $120,000
    Depreciation taken during the first 3 years
    {[($120,000 – $15,000) ÷ 7] × 3}   45,000
    Book value   75,000
    Current disposal price: 60,000
    Loss on disposal $ 15,000
    Tax rate   ×   0.40
    Tax savings in cash from loss on current disposal of old machine $ 6,000

1b. Difference in recurring after-tax variable cash-operating savings, with 40% tax rate:
    ($0.20 – $0.14) × (450,000) × (1– 0.40) = $16,200 (in favor of new machine)

Difference in after-tax fixed cost savings, with 40% tax rate:
    ($22,500 – $21,000) × (1 – 0.40) = $900 (in favor of new machine)

1c.

	Old Machine	**New Machine**
Initial machine investment	$120,000	$180,000
Terminal disposal price at end of useful life	15,000	30,000
Depreciable base	$105,000	$150,000
Annual depreciation using straight-line (7-year life)	$ 15,000	
Annual depreciation using straight-line (4-year life):		$ 37,500

Year (1)	Depreciation on Old Machine (2)	Depreciation on New Machine (3)	Additional Depreciation Deduction on New Machine (4) = (3) – (2)	Income Tax Cash Savings from Difference in Depreciation Deduction at 40% (4) × 40%
2009	$15,000	$37,500	$22,500	$9,000
2010	15,000	37,500	22,500	9,000
2011	15,000	37,500	22,500	9,000
2012	15,000	37,500	22,500	9,000

1d.

	Old Machine	New Machine
Original cost	$120,000	$180,000
Total depreciation	105,000	150,000
Book value of machines on Dec. 31, 2012	15,000	30,000
Terminal disposal price of machines on Dec. 31, 2012	10,500	30,000
Loss on disposal of machines	4,500	0
Add tax savings on loss (40% of $4,500; 40% of $0)	1,800	0
After-tax cash flow from terminal disposal of machines ($10,500 + $1,800; $30,000 + $0)	$ 12,300	$ 30,000

Difference in after-tax cash flow from terminal disposal of machines: $30,000 − $12,300 = $17,700.

2. Considering financial information only, the Smacker Company should *retain the old equipment* because the *net present value of the incremental cash flows from the new machine is negative*. The computations, using the results of requirement 1, are presented below. In this format the present value factors appear at the bottom. All cash flows, year by year, are then converted into present values.

	After-Tax Cash Flows				
	2008[a]	2009	2010	2011	2012
Initial machine investment	$(180,000)				
Current disposal price of old machine	60,000				
Tax savings from loss on disposal of old machine	6,000				
Recurring after-tax cash-operating savings					
Variable		$16,200	$16,200	$16,200	$16,200
Fixed		900	900	900	900
Income tax cash savings from difference in depreciation deductions		9,000	9,000	9,000	9,000
Additional after-tax cash flow from terminal disposal of new machine over old machine					17,700
Net after-tax cash flows	$(114,000)	$26,100	$26,100	$26,100	$43,800
Present value discount factors (at 16%)	1.000	0.862	0.743	0.641	0.552
Present value	$(114,000)	$22,498	$19,392	$16,730	$24,178
Net present value	$ (31,202)				

[a]Actually January 1, 2009

3. Let $X be the *additional* recurring after-tax cash operating savings required each year to make NPV = $0.

The present value of an annuity of $1 per year for 4 years discounted at 16% = 2.798

To make NPV = 0, Smacker needs to generate cash savings with NPV of $31,202.
That is $X (2.798)   = $31,202
              X   =   31,202 ÷ 2.798 = $11,152

Smacker must generate additional annual after-tax cash operating savings of $11,152.

378

21-34 (35 min.) **Recognizing cash flows for capital investment projects.**

1.   Partitioning relevant cash flows into categories:

   (1)   Net initial investment cash flows:
   - The $98,000 cost of the new Flab-Buster 3000
   - The disposal value of the old machine, $5,000, is a cash inflow
   - The book value of the old machine $4,000 ($50,000 − $46,000), relative to the disposal value of $5,000, yields a taxable gain of $1,000 ($5,000 − $4,000) that leads to a cash outflow for taxes of $1,000 × Tax Rate

   (2)   Cash flow savings from operations:
   - The 30% savings in utilities cost per year of $4,320 (30% × $1,200 per month × 12 months) results in cash inflow from operations after tax of $4,320 × (1 − Tax Rate)
   - The savings of half the maintenance costs per year of $5,000 (50% × $10,000) results in a cash inflow from operations after tax of $5,000 (1 − Tax Rate)
   - Annual depreciation of ($98,000 − $10,000) ÷ 10 years = $8,800 on Flab-Buster 3000, relative to the ($4,000 − $0) ÷ 10 years = $400 depreciation on current Fit-O-Matic leads to additional tax savings of $8,400 × Tax Rate

   (3)   Cash flows from terminal disposal of investment:
   - The $10,000 salvage value of Flab-Buster 3000 minus the $0 salvage value of the old Fit-O-Matic is a terminal cash flow at the end of Year 10. There are no tax effects because both machines are planned to be disposed of at book value.

   (4)   Data not relevant to the capital budgeting decision:
   - The $10 charge for customers, since it would not change whether or not Ludmilla got the new machine
   - The $78,000 cost of the machine Ludmilla does not intend to buy
   - The $50,000 original cost of the Fit-O-Matic machine

2.   Net present value of the investment:

Net initial investment

Initial investment in Flab-Buster 3000	$(98,000)
Current disposal value of Fit-O-Matic	5,000
Tax on gain on sale of Fit-O-Matic, 40% × $1,000	(400)
Net initial investment	$(93,400)

Annual after-tax cash flow from operations (excl. deprn. effects)

After-tax savings in utilities costs, $4,320 (1−0.40)	$ 2,592
After-tax savings in maintenance costs, $5,000 (1−0.40)	3,000
Annual after-tax cash flow from operations	$ 5,592
Income-tax cash savings from annual additional depreciation deductions ($8,800 − $400) × 40%	$ 3,360

After-tax cash flow from terminal disposal of machines	$ 10,000

These four amounts can be combined to determine the NPV at an 8% discount rate.

Present value of net initial investment, $(93,400) × 1.000	$(93,400)
Present value of 10-year annuity of annual after-tax cash flow from operations (excl. deprcn. effects), $5,592 × 6.710	37,522
Present value of 10-year annuity of income-tax cash savings from annual depreciation deductions, $3,000 × 6.710	22,546
Present value of after-tax cash flow from terminal disposal of machines, $10,000 × 0.463	4,630
Net present value	$(28,702)

At the required rate of return of 8%, the net present value of the investment in the Flab-Buster 3000 is substantially negative. Considering financial information only, Ludmilla should therefore not make the investment.

21-36 (20 min.) **NPV and inflation.**

1. Without inflation or taxes, this is a simple NPV problem with a 10% discount rate.

Present value of initial investment, $(600,000) × 1.000	$(600,000)
Present value of 6-year annuity of annual cash savings ($140,000 × 4.355)	609,700
Net present value	$ 9,700

2. With inflation, we adjust each year's cash flow for the inflation rate to get nominal cash flows and then discount each cash flow separately using the nominal discount rate.

Nominal rate = $(1 + \text{real rate}) \times (1 + \text{inflation rate}) - 1$
Nominal rate = $(1.10)(1.055) - 1 = 1.16 - 1 = .16$ or 16%

Period	Cash Flow (Real Dollars) (1)	Cumulative Inflation Rate (2)	Cash Inflows (Nominal Dollars) (3) = (1) × (2)	Present Value Factor, 16% (4)	Present Value (5) = (3) × (4)
1	140,000	1.055	147,700	0.862	$127,317
2	140,000	1.113[1]	155,824	0.743	115,777
3	140,000	1.174	164,394	0.641	105,376
4	140,000	1.239	173,435	0.552	95,736
5	140,000	1.307	182,974	0.476	87,096
6	140,000	1.379	193,038	0.410	79,146

Total present value of annual net cash inflows in nominal dollars   610,448
Present value of initial investment, $(600,000) × 1.000   (600,000)
Net present value $ 10,448
[1]$1.113 = (1.055)^2$

3. Both the unadjusted and adjusted NPV are positive. Based on financial considerations alone, Cost-Less should buy the new cash registers. However, the effect of taxes should also be considered, as well as any pertinent non-financial issues, such as potential improvements in customer response time from moving to the new cash registers.

21-38 (45 min.) **Net present value, Internal Rate of Return, Sensitivity Analysis.**

1. Given the annual operating cash outflows of $160,000 and the payment of 10% of revenues (10% × $260,000 = $26,000), the net cash inflows for each period are as follows:

	Period	
	0	1 - 12
Cash inflows		$260,000
Cash outflows	$(500,000)	(186,000)
Net cash inflows	$(500,000)	$ 74,000

The NPV of the investment is:

Annual net cash inflows	$ 74,000
Present value factor for annuity, 12 periods, 8%	× 7.536
Present value of net cash inflows	$557,664
Initial investment	(500,000)
Net present value	$ 57,664

And the IRR will be: $500,000 ÷ $74,000 = present value factor of 6.76, yielding a return just over 10% from the table, or using a calculator, a return of 10.17%.

2. For revenues of $240,000, the cash flows and NPV computation are given below.

	Period	
	0	**1 - 12**
Cash inflows		$240,000
Cash outflows	$(500,000)	(184,000)
Net cash inflows	$(500,000)	$ 56,000

Annual net cash inflows	$ 56,000
Present value factor for annuity, 12 periods, 8%	× 7.536
Present value of net cash inflows	$422,016
Initial investment	(500,000)
Net present value	$ (77,984)

And the IRR will be: $500,000 ÷ $56,000 = present value factor of 8.93, yielding a return between 4% and 6% from the table, or using a calculator, a return of 4.87%.

For revenues of $220,000:

	Period	
	0	**1 - 12**
Cash inflows		$220,000
Cash outflows	$(500,000)	(182,000)
Net cash inflows	$(500,000)	$ 38,000

Annual net cash inflows	$ 38,000
Present value factor for annuity, 12 periods, 8%	× 7.536
Present value of net cash inflows	$ 286,368
Initial investment	(500,000)
Net present value	$(213,632)

And the IRR will be: $500,000 ÷ $38,000 = present value factor of 13.16, yielding a return of less than 2% from the table or −1.35% using a calculator.

3. For revenues of $240,000, lower costs of $150,000, and payments of only 6% of revenues equal to $14,400:

	Period	
	0	**1 - 12**
Cash inflows		$240,000
Cash outflows	$(500,000)	(164,400)
Net cash inflows	$(500,000)	$ 75,600

Annual net cash inflows	$ 75,600
Present value factor for annuity, 12 periods, 8%	× 7.536
Present value of net cash inflows	$569,722
Initial investment	(500,000)
Net present value	$ 69,722

And the IRR will be: 500,000 ÷ 75,600 = present value factor of 6.61, yielding a return between 10% and 12% from the table, or using a calculator, a return of 10.61%.

For revenues of $220,000, lower costs of $150,000, and payments of only 6% of revenues equal to 13,200:

	Period	
	0	**1 - 12**
Cash inflows		$220,000
Cash outflows	$(500,000)	(163,200)
Net cash inflows	$(500,000)	$ 56,800

Annual net cash inflows	$ 56,800
Present value factor for annuity, 12 periods, 8%	× 7.536
Present value of net cash inflows	$428,045
Initial investment	(500,000)
Net present value	$ (71,955)

And the IRR will be: 500,000 ÷ 56,800 = present value factor of 8.80, yielding a return between 4% and 6% from the table, or using a calculator, a return of 5.12%.

4. Under the scenario of higher costs, _Francesca will only be well off making the investment if she can reach the sales revenue goal of $260,000_. Otherwise she will earn less than her desired return of 8%. If Francesca is able to lower the operating costs to $150,000 and pay out a smaller share of her revenues, the project will be profitable unless she only reaches the revenue level of $220,000; in that case, she will fall short not only of her desired return, but also her cost of capital of 6%. In summary, unless Francesca is either fairly certain to reach the $260,000 revenue level or fairly certain to lower her costs, it is advised that she not make the investment.

It is not necessary to redo the NPV with different interest rates if you already calculated the IRR, since the IRR will not change with changes in desired rate of return. All you need to do is compare the IRR of the project to different desired returns if you are changing the required rate of return and not the cash flows themselves.

CHAPTER 22
MANAGEMENT CONTROL SYSTEMS, TRANSFER PRICING, AND MULTINATIONAL CONSIDERATIONS

22-2 An **effective management control system** is:

(a) closely *aligned* to an organization's strategies and goals

(b) designed to *support* the organizational responsibilities of individual managers

(c) able to *motivate* managers and employees to put in effort to attain selected goals desired by top management.

22-4 The chapter cites five **benefits of decentralization**:

1. Creates greater *responsiveness to local needs*
2. Leads to gains from *faster decision making*
3. Increases *motivation* of subunit managers
4. Assists *management development* and learning
5. Sharpens the *focus* of subunit managers

The chapter cites four costs of decentralization:

1. Leads to *suboptimal decision making*
2. Focuses managers' *attention on the subunit* rather than the company as a whole
3. Increases *costs of gathering information*
4. Results in *duplication* of activities

22-6 **No**. *A transfer price is the price one subunit of an organization charges for a product or service supplied to another subunit of the same organization*. The two segments can be cost centers, profit centers, or investment centers.

22-8 **Transfer prices** should have the following **properties**:

1. promote *goal congruence*,
2. be useful for *evaluating* subunit *performance*,
3. *motivate* management effort, and
4. *preserve* a high level of subunit *autonomy in decision making*.

22-10 **Market based transfer pricing** is optimal when

(a) the market for the intermediate product market is perfectly *competitive*

(b) *interdependencies* of subunits are *minimal*

(c) there are *no additional costs or benefits to the company as a whole* from buying or selling in the external market instead of transacting internally.

22-12 Reasons why a **dual-pricing** approach to transfer pricing is **not widely used** in practice include:

1. In this approach, the manager of the *supplying* division uses a cost-based method to record revenues and *does not have sufficient incentives to control costs*.
2. This approach *does not provide clear signals* to division managers *about* the level of *decentralization* top management wants.
3. This approach tends *to insulate managers* from the frictions of the marketplace because costs, not market prices, affect the revenues of the supplying division.
4. It leads to *problems in computing the taxable income* of subunits located in different tax jurisdictions.

22-14 **Yes**. Under the general transfer-pricing guideline the minimum transfer price will vary. The minimum transfer price equals the *incremental cost per unit* incurred up to the point of transfer *plus* the *opportunity cost per unit* to the supplying division. When the supplying division has idle capacity, its opportunity cost per unit is zero; when the supplying division has no idle capacity, its opportunity cost per unit is positive.

22-16 (15 min.) **Management control systems, balanced scorecard.**

Greystone follows a *low-cost strategy* that emphasizes *high quality*, *timeliness*, and a *multi-skilled workforce*. Accordingly, Greystone should adopt financial and non-financial performance measures in its balanced scorecard that support this strategy. Examples of performance measures in each perspective are identified below.

Financial perspective	Revenue growth
	Operating income from productivity gain
	Operating income, EVA, ROI
	Gross margin percentage
Customer perspective	Growth in market share
	Customer satisfaction ratings
	Customer response time
	Number of customer complaints
	Number of new customers
Internal-business processes perspective	Yield
	Percent of defective tiles
	Manufacturing cycle efficiency
	On-time delivery
	Number of design and process changes made
Learning and growth perspective	Employee turnover
	Employee satisfaction ratings
	Percent of employees trained in quality management
	Hours of training
	Percent of compensation based on team incentives
	Information systems availability

22-18 (15 min.)   **Decentralization, goal congruence, responsibility centers.**

1.   The environmental-management group appears to be _decentralized_ because its managers have considerable _freedom to make decisions_. They can choose which projects to work on and which projects to reject.

2.   The environmental-management group is a _cost center_. The group is required to charge the operating divisions for environmental services at cost and not at market prices that would help earn the group a profit.

3.   The **benefits** of structuring the environmental-management group in this way are:
   a.   The _operating managers_ have _incentives_ to carefully weigh and conduct _cost-benefit_ analyses before requesting the environmental group's services.
   b.   The _operating managers_ have an _incentive_ to _follow the work and the progress_ made by the environmental team.
   c.   The _environmental group_ has _incentives_ to fulfill the contract, to do a good job in terms of cost, time, and quality, and to _satisfy the operating division_ to continue to get business.

The **problems** in structuring the environmental-management group in this way are:
   a.   The contract requires _extensive_ internal _negotiations_ in terms of cost, time, and technical specifications.
   b.   The _environmental group needs to continuously "sell" its services_ to the operating division, and this could potentially result in loss of morale.
   c.   Experimental _projects that have long-term potential may not be undertaken_ because operating division managers may be reluctant to undertake projects that are costly and uncertain, whose benefits will be realized only well after they have left the division.

To the extent that the focus of the environmental-management group is on short-run projects demanded by the operating divisions, the current structure leads to goal congruence and motivation. Both operating divisions and the environmental-management group are motivated to work toward the organizational goals of reducing pollution and improving the environment.

22-20 (30 min.)   **Transfer-pricing methods, goal congruence.**

1.   _Alternative 1:_ Sell as raw lumber for $200 per 100 board feet:

Revenue	$200
Variable costs	100
Contribution margin	$100 per 100 board feet

Alternative 2: Sell as finished lumber for $275 per 100 board feet:

Revenue		$275
Variable costs:		
Raw lumber	$100	
Finished lumber	125	225
Contribution margin		$ 50 per 100 board feet

British Columbia Lumber will maximize its total contribution margin by selling raw lumber.

2.   Transfer price at 110% of variable costs:

$$= \$100 + (\$100 \times 0.10)$$
$$= \$110 \text{ per 100 board feet}$$

	Sell as Raw Lumber	Sell as Finished Lumber
Raw Lumber Division		
Division revenues	$200	$110
Division variable costs	100	100
Division operating income	$100	$ 10
Finished Lumber Division		
Division revenues	$ 0	$275
Transferred-in costs	—	110
Division variable costs	—	125
Division operating income	$ 0	$ 40

The Raw Lumber Division will maximize reported division operating income by selling raw lumber, which is the action preferred by the company as a whole. The Finished Lumber Division will maximize division operating income by selling finished lumber, which is contrary to the action preferred by the company as a whole.

3.   Transfer price at market price = $200 per 100 board feet.

	Sell as Raw Lumber	Sell as Finished Lumber
Raw Lumber Division		
Division revenues	$200	$200
Division variable costs	100	100
Division operating income	$100	$100
Finished Lumber Division		
Division revenues	$ 0	$275
Transferred-in costs	—	200
Division variable costs	—	125
Division operating income	$ 0	$ (50)

Since the Raw Lumber Division will be indifferent between selling the lumber in raw or finished form, it would be willing to maximize division operating income by selling raw lumber, which is the action preferred by the company as a whole. The Finished Lumber Division will maximize division operating income by not further processing raw lumber and this is preferred by the company as a whole. Thus, transfer at market price will result in division actions that are also in the best interest of the company as a whole.

22-22 (30 min.) **Transfer pricing, general guideline, goal congruence.**

1. Using the general guideline presented in the chapter, the minimum price at which the Airbag Division would sell airbags to the Tivo Division is $90, the incremental costs. The Airbag Division has idle capacity (it is currently working at 80% of capacity). Therefore, its opportunity cost is zero.

2. Transferring products internally at incremental cost has the following properties:

   a. Achieves *goal congruence—Yes*, as described in requirement 1 above.
   b. Useful for *evaluating division performance—No*, because this transfer price does not cover or exceed full costs. By transferring at incremental costs and not covering fixed costs, the Airbag Division will show a loss, which is not a good measure of the economic performance of the subunit.
   c. *Motivating management effort—Yes*, if based on budgeted costs (actual costs can then be compared to budgeted costs). If, however, transfers are based on actual costs, Airbag Division management has little incentive to control costs.
   d. *Preserves division autonomy—No*. Because it is rule-based, the Airbag Division has no say in the setting of the transfer price.

3. If the two divisions were to negotiate a transfer price, the range of possible transfer prices will be between $90 and $125 per unit. The Airbag Division has excess capacity that it can use to supply airbags to the Tivo Division. The Airbag Division will be willing to supply the airbags only if the transfer price equals or exceeds $90, its incremental costs of manufacturing the airbags. The Tivo Division will be willing to buy airbags from the Airbag Division only if the price does not exceed $125 per airbag, the price at which the Tivo division can buy airbags in the market from external suppliers.

   a. Achieves *goal congruence—Yes*, as described above.
   b. Useful for *evaluating division performance—Yes*, because the transfer price is the result of direct negotiations between the two divisions. Of course, the transfer prices will be affected by the bargaining strengths of the two divisions.
   c. *Motivating management effort—Yes*, because once negotiated, the transfer price is independent of actual costs of the Airbag Division. Airbag Division management has every incentive to manage efficiently to improve profits.
   d. *Preserves subunit autonomy—Yes*, because the transfer price is based on direct negotiations between the two divisions and is not specified by headquarters on the basis of some rule (such as Airbag Division's incremental costs).

4. *Neither method is perfect*, but negotiated transfer pricing (requirement 3) has more favorable properties than the cost-based transfer pricing (requirement 2). Both transfer-pricing methods achieve goal congruence, but negotiated transfer pricing facilitates the evaluation of division performance, motivates management effort, and preserves division autonomy, whereas the transfer price based on incremental costs does not achieve these objectives.

22-24 (30 min.) **Multinational transfer pricing, goal congruence (continuation of 22-23).**

1. After-tax operating income if Mornay Company sells all 1,000 units of Product 4A36 in the United States:

Revenues, $600 × 1,000 units	$600,000
Full manufacturing costs, $500 × 1,000 units	500,000
Operating income	100,000
Income taxes at 40%	40,000
After-tax operating income	$ 60,000

From Exercise 22-23, requirement 1, Mornay Company's after-tax operating income if it transfers 1,000 units of Product 4A36 to Austria at full manufacturing cost and sells the units in Austria is $112,000. Therefore, Mornay should sell the 1,000 units in Austria.

2. Transferring Product 4A36 at the full manufacturing cost of the U.S. Division minimizes import duties and taxes (Exercise 22-23, requirement 2), but creates zero operating income for the U.S Division. Acting autonomously, the U.S. Division manager would maximize division operating income by selling Product 4A36 in the U.S. market, which results in $60,000 in after-tax division operating income as calculated in requirement 1, rather than by transferring Product 4A36 to the Austrian division at full manufacturing cost. Thus, the transfer price calculated in requirement 2 of Exercise 22-23 will not result in actions that are optimal for Mornay Company as a whole.

3. The minimum transfer price at which the U.S. division manager acting autonomously will agree to transfer Product 4A36 to the Austrian division is $600 per unit. Any transfer price less than $600 will leave the U.S. Division's performance worse than selling directly in the U.S. market. Because the U.S. Division can sell as many units that it makes of Product 4A36 in the U.S. market, there is an opportunity cost of transferring the product internally equal to $250 (selling price $600 – variable manufacturing costs, $350).

$$\begin{array}{lcl} \text{Minimum transfer} \\ \text{price per unit} \end{array} = \begin{array}{c} \text{Incremental cost per} \\ \text{unit up to the point of} \\ \text{transfer} \end{array} + \begin{array}{c} \text{Opportunity cost per} \\ \text{unit to the selling} \\ \text{(U. S.) division} \end{array}$$

$$= \quad \$350 + \$250 = \$600$$

This transfer price will result in Mornay Company as a whole paying more import duties and taxes than the answer to Exercise 22-23, requirement 2, as calculated below:

U.S. Division

Revenues, $600 × 1,000 units	$600,000
Full manufacturing costs	500,000
Division operating income	100,000
Division income taxes at 40%	40,000
Division after-tax operating income	$ 60,000

390

Austrian Division

Revenues, $750 × 1,000 units		$750,000
Transferred in costs, $600 × 1,000 units		600,000
Import duties at 10% of transferred-in price,		
$60 × 1,000 units		60,000
Division operating income		90,000
Division income taxes at 44%		39,600
Division after-tax operating income		$ 50,400

Total import duties and income taxes at transfer prices of $500 and $600 per unit for 1,000 units of Product 4A36 follow:

		Transfer Price of $500 per Unit (Exercise 22-23, Requirement 2)	Transfer Price of $600 per Unit
(a)	U.S. income taxes	$ 0	$ 40,000
(b)	Austrian import duties	50,000	60,000
(c)	Austrian income taxes	88,000	39,600
		$138,000	$139,600

The minimum transfer price that the U.S. division manager acting autonomously would agree to results in Mornay Company paying $1,600 in additional import duties and income taxes.

22-26 (5 min.)   Transfer-pricing problem (continuation of 22-25).

The company as a whole would benefit in this situation if Division C purchased from external suppliers. The $15,000 disadvantage to the company as a whole as a result of purchasing from external suppliers would be more than offset by the $30,000 contribution margin of Division A's sale of 1,000 units to other customers:

Purchase costs paid to external suppliers, 1,000 units × $135		$135,000
Deduct variable cost savings, 1,000 units × $120		120,000
Net cost to the company as a result of purchasing from external suppliers		$ 15,000
Division A's sales to other customers, 1,000 units × $155		$155,000
Deduct:		
Variable manufacturing costs, $120 × 1,000 units	$120,000	
Variable marketing costs, $5 × 1,000 units	5,000	
Total variable costs		125,000
Contribution margin from selling units to other customers		$ 30,000

22-28 (20–30 min.) **Pertinent transfer price.**

1. No, transfers should not be made to Division B if there is no unused capacity in Division A. An incremental cost approach shows a positive contribution for the company as a whole:

Selling price of final product		$300
Incremental cost per unit in Division A	$120	
Incremental cost per unit in Division B	150	270
Contribution margin per unit		$ 30

However, if there is no excess capacity in Division A, any transfer will result in diverting products from the market for the intermediate product. Sales in this market result in a greater contribution for the company as a whole.

Selling price of intermediate product	$200
Incremental (outlay) cost per unit in Division A	120
Contribution margin per unit	$ 80

Using the general guideline described in the chapter,

$$\text{Minimum transfer price} = \left(\begin{array}{c}\text{Additional } \textit{incremental } \text{cos}t \\ \textit{per unit} \text{ incurred up} \\ \text{to the point of transfer}\end{array}\right) + \left(\begin{array}{c}\textit{Opportunity } \text{cos}t \\ \textit{per unit} \text{ to the} \\ \text{supplying division}\end{array}\right)$$

$$= \$120 + (\$200 - \$120)$$
$$= \$200, \text{ which is the market price}$$

The market price is the transfer price that leads to the correct decision; that is, do not transfer to Division B unless there are extenuating circumstances for continuing to market the final product. Therefore, Division B must either drop the product or reduce the incremental costs of assembly from $150 per bicycle to less than $100 (selling price, $300 – transfer price, $200).

2. If A has excess capacity, there is intermediate external demand for only 800 units at $200, and the $200 price is to be maintained, then the opportunity costs per unit to the supplying division are $0. The general guideline indicates a minimum transfer price of: $120 + $0 = $120. B would buy 200 units from A at a transfer price of $120 because B can earn a contribution of $30 per unit [$300 – ($120 + $150)].

3. Division B would show zero contribution [$300 – ($150 + $150)], but the company as a whole would generate a contribution of $30 per unit on the 200 units transferred. Any price between $120 and $150 would induce the transfer that would be desirable for the company as a whole. A motivational problem may arise regarding how to split the $30 contribution between Division A and B. Unless the price is below $150, B would have little incentive to buy.

22-30 (30–35 min.) **Effect of alternative transfer-pricing methods on division operating income.**

1.

Pounds of cranberries harvested	400,000
Gallons of juice processed (500 gals per 1,000 lbs.)	200,000
Revenues (200,000 gals. × $2.10 per gal.)	$420,000
Costs	
Harvesting Division	
Variable costs (400,000 lbs. × $0.10 per lb.)	$ 40,000
Fixed costs (400,000 lbs. × $0.25 per lb.)	100,000
Total Harvesting Division costs	140,000
Processing Division	
Variable costs (200,000 gals. × $0.20 per gal.)	$ 40,000
Fixed costs (200,000 gals. × $0.40 per gal.)	80,000
Total Processing Division costs	120,000
Total costs	260,000
Operating income	$160,000

2.

	200% of Full Costs	Market Price
Transfer price per pound (($0.10 + $0.25) × 2; $0.60)	$0.70	$0.60
1. Harvesting Division		
Revenues (400,000 lbs. × $0.70; $0.60)	$280,000	$240,000
Costs		
Division variable costs (400,000 lbs. × $0.10 per lb.)	40,000	40,000
Division fixed costs (400,000 lbs. × $0.25 per lb.)	100,000	100,000
Total division costs	140,000	140,000
Division operating income	$140,000	$100,000
Harvesting Division manager's bonus (5% of operating income)	$7,000	$5,000
2. Processing Division		
Revenues (200,000 gals. × $2.10 per gal.)	$420,000	$420,000
Costs		
Transferred-in costs	280,000	240,000
Division variable costs (200,000 gals. × $0.20 per gal.)	40,000	40,000
Division fixed costs (200,000 gals. × $0.40 per gal.)	80,000	80,000
Total division costs	400,000	360,000
Division operating income	$ 20,000	$ 60,000
Processing Division manager's bonus (5% of operating income)	$1,000	$3,000

3. Bonus paid to division managers at 5% of division operating income is computed above and summarized below:

	Internal Transfers at 200% of Full Costs	Internal Transfers at Market Prices
Harvesting Division manager's bonus (5% × $140,000; 5% × $100,000)	$7,000	$5,000
Processing Division manager's bonus (5% × $20,000; 5% × $60,000)	$1,000	$3,000

The Harvesting Division manager will prefer to transfer at 200% of full costs because this method gives a higher bonus. The Processing Division manager will prefer transfer at market price for its higher resulting bonus.

Crango may resolve or reduce transfer pricing conflicts by:

- Basing division managers' *bonuses on overall Crango profits in addition to division operating income.* This will motivate each manager to consider what is best for Crango overall and not be concerned with the transfer price alone.
- Letting the two divisions *negotiate the transfer price* between themselves. However, this may result in constant re-negotiation between the two managers each accounting period.
- Using *dual transfer prices.* However, a cost-based transfer price will not motivate cost control by the Harvesting Division manager. It will also insulate that division from the discipline of market prices.

22-32 (40 min.) Multinational transfer pricing, global tax minimization.

This is a two-country two-division transfer-pricing problem with two alternative transfer-pricing methods. The summary data in U.S. dollars are:

South Africa Mining Division

Variable costs:	560 ZAR ÷ 7 =	$80 per lb. of raw diamonds
Fixed costs:	1,540 ZAR ÷ 7 =	$220 per lb. of raw diamonds
Market price:	3,150 ZAR ÷ 7 =	$450 per lb. of raw diamonds

U.S. Processing Division

Variable costs	=	$150 per lb. of polished industrial diamonds
Fixed costs	=	$700 per lb. of polished industrial diamonds
Market price	=	$5,000 per lb. of polished industrial diamonds

1. The transfer prices are:
   a. *200% of full costs*
      Mining Division to Processing Division
         = 2.0 × ($80 + $220) = $600 per lb. of raw diamonds
   b. *Market price*
      Mining Division to Processing Division
         = $450 per lb. of raw diamonds

	200% of Full Cost	Market Price
South Africa Mining Division		
Division revenues, $600, $450 × 4,000	$2,400,000	$1,800,000
Costs		
Division variable costs, $80 × 4,000	320,000	320,000
Division fixed costs, $220 × 4,000	880,000	880,000
Total division costs	1,200,000	1,200,000
Division operating income	$1,200,000	$ 600,000
U.S. Processing Division		
Division revenues, $5,000 × 2,000	$10,000,000	$10,000,000
Costs		
Transferred-in costs, $600, $450 × 4,000	2,400,000	1,800,000
Division variable cost, $150 × 2,000	300,000	300,000
Division fixed costs, $700 × 2,000	1,400,000	1,400,000
Total division costs	4,100,000	3,500,000
Division operating income	$ 5,900,000	$ 6,500,000

2.

	200% of Full Cost	Market Price
South Africa Mining Division		
Division operating income	$1,200,000	$600,000
Income tax at 18%	216,000	108,000
Division after-tax operating income	$ 984,000	$492,000
U.S. Processing Division		
Division operating income	$5,900,000	$6,500,000
Income tax at 30%	1,770,000	1,950,000
Division after-tax operating income	$4,130,000	$4,550,000

3.

	200% of Full Cost	Market Price
South Africa Mining Division:		
After-tax operating income	$ 984,000	$ 492,000
U.S. Processing Division:		
After-tax operating income	4,130,000	4,550,000
Industrial Diamonds:		
After-tax operating income	$5,114,000	$5,042,000

The South Africa Mining Division manager will prefer the higher transfer price of 200% of full cost and the U.S. Processing Division manager will prefer the lower transfer price equal to market price. Industrial Diamonds will maximize companywide net income by using the 200% of full cost transfer-pricing method. This method sources more of the total income in South Africa, the country with the lower income tax rate.

4.   Factors that executives consider *important in transfer pricing* decisions include:
     a. Performance evaluation
     b. Management motivation
     c. Pricing and product emphasis
     d. External market recognition

Factors specifically related to ***multinational** transfer pricing* include:
     a. Overall income of the company
     b. Income or dividend repatriation restrictions
     c. Competitive position of subsidiaries in their respective markets

22-34 (30 min.) **Transfer pricing, goal congruence.**

	Transfer 10,000 tape players to Assembly. Sell 2,000 in outside market at $35 each	Buy 10,000 tape players from Johnson at $38. Sell 12,000 tape players in outside market at $35 each	Buy 10,000 tape players from Johnson at $40. Sell 12,000 tape players in outside market at $35 each	Buy 10,000 tape players from Johnson at $45. Sell 12,000 tape players in outside market at $35 each
	(1)	(2a)	(2x)	(2b)
Incremental cost of Cassette Division supplying 10,000 tape players to Assembly Division $25 × 10,000; 0; 0; 0	$(250,000)	$ 0	$ 0	$ 0
Incremental costs of buying 10,000 tape players from Johnson $0; $38 × 10,000; $40 × 10,000; $45 × 10,000	0	(380,000)	(400,000)	(450,000)
Revenue from selling tape players in outside market $35 × 2,000; 12,000; 12,000; 12,000	70,000	420,000	420,000	420,000
Incremental costs of manufacturing tape players for sale in outside market $25 × 2,000; 12,000; 12,000; 12,000	(50,000)	(300,000)	(300,000)	(300,000)
Revenue from supplying head mechanism to Johnson $20 × 0; 10,000; 10,000; 10,000	0	200,000	200,000	200,000
Incremental costs of supplying head mechanism to Johnson $15 × 0; 10,000; 10,000; 10,000	0	(150,000)	(150,000)	(150,000)
Net costs	$(230,000)	$(210,000)	$(230,000)	$(280,000)

1. Column 1 shows the incremental costs of $230,000.
2. Columns (2a) and (2b) show that if Johnson Corporation offers a price of $38 per tape player, Orsilo Corporation should purchase the tape players from Johnson; this will result in an incremental net cost of $210,000 (column 2a). If Johnson Corporation offers a price of $45 per tape player, Orsilo Corporation should manufacture the tape players in-house; this will result in an incremental net cost of $280,000 (column 2b).

Comparing columns (1) and (2a), at a price of $38 per tape player from Johnson, the net cost of $210,000 is less than the net cost of $230,000 to Orsilo Corporation if it made the tape players in-house. So, Orsilo Corporation should outsource to Johnson.

Comparing columns (1) and (2b), at a price of $45 per tape player from Johnson, the net cost of $280,000 is greater than the net cost of $230,000 to Orsilo Corporation if it made the tape players in-house. Therefore, Orsilo Corporation should reject Johnson's offer.

Now consider column (2x). It shows that at a price of $40 per tape player from Johnson, the net cost is exactly $230,000, the same as the net cost to Orsilo Corporation of manufacturing in-house (column 1). Thus, for prices between $38 and $40, Orsilo will prefer to purchase from Johnson. For prices greater than $40 (and up to $45), Orsilo will prefer to manufacture in-house.

3. The Cassette Division can manufacture at most 12,000 tape players and it is currently operating at capacity. The incremental costs of manufacturing a tape player are $25 per unit. The opportunity cost of manufacturing tape players for the Assembly Division is (1) the contribution margin of $10 (selling price, $35 minus incremental costs $25) that the Cassette Division would forgo by not selling tape players in the outside market plus (2) the contribution margin of $5 (selling price, $20 minus incremental costs, $15) that the Cassette Division would forgo by not being able to sell the head mechanism to external suppliers of tape players such as Johnson (recall that the Cassette division can produce as many head mechanisms as demanded by external suppliers, but their demand will fall if the Cassette Division supplies the Assembly Division with tape players). Thus, the total opportunity cost to the Cassette Division of supplying tape players to Assembly is $10 + $5 = $15 per unit.

Using the general guideline,

$$\begin{array}{c} \text{Minimum transfer} \\ \text{price per tape player} \end{array} = \begin{array}{c} \text{Incremental cost per} \\ \text{tape player up to the} \\ \text{point of transfer} \end{array} + \begin{array}{c} \text{Opportunity cost per} \\ \text{tape player to the} \\ \text{selling division} \end{array}$$

$$= \$25 + \$15 = \$40$$

Thus, the minimum transfer price that the Cassette Division will accept for each tape player is $40. Note that at a price of $40, Orsilo is indifferent between manufacturing tape players in-house or purchasing them from an external supplier.

4a. The transfer price is set to $40 + $1 = $41 and Johnson is offering the tape players for $40.50 each. Now, for an outside price per tape player below $41, the Assembly Division would prefer to purchase from outside; above it, the Assembly Division would prefer to purchase from the Cassette Division. So, the Assembly division will buy from Johnson at $40.50 each and the Cassette Division will be forced to sell its output on the outside market.

4b. But for Orsilo, as seen from requirements 1 and 2, an outside price of $40.50, which is greater than the $40 cut-off price, makes inhouse manufacture the optimal choice. So, a mandated transfer price of $41 causes the division managers to make choices that are sub-optimal for Orsilo.

4c. When selling prices are uncertain, the transfer price should be set at the minimum acceptable transfer price. It is only if the price charged by the external supplier falls below $40 that Orsilo Corporation as a whole is better off purchasing from the outside market. Setting the transfer price at $40 per unit achieves goal congruence. The Cassette division will be willing to sell to the Assembly Division, and the Assembly Division will be willing to buy in-house and this would be optimal for Orsilo, too.

22-36 (40–50 min.)   **Transfer pricing, utilization of capacity.**

1.

	Super-chip	**Okay-chip**
Selling price	$60	$12
Direct material cost per unit	2	1
Direct manufacturing labor cost per unit	28	7
Contribution margin per unit	$30	$ 4
Contribution margin per hour		
($30 ÷ 2; $4 ÷ 0.5)	$15	$ 8

Because the contribution margin per hour is higher for Super-chip than for Okay-chip, CIC should produce and sell as many Super-chips as it can and use the remaining available capacity to produce Okay-chip.

The total demand for Super-chips is 15,000 units, which would take 30,000 hours (15,000 × 2 hours per unit). CIC should use its remaining capacity of 20,000 hours (50,000 – 30,000) to produce 40,000 Okay-chips (20,000 ÷ 0.5).

2.   Options for manufacturing process-control unit:

	Using Circuit Board	**Using Super-chip**
Selling price	$132	$132
Direct material cost per unit	60	2
Direct manufacturing labor cost per unit (Super-chip)	0	28
Direct manufacturing labor cost per unit (process-control unit)	50	60
Contribution margin per unit	$ 22	$ 42

Overall Company Viewpoint
Alternative 1: No Transfer of Super-chips:

Sell 15,000 Super-chips at contribution margin per unit of $30	$450,000
Transfer 0 Super-chips	0
Sell 40,000 Okay-chips at contribution margin per unit of $4	160,000
Sell 5,000 Control units at contribution margin per unit of $22	110,000
Total contribution margin	$720,000

Alternative 2: Transfer 5,000 Super-chips to Process-Control Division. These Super-chips would require 10,000 hours to manufacture, leaving only 10,000 hours for the manufacture of 20,000 Okay-chips (10,000 ÷ 0.5):

Sell 15,000 Super-chips at contribution margin per unit of $30	$450,000
Transfer 5,000 Super-chips to Process-Control Division	0
Sell 20,000 Okay-chips at contribution margin per unit of $4	80,000
Sell 5,000 Control units at contribution margin per unit of $42	210,000
Total contribution margin	$740,000

CIC is better off transferring 5,000 Super-chips to the Process-Control Division.

3. For each Super-chip that is transferred, two hours of time (labor capacity) are given up in the Semiconductor Division, and, in those two hours, four Okay-chips could be produced, each contributing $4.

$$\begin{array}{rcl}\text{Minimum transfer price} \\ \text{per Super - chip}\end{array} = \begin{array}{c}\text{Incremental cost} \\ \text{per unit to} \\ \text{the point of transfer}\end{array} + \begin{array}{c}\text{Opportunity cost per unit for} \\ \text{the Semiconductor Division}\end{array}$$

$$= \quad \$30 + \$16$$
$$= \quad \$46 \text{ per unit}$$

If the selling price for the process-control unit were firm at $132, the Process-Control Division would accept any transfer price up to $50 ($60 price of circuit board − $10 incremental labor cost if Super-chip used).

However, consider what happens if the transfer price of Super-chip is set at, say, $49, and the price of the control unit drops to $108. From CIC's viewpoint:

	Using Circuit Board	Using Super-chip
Selling price	$108	$108
Direct material cost per unit	60	49
Direct manufacturing labor cost per unit	50	60
Contribution margin per unit	$ −2	$ −1

Process-Control Division will not produce any control units. From the company's viewpoint, the contribution margin on the control unit if the Super-chip is used is:

Selling price	$108
Direct material cost per unit	2
Direct manufacturing labor cost per unit (Super-chip)	28
Direct manufacturing labor cost per unit (process-control unit)	60
Contribution margin per unit	$ 18

The contribution margin per unit from producing Super-chips for the process-control unit exceeds the contribution margin of $16 from producing 4 Okay-chips, each yielding a contribution margin of $4 per unit. Therefore, the Semiconductor Division should transfer 5,000 Super-chips as the following calculations show:

Alternative 1—No transfer (and, therefore, no sales of process-control units):

Sell 15,000 Super-chips at contribution margin per unit of $30	$450,000
Sell 40,000 Okay-chips at contribution margin per unit of $4	160,000
	$610,000

Alternative 2—Transfer 5,000 Super-chips:

Sell 15,000 Super-chips at contribution margin per unit of $30	$450,000
Sell 20,000 Okay-chips at contribution margin per unit of $4	80,000
Sell 5,000 control units at contribution margin per unit of $18	90,000
	$620,000

So, if the price for the control unit is uncertain, the transfer price must be set at the minimum acceptable transfer price of $46.

4. For a transfer of any amount between 0 and 10,000 Super-, the opportunity cost is the production of Okay-chips. In this range, the relevant costs are equal to the transfer price of $46 established in part 3.

If more than 10,000 Super-chips are transferred, the opportunity cost becomes the sale of Super-chips on the outside market.

Incremental cost per Super-chip up to the point of transfer + Opportunity cost per Super-chip to the Semiconductor Division = $30 + ($60 – $30) = $60, the market price.

At this transfer price, it is cheaper for the Process-Control Division to buy the circuit board for $60, since $10 of additional direct manufacturing labor cost is saved. The Semiconductor Division should at most transfer 10,000 Super-chips:

Internal Demand	Transfer Price
0–10,000	$46
10,000–25,000	60

CHAPTER 23
PERFORMANCE MEASUREMENT, COMPENSATION, AND
MULTINATIONAL CONSIDERATIONS

23-2 The **six steps** in designing an **accounting-based performance measure** are:
1. Choose performance measures that *align* with top management's financial goals
2. Choose the *time horizon* of each performance measure in Step 1
3. Choose a *definition of the components* in each performance measure in Step 1
4. Choose a *measurement alternative* for each performance measure in Step 1
5. Choose a *target* level of performance
6. Choose the *timing of feedback*

23-4 **Yes**. Residual income (RI) is not identical to return on investment (ROI). *ROI is a percentage* with investment as the denominator of the computation. *RI is an absolute monetary amount* which includes an imputed interest charge based on investment.

23-6 Definitions of **investment** used in practice when computing ROI are:
1. Total *assets available*
2. Total *assets employed*
3. Total *assets employed minus current liabilities*
4. Stockholders' *equity*

23-8 Special problems arise when evaluating the **performance** of divisions in **multinational companies** because
a. The economic, legal, political, social, and cultural *environments* differ significantly across countries.
b. *Governments* in some countries may impose *controls* and limit selling prices of products.
c. *Availability* of *materials* and skilled *labor,* as well as *costs* of materials, labor, and infrastructure may differ significantly across countries.
d. Divisions operating in different countries keep score of their performance in different *currencies.*

23-10 **Moral hazard** describes situations in which an *employee prefers to exert less effort* (or to report distorted information) compared with the effort (or accurate information) desired by the owner *because* the employee's effort (or validity of the reported information) *cannot be accurately monitored* and enforced.

23-12 **Benchmarking** or relative performance evaluation is the process of *evaluating a manager's performance against the performance of other similar operations.* Benchmarking cancels the effects of the common noncontrollable factors and provides better information about the manager's performance.

23-14 <u>Executive compensation disclosures</u> required by the Securities and Exchange Commission are:

a. A *summary compensation table* showing the salary, bonus, stock options, other stock awards, and other compensation earned by the five top officers in the previous three years

b. The *principles* underlying the executive compensation plans, and the *performance criteria*, such as profitability, sales growth, and market share used in determining compensation

c. How well a company's *stock performed relative* to the stocks of other companies in the same industry

23-16 (30 min.) ROI, comparisons of three companies.

1. The **separate components** highlight several features of return on investment not revealed by a single calculation:

    a. The importance of *investment turnover* as a key to income is stressed.
    b. The importance of *revenues* is explicitly recognized.
    c. The important components are expressed as *ratios* or percentages instead of dollar figures. This form of expression often enhances comparability of different divisions, businesses, and time periods.
    d. The breakdown stresses the possibility of *trading off investment turnover for income as a percentage of revenues* so as to increase the average ROI at a given level of output.

2. (Filled-in blanks are in bold face.)

	Companies in Same Industry		
	A	**B**	**C**
Revenue	$1,000,000	$ 500,000	**$10,000,000**
Income	$ 100,000	$ 50,000	**$ 50,000**
Investment	$ 500,000	**$5,000,000**	$ 5,000,000
Income as a % of revenue	**10%**	**10%**	0.5%
Investment turnover	**2.0**	**0.1**	2.0
Return on investment	**20%**	1%	**1%**

Income and investment alone shed little light on comparative performances because of disparities in size between Company A and the other two companies. Thus, it is impossible to say whether B's low return on investment in comparison with A's is attributable to its larger investment or to its lower income. Furthermore, the fact that Companies B and C have identical income and investment may suggest that the same conditions underlie the low ROI, but this conclusion is erroneous. B has higher margins but a lower investment turnover. C has very small margins (1/20th of B) but turns over investment 20 times faster.

23-18 (10–15 min.) **ROI and RI**.

1. Operating income = (Contribution margin per unit $\times$ 150,000 units) – Fixed costs
    $$= (\$720 - \$500) \times 150{,}000 - \$30{,}000{,}000 = \$3{,}000{,}000$$

    $$\text{ROI} \;=\; \frac{\text{Operating income}}{\text{Investment}} = \$3{,}000{,}000 \div \$48{,}000{,}000 = 6.25\%$$

2. Operating income = ROI $\times$ Investment

    [No. of pairs sold (Selling price – Var. cost per unit)] – Fixed costs = ROI $\times$ Investment

    Let \$X = minimum selling price per unit to achieve a 25% ROI

    $$
    \begin{aligned}
    150{,}000\,(\$X - \$500) - \$30{,}000{,}000 &= 25\%\,(\$48{,}000{,}000) \\
    \$150{,}000X &= \$12{,}000{,}000 + \$30{,}000{,}000 + \$75{,}000{,}000 \\
    X &= \$780
    \end{aligned}
    $$

3. Let \$X = minimum selling price per unit to achieve a 20% rate of return

    $$
    \begin{aligned}
    150{,}000\,(\$X - \$500) - \$30{,}000{,}000 &= 20\%\,(\$48{,}000{,}000) \\
    \$150{,}000X &= \$9{,}600{,}000 + \$30{,}000{,}000 + \$75{,}000{,}000 \\
    X &= \$764
    \end{aligned}
    $$

23-20 (25 min.) **Financial and nonfinancial performance measures, goal congruence**.

1. *Operating income is a good summary measure of short-term financial performance*. By itself, however, it does not indicate whether operating income in the short run was earned by taking actions that would lead to long-run competitive advantage. For example, Summit's divisions might be able to increase short-run operating income by producing more product while ignoring quality or rework. Harrington, however, would like to see division managers increase operating income without sacrificing quality. The new performance measures take a balanced scorecard approach by evaluating and rewarding managers on the basis of direct measures (such as rework costs, on-time delivery performance, and sales returns). This motivates managers to take actions that Harrington believes will increase operating income now and in the future. *The nonoperating income measures serve as surrogate measures of future profitability*.

2. The semiannual installments and total bonus for the Charter Division are calculated as follows:

Charter Division Bonus Calculation
For Year Ended December 31, 2009

January 1, 2009 to June 30, 2009

Profitability	$(0.02 \times \$462,000)$	$ 9,240
Rework	$(0.02 \times \$462,000) - \$11,500$	(2,260)
On-time delivery	No bonus—under 96%	0
Sales returns	$[(0.015 \times \$4,200,000) - \$84,000] \times 50\%$	(10,500)
Semiannual installment		$ (3,520)
Semiannual bonus awarded		$ 0

July 1, 2009 to December 31, 2009

Profitability	$(0.02 \times \$440,000)$	$ 8,800
Rework	$(0.02 \times \$440,000) - \$11,000$	(2,200)
On-time delivery	96% to 98%	2,000
Sales returns	$[(0.015 \times \$4,400,000) - \$70,000] \times 50\%$	(2,000)
Semiannual installment		$ 6,600
Semiannual bonus awarded		$ 6,600
Total bonus awarded for the year		$ 6,600

The semiannual installments and total bonus for the Mesa Division are calculated as follows:

Mesa Division Bonus Calculation
For Year Ended December 31, 2009

January 1, 2009 to June 30, 2009

Profitability	$(0.02 \times \$342,000)$	$ 6,840
Rework	$(0.02 \times \$342,000) - \$6,000$	0
On-time delivery	Over 98%	5,000
Sales returns	$[(0.015 \times \$2,850,000) - \$44,750] \times 50\%$	(1,000)
Semiannual bonus installment		$10,840
Semiannual bonus awarded		$10,840

July 1, 2009 to December 31, 2009

Profitability	$(0.02 \times \$406,000)$	$ 8,120
Rework	$(0.02 \times \$406,000) - \$8,000$	0
On-time delivery	No bonus—under 96%	0
Sales returns	$[(0.015 \times \$2,900,000) - \$42,500]$ which is greater than zero, yielding a bonus	3,000
Semiannual bonus installment		$11,120
Semiannual bonus awarded		$11,120
Total bonus awarded for the year		$21,960

3. The manager of the Charter Division is likely to be frustrated by the new plan, as the division bonus has fallen by more than $20,000 compared to the bonus of the previous year. However, the new performance measures have begun to have the desired effect—both on-time deliveries and sales returns improved in the second half of the year, while rework costs were relatively even. If the division continues to improve at the same rate, the Charter bonus could approximate or exceed what it was under the old plan.

The manager of the Mesa Division should be as satisfied with the new plan as with the old plan, as the bonus is almost equivalent. On-time deliveries declined considerably in the second half of the year and rework costs increased. However, sales returns decreased slightly. Unless the manager institutes better controls, the bonus situation may not be as favorable in the future. This could motivate the manager to improve in the future but currently, at least, the manager has been able to maintain his bonus with showing improvement in only one area targeted by Harrington.

Ben Harrington's revised bonus plan for the Charter Division fostered the following improvements in the second half of the year despite an increase in sales:
- An increase of 1.9% in on-time deliveries.
- A $500 reduction in rework costs.
- A $14,000 reduction in sales returns.

However, operating income as a percent of sales has decreased (11% to 10%).

The Mesa Division's bonus has remained at the status quo as a result of the following effects:
- An increase of 2.0 % in operating income as a percent of sales (12% to 14%).
- A decrease of 3.6% in on-time deliveries.
- A $2,000 increase in rework costs.
- A $2,250 decrease in sales returns.

This would suggest that revisions to the bonus plan are needed. Possible changes include:
- increasing the weights put on on-time deliveries, rework costs, and sales returns in the performance measures while decreasing the weight put on operating income;
- a reward structure for rework costs that are below 2% of operating income that would encourage managers to drive costs lower;
- reviewing the whole year in total. The bonus plan should carry forward the negative amounts for one six-month period into the next six-month period incorporating the entire year when calculating a bonus; and
- developing benchmarks, and then giving rewards for improvements over prior periods and encouraging continuous improvement.

23-22 (25 min.)   **ROI, RI, EVA®.**

1.

	New Car Division	Performance Parts Division
Total assets	$33,000,000	$28,500,000
Current liabilities	$6,600,000	$8,400,000
Operating income	$2,475,000	$2,565,000
Required rate of return	12%	12%
Total assets – current liabilities	$26,400,000	$20,100,000
1. ROI (based on total assets) ($2,475,000 ÷ $33,000,000; $2,565,000 ÷ $28,500,000)	7.5%	9.0%
2. RI (based on total assets – current liabilities) ($2,475,000 – (12% × $26,400,000); $2,565,000 – (12% × $20,100,000))	($693,000)	$153,000
3. RI (based on total assets) ($2,475,000 – (12% × $33,000,000); $2,565,000 – (12% × $28,500,000))	($1,485,000)	($855,000)

3. Division RIs using assets is an alternate a measure of investment. Even with this new measure that is insensitive to the level of short-term debt, the New Car Division has a relatively worse RI than the Performance Parts Division. Both RIs are negative, indicating that the divisions are not earning the 12% required rate of return on their assets.

4. After-tax cost of debt financing = $(1 - 0.4) \times 10\% = 6\%$
After-tax cost of equity financing = 15%

$$\text{Weighted average cost of capital} = \frac{(\$18,000,000 \times 6\%) + (\$12,000,000 \times 15\%)}{\$18,000,000 + \$12,000,000} = 9.6\%$$

Operating income after tax		
0.6 × operating income before tax	$ 1,485,000	$1,539,000
(0.6 × $2,475,000; 0.6 × $2,565,000)		
Required return for EVA		
9.6% × Investment		
(9.6% × $26,400,000; 9.6% × $20,100,000)	2,534,400	1,929,600
EVA (Optg. inc. after tax – reqd. return)	$(1,049,400)	$ (390,600)

5. Both the residual income and the EVA calculations indicate that the Performance Parts Division is performing nominally better than the New Car Division. The Performance Parts Division has a higher residual income. The negative EVA for both divisions indicates that, on an after-tax basis, the divisions are destroying value—the after-tax economic returns from them are less than the required returns.

23-24 (20 min.) **Multinational performance measurement, ROI, RI.**

1a. U.S. Division's ROI in 2011 $= \dfrac{\text{Operating income}}{\text{Total assets}} = \dfrac{\text{Operating income}}{\$8,000,000} = 15\%$

Hence, operating income = 15% × $8,000,000 = $1,200,000.

1b. Norwegian Division's ROI in 2011 (based on kroners) $= \dfrac{8,100,000 \text{ kroners}}{52,500,000 \text{ kroners}} = 15.43\%$

2. Convert total assets into dollars using the December 31, 2010 exchange rate, the rate prevailing when the assets were acquired (6 kroners = $1):

$$\dfrac{52,500,000 \text{ kroners}}{6 \text{ kroner per dollar}} = \$8,750,000$$

Convert operating income into dollars at the average exchange rate prevailing during 2011 when operating income was earned (6.5 kroners = $1):

$$\dfrac{8,100,000 \text{ kroners}}{6.5 \text{ kroners per dollar}} = \$1,246,154$$

$$\text{Comparable ROI for Norwegian Division} = \dfrac{\$1,246,154}{\$8,750,000} = 14.24\%$$

The Norwegian Division's ROI based on kroners is helped by the inflation that occurs in Norway in 2011 (that caused the Norwegian kroner to weaken against the dollar from 6 kroners = $1 on 12-31-2010 to 7 kroners = $1 on 12-31-2011). Inflation boosts the division's operating income. Since the assets are acquired at the start of the year 2011, the asset values are not increased by the inflation that occurs during the year. The net effect of inflation on ROI calculated in kroners is to use an inflated value for the numerator relative to the denominator. Adjusting for inflationary and currency differences negates the effects of any differences in inflation rates between the two countries on the calculation of ROI. After these adjustments, the U.S. Division earned a higher ROI than the Norwegian Division.

3. U.S. Division's RI in 2011 = $1,200,000 – (12% × $8,000,000)
    = $1,200,000 – $960,000 = $240,000

Norwegian Division's RI in 2011 (in U.S. dollars) is calculated as:

$1,246,154 – (12% × $8,750,000) = 1,246,154 – $1,050,000 = $196,154.

The U.S. Division's RI also exceeds the Norwegian Division's RI in 2011 by $43,846.

23-26 (20–30 min.) Risk sharing, incentives, benchmarking, multiple tasks.

1. An evaluation of the three proposals to compensate Marks, the general manager of the Dexter Division follows:

   (i) Paying Marks a *flat salary* will not subject Marks to any *risk*, but it will provide no *incentives* for Marks to undertake extra physical and mental effort.

   (ii) Rewarding Marks only on the basis of Dexter *Division's ROI* would *motivate* Marks to put in *extra effort* to increase ROI because. But compensating Marks solely on the basis of ROI subjects Marks to *excessive risk* because the division's ROI depends not only on Marks's effort but also on other random factors over which Marks has no control.

   (iii) The motivation for having *some salary and some performance-based bonus* in compensation arrangements is to *balance the benefits of incentives* against the extra *costs of imposing risk* on the manager.

2. Marks's complaint does not appear to be valid. The senior management of AMCO is proposing to benchmark Marks's performance using a relative performance evaluation (RPE) system. RPE controls for common uncontrollable factors that similarly affect the performance of managers operating in the same environments (for example, the same industry). If business conditions for car battery manufacturers are good, all businesses manufacturing car batteries will probably perform well. A superior indicator of Marks's performance is how well Marks performed relative to his peers of the same size and situation.

3. If Marks has no authority for making capital investment decisions, then ROI is not a good measure of Marks's performance—it varies with the actions taken by others rather than the actions taken by Marks. AMCO may wish to evaluate Marks on the basis of operating income rather than ROI.

4. There are two main concerns with Marks's plans. First, creating very strong sales incentives imposes excessive risk on the sales force because a salesperson's performance is affected not only by his or her own effort, but also by random factors that are beyond the salesperson's control. If salespersons are risk averse, the firm will have to compensate them for bearing this extra uncontrollable risk. Second, compensating salespersons only on the basis of sales creates strong incentives to sell, but may result in lower levels of customer service and sales support.

23-28 (40–50 min.) ROI performance measures based on historical cost and current cost.

1. ROI using historical cost measures:

Passion Fruit	$260,000 ÷ $680,000	=	38.24%
Kiwi Fruit	$440,000 ÷ $2,300,000	=	19.13%
Mango Fruit	$760,000 ÷ $3,240,000	=	23.46%

The Passion Fruit Division appears to be considerably more efficient than the Kiwi Fruit and Mango Fruit Divisions.

2. The gross book values (i.e., the original costs of the plants) under historical cost are calculated as the useful life of each plant (12 years) × the annual depreciation:

Passion Fruit	12 × $140,000	=	$1,680,000
Kiwi Fruit	12 × $200,000	=	$2,400,000
Mango Fruit	12 × $240,000	=	$2,880,000

Step 1: Restate long-term assets from gross book value at historical cost to gross book value at current cost as of the end of 2008:

(Gross book value of long-term assets at historical cost) × (Construction cost index in 2008 ÷ Construction cost index in year of construction).

Passion Fruit	$1,680,000 × (170 ÷ 100)	=	$2,856,000
Kiwi Fruit	$2,400,000 × (170 ÷ 136)	=	$3,000,000
Mango Fruit	$2,880,000 × (170 ÷ 160)	=	$3,060,000

Step 2: Derive net book value of long-term assets at current cost as of the end of 2008. (Estimated useful life of each plant is 12 years.)

(Gross book value of long-term assets at current cost at the end of 2008) × (Estimated remaining useful life ÷ Estimated total useful life)

Passion Fruit	$2,856,000 × (2 ÷ 12)	=	$ 476,000
Kiwi Fruit	$3,000,000 × (9 ÷ 12)	=	$2,250,000
Mango Fruit	$3,060,000 × (11 ÷ 12)	=	$2,805,000

Step 3: Compute current cost of total assets at the end of 2008. (Assume current assets of each plant are expressed in 2008 dollars.)

(Current assets at the end of 2008 [given]) + (Net book value of long-term assets at current cost at the end of 2008 [Step 2])

Passion Fruit	$400,000 + $476,000	=	$ 876,000
Kiwi Fruit	$500,000 + $2,250,000	=	$2,750,000
Mango Fruit	$600,000 + $2,805,000	=	$3,405,000

Step 4: Compute current-cost depreciation expense in 2008 dollars.

Gross book value of long-term assets at current cost at the end of 2008 (from Step 1) ÷ 12

Passion Fruit	$2,856,000 ÷ 12 = $238,000
Kiwi Fruit	$3,000,000 ÷ 12 = $250,000
Mango Fruit	$3,060,000 ÷ 12 = $255,000

Step 5: Compute 2008 operating income using 2008 current-cost depreciation expense.

(Historical-cost operating income – [Current-cost depreciation expense in 2008 dollars (Step 4) – Historical-cost depreciation expense])

Passion Fruit	$260,000 – ($238,000 – $140,000)	= $162,000
Kiwi Fruit	$440,000 – ($250,000 – $200,000)	= $390,000
Mango Fruit	$760,000 – ($255,000 – $240,000)	= $745,000

Step 6: Compute ROI using current-cost estimates for long-term assets and depreciation expense (Step 5 ÷ Step 3).

Passion Fruit	$162,000 ÷ $ 876,000	= 18.49%
Kiwi Fruit	$390,000 ÷ $2,750,000	= 14.18%
Mango Fruit	$745,000 ÷ $3,405,000	= 21.88%

	ROI: Historical Cost	ROI: Current Cost
Passion Fruit	38.24%	18.49%
Kiwi Fruit	19.13	14.18
Mango Fruit	23.46	21.88

Use of current cost results in the Mango Fruit Division appearing to be the most efficient. The Passion Fruit ROI is reduced substantially when the ten-year-old plant is restated for the 70% increase in construction costs over the 1998 to 2008 period.

3. Use of **current costs** increases the *comparability* of ROI measures across divisions' operating plants built at different construction cost price levels. Use of current cost also will increase the willingness of managers, evaluated on the basis of ROI, to *move between divisions* with assets purchased many years ago and divisions with assets purchased in recent years.

23-30 (20 min.) **ROI, RI, and multinational firms**.

1. Calculation of ROI and RI before currency translation:

	United States	France
Investment in assets	$3,490,000	2,400,000 eu
Income for current year	$ 383,900	266,400 eu
ROI ($383,900 ÷ $3,490,000; 266,400 eu ÷ 2,400,000 eu)	11.0%	11.1%
RI ($383,900 − 0.10 × $3,490,000; 266,400 eu − 0.10 × 2,400,000 eu)	$ 34,900	26, 400 eu

	United States	France
Investment in assets	$3,490,000	$2,880,000 (2,400,000 eu × $1.20)
Income for current year	$ 383,900	$ 346,320 (266,400 eu ×$1.30)
ROI ($383,900 ÷ $3,490,000; $346,320 ÷ $2,880,000)	11.0%	12.0%
RI ($383,900 − 0.10 × $3,490,000; $346,320 − 0.10 × $2,880,000)	$ 34,900	$ 58,320

Without currency translation, the ROIs in the United States and France are similar, but after currency translation the ROI of France is substantially higher. Residual income is not comparable before currency translation given the different currencies used by the units. After translation, RI is higher in France. Together with the higher ROI, the RI results suggest that performance was better in France than in the United States.

2. Adjusting for differences in currency values makes the *comparison of performance between foreign countries more meaningful* since the accounting measures being examined are more comparable. However, changes in relative currency values can lead to *misleading performance evaluations if interdependencies exist* across units in different countries.

23-32 (30–40 min.) ROI, RI, DuPont method, investment decisions, balanced scorecard.

1.

2009	$\dfrac{\text{Revenue}}{\text{Total Assets}}$	×	$\dfrac{\text{Operating Income}}{\text{Revenues}}$	=	ROI = $\dfrac{\text{Operating Income}}{\text{Total Assets}}$
Print	0.939 ($19,320 ÷ $20,580)		0.239 ($4,620 ÷ $19,320)		0.224 ($4,620 ÷ $20,580)
Internet	2.133 ($26,880 ÷ $12,600)		0.025 ($ 672 ÷ $26,880)		0.053 ($ 672 ÷ $12,600)

The Print Division has a relatively high ROI because of its high income margin relative to Internet. The Internet Division has a low ROI despite a high investment turnover because of its very low income margin.

2. Although the proposed investment is small, relative to the total assets invested, it earns less the 2009 return on investment (0.224) (All dollar numbers in millions):

2009 ROI (before proposal) $= \dfrac{\$4,620}{\$20,580} = 0.224$

Investment proposal ROI $= \dfrac{\$120}{\$800} = 0.150$

2009 ROI (with proposal) $= \dfrac{\$4,620+\$120}{\$20,580+\$800} = 0.222$

411

Given the existing bonus plan, any proposal that reduces the ROI is unattractive.

3a. Residual income for 2009 (before proposal, in millions):

	Operating Income		Imputed Interest Charge	Division Residual Income
Print	$4,620	–	$2,470 (0.12 × $20,580) =	$2,150
Internet	672	–	1512 (0.12 × $12,600) =	(840)

3b. Residual income for proposal (in millions):

	Operating Income		Imputed Interest Charge	Residual Income
	$120	–	$120 (0.15 × $800) =	$0

Investing in the fast-speed printing press will have no effect on the Print Division's residual income. As a result, if Mays is evaluated using a residual income measure, Mays would be indifferent to adopting the printing press proposal.

4. As discussed in requirement 3b, Turner could *consider using RI*. The use of RI motivates managers to accept any project that makes a positive contribution to net income after the cost of the invested capital is taken into account. Making such investments will have a positive effect on News Mogul Group's customers.

Turner may also want to consider *nonfinancial measures* such as newspaper subscription levels, internet audience size, repeat purchase patterns, and market share. These measures will require managers to invest in areas that have favorable long-run effects on News Mogul Group's customers.

23-34 (20 min.) **Executive compensation, balanced scorecard.**

The percentage changes in net income and customer satisfaction in the three business units between 2008 and 2009 are:

	Retail Banking	Business Banking	Credit Cards
Percentage change in net income			
($3,220,000 − $2,800,000) ÷ $2,800,000;			
($3,016,000 − $2,900,000) ÷ $2,900,000;			
($2,722,500 − $2,750,000) ÷ $2,750,000	15%	4%	(1%)
Percentage change in customer satisfaction			
(73 − 73) ÷ 73; (75.6 − 70) ÷ 70; (79.35 − 69) ÷ 69	0%	8%	15%

1. The bonus formula indicates that the executives of the three units will receive the following 2009 bonuses as a percent of salary:

    Retail Banking: 15% + 0% = 15% of salary
    Business Banking: 4% + 8% = 12% of salary
    Credit Cards: 0% + 15% = 15% of salary

2. The results show an inverse relation between changes in net income and changes in customer satisfaction. This suggests that some units may be making investments in customer satisfaction to increase long-term financial performance, even though these investments cause short-term net income to decline. Alternatively, some units may be over-investing in customer satisfaction initiatives, causing overall financial performance to decline.

3. The board of directors can *set targets for changes in both net income and customer satisfaction*. This would allow the company to take differences in the units, their competitive environments, and their customers into account when assessing performance. Target setting would also allow the company to reward managers when desirable investments in one dimension lead to short-term declines in the other.

23-36 (15 min.) **Ethics, levers of control.**

1. If Amy Kimbell "turns a blind eye" toward what she has just observed at the UFP log yard, she will be violating the competence, integrity, and objectivity standards for management accountants.
    Competence
    - Perform professional duties in accordance with technical standards

    Integrity
    - Communicate unfavorable as well as favorable information and professional judgments or opinions
    - Refrain from engaging in or supporting any activity that would discredit the profession

    Credibility
    - Communicate information fairly and objectively
    - Disclose fully all relevant information that could reasonably be expected to influence an intended user's understanding of the reports, comments, and recommendations.

Kimbell should:

    a. Try to follow established UFP policies to try to bring the issue to the attention of UFP management through regular channels; then, if necessary,

    b. Discuss the problem with the immediate superior who is not involved in the understatement of quality and costs.

    c. Clarify relevant ethical issues with an objective advisor, preferably a professional person outside UFP.

    d. If all the above channels fail to lead to a correction in the organization, she may have to resign and become a "whistle-blower" to bring UFP to justice.

2.   UFP is clearly emphasizing profit, driving managers to find ways to keep profits strong and increasing. This is a *diagnostic measure*, and over-emphasis on diagnostic measures can cause employees to do whatever is necessary—including unethical actions—to keep the measures in the acceptable range, not attract negative senior management attention and possibly improve compensation and job reviews.

    To **avoid problems like this in the future**, UFP needs to establish some *strong boundary systems and codes of conduct*. There should be a clear message from upper management that unethical behavior will not be tolerated. Training, role-plays, and case studies can be used to raise awareness about these issues, and strong sanctions should be put in place if the rules are violated. An effective boundary system is needed to keep managers "on the right path."

    UFP also needs to *articulate a belief system of core values*. The goal is to inspire managers and employees to do their best, exercise greater responsibility, take pride in their work, and do things the right way.